TRASH

AFRICAN CINEMA FROM BELOW

KENNETH W. HARROW

INDIANA UNIVERSITY PRESS

Bloomington and Indianapolis

This book is a publication of

Indiana University Press
601 North Morton Street
Bloomington, Indiana 47404-3797 USA

iupress.indiana.edu

Telephone orders   800-842-6796
Fax orders   812-855-7931

♻ The paper used in this publication meets the minimum requirements of the American
National Standard for Information Sciences—Permanence of Paper for Printed Library
Materials, ANSI Z39.48-1992.

Manufactured in the United States of America

Library of Congress Cataloging-in-Publication Data

Harrow, Kenneth W.
    Trash : African cinema from below / Kenneth W. Harrow.
      p. cm.
    Includes bibliographical references and index.
    ISBN 978-0-253-00744-5 (cl : alk. paper) — ISBN 978-0-253-00751-3 (pb : alk. paper) — ISBN 978-0-253-
00757-5 (eb) 1. Refuse and refuse disposal in motion pictures. 2. Motion pictures—Africa. I. Title.
    PN1993.5.A35H375 2013
    791.43096—dc23

                                                                                    2012037383

1 2 3 4 5   18 17 16 15 14 13

For Alexander, Sharon, Aram, and Joseph

Contents

Preface and Acknowledgments

In a strange way *Trash: African Cinema from Below* came about due to an off-chance remark of Jude Akudinobi, who was troubled by my words in *Postcolonial African Cinema* (2007) that it was time for some real trash in African cinema. What I meant was that the system needed to be shaken up: that we had to be shaken out of our historical need to read African cinema in narrow political terms, as subject to the exigencies of nation building, of meliorism, of Truth, with serums delivered by Authentic African voices performed by Griots.

I felt we needed to expand our critical readings beyond the educational imperative, and African cinema needed to become something other than dogmatic. It was indeed becoming such, as Bekolo had already launched us on the path with *Quartier Mozart,* and the late Djibril Diop Mambety had never succumbed to reductionist formulae; Henri Duparc had always worked toward a popular cinema. By the 1990s, Nollywood was making itself known. Things had moved, had changed. It was indeed time for a revolution in African critical approaches.

Now there are many significant studies, like Haynes and Okome's *Nigerian Video Film* and Larkin's *Signal and Noise,* that recognize the presence of Nollywood and its "trashy" films. There are new understandings of the cinema scene as entailing more auteurist film as well as popular film, as Diawara has shown in his latest study *African Film: New Forms of Aesthetics and Politics,* which radically revises the schematic, influential program he set out thirty years ago when he defined African cinema by its thematic approaches, its serious agendas—that now cries out for more. Diawara has worked in some ways more than anyone to get us there by the creation of his public voice in documentary films, beginning with the important *Rouch in Reverse,* in his compelling memoirs in the form of films, the book-length essays, journal articles and blog entries, and finally his own major study on African cinema that are intended to lead us to current groundbreaking films that are auteurist as well as popular.

This book began by wondering about trashy aesthetics, graffiti, popular cinemas, and imperfect cinemas that enriched our reactions to African visual culture, with its Mammy Wattas and its mammy wagons, its posters of Amadou Bamba and Mourid icons, an entire creative world of public African iconography, so free, so uninhibited, so much beyond the limited understandings in the west of public versus private spaces, so much more fully political than our older ideological thinking permitted, following what our earlier gods, Fanon,

Cabral, Nkrumah, Cheikh Anta Diop, had set out for us during the period of national liberation and revolutionary struggle. Alan and Mary Noor Roberts must be acknowledged as crucial in their work on public art, Mouridism, and popular images.

Focusing on trash does not constitute a rejection but an advance on positions we all shared in the 1970s and 1980s. The change is signaled in Gerima's latest brilliant film *Teza,* which revisits where we had been, and how more rethinking on our absolutist, grand narratives of liberation is required. The Bataille who inspires the early chapters of this book wanted to turn his bourgeois world upside-down. That was in the 1920s! We now have Bekolo's *Saignantes* to point us to a new, crazy, noir, exciting world. We have the graffiti images of Nacro's *Nuit de la vérité.* We need this visual trash to come alive. We have Hell in all its glory lighting up the screens of Nollywood, despite the imams of Kano. The screens were moribund with deadening Hollywood blockbusters until the movie theaters closed down. Nollywood has created a miraculous resurrection of the popular visual image of the self, in all its imaginary formulations, just as Africans fed the visual images of Others since the inception of cinema. Indeed both popular and auteur cinema today trade on images of melodrama, garbage, loss, and emotion, in ways that were inconceivable when a stately group of African students sat around the table in *Afrique sur Seine,* Paulin Vieyra's 1955 film that kicked things off with sketches of African lives in exile.

But what is trash? I discovered that it is not a simple term. What follows is an attempt to understand it, and in ways that make sense of African cinema, then and now. And it is an attempt to bring various approaches to such concrete things as waste management and toxic dumping into relation with globalization, current cultural trends in popular commercial filmmaking, and the tropes and styles that borrow from the rubbish bins, trash heaps, garbage cans of the world. And trash, above all, applies to people who have been dismissed from the community, marginalized and forgotten, turned into "bare lives" in "states of exception" for others to study and pity. Trash encompasses the turning of that reduced status into the basis for revolt, change, and the turning away from regimes that produce definitions of trash to newly formulated regimes that force us to reconsider the criteria for assigning value, not only to people, to culture, but to African films in particular.

Thanks, Jude, for making me think this through. Thanks also to Carmela Garritano, who inspired and encouraged me to take Nollywood and Gollywood seriously, and who has persevered in making this a field of study that has passed from being casually dismissed to perhaps the most compelling area of African popular culture and African cinema. It is daunting for those of us accustomed to auteur cinema to take on something as radically different as popular Nollywood cinema, and Carmela's support helped me dare to attempt to bridge the distance between the two.

Jonathan Haynes, the doyen in Nollywood film studies, has done more than anyone to open up this field to film scholars trained in conventional film studies. His work has inspired me for a long time.

Thanks to my students of ENG 478, Fall 2010, especially Carol Ross and Sean Walsh, who were superb thinkers about trash and the study of its manifest features as a trope, as an aesthetic, as key to the material dimensions of society and culture. Thanks to Scott Michaelsen for his challenging reading of the chapters on Bataille and Agamben and his brilliant work on hybridity and its misconceptions. Thanks to Salah Hassan for his support from my first talk on "high and low" in Bataille, and the years of trashy examples I couldn't resist citing—and for his faith in my scholarship. Especially thanks to Salah for making a political commitment in scholarship seem like our imperative and raison d'être as scholars.

Thanks to another wonderful colleague in the Michigan State University Department of English, Karl Schoonover, whose knowledge of cinema seems endless and whose complementary work on trash opened us to wonderful discussions. Thanks to Pat O'Donnell not only for sharing his work on trash in Delillo's *Underworld,* but for his steady support over the years. Thanks to Safoi Babana-Hampton for helping me with the translation of the untranslatable Lacan and helping in my questions with the French language. Thanks to Bill Vincent for his suggestions on how to format my "film-script style" descriptive passages, his understanding of suturing, and of film sensibilities over the years of our friendship. And thanks to the scholars in the field who continue to make it a vibrant and important part of my life, Odile Cazenave, Susan Andrade, Eileen Julien, Charlie Sugnet, Alexie Tcheuyup, and Manthia Diawara. Thanks for the praises and the challenges from Keyan Tommaselli, another doyen of South African cinema and a bedrock for scholars in African cinema. Olivier Barlet and his dynamic *Africultures* and his study of African cinema have also inspired me.

I owe a real debt to my chair, Steve Arch, for working out my schedule to get me the semester off in 2010, enabling me to complete this book in something less than the decade it took for my previous books—and for believing in the value of a study called "Trash" when I applied for grants to work on it.

I am grateful for the grant from the Center for the Advanced Study of International Development and Rob Glew, which permitted me to have a reduced teaching load in 2010.

For assiduous work on the index and bibliography sections, and generally enthusiastic support, my thanks to Emilie Diouf. And thanks to Connor Ryan for his commitment to African studies and generally to the issues that excite me in the field.

I continue to look to the work of the exciting new filmmakers like Abderrahmane Sissako, Jean Pierre Bekolo, Mahamet-Saleh Haroun, Jean Marie Teno, Fanta Nacro, Jo Ramaka, Zeze Gamboa, Kingsley Ogoro, Tejani Kelani, Teco

Benson; and to the host of African film critics who insist on sustaining the labor of understanding how the heritage of Sembène Ousmane continues to be important for us today, without being held back by the ideological constructions of the past. The work of emancipation, to be enriched, must follow that trajectory for African studies, just as Rancière sees it as necessary for the European in his *Emancipated Spectator*. His notions of a human community founded in notions of equality underlie the spirit of rebellion that caused me to first turn to trash. I was inspired by Sembène's fidelity to *les déchets humains* in *Xala*, and by the image of Jimmy Cliff standing wearily on the edges of the dungle in *The Harder They Come*. I hope I succeeded in turning that initial simple sympathy for the underprivileged into a more solid basis of inspiration that marks the reversals of dominant ideological discourses, and that carries the exuberance of Nollywood craziness in the way that John Waters was carried by Devine in his creation of a "trash aesthetics."

Sarah Jacobi, assistant sponsoring editor at Indiana University Press, has patiently and assiduously answered my questions about how to put the book together properly, how to address the thorny issues of permissions, and many more queries, and I am grateful to her. Dee Mortensen supported this project when I first told her about my crazy idea of writing about trash; she helped me enormously, whether she knows it or not, by assuring me of the desire of the press to see the book be published, and she always sustained me in my work. She has created a major African list, and I am very grateful to be part of it. I am particularly grateful to Ann Youmans, whose copyediting provided great assistance and final polish to the manuscript.

The project of this book is silly and serious. My wife Liz told me to go for it, and made it possible to work and write and view films, and then write some more. And she read what I wrote and told me when to rethink. She has always been doing this; the thanks have to be told in silence.

TRASH

Introduction

The trash was always there, only we never noticed it. In *Nyamanton* (1987), Cheick Oumar Sissoko positions children between garbage cans for the cameras, has children acting as trash pickers, and moves the representation of street children from sweet victims to streetwise survivors. The use of the trope of trash to define the lives of the poor was there from the start as well, for if trash is dirt, matter that is "out of place" as Mary Douglas (2002) says, if it is the jetsam of a material world, what's left over when the rich have eaten, then trash must define not only the scraps but the eaters of scraps as well. Early African filmmakers turned to the quartier not just to evoke home, as Sembène Ousmane and Djibril Diop Mambety do in their earliest films, but also to contrast its poverty with the wealth of the white neighborhoods. From "Borom Sarret" (1963) and *La Noire de . . .* (1966) that contrast is portrayed: the wealthy quartier of high rise apartments and villas, with the appropriate high-cultural signifiers, its classical music and quiet orderliness on the forbidden grounds of the Plateau, versus the dirt streets, the mules, chickens, goats, the modest homes patched from leftover materials in the Medina. Borom Sarret's wife goes off at the end of the film when her husband has returned home broke at night. She tells him she will get what they need for dinner, and he asks himself where she is going. What will she be doing, a question left unanswered. Trash is hidden in the unspoken words.

Trash has haunted African cinema from the start, when the decision was made not to make films that would be Hollywood dream machines, not films of escapism but of reality, even of harsh reality, daring to portray those who take advantage of their power and means to cheat others; of thieves who come to define the nature of the ruling classes; of conniving and unscrupulous people, immoral figures for whom notions of community are lost. Trash was there in all those films dealing with the unjust pressures placed on women for sex; on children who beg, street children victims of marabouts, abandoned by foolish or credulous parents. And the handicapped, the paraplegics, the lepers without hands, the squint-eyed—*les déchets humains*. These are the images Sembène had the courage to create, and that recurred in the films of Cissé, Ouédraogo, Sissoko, Traore, and others.

With Independence came a body of films that were fiercely liberationist, like those of Med Hondo, that celebrated revolution, or those of Sarah Maldoror or Haile Gerima, films of radical political engagement. Films of struggle and protest against the nation betrayed by neocolonialism and comprador rulers, by capitalist greed. Now contemporary films by Sissako and Djadjam show

Africans as illegal immigrants striving to get to Europe's shores where they will either drown in the attempt, wash up with the flotsam and jetsam, or wind up selling sunglasses and balloons in the street; hopes trashed; victims of power in a globalized world system. Bare life on the edges of the state of exception, they will carry out Benjamin's prediction that the twentieth century will be marked by those spaces where people without value will live out their lives barely existing under the power of sovereigns whose rule over them had no check.

A cinema of struggle, of oppositionality, of revolt, of cries as in Med Hondo's *Soleil O* (1967). A Third Cinema, a neorealist cinema, an African cinema, a Black Cinema, and even a Third World Cinema. Trash had to be present for the struggle to be given meaning, to show the face of oppression and of worthlessness that had never been seen before because the maids, the servants, the lower classes, the laborers' hardscrabble lives did not make for good entertainment in an economy run by dream machines.

Trash has its trajectory. When measured in terms of loss and lack of value, the trajectory has to be downward, the title "La Noire de . . ." suggesting the anonymity of the servant when seen through the eyes of the master. Even there, from her low status, she descends from nanny in Dakar to maid and desperate prisoner in a Côte d'Azur apartment, and finally corpse found in a bathtub. Like the Borom Sarret who returns home without any money, empty.

But all this changed in a cinema devoted to revolutionary struggle. In the films of revolt, the exhibition of the trashed lives served to educate and motivate the audience to seek change, not simply to commiserate and then leave the movie theater the same as when they entered. Trash was there for a reason: to provide the *damnés de la terre* with the power to stimulate change—the heritage of Césaire's *Cahier d'un Retour au Pays Natal* (1939) now given image and voice on the screen. There is more here than loss; more than decay and a descent. In fact, the descent is here only because of the belief that the depiction of it will serve to enable a change, an ascent, to become possible.

Trash is a stage in the trajectory attached to objects of worth in the economies of value, the economics of trash. While there are limitless economies one might evoke in this study, three in particular receive attention: those of the market, art, and memory (Assman 2002). The theorizing around trash moves from the material to the psychological, sociological, and political, with regimes of trash recycling discarded objects from one order to another: discarded, worthless people from one community to another; states of exception returning the margin to new centers; worthless films from sites where they lie forgotten, and then revived, reformulated, redeemed. A range of theories of history that entail forgetting in the forging of rule and national identity and in the creation of archives, order, and disorder converge around the tropes of trash in the central paradigms of Derrida's *Archive Fever* (1996), Agamben's *Homo Sacer* (1998), Bataille's *Visions of Excess* (1989), Mbembe's "Necropolitics" (2003) and *On the Postcolony* (2001), Mary Douglas's *Purity and Danger* (2002), Timothy Mitchell's *Rule of Experts* (2002), and particularly those dealing explicitly in waste, like *The History of Shit* (LaPorte 2002) and *Waste-Site Stories* (Neville and Villeneuve 2002). Above all, in considering questions of aesthetics and inclusion or exclusion from the community, this book has turned to the theories of Rancière on art, politics, and cinema. Finally, bizarrely, in coming to terms with issues of subjectivity in the trashiest of popular commercial African cinema, Nollywood, I depended on Judith Butler's *Psychic History of Power* (1997).

Work on this project began before I encountered Robert Stam's key essay on the topic, "Beyond Third Cinema: The Aesthetics of Hybridity" (2003), or Chakrabarty's "Of Garbage, Modernity, and the Citizen's Gaze" (2002), an invaluable study of the topic in India. Stam's essay precedes this study in its evocation of garbage, hybridity, and heterophony, taking the same path as *Trash: African Cinema from Below* does in validating those people, those cultural artifacts, considered trash by dominant political and aesthetic discourses. Stam concludes with a celebration of hybridity. I leave to him and Bhabha, as well as my colleague Scott Michaelsen, the issues of hybridity, and take from Stam's essay the inspiration for an approach to postcolonial cinema that frees us from conventional cinema readings of dominant western forms of commercial or of auteur cinema. The wealth of references and knowledge of cinema that emerges in Stam's essay testifies to the considerable impact his work has had on the field for twenty or more years.

Reading contemporary African cinema around the issues of power, subjectivity, exclusion, and above all value led me to a cinema Diawara highlighted in his recent *African Film: Politics and Culture* (2010). Films analyzed here include Joseph Ramaka's *Karmen Gei* (2001), Zeze Gamboa's *O Herói* (2004), Mahamet-Saleh Haroun's *Daratt* (2006), Abderrahmane Sissako's *Bamako* (2006), Fanta Nacro's "Puk Nini" (1995) and her major recent work *La Nuit de la vérité* (2004), Carl Deal and Tia Lessin's *Trouble the Water* (2008), Perry Henzell's *The Harder They Come* (1972), and a host of Nollywood films, including specifically Teco Benson's *Formidable Force* (2002) and Kingsley Ogoro's *Osuofia in London* (2004).

Reading contemporary African cinema around issues of power and trash leads also inevitably to considerations of globalization, to Africa's location in the dumping of toxic waste, and in this study in particular the infamous case of Trafigura's dumping of poisonous containments in Côte d'Ivoire.

Garbology has become a field of study, one that joins the patient examination of dumps from the past to contemporary issues of garbage disposal. From the material to the trope within the economy of the visual image, trash has functioned as the organizing principle for a study that is intended to enable us to engage African cinema in fresh ways.

Certainly the ground for such an approach was already prepared by the magnum opus of Achille Mbembe, *On the Postcolony* (2001). With chapters on "The Aesthetics of Vulgarity," "The Thing and Its Doubles," "Out of the World," and "God's Phallus," Mbembe created images of contemporary power in Africa, and most unforgettably the autocrat, whose body became the site for pleasure and pain, or, in Bataille's terms, consumption and excretion or expenditure. Mbembe's sensibilities are very similar to those expressed in Nollywood, that is, a visual expression of excess, extravaganza, the baroque, or more especially the neo-baroque, all in the service of decimating the gross figure that African rule has come to embody in the contemporary postcolonial period.

He evokes the horrific figures of the Africans created by Europeans in the past—the acephalous man (Mbembe 3), reminding us of Bataille's own imaginary figure of the surrealistic monstrosity to which bourgeois European culture gave rise. In summarizing this negative portrait of Africa concocted by the Europeans, Mbembe describes it as comprising a "bottomless abyss where everything is noise, yawning gap, and primordial chaos" (3). Here, as throughout *On the Postcolony,* there is an immediate link to the broad notion of trash: trashy music ("noise," as in Larkin's *Signal and Noise* [2008]); trashy people (as in Sembène's *déchets humains* or beggars, in *Xala* [1974], "Tauw" [1970], "Borom Sarret" [1963]), and also in the "bare lives" of Agamben's *Homo Sacer* (1998); the forgotten ones whom Buñuel called *Los Olvidados* (1950), the street children of Third World city streets, and Cheikh Oumar Sissoko's "garbage boys," or *Nyamanton* (1986). In these films, precursors to Gamboa's *O Herói* (2004), the urban chaos reflects the larger sense of a social disintegration.

Mbembe senses the risks of an Afro-pessimism in writing about these abuses using the extravagant images of trashiness, and underscores the role of critique in evoking the seamy side of power. But as in a Nollywood film, the boldness of the images and discourse lead him to focus on "the mouth, the belly, and the phallus" (107) in terms that evoke hilarity, even in its most disturbing features. Trash not only describes this iconography that he reads in *Le Messager*'s cartoons of Biya, "Popaul," but also and especially the effects, the aftereffects, the expenditure that *commandement* entails: "For the most part, those who laugh are only reading the signs left, like rubbish, in the wake of the *commandement*" (108). The logorrhea of the autocrats spills over into the discourse of its critique, which is never content with a single expletive but a series of explosions that prepare the way for true vulgarity to follow. Thus the west's construction of Africa, as in the heritage carried on by the autocrat, is marked by an obsessiveness with "the facts of 'absence,' 'lack,' and 'non-being,' of identity and difference, or negativeness—in short of nothingness" (4). For Mbembe, this goes beyond mere oppositionality since difference implies something of substance. But in our larger view of trash as encompassing "bare life" or forgotten histories, nothingness is yet another description of people who do not count, as Rancière puts it. The dead body that washes up on the beach in Sissako's *Heremakono* (2002), as the émigrés wait for another boat to take them north in hopes of reaching Spain, is multiplied in Mbembe's feverish purple prose that gives us the features of an imaginary fit-for-Nollywood version of Evil Powers, Greed, and Utter Destruction: "Terrible movement, laws that underpin and organize tragedy and genocide, gods that present themselves in the guise of death and destitution, monsters lying in wait, corpses coming and going on the tide, infernal powers, threats of all sorts, abandonments, events without response, monstrous couplings, blind waves, impossible paths, terrible forces that every day tear human beings, animals, plants, and things from their sphere of life and condemn them to death" (8). The trailers that run endlessly before each part of Nollywood VCDs give us all the above, in voices filled with the apprehension and excitement that precedes viewing all trashy film, all images of trashy people who behave in the trashiest way. If, as Mbembe mildly concludes, it is true that Africa is not an "incomparable monster" or a "mute place of darkness," he has evoked this untruth in ways that speak in loud decibels, as befits the gothic ruins of thundering detritus. All we need are the titles—"Blood Sisters," "Dangerous Sisters," "Jezebell," "Formidable Force," "Mark of the Beast," or "Witches .com"—and we are prepared to enter into the "mute places of darkness of the heart" that the beast will feed upon. This is the side of Lagos that hosts Djibril Diop Mambety's "hyenas," the beasts of today's urban streets where "saignantes" strut and the rich race through the night in their Mercedes, dressed to kill.

Mbembe's study is ultimately about how the autocratic societies that have emerged in Nigeria, Cameroon, Togo, the DRC, and elsewhere in the continent have joined together the two features of globalization that are ultimately most destructive: the violence of the state and its insatiable greed for consuming commodities of high monetary and low moral value. Thus, through the police and army, violence insures "their grip, through drug trafficking, counterfeiting money, trade in arms and toxic waste, customs frauds, etc." (85). Rubbish and waste alternate from the realm of the literal (toxic waste) to the figurative resonances of words that denote false value (counterfeiting), all in the service of "business" (trade) and death (arms).

By turning to *Le Messager,* Mbembe takes a direction also followed in this study, namely the exploration of the iconography and visual images of trashiness in its manifold features, so that resistance to autocracy might be encouraged. He cites Bakhtin, who looked to the grotesque and obscene in popular cultural performances for "parodies that undermine officialdom" (2001: 103), and where better to look for the obscene than "the mouth, the belly, and the phallus."

Just as Stam looked to the body of Brazilian films to lead him to figures deemed worthless by high society, and just as Mbembe looked to the "belly of the beast," just as Bataille to the acephalic man, the "big toe" that digs into the mud, to every obscure feature of the obscene body so as to free himself, so too will this study engage the materiality of trash as it informs the visual images of contemporary African cinema. It may appear strange to take this approach so as to celebrate that cinema, but the old paths of celebration are no longer living, they are largely zombified, and where better to seek out the zombies than in the monstrous images of a "Nuit de la vérité" with its powerful graffiti and still more powerful nightmarish Walpurgisnacht.

Nollywood is not the answer to trash: it is the answer to African culture's quest for a viable economic basis that rests upon an African audience and its taste. *Trash: African Cinema from Below* attempts to establish a critical basis for reading African cinema beyond the narrow ideological and dogmatic base on which it originally depended. The work of Rancière, Agamben, and Mbembe provides us with approaches to globalized cinema; the work of "garbologists" and anthropologists like Richard Thompson and Mary Douglas and others enables us to deploy notions about that which is "out of place" so as to decipher the themes and images that mark contemporary cinema as a new generation of brilliant filmmakers, beginning with Sissako, Haroun, Kelani, Ramaka, and Nacro, enable us to rethink what we encounter when we view African cinema today.

1 Bataille, Stam, and Locations of Trash

If loving these islands must be my load
Out of corruption my soul takes wings

—Derek Walcott

In *Postcolonial African Cinema* (2007), I threw down the following challenge:

> It is time for a revolution in African film criticism. A revolution against the old tired formulas deployed in justification of filmmaking practices that have not substantially changed in forty years. Time for new voices, a new paradigm, a new view—a new Aristotle to invent the poetics we need for today.
>
> Something trashy, to begin, straight out of the Nigerian video handbook. Something sexy, without the trite poses of exotic behinds spinning the *ventilateur* for the tourists. Something violent, without the obscenity of trivializing brutality, trivializing phallocentric abuse, without the accompanying violence of Truth holding the whiphand over thought or difference.
>
> Most of all, it is the retreat into safe and comfortable truisms that must be disrupted by this new criticism, this new third cinema challenge. (xi)

These words engendered a certain controversy when I was called to account, at an African Studies Association conference, for describing the new cinema I was seeking as "trashy." My goal here is to hold fast to the term "trash," to push into the heart of the rubbish tip until we have reached the breaking point where it will be then possible to return to such phenomena as Nigerian video films, to the melodramatic, not only in Nollywood but elsewhere, to the popular and the popularized. Furthermore, I want to deploy a new paradigm appropriate to the "tip" and the Dungle,[1] where it will be possible to understand trash on its own terms, not in the terms of its opposite, that which produces trash.

It turns out there are a million ways to evoke this concept. The easiest place to begin is with the paradigm of high and low deployed by Bataille in his early writings, published in *Visions of Excess* (1989). At the time, he was very much under the influence of the surrealists, of de Sade, and probably of youthful libidinal energy as he eulogized repeatedly the value of orgies in disrupting western bourgeois society and its orders of height: high culture, high society, and high philosophical thought. I am interested in building on Stam's crucial work on third cinema, like those of Espinosa's "imperfect cinema,"[2] but without subordinating the disruptive quality of imperfection to the ideological or doctrinal program of third cinema.

Bataille's writings in the 1920s and 1930s reflect the influence of surrealism and notions of class as well as social subversions that belong to that period. His is a studied attack on the bourgeoisie and its conventionality, especially its conventional thinking. He sought to remain true to the early principles of a Dadaism and an early surrealism perhaps best summed up in Breton's famous comment that "the simplest surrealist act consists of dashing into the street, pistol in hand, and firing blindly, as fast as you can pull the trigger, into the crowd" (125). When the surrealists took little notice of Bataille's attempts at outrageous writing, and when their artistic successes resulted in wide acceptance in the world of culture, Bataille became disillusioned with them. Our interest in his work lies in his studied fidelity to a discourse whose site of enunciation is associated with everything the comfortable bourgeois would regard as "below."[3]

"Below" is one location for trash. Its value shapes the ways in which one might view the world and speak. Bataille's rigorous adherence to this site and all the ramifications he finds there for enabling revolutionary, disruptive acts to be performed, for subversive speech to be articulated, provides a valuable approach to thinking through trash in its various permutations in the African context.

Stam could not be more different, though he too embraces trash as a point of departure. Whereas Bataille writes out of the post–World War I period with the rise to dominance of bourgeois culture, and its period of ensuring economic and political crisis in the 1930s before communist ideals had been tarnished by reports about the gulag, Stam's work might be dubbed post-Vietnam. It is grounded in the values of the counterculture of the 1960s, coming to fruition with his studies of postcolonial media, especially cinema, as his work helped define the core of left cultural politics that developed in the 1980s and 1990s. His joint publications with Ella Shohat are emblematic of a Third Worldism and its cultural and political critiques of late capitalism (for example, *Unthinking Eurocentrism: Multiculturalism and Media* 1994; *Multiculturalism, Postcoloniality, and Transnational Media* 2003). The earliest version of Stam's essay on trash cited here was given in a conference paper in 1997, and it was published in Guneratne and Dissanayake's *Rethinking Third Cinema* (2003).

The essay offers a broad compendium of positions on culture produced from below, and in particular provides three examples of Brazilian films in which Stam also locates examples of a "cinema of garbage." The range of positions he embraces includes critiques of commodity capitalism, the literal and figurative dumping of Euro-American toxic waste, from commercial films to dominant ideological codes. In contrast to high culture and its pretensions of value centered on purity and presence, he opposed hybridity and contamination, or garbage, as a site of resistance. Like Bataille, his favored site of enunciation is from below—Bataille stressing the erotic and abject, Stam the wretched of the earth and their oppression. But Bataille's scorn is ultimately for bourgeois culture and social domination, whereas Stam's is located in Third World resistance, what he terms a "social indictment."

This study will depend upon both, using the earlier thinker for his focus on the notion of what is "below" and the images associated with such a position as emblematic of what is trash. The later thinker laid the groundwork for a politics that exceeds the easy, early dogmatic positions that limited the notion of what was possible as politics in the 1960s and 1970s. But this study will also see in Bataille and Stam the limits of positions that depend systematically upon binary oppositions to provide a location for what is "below." Spivak's critique of a postcolonialism that depends upon the categories of the very thing it is opposing will apply here as well. No one sums up more succinctly than Stam the world of political engagement for today, from AIDS to poverty to late capitalist exploitation. No one situates it better in a global context. But we can't stop there if trash is to be engaged in its fullness. For a transformative epistemology to be formulated, we have to consider the location of trash not simply on the axis of above and below, the one rotating above the other. There needs to be a disconnection, as in the loss of a limb to a land mine, or a paralysis suffered by the use of a medicine that is out of date. For this, the larger readjustment of what is seen to be normal and natural has to occur.

I wish to "trouble the waters" of the binary, above-below, by aligning not simply with the hybrid, mestizo, métis counter to the racially pure, or by placing an African ideal against a western one. This will require seeing the moon in more than two opposed locations, as Dionne Brand envisages in her title *In the Full and Change of the Moon* (1999), which was meant to encapsulate the passage of diaspora generations from the past into the present with the motion from the total and pure heights and the darkened bottom of the cycle of change. I want to situate trash not simply in the Sierra Madre mountains of revolt but in some more indefinite, ill-defined, uncomfortable position where the grain of sand comes to trouble and destabilize the oyster's sense of wholeness. That location, then, pace Bataille, is an alternative kind of belowness, a Bottoms that cannot be set in opposition to an Icarus above. Similarly, it is a personal space this is occupied by someone who is neither racially pure or hybrid, a person who sees herself in a mirror that is slanted in respect to the other two positions. Whereas purity and hybridity can reflect back a place or identity for the viewer to safely occupy with an assurance of knowing where you are—a Creole, for instance—trash is more like the ghostly presence of a missing limb, an object of desire that cannot be directly perceived, that is lost like a beloved child or mother to whose presence one makes an appeal on a TV show dedicated to reuniting lost members of a family, without a connection made at the end.

So Bataille and Stam will offer us the first steps on a program that will gesture toward a fuller readjustment of our vision when viewing African cinema. For that fuller readjustment, our shared manner of perceiving will have to shift its coordinates, in the manner suggested by Rancière along the lines of what he terms "le partage du sensible." That will be developed in subsequent chapters.

We begin with Stam and his garbage. For Stam, the value of garbage lies in its ability to disrupt the easy codes of domination. He writes, "Garbage, like death and excrement, is a great social leveler" (41). While he emphasizes the materiality of garbage, its function as the id, placing it "below" in every sense—"it steams and smells below the threshold of ideological rationalization and sublimation" (40)—his purpose is always to evoke its disruptive qualities in relation to the high points that serve as its referential marker: "garbage is reflective of social prestige; wealth and status are correlated with the capacity of a person (or a society) to discard commodities, i.e., to generate garbage" (40). The advantage of this low vantage point is that it illuminates what goes unperceived by those who so casually discard their wrappers while tasting the delectable candies: "The third shared feature of these hybrid bricolage aessthetics is their common leitmotif of the strategic redemption of the low, the despised, the imperfect, and the 'trashy' as part of a social overturning" (35). Even when denying its ideological or subliminal qualities, he still returns to a functionality, such as "social overturning" or conscientization clothed in the language of lucidity. He writes, "In these films, the garbage dump becomes a critical vantage point from which to view society as a whole" (45), and in so doing, he does not indicate the partial perspective from the vantage point, but its ability to reveal the false consciousness constructed from above: "It reveals the social formation as seen 'from below'" (45). Thus, "garbage defines and illuminates the world" (45). And although its materiality cannot be denied, its legibility reveals a metaphorical function: "It can also be read symptomatically, as a metaphorical figure for social indictment . . . an allegorical text to be deciphered, a form of social colonics where the truth of a society can be 'read' in its waste products" (45).

Stam sees in hybridity the correlate to garbage, inasmuch as mixture is framed by its opposition to purity. The colonial scene validates pure racial identities: as Robert Young confirmed in *Colonial Desire* (1995), colonialism presented métissage as life-negating in the belief held in the eighteenth century that mixed races eventually bred sterility in the species, in contrast to the notion that reproduction of pure races was life affirming. If mixed-race people were the lowest types to emerge in the dominant discourse of the nineteenth century, their status as wretched victims of racist ideologies best positioned them as figures for resistance and ultimately liberation in the postcolonial twentieth century. Thus Stam finds in "hybrid bricolage" the common theme of the "strategic redemption of the low, the despised, the imperfect, and the 'trashy' as part of social overturning" (35).

Stam's archive of the low and the despised is vast. Whether he evokes Bakhtin's "redeeming filth," Derrida's marginalia, Benjamin's "trash of history," Deleuze and Guattari's schizophrenia, or Camp's recuperation of kitsch (Stam 35), he is able to move from the aesthetics of trash to the politics of the low and the despised, from a cinema of the despised to garbage aesthetics—all the time evoking a politics of resistance not far from the initial impulses of Third Worldism. The readings he gives of what is seen as low life, low culture, low and debased forms of art, film, society—"the low, the despised, the imperfect, and the 'trashy'"—are converted into gold and silver: "the base metals of titles, blank frames, and wild sound [are transformed] into the gold and silver of rhythmic virtuosity" (35). A people's art transformed from "history" and memory into a People's History, into a moment in modernism's quilt, a "para-modern" aesthetic that reconfigures the temporalities and cultural practices of the underclass into positive terms. Every debased moment becomes an occasion for its sublation, its "negation of the negation" (36) through its immersion in the mixed, the heterogeneous, the heterological, the multiple, the "palimpsestic overlay" of polyphonous and hybridized "multichronotopicality" (37). The evocations of hybrid forms in music, art, cinema, history, society are multilayered and above all marked by immiscion in the avant-gardism of the postmodern moment, or more, in the postcolonial moment since the points of reference repeatedly return to cinema's Third locations, be they in independent western film, or Latin American and African film.

The joining of the low or debased and the mixed is captured in the phrase, "garbage is hybrid" (40), which encapsulates a plethora of combinatory possibilities, all marked by the three qualities Stam highlights in his essay, hybridity, chronotopic multiplicity, and the redemption of detritus. Here is his culminating list of hybridity's properties: it is "the diasporized, heterotopic site of the promiscuous mingling of rich and poor, center and periphery, the industrial and the artisanal, the domestic and the public, the durable and the transient, the organic and the inorganic, the national and the international, the local and the global." To cap it, he proclaims garbage the "ideal postmodern and postcolonial metaphor" as it is "mixed, synchretic, a racially decentered social text"(40). Detritus becomes more than an aspect of society and culture here; it is the moment of our times that proclaims a new cultural dominant, the defining quality of the socius. This is particularly apt when socius is viewed as the site for nonproductive expenditure and excess: "It [socius] appropriates the excessive forces of production, distributing some for the reproduction of society and wasting most (in the form of tribal honors, palaces, and ultimately war)" (Holland 62). Eugene Holland underscores the centrality of "'anti-production' of an expenditure that is at once useless (constituting a vast appropriation of productive forces for excess and expenditure) and useful (reproducing the relations) and thus does not fit within a neat Marxist conceptualization of 'forces' and 'relations' of production" (Holland 1999: 62–63).[4]

Hybridity can accomplish this decentering because of two qualities that continually mark Stam's listings: the binary opposition of detritus to the cultural norm that privileges and naturalizes aesthetic and economic dominants—the upper classes and higher social manifestations of their cultural lives, the performances of high culture and high society as located in the authorized social sites, the theaters and stages of wealth and value. Stam's garbage is set against these sites, not ensconced within its own locations. Dirt, as Stam approvingly notes, citing Douglas, is "matter out of place." And secondly, because it is in conflict with the upper social and cultural reaches, it is naturalized as subversive if not revolutionary, and ultimately as "redemptive" as well as redeemable.

For Stam, oppositionality and redemptiveness sustain the frame of intelligibility that defined the lowly and trashy, that gave their aesthetic and ethic meaning. As the "ideal postmodern and postcolonial metaphor," they remain positioned by modernity and colonial discourse. In short, they are not independent from the very thing against which they have positioned themselves. (This is essentially Spivak's argument about the discourse of postcolonialism as being indebted to the very frame that it seeks to resist.) Hybridity thus fails to extract itself from a location that promises the continuity and presence of what detritus was intended to undermine.

The undermining could not take place, the abjection could only be incomplete, only "juxtaposed" as Stam recognizes in his use of Foucault's term "heterotopia," which he glosses as "the juxtaposition in a real place of 'several sites that are themselves incompatible'" (40). Kristeva signals this partial distancing move—mixing, juxtaposing, syncretizing—in her presentation of the abject as necessary to sustain the same border through which the abject was expelled. The border requires the presence of the abject alongside its expulsion and absence in order that the clean and clear center, the ego, the self, might sustain itself. But the self "itself" must be positioned against its other, its own other, its self and its own different dimensions, in order to give presence to itself. Garbage becomes the needed feature and location against which the discriminatory intellect can establish its difference, its claim to being special, worthy, separate. Where all is indiscriminately merged, social and psychic difference becomes polluted:

> Garbage, like death and excrement, is a great social leveler, the trysting point of the funky and the shi shi. It is the terminus for what Mary Douglas calls "matter out of place." In social terms, it is a truth-teller. As the lower stratus of the socius, the symbolic "bottom" or *cloaca maxima* of the body politic, garbage signals the return of the repressed; it is the place where used condoms, bloody tampons, infected needles and unwanted babies are left, the ultimate resting place of all that society both produces and represses, secretes and makes secret. (Stam 41)

Again Stam sees this leveling as a function of juxtaposing, with "violent, surprising juxtapositions" (41), or neobaroque combinations that startle and shock, often enough in their revolting disclosures of the ugly and deformed.

Stam's list of detritus continues, with the psychic location becoming that of the "return of the repressed," and with society's "bloody tampons" and "infected needles"—that is, the abject. In Stam's closest formulation to Bataille's, this becomes the "grossly material" as it "steams and smells below the threshold of ideological rationalization and sublimation" (41). At this point, it is hard to see where the negation of the negative can occur or where the redemption of the excremental can take place. Stam turns to the Brazilian aesthetic of garbage, the "boca de lixo" which he sets in contrast to the "boca de luxo" (mouth of garbage versus mouth of luxury), evoking Sganzerla's film *Red Light Bandit* (1968) (41–42). But the qualities he indicates in this aesthetic of trash remain dialectically positioned, inevitably, even when not sublated. The low remains, but set within the binary's frame, its *partage du sensible*. Thus Eduardo Coutinho's *O Fio da Memoria* (The Thread of Memory, 1991) is described as offering "a history based on disjunctive scraps and fragments" *instead of* "a history as a coherent, linear narrative" (42). Returning to his central trope of redemption (again in contrast to Bataille for whom the "Icarian" impulse betrays the disruptive force of trash), Stam describes how garbage in the film is recuperated: "a transformative impulse takes an object considered worthless and turns it into something of value. Here the restoration of the buried worth of a cast-off object analogizes the process of revealing the hidden worth of the despised, devalued artist himself. . . . The trash of the haves becomes the treasure of the have-nots; the dank and unsanitary is transmogrified into the sublime and the beautiful" (42).

Redemption and sublimation, in fact, have their day, as one side or another of the consumerist proclivities of the wealthy are overturned by the return of their repressed detritus against them. Hybridity becomes revolutionary, but the revolution revolves within the same framework established when the initial Hegelian moment of domination had its day. That day comes to light thanks to garbage since garbage "defines and illuminates the world" (45), and in so doing enables the lucid exposure of history to occur. But the limits of the illumination remain as they had been from the outset: the society is indicted, its "truth" revealed, its contours made plain, and its sensibilities, along with the community of those sharing those sensibilities, retained.

For Scott Michaelsen, hybridity theory reaches its limits precisely because of its "logic of cultural resistance" (*Anthropology's Wake* 174). Racial theorizing of the nineteenth century turns on this question of resistance when hybridity is viewed as either the result of different species of humans intermingling, or of the formation of separate races by the differentiation of descendants of the same species. The texts of mingling or separating turned on the positioning of one race against another, be they the product of mono-or polygenetic origins. Similarly, Stam's hybrid structures inevitably were positioned against other non-hybrid forms—those typically placed in superior, dominating, authorized roles. The disruptions caused by hybridity were intended to reveal the consequences of the actions of the dominant social classes. Logically, Michaelsen points out that the mere act of mixing doesn't produce hybridity as long as the individual elements can still be identified as such: "A hybrid that can be disarticulated, then, is a compound without mixture, is not a hybrid" (175). As long as the métis is half and half, the quadroon one-quarter and three-quarters, the octroon one-eighth, and so forth, the compound remains unmixed, disarticulated. As long as the "lixo" is set against the "luxo," we have a difference that is not a "différance," that is, a difference that is finite and temporal—a difference that gives definition to identities. The trash here is not disruptive of the definition, it gives definition; it is not indefinite, but finite and definitive. It remains within the system that gives it definition; it is oppositional trash.

But there is another reading to trash, one on which Bataille insists even as he is trapped within the same logic of high and low. He holds to a non-sublimated and non-sublated materiality, one that cannot be conflated with the redemptive idea. We can explore his metaphors and notions of this trash as well, noting in the process that as long as the hybrid is set against the pure, the low against the high, there is always the possibility of reading trash as not simply that which is set against its opposite, but as the troubling factor, the grain of sand or dirt within the oyster's shell, that remains without being absorbed or transformed into the pearl.

Michaelsen reaches for this extra-systemic figure by citing Samira Kawash's notion of the hybrid that is not a mixture but rather as that which "appears for the racially constituted subject as that which cannot appear" (*Dislocating the Color Line*, 184). Michaelsen presents this alternative figure of hybridity as one that is not a mixture, not a figure that arrives as a determined definition, but which resists "positive determination of the subject" to the ultimate degree, that is, "all the way down" (184).

Michaelsen's other example is that of Agamben's "quodlibet" or "whatever being," a being that cannot coalesce into someone with an identity (185). It might be possible to read the figure of the hero without a leg as a man without an identity (*O Herói* [2004]), or the beggars who chant their curses against Al Hadj as nameless figures excluded from the state (*Xala* [1974]). The possibilities offered by African cinema for a reading of trash as both resistant and more than simply oppositional, as a thing, not simply wretched but "damné" *all the way down;* as a marinated colonel, literally and figuratively grilled all the way to his scarlet death, all the way down (*La Nuit de la vérité* [2004]). These are the possibilities both for a revolution and for a Bataillean erotic abjection. For Michaelsen, this figure conjured up by Kawash presents "a form of hybridity that breaks with liberal-democratic politics of recognition, rights, cultural citizenship, and the like" (184). We can say that the aesthetics of trash engender a similar break, and paradoxically make possible a politics of the common, of the community of those viewing the world from below, and who remain situated there, without the Hollywoodian finality of being raised to the status of the saved, the redeemed at the end; without the angels of *Miracle in Milan* (1951).

With such a tour de force of references to garbage mustered by Stam, it is difficult to construct an additional locus from which to approach the role of trash. However, Bataille's youthful revolutionary rejection of the high points of society extends to the work of theorizing or intellectualizing itself—not so as to achieve a desublimation, which for Marcuse was the effect of popular culture's repressive mechanisms—but to challenge the status of the intellectualized concept in relation to the material function. Bataille writes about the upper classes as making almost exclusive use of ideas, so that "even when those ideas have a low origin they are no less elaborated *in a high place,* in high intellectual spheres, before taking on universal value" (36). In contrast to this reaching upward, he counterposes the actions of the plant whose roots reach down into the soil: a plant's "obscene-looking roots" are thrust down "into the earth in order to assimilate the putrescence of organic matter, and a man experiences, in contradiction to strict morality, urges that draw him to what is low, placing him in open antagonism to all forms of spiritual elevation" (36). The tendency to seek the transcendental moment he terms the "Icarus adventure" (37), the desire to rise above social conditions generates a category of the sublime that "has become useless to industrial and commercial development in ordinary times" (37). Ultimately for Bataille, writing at the high point of western industrial capitalism, the power of this economic order is measured in its drive to render abstract that power in the form of the concept of bank capital, capitalist power "constitut[ing] a perfect incarnation of this idea, i.e., what is most elevated and free of the intervention of any values other than material utility" (37). The rage to seek elevation is futile, in this regard: Nietzsche's exertions to do so, in a modern capitalist age, could only find anachronistic adherents, those who found in his "romantic exaltation" the "improbable soaring of archaic values" (38) whose quaintness only confirms the dominant order and its crass forms of exploitation and rule. For Bataille, treating modes of resistance as higher incarnations than the system it opposes results in elevated postures that reinforce that very system. Thus, when de Sade's grossest interventions are turned by the surrealists into gestures of revolt, when the surrealists' own materialism is subordinated to that program, they too succumb to the "Icarian pose" with which Bataille identifies the "moralistic idealist": "that Sade, emasculated by his cowardly apologists, takes on the form of a moralising idealist. . . . All claims from below have been scurrilously disguised as claims from above: and the surrealists, having become the laughing-stock of those who have seen close up a sorry and shabby failure, obstinately hold on to their magnificent Icarian pose" (39).

If, as Stam would have it, "garbage illuminates the world," it is the deployment of "illumination" for ideological purposes that betrays the base status of the garbage: its illuminations raise it to the very heights that cast shadows of obscurantisms, false consciousness, Reaganomics, and ultimately the nets of structural adjustments over the lower economies of the trashed. Icarus rises to fall; he falls into the obscurity from which he arose. That is, in the attempt to deploy the material, Stam's ideal of illumination elevates the idea in its place. I cannot guarantee that I will avoid the same reversion into this position since I share substantially the values of Stam, his co-editor Shohat, and indeed that familiar list of Third Worldist cinema critics, including Paul Willemen, Julianne Burton, and others for whom the rigidities of Teshome Gabriel's ideological approach proved too much of a straitjacket. And although I find sympathetic Bataille's anti-idealist images—setting the mole against the eagle, bringing Icarus back to earth—it isn't clear how one is to enter into the materiality of, say, Sissako's *Bamako* (2006) without simultaneously entering the courtyard of the idealistic mock trial being held in the film, where the World Bank will have to answer for its maladjustments of African societies. The repudiation of dogma cannot permit us to do away with a politics of resistance, and it is difficult to see where resistance can itself resist being cast into ideological form, where the earlier attempts of the surrealists and dadaists failed to do so. Bataille images this conundrum for us, centering his thought on the figure of the eagle, an appropriate one for the age of the American imperium:

> From the point of view of appearance and brilliance, the eagle is obviously the more virile conception of the two [eagle and "old mole"]. Not only does it rise in radiant zones of the solar sky, but it resides there with uncontested glamour. The eagle's hooked beak, which cuts all that enters into competition with it and cannot be cut, suggests its sovereign virility. Thus the eagle has formed an alliance with the sun, which castrates all that enters into conflict with it (Icarus, Prometheus, the Mithraic bull). Politically the eagle is identified with imperialism, that is, with the unconstrained development of individual authoritarian power, triumphant over all obstacles. And metaphysically the eagle is identified with the *idea,* when, young and aggressive, it has not yet reached a state of pure abstraction, when it is still only the unbounded development of concrete fact disguised as divine necessity.
>
> Revolutionary idealism tends to make of the revolution an eagle above eagles, a *supereagle* striking down authoritarian imperialism, an idea as radiant as an adolescent eloquently seizing power for the benefit of utopian enlightenment. This detour naturally leads to the failure of the revolution and, with the help of military fascism, the satisfaction of the elevated need for idealism. (34)

The upshot of this revolution betrayed is, for Bataille, the inevitable reiteration of a value placed on the heights where ideas reside, despite all attempts to ground them in the material. Pace Stam, it is as though Bataille's lament were written to critique his brilliant exegesis on garbage:

> It is true that is seems easy to characterize in this manner the antinomy of high and low, but this antinomy, more than any other, is thereby immediately deprived of interest and meaning. All of its interest and meaning are linked to the irreconcilable nature of its specific forms: the terrifying darkness of tombs or caves and the luminous splendor of heaven, the impurity of earth where bodies rot and the purity of lofty space; on the order of the individual the base and noble faculties, on the political order the imperialist eagle and the "old-

mole" revolution, as on the universal order matter, vile and base reality, and elevated spirit. (35)

His lament would thus be with the loss of what, in its lowness, lacks the elevation necessary to generate illumination and sublimity: "Even in its most general form, the opposition which runs from the Very-High to the Very-Low has disappeared with the success of secular philosophy" (35).

In his attempt to remain faithful to this opposition, to attend to the "old-mole" as Very-Low, Bataille generates categories that lend themselves to Stam's validation of the hybrid, that is, the heterogeneous as opposed to the homogeneous. Bataille associates with the former the lawless, the lacerated—a series of categories Stam figured effectively in the urban barrios or favelas of many recent third cinema or postcolonial productions (including most recently *Slumdog Millionaire* [2008]). The recent Angolan film *O Herói* (2004) might well serve to elucidate how Bataille's old-mole underground translates into the postwar setting of Luanda. A combination of wounded souls fit into the city's depleted spaces: Vitorio, the protagonist whose leg was blown off in the wars of Angola; Manu, the child of a soldier who is missing in action and whom we can assume to be dead. Manu is gradually turning into a street child, with a gang that seizes opportunities to steal whenever they can. Vitorio's love interest is Judite, a prostitute who has lost her child in the war. There is also Manu's grandmother who was left with no children. In one key scene, we witness the telecasting of appeals to locate lost relatives made before the cameras by an endless line of orphans, widows, and bereaved relatives. The tropes of loss, disconnection, and the discarded are made manifest by Vitorio's prosthesis which is stolen early in the film. As the stolen prosthesis makes its way through the hands of a street gang, a fence, and Manu who trades a stolen radio for it, we come to appreciate how the system of exchanges on which the economy depends has had to go underground in order for people to survive. The old mole works through the used trash refashioned by the fence whose goods include an AK-47, a wicked knife, and an endless heap of stolen goods that are gradually recycled back into circulation. The prosthesis enters into the orbit of recycling, and as such functions as a trope for the nation of Angola and its people, whose lives were wrecked by a quarter century of civil war and whose limbs were lost to an endless supply of landmines.

The lives of *O Herói*'s characters are the products of a process that cannot be dissociated from the global strategies of the great powers and from the global economics that ignite the wars that rely upon diamonds and gold to provide money to purchase arms. Angola has added vast oil reserves to this mix, and as a result suffered from a civil war, a proxy war for China, the United States, the Soviet Union, Cuba, and South Africa, for a quarter century—a war that cost hundreds of thousands of lives and left the landscape littered with landmines. The "heterogeneous" trash generated by the conflict was embodied by the characters mentioned above. It is important to situate the specter of these, the Very-Low, whose relationships to others in the film serve to situate the aspects of detritus within the economy of appropriation and expenditure.[5]

At every point, Bataille worries about the vertical structure marked by high or privileged sectors and low or diminished sectors. The thought that elevates, that collapses all ecstasies into one heaven, one hell, stands in contrast to the multiplicities of demonical representations to which undeveloped thought gives rise. Bataille always want to associate the orgiastic, the sexually excited impulse, with this lower domain, and with it a servility that can only know revolt in opposition to that which would reduce its excitability. Like Hegel, he looks to the classes of slaves for some advancement beyond the stasis of the homogeneous. In his conception of this revolt, ecstasy and frenzy play central roles:

> All organizations that have ecstasy and frenzy as their goal (the spectacular death of animals, partial tortures, orgiastic dances, etc.) will have no reason to disappear when a heterological conception of human life is substituted for the primitive conception: they can only transform themselves while they spread under the violent impetus of a moral doctrine of white origin, taught to blacks by all those whites who have become aware of the abominable inhibitions paralyzing their race's communities. It is only starting from this collusion of European scientific theory with black practice that institutions can develop which will serve as the final outlets (with no other limitations than those of human strength) for the urges that today require worldwide society's fiery and bloody Revolution. (102)

This was not exactly Senghor's "Civilization of the Universal," but it can find perverse companionship with Sartre's desire, in "Black Orpheus," to find the negation in Negritude so needed by a post–World War II Europe.

"Urges" that result in "fiery and bloody Revolution" inform the lives of the slaves, for Bataille. Following Hegel, he envisions the masters as having distanced themselves from work, the material realm, and ultimately those primeval urges to which black people still have greater access. These repellant notions that divide "civilized" and "colonized" peoples, which want to see in the colonized something less alienated from nature, have long degraded European thought, especially during the colonial period, as we have seen in writers like Joyce Cary with his lamentable visions of the "semi-civilized" Mr. Johnson, or like V. S. Naipaul with his mimic men. Bataille's infatuation with "being" reflects this conception as he views the slave's existence as more fully engaged in the processes of creation and destruction: "Being," he states, "increases in the tumultuous agitation of a life that knows no limits; it wastes away and disappears if he who is at the same time 'being' and knowledge mutilates himself by reducing himself to knowledge" (172).

Being is dynamic, heterological: the sustenance of the foreign elements that accentuate the function of expenditure—of excretion, including sexual activity, the abjecting of bodily fluids, the disruption of the static equilibrium sought in the sublimation of thought—all serve the "universe's sources of excitation" and at the same time "the development of a servile human species" (97).[6] As Bataille puts it in more inspired terms, "Being attains the blinding flash in tragic annihilation . . . It is not only the composition of elements that constitutes the incandescence of being, but its decomposition in its mortal form" (177). This process is echoed in laughter that is "assumed by the totality of being" (177). The figure of the bull, throwing itself into the void, like laughter, makes possible the heterogeneous in its most ecstatic phase, where "the void it meets is also the nudity it espouses TO THE EXTENT THAT IT IS A MONSTER lightly assuming many crimes," at which point "nothingness itself is its plaything." It thus illuminates the night for a moment "with an immense laugh" (177). For Senghor, that is the Negro's great laugh: "Et les oreilles, surtout les oreilles de Dieu qui d'un rire de saxophone créa le ciel et la terre en six jours. / Et le septième jour, il dormit du grand sommeil nègre" ("And to hear, especially to hear the Lord, who with a saxophonic laugh, created heaven and earth in six days / And on the seventh, slept a great Negro sleep"; 141).

In an alternative reading of the ex-stasis and heterogeneous, Jonathan Boulter reads Bataille (and especially his "Story of the Eye") as exhibiting all the elements of trauma whose inner experience is constituted by "the profound, unmediated confrontation with loss, degradation." Most tellingly, trauma, and anguish mark the inner experience defined as "the encounter with anguish removed from the possibility of transcendence" (14).

We can term this embrace of trash, of the "orgiastic dances" of slaves, as with Senghor's images of trashy used condoms in the gutters of New York, of its wailing saxophones and the great black belly laugh, as the romantic version of what Bataille envisions by the term "excess." If Senghor wants to turn the ashes of the "femme noire" into "cendres pour nourrir les racines de la vie" (ashes to nourish the roots of life), it is only because his Negritude, unlike Bataille's excrement, is dialectically placed in his poem "Femme noire" in the service of the Higher Idea, commensurate with the poet's emplacement high on a parched hill from which he can hold the vision of the black woman. This is the beautiful negation embodied by the black man, the "barbare," of whom Césaire speaks directly: "Barbare / du langage sommaire / et nos faces belles comme le vrai pouvoir opératoire / de la négation" (Barbarous/ rough language / and our beautiful faces like the true, surgical power / of negation; 78). Bataille's epigraph to the essay cited above concerning Being and laughter again celebrates the dialectical negative: "Negativity, in other words, the integrity of determination" (Hegel cited in Bataille 171).

The dialectic emerges in "Story of the Eye" as defined by the relationship between the taboo and its transgression, each needing the other, both completing the anguish of trauma, according to Boulter: "Without transgression there is no taboo, without taboo there is no transgression: The Transgression does not deny the taboo but transcends it and completes it." "The reciprocal and symbiotic relation between taboo and transgression reinforces the taboo by sanctifying it. And this reciprocal relation is continually mediated by anguish or the realization of the trauma that instigates both the taboo and its transgression" (12). Transgression functions as negation without sublation, freezing the dialectic in a completed reciprocity, one unmediated by ethics or salvation but nevertheless sanctified in the erotic ecstasy of the trauma.

Like all celebrations, the romantic embrace of the negative occludes as much as it exhibits. The laughter's creative burst, the light that illuminates the night, the power and determining force that enables the monstrous to assume the totality of being, leaves the partially assumed being in the twilight edges of the celebratory vision. As always, the oppositional powers of negation illuminate the path hidden by the dominant class in its affirmation of value, its rationalization for its position, its deployment of the forces of order, so scorned by Césaire in his opening of the great poem the *Cahier d'un retour au pays natal:* "Au bout du petit matin . . . / Va-t-en, lui disais-je, gueule de flic, gueule de vache, va-t-en je déteste les larbins de l'ordre et les hannetons de l'esperance" (At the end of twilight . . . / beat it, I told him, mug of a cop, mug of a cow, beat it I detest flunkies of order and beetles of hope; 7). "Flunkies of order," "beetles of hope," with their "cops' mugs"—these are the true faces of romantic negation, a posturing of negation to combat the depressingly ordinary forms of subjugation that Césaire will encounter later in his recollection of a moment of complicity, when he laughed along with the bourgeois women on board a bus at the sight of a large, beaten-down black man, sitting alone with his fatigue: "Il était COMIQUE ET LAID, / COMIQUE ET LAID pour sûr. / J'arborai un grande sourire complice . . . / Ma lâcheté retrouvée!" (He was comic and ugly, / comic and ugly for sure. / I would wear a great smile of complicity . . . / My cowardice rediscovered!; 41).

For a range of Caribbean authors, the totalizing gestures of negation need to be attenuated so as to accommodate those in-between spaces that define their ontological status. For Derek Walcott, in his celebrated essay "What the Twilight Says," it is at dusk, at the edges of the day, that the light best captures the tints of ordinary people's lives: "When dusk heightens, like amber on a stage set, those ramshackle hoardings of wood and rusting iron which circle our cities, a theatrical sorrow rises with it. . . . Deprivation is made lyrical, and twilight, with the patience of alchemy, almost transmutes despair into virtue" (3). Against this backdrop, he opposes the vision of those enthused over the "African" phase for whom the celebration of a "romantic darkness" is ultimately little more than "another treachery, this time perpetuated by the intellectual" (8). The refusal of an absolute politics of racial identity grounded in dogmatic affectation led Walcott to a theatre of ironic demystification rather than of revolt. For Glissant and subsequently for the Creolists, twilight bred shades of contamination etching figures of hybridity, and for Chamoiseau, créolité. The system of exchanges on which Negritude is based leaves out systems not reducible to black and white or colonized, colonizer binaries. In *Dream on Monkey Mountain* (1967), Walcott's Corporal Lestrade, the mixed-race jailor, embodies this métissage as a condemned man's sentence, one that Makak can redeem only at the price of the pure face of negation: "They [the whites] reject half of you. We accept all" (300). Similarly, the police sergeant and inspector in Chamoiseau's *Solibo* (1997), Boisfesse and Pilon, turn away from the creole to a French that they cannot embrace and cannot deny: Pilon "petitions for Creole in the schools but jumps when his children use it to speak to him, crowns Césaire a great poet without ever having read him, venerates the Antilleanity of the July cultural festival with its outdoor theater but dreams of Jean Gosselin's variety shows.... He lives like all of us, at two speeds, not knowing whether he should put on the brakes when going uphill or accelerate going down" (76).

If every system is marked by occlusions that give it definition, by supplements that fill what is lacking to complete the system, virtual centers without points of origin or histories without originary moments, the simulacra of totalized structures, then oppositionality and the politics of resistance are threatened with an endless coil of differences, substitutions, incompleteness. James Ferguson enables us to hold onto the thread of resistance by focusing on one clear issue, social inequality. For Ferguson, the ideals of development as forms of generosity function in a similar way to that of the romanticization of negation. With his discovery of his cowardice, Césaire sought to move away from his earlier egotistical assumption of the role of superior spokesman for his people. Ferguson would ask what occlusions of social inequality are enacted by the romantic versions of development; what less dramatic posture might be uncovered if the production of wealth is the outcome of appropriations that entail and sustain social inequalities. Césaire turns toward his complicity with the class-based values of the colonialist, and furiously disgorges both them and his cowardice. The gueule de flic, de vache, is revealed to be his own—the great discovery of the Negritude poet in his inward gaze. By turning to Ferguson, we can move on, past the fascination, revulsion, and self-overcoming that that gaze engenders. The gueule de flic may become a metaphor for the colonized subject's own subjection, and the pouvoir opératoire needed to reject it; but the flic is still there at the end of the twilight, au bout du petit matin, still walking his beat. Ferguson's look into what he calls the "global shadows" involves not the liberation from false consciousness but the opening of the vision onto the powers at work in the global enterprises that continue to dump their toxic wastes on the continent. For this we can begin with Lawrence Summers.

In December 1991, Summers sent a memo that was later made public in which he scandalously stated that since "the measurement of the costs of health-impairing pollution depends on the foregone earnings from increased morbidity and mortality, a given amount of health-impairing pollution should be done in the country with the lowest cost, which will be the country with the

lowest wages" (cited in Ferguson 70). Between illegal dumping and this pre-
scription for legal polluting, there is not a shred of moral difference since, as
Summers goes on to say, moral reasons and social concerns "could be turned
around and used more or less effectively against every Bank proposal for lib-
eralization" (cited in Ferguson 70–71). The view *of* the garbage dump is clearly
different from the view *from* the garbage dump. And if that were not clear
enough from the outrage his words engendered, we might also consider, from
the dumpside, the status not only of life for those "with the lowest wages" but
of what they make of that which others discard. For example, junk art—not the
old variety, meaning tourist or airport art, but the new, aesthetically validated
variety in which "recupérés" or art made from recuperated trash is now being
sold on the tourist and art markets. In Dakar, the largest, oldest of dumps was
functioning long enough for entire families to take up residence on its prem-
ises, and for generations to live off its resources. As President Wade contemplated closing the public dump in 2005–2006, marginal expressions of concern
for those families echoed in the press—the opposition press. Ferguson's vision
requires that we first examine that dump, à la Summers, to see what benefits
might accrue from its existence and resources, to view it within the perspective
of the community, of the city authorities, of the local inhabitants and local experts, and then the development community. This could be taken as the Summers trash story: the one that takes into account the costs and benefits of living
off trash, of contributing trash to an impoverished community whose assets and
benefits cannot be offset by becoming the recipient of others' waste—indeed,
who are judged to be so diminished that any increase in radioactive exposure
cannot seriously constitute a risk since they wouldn't live long enough to contract prostate cancer anyway. Thus, such countries, such humble village people,
must be understood to be "*under*-polluted" in proportion to their "underpopu-
lation" (70). Between Bataille's romanticism and Summers' realpolitik, Ferguson
reminds us that there is a larger economic order in place, one in which the polluted waste has a place, in which the places of those "under-populated," low-
density, under-radiated populations are affixed as surely as the privileges of
those whose need to dispose of the waste takes priority. There is no "under"
without those "over" them insuring the imposition of a rule with their "larbins
d'ordre."

Ferguson tells us, logically, that the production of wealth is inseparable from
the production of social relations (72), by which he means that the social values associated with the wealthy and powerful, and which define their relationship with their subordinates—their authority, their generosity, their superior
judgments—are given definition by their relationship to those over whom they
rule. Our eyes are turned to the fetishized glories of their mansions, to the mansions of their minds, to the glittering gowns with which they adorn themselves,
turning us away from the sordid conditions of production from which they derive their benefits.

Trash can serve to soil their glitter, but if that is the only function to which it is put, all that will be needed to deal with it is a better cleaning service. Ferguson notes Marx's classic notion of commodity fetishism as the capitalist technique that functions to obscure the social origins of the value of the commodity, "imputing value to the object itself as a natural property" (73). But in Africa, he tells us, the natural itself is subordinated to human agency, to human intentions. Poverty and bad luck are not chance events; and even effort itself cannot always alleviate suffering. Rather, it is the ill will of others that is viewed as supplanting any material explanations; it is the power of the powerful, not their inherent natural value, that accounts for their surpassing others. The video dramas of Nigeria remind us incessantly how these occult powers are employed to account for the extravagant appurtenances of the wealthy. And the moral impulse not to do so is cited in Nyerere's inspiring words, to the effect that a true leader will not live off the sweat of others but will, rather, feed them (Ferguson 75).[7] Ferguson's point is that a moralistic discourse comes to the fore in these African judgments about human relations—the morality of not consuming others in one's greed—in opposition to the "scientific" discourse of the president of the World Bank who was able to move "moral" or "social" concerns off the table in considering the cost-benefit analysis of toxic waste removals to Africa. In his analysis of this discourse, Ferguson moves the discourse analysis onto the level of larger world systems perspective, refusing to locate his gaze on the details of the analysis:

> Notions of the inviolate rights of individuals, the sanctity of private property, the nobility of capitalist accumulation, and the intrinsic value of "freedom" (understood as the freedom to engage in economic transactions) lie just below the surface of much of the discourse of scientific capitalism. Often, too, there seems to be a puritan undertone of austerity as punishment for past responsibility: having lived high on the hog for so long, say the stern bankers and economists (safely ensconced in their five-star hotels and six-figure incomes), it is time for Africans to pay for their sins. (80)

Both moral and scientific discourses are concerned with sweat. For the former, it is a sign of evil accumulation to live off the sweat of others, that is, to "eat" others, to consume their labor, their flesh—and then to expel one's own feces. For the latter, it is in the order of things that there would be those who sweat without real accumulation, who might even sweat and fail to accumulate enough to sustain themselves and their families. For them, an adjustment in the structure that requires more sweat for the same sack of rice might be prescribed; while the same city that holds its masses in poverty will naturally also be home to those who return at night to their well-guarded compounds where the generators insure that the lights will never go off.

I cannot find any easy reconciliation between this Bataille, this Summers, and this Ferguson, especially since each insists on holding in prominence their own evaluations of trash. For Bataille, it is an inevitable factor in resistance to the oppressive dominant order, an order that extends well into the symbolic order that molds the inhabitants of the city into docile subjects. For Summers, it isn't a matter of subject or citizen, but statistical figures wherein sentiments about trashy values, or lives, cannot be taken into account in making decisions for the powerless, for their lives. For Ferguson, our conceptions of cultures, societies, and the conventional anthropological field function to produce knowledge in such a way as to occlude questions of a larger economic and historical order, that is, to naturalize the social values without considering their relationship to larger systems that generate poverty and wealth.

So our task will be to bear that question in mind when we review the production of trash, of trashiness, of trashy films, of films with trash in the eye of the camera, so that we are not transfixed by its glamorousness/repulsiveness, not transfixed or repelled into a forgetfulness of what produces it—remembering the material universe won't suffice, although it is the place where we must begin. Bataille is right in seeking to bring forth the bull in all its immoral splendor, right, like Césaire, about the larbins de l'order. But not so right that Césaire's Rue Paille and all its demands are forgotten.

To end this chapter, I want to signal the presence of this trope of trash in a wide range of African films. It would be impossible not to begin with Armah's excremental imagery in *The Beautyful Ones* (1969) that translates all the forms of corruption in Nkrumah's Ghana into an unforgettable shit-stained handrail. The passage of The Man through the slimy pits of an outhouse preceded *Slumdog Millionaire*'s echo of that scene by some forty years. Trash, the abject, the discarded detritus of society can range over a lost limb, a lost prosthesis, or a lost soul.

In *Daratt* (2006), the primal loss is of the protagonist's father, killed by government forces in Chad's wars. The film begins with the government's decision not to pursue those responsible, to discard the body of the father, as it were, along with the appeals for justice. As Atim, the son who is charged by his grandfather with taking revenge, meets his father's killer and establishes a relationship with him, he finds he cannot carry out the killing. The Law of the Father fades, and the Father is discarded as the son tricks his blind grandfather into thinking the revenge has taken place.

Trash enters into the imagery early in the film. When the general amnesty for those having committed crimes during the civil war is announced, crowds cry out and there are bursts of shots. Atim goes out into the street, which is now littered with shoes, as we see a few men continuing to run down the street. Atim's grandfather follows Atim out, turning his face up as he hears the shooting. He is thin and striking looking. He can't see the street since he is blind. For him, a believer, the sky above is where the indefinite, unreachable distance of power extends. For Atim, the street with the shoes signifies what is below, the remainders of the fear of the people fleeing. Atim picks up shoes and drops them.

The grandfather then arms Atim with his father's gun, saying, "I shall pray God to watch over you." He tells Atim he will go to wait in the desert while Atim is to take revenge. "You will find me under the jujube tree." All is configured in tropes of above and below.

Atim sets out for Ndjamena on a bus. A soldier gets on, and Atim, who is sitting across from him, stares at the soldier. The soldier asks Atim what he is staring at, and Atim doesn't answer. The soldier points a gun at him. The camera is placed directly in front of Atim's face, so that the gun points directly at the audience. The soldier says, "You're scared, aren't you." Atim doesn't answer. Subsequently, in a voice-over, Atim tells us he was born after his father died, which is why he is called Atim, the orphan. "Daratt" means dry season.

Atim arrives at Ndjamena, descends, and pisses against a wall. Two soldiers who are watching get up and beat him; we see a large sign painted on wall, "interdit d'uriner"—no urinating. This marks Atim's arrival in the city.

After some brief encounters, Atim finally arrives at the home of Nassara, his father's killer, for the first time. He is pacing back and forth, his hand in his pocket where we know he has a gun. There are plastic bags blowing across the ground right behind him as he paces back and forth. His pacing moves him temporarily off screen as the static camera holds its position, leaving the plastic trash bags blowing across the scene. For a second or two, the screen is filled with nothing but plastic bags blowing about. Atim's shadow and then he himself reappear. The camera shifts 180 degrees to face Nassara's door. Barefooted boys are playing soccer, moving in and out of the frame, as Atim had been doing. Their motions become parallel to those of the garbage bags blown by the wind. Nassara emerges: the plot resumes; the trash of the moment remains like a frozen space in time.

Atim follows Nassara. Shortly thereafter Nassara crosses a field filled with plastic bags (15:55). It is a field of trash, with nothing there but the bags. The trash becomes the mise-en-scène for the pursuit. Atim appears following Nassara as they cross the screen from right to left, with Nassara at one end, Atim at the other, and the trash field between them. In the background, we hear the call to prayer. It increases in volume, and the subsequent shot is that of the top of the minaret. The camera tracks down, moving us from a long crane shot down to the scene on the ground. From the field of trash and the tracking of revenge to the tracking shot of the believers in front of the mosque, we are moved into the spaces where the relationship between the two men is to be formed. Trash mediates the scene for the camera, setting its stage in a location that we read primarily as a trope. Its materiality remains, however the trope may be constructed, and it holds us in the concreteness of this Ndjamena where this Hamlet and his Claudius can act out a revenge plot on their own terms. Through it the trash perseveres as an image that we will identify later, on Rancière's terms, as more than ethical or representative, but rather a figure in the aesthetic regime. The film has only begun, and we are compelled to read what follows along the lines sketched for us at the outset, delimited by more than the plot. The key moments, when the narrative freezes momentarily, are marked by the inertness of what has been discarded; the street of shoes, the field of plastic bags: the detritus that will frame the aftereffects of Chad's civil war.

The series of films made by Abderrahmane Sissako are marked by grace and beauty, but not without their own figures of trash. The basic globalized tropes for waste depend upon a vision of commodity capitalism based on overconsumption. Thus *La Vie sur terre* (1999), a film that ultimately celebrates the passages of life in a rural African town, begins in Paris with visions of excess in a supermarket where the camera captures row after row of different brands of camembert and rich butter from which the sated consumers are to choose. Set against this scene, we pass to Mali where broken systems of all sorts—breaks in communication lines, failing telephone calls, rudimentary radio transmissions—are interposed with inspiring, humanistic quotations from Césaire's *Retour*.

The opening in the supermarché offers a full two minutes of consumerism during which the rows of cheese and butter get a thirty-second tracking shot. Shot from above, Dramane, dressed in an overcoat and fedora, appears lost amid the bric-a-brac of consumer goods. At 2:30 into the film, Malian stringed music discretely begins, and after twenty seconds, as Dramane ascends an escalator, the camera passes to Africa, panning up a magnificent tree. A beautiful moving transition from the north to the south, from one regime of sensibility to another. The sound of the single stringed instrument is followed by discrete atmospheric sounds, first of a rooster then goats or cows. We gain an entrée into another realm through the magic of this tree, the image of which enables the crossing from Europe to Africa. The single tree standing tall, as Bataille would imagine it, crowns the heights of Sissako's love for his homeland, while shots of the traveler passing through the countryside reveal a world pleasantly devoid of waste—no plastic bags, no signs of dead animals or their droppings, a world without sewage. The counterpoint of Europe's wealthy but degraded culture is an Africa of simplicity and beauty. Each requires the other.

The title credits return over the sounds of the instrument and cows lowing. A pastoral atmosphere, opening onto a shot at night of an old man reading a letter on the edge of his bed, the mosquito net tucked up. "Cher père," the letter begins. The father is reading what we suppose is the letter of our cineaste who announces his return, like that of Césaire, with the words, "Il faut partir" (It is necessary to leave). The father smiles. Music returns. His son, Dramane (played by Sissako himself in the film) recites the well-known lines: "Partir. Mon Coeur bruissait de générosités emphatiques. Partir . . . j'arriverais lisse et jeune dans ce pays mien et je dirais à ce pays dont le limon entre dans la composition de mon chair: 'J'ai longtemps erré et je reviens vers la hideur désertée de vos plaies'" (To leave. My Heart burst with empathetic feelings of generosity. To leave . . . I would arrive smooth and young in this country of mine, and I would say to this country whose mud enters into the composition of my flesh:

"I have long wandered and I am returning to the deserted hideousness of your wounds"; 8 Irele version).

Here the cineaste's voice stops, singing begins, and we are there, in the moment of the return. The lines that follow the above in Césaire's *Retour,* where the poet vaunts his newly gained position as educated retourné and announces he will become his people's mouthpiece, are glossed over. The mood of the singing and images, the regime into which we enter *this* Africa, is one of nostalgia, deep nostalgia, and relief at a homecoming long overdue. Instead of the vaunting of the Negritude poet, Sissako's next lines begin with Césaire's warning to himself, and to the educated, assimilated generation of his day, the ones who had known what plenty there was to be found in the European supermarket: "Et surtout mon corps aussi bien que mon âme, gardez-vous de vous croiser les bras en l'attitude stérile du spectateur, car la vie n'est pas un spectacle, car une mer de douleurs n'est pas un proscenium, car un homme qui crie n'est pas un ours qui danse" (And especially my body as well as my soul, beware of crossing your arms in the sterile posture of a spectator, because life is not a spectacle, because a sea of sorrows is not a proscenium stage, because a man who screams is not a dancing bear; 9).

How do we move from one regime of representation, the surrealist autobiographical one of Césaire, to this familiar regime of the return home, with the intimacy of its voice-over, and the triste nostalgia of the music and images? How are these two regimes produced differently, and what happens when the later one turns the former into its intertext? How can the 1930s catch us in the turn-of-the-millennium moment when the voice of the exile announces his desire to film Sokolo and immediately presents us with those images: the cattle, the children, and then the watery reflection of the man on a bicycle. Traveling into this new old world of the father, the past and yet the home, comes with a warning not to regard it as a spectacle because "man is not a performing bear." For the poet, the hideous wounds and mud are mud of his flesh, wounds of his heart. These are the opening refrains of this return that immediately turn "limon" (mud), "hideur" (hideousness), "ours" (bear) into the elements of a humanist composition intended to overturn that other regime, the "civilized" one of Paris, that produced the possibility for an African homecoming from Europe to be imperative for this poet, for this filmmaker at the turn of the millennium. Even in this idyllic film about home, the hideous wounds cannot be ignored. Bataille's toe is located in the mud (*limon*); Sissako's nostalgia can only work when set against the alienation of the global images of commodity consumerism and in the familiar embrace of Negritude's negation.

The "trash" in Sissako's *Bamako* (2006) abounds in story after story. The frame story deals with a couple in the process of breaking up, with the husband, Chaka, set on a trajectory of despair that leads to his suicide at the end of the film. Chaka's body finishes up in the street, matching the image of a dead dog captured in the opening tracking shot. Within Chaka's compound, a mock trial of the World Bank is staged, and a series of "witnesses" attest to the destruction wrought on their lives in an Africa suffering from the malfeasance of neoliberal banking policies. In one instance, a young man describes his experience of attempting to emigrate to Europe through illegal channels. He and a group of others find themselves stranded in the desert, expelled and left to die by the frontier guards of the great Western Fortress. In one of the most striking images of the film, we see the body of a dead young woman stretched across the sands with scarabs approaching her face.

In another scene, we witness the youth of Bamako watching a mock version of a cheap Hollywood Western, a dead cinema of meretricious imitations capturing their imagination. Death limns each plotline of *Bamako,* with the triste song of a moribund love echoing throughout the narrative; lethargic figures listen half-heartedly outside the courtyard to the rhetoric of the high ideals of Justice being reiterated by the prosecution as the World Bank is denounced. The productive labor of the women in the film is crowned by the work of dyers whose beautiful cloths are displayed drying on laundry lines; simultaneously we see the dyed cloths' liquids running off, staining the pavement—the discharged substance of the process of dying. A white lawyer who is on the defense team for the World Bank purchases a pair of sunglasses while images of an Africa decimated by the effects of structural adjustment are continually evoked. The Bataillian dichotomy of high and low, of idea and material, of consumption and expenditure, set the pace for the rhythm of the film.

In Djibril Diop Mambety's *Le Franc* (1994), the musician passes through a garbage field on his way to town. We see a plastic bag hanging out of the mouth of a cow. The degradation of the former symbol of status is the condition for the development of the urban centers. In Sembène's *Xala* (1974), the commissaire responds to El Hadj's complaints about the beggars and rids him of the *déchets humaines,* the street's human garbage, by throwing the beggars and handicapped out of town. In *Faat Kine* (2000), when Kine and her business colleagues hold a meeting, one of their number, an injudicious man with many wives who has overspent his means, asks for a loan. He is rejected as a figure of the "Old Africa" that must be discarded to make way for the New African Man and Woman. Thirty years earlier, another banker who refused a loan, in *Xala,* symbolized neocolonial corruption. Now the New has passed over that accusation and integrated itself into the New Economic Order.

Discarded bodies appear in Bekolo's *Aristotle's Plot* (1996), including an African American who is shot and then staggers off like a zombie, E.T. who is run over by a car only to rise again, and an entire series of gangsters who are killed in a dramatic shootout. But the most spectacular figure in Bekolo's oeuvre is that of the government official, the SGCC, in *Les Saignantes* (2005), whose body is dissected with a chain saw and later pieced back together with the wrong head attached. Amid a series of shots set in a morgue, in back alleys, in noir locations, Bekolo intersperses billboard messages articulating his ideals and judgments on an Africa whose future has been compromised by corrupt politicians and authoritarian government.

Trash abounds, with excessive bodies cast off the continent, languishing in Europe or in the new Middle Passage, unable to make the *retour* to a native homeland. Figures of rebellious children seen in earlier films, as in Souleyman Cissé's *Baara* (1978), now return increasingly with visions of street urchins, as in Cheikh Oumar Sissoko's *Nyamanton* (1986) or, in more romantic mode, in Ouédraogo's *Yaaba* (1989), where those on the margins of society hold the keys to its regeneration or survival. In Kaboré's *Zan Boko* (1988), the New City discards what is left of the Old African Village as progress is marked by the powerful and corrupt politicians who take the land, the people, the past. The last, everlastingly poignant shot of *Hyenas* (1992) is that of the plowed field, the elimination of Colobane's old presence, making way to the New City on the horizon, a Dakar soon to be overwhelmed by new ghettos and their urban poverty. For Fanta Nacro in *Puk Nini* (1995), it is the family that is trashed when a Senegalese prostitute comes to town and steals the husband. In her *Nuit de la vérité* (2004), it is soldiers, the ethnic wars, that leave the land devastated. Child soldiers in *Ezra* (2007) mark the descent from the innocent figures of urban children in Sembène's earlier films like *Tauw* (1970) to a series of monsters in a veritable inferno of destruction where a son shoots into his house, killing his father, and has the house blown up. His village is destroyed by his platoon and he himself is traumatized by the brutalities he commits. Eventually he develops amnesia and PTSD.

The question of the conjunction of the high and the low marks each of these films: the baobab tree of Africa's glory, its proud head, as David Diop would have it, is increasingly matched with the images of a New Day that cannot disguise its rivulets of despair. *Pièces d'identité* (1998) evokes that fall from an earlier day of freedom and glorious rule to the sad state of an African king lost in an indifferent Europe, his signs of royalty now languishing in a pawn shop in Brussels. The question before us is not how to avoid Afro-pessimism in reading these films, since every act of global consumption must be marked by an equal discharge of global proportions. It is the only way to read the global system within which African films are produced and consumed, films whose materiality captures those processes by inevitably engaging with the end products of commodity acquisition. The figuration of trash is both an end point and a starting point for an inquiry that will insist that the trashiness of the popular visual culture is the condition for "art récupéré," recycled art, as well as of film récupéré, and that in a larger sense these supplements to the high forms of "cinema" are now functioning to destabilize the former systems of culture and enable new space-clearing gestures in African film criticism to emerge.

2 Rancière: Aesthetics, Its Mésententes and Discontents

There is one question for trash that has to be addressed before any other if we are to relate the trope to African cinema without falling into the traps of earlier paradigms and their discontents. The first trap for trash arises when African cinema, or any art form, is judged to be inadequately serious in addressing social issues. That is the trap of "art for art's sake," that sets art against politics in a binary fashion.[1] Secondly, when African cinema is judged to be adequately serious, successfully raising social issues but failing to meet aesthetic standards, it is taken as a second-rate cinema that must resort to special pleading in order to be taken seriously as art, as "cinema." Here the issues supplant the art, and the question of "good cinema" must be put on hold because addressing AIDS, child soldiers, genocide, blood diamonds, and so forth, outweighs the trivial question of whether the film meets international norms for "cinema." In the first case of aesthetic value, African cinema is measured in terms of the standards of high culture, which defines itself against trashy, commercial, porno, amateurish, or overtly didactic cinema. In the second, trash is equated with subjectivity, asocial dispositions, introspection, and individualism—that is, film as entertainment, as "the movies"—with its fascination with emotion and personal relations that have no importance in terms of social meliorism. Both kinds of trash are failures of teleological projects that see society as struggling to improve and art as struggling for ever higher accomplishments. Both are tied to the same sets of values, even if they are completely at odds over which matters the most. Both predetermine an outcome in which African cinema maintains its marginal status.

In a sense, few would want to take these questions seriously for several reasons. Special pleading for an African exceptionalism—for what is taken to be, by implication, inferior art, inferior talents, and so on—creates a tedious, specious label tied to African cultural production when measured by western standards as has long been the case. Special pleading also raises the question of whose standards constitute "international norms," and whether there isn't such a thing as an African film practice, an African aesthetic, recognizable since its qualities were first identified by Teshome Gabriel (1982) in a series of discrete propositions dealing with the predominance of certain kinds of shots, African temporality, a culturally determined mode of editing, and African subjectivities centered on group identities as opposed to individuals.[2] The work of Senegalese, Malian, and Burkinabe directors would typically be cited as exemplary in having established this style of "authentic" African cinema practice. Nonetheless, African filmmakers never abjured their roles as artists as well as militants: "I'm both a militant and an artist. . . . I'm a militant through my art" (Sembène, cited in Gadjigo).

"Third Cinema" initially conveyed a commitment and revolution and national liberation, cultural affirmation and social meliorism. Anticolonial arguments yielded, with time, to postcolonial theorizing, which eventually had to deal with the problematic issue of how to approach commercial productions such as television series and ultimately Nollywood films that proved indifferent to political agendas. Art and politics remained dueling partners but were increasingly sidelined by the overwhelming problem of the financing of serious African filmmaking and by the competing commercial success of Nollywood. Consumerism and commodification, as the key ideological issues for a postmodern economy, rose to prominence, and found their definitions in terms supplied by the vocabulary of globalization and its accompanying neoliberal agendas. Orienting theory around the critique of commodification of women, joined to stereotypical depictions of women as witches, whores, and abused victims, led to calls to censor Nollywood and its negative depictions of women.[3] Commodification was also linked to the concerns of globalization critics and activists over mineral resource extraction and the conflicts that engaged child-soldiers, violence against women, and the arms trade. Even without the blood diamonds, it was inevitable that a Fanta Nacro would produce *La Nuit de la vérité* (2004), and that Nollywood would engender an *Ezra* (2007). African politics drove the issues depicted in African films until Nollywood changed the formulae and gave prominence to the appeal to mass audience taste. Art and politics remained at loggerheads as long as the issues surrounding their exigencies were addressed in frozen terms of aesthetics and political commitment, or commercial versus serious cinema.

Using Rancière, we will revisit the art/politics binary so as to permit the trope of trash to escape the conundrum of being regarded as either failed political thought or failed art. To do this, both "art" and "politics" must be problematized and reconceptualized in new definitions.

"Aesthetics," which Rancière chooses to defend as a conceptual field in *Aesthetics and Its Discontents* (2009a), is understood through the particular way we approach texts, objects, or installations when defined as art. His goal is to establish that politics and art each has its own autonomous realm: that not everything can be subsumed under the auspices of a regime of power: "What the term 'art' designates in its singularity is *the framing of a space of presentation* by which things of art are identified as such" (23; my emphasis). African literature and cinema initially worked through their own struggle to be taken as more than ethnography or sociology, to be accorded the identification of "literature," of "cinema," and to be read as more than thinly disguised documentary renditions of "authentic" culture. The blurring of the boundaries between documentary cinema and fiction accentuates the problematic nature of this approach, and has been heightened in recent African films.[4] Understanding these works entails more than classifying them according to specific genres. Prior to classification, including what belongs to a category of "art" or "politics," there must be acts of recognition and understanding of what we perceive, and these depend on how we have created a common set of terms for our perceptions, a shared world or perceptions, a "distribution of the sensible" (*le partage du sensible*) that can be understood thus: "This distribution is composed of the *a priori* laws which condition what is possible to see and hear, to say and think, to do and make ... the distribution of the sensible is literally the conditions of possibility for perception, thought, and activity, what it is possible to apprehend by the senses. The sensible is partitioned into various regimes and therefore delimits forms of inclusion and exclusion in a community" (Bornowsky). In Rancière's terms, the distribution of the sensible encompasses the "implicit law governing the sensible order that parcels out *places and forms of participation in a common world by first establishing the modes of perception within which these are inscribed.* The distribution of the sensible thus produces a system of self-evident facts of perception based on the set horizons and modalities of what is visible and audible as well as what can be said, thought, made, or done" (2009b: 85; my emphasis). "Distribution" refers both to forms of inclusion and to forms of exclusion—it is the weak translation of the French term *partage,* which emphasizes more the notion of sharing, of what is shared or held in common, and by extension what is situated outside that which is held in common, by a community of perceivers, performers, participants in the experience. "Sensible" is even more misleading in translation, coming from the French *sensible,* which means what we can perceive or sense, what is tangible, not what in English means reasonable or that which makes sense. We perceive and make sense of art only after we fit the object of art into a category called art or aesthetics. Before such categories existed, we had no slot with which to distinguish an object as a work of art or a documentary film, or distinguish a citizen from one who is not.

For Rancière, the productions of Greek sculpture or drama, which we now call art, would have functioned more as an expression of the community's ethos than something that belonged to the aesthetic realm, and thus he calls this the ethical regime. The goal in making objects like sculptures or plays was to educate the community concerning their role in the communal body, and the origin and telos of imagery were emphasized: artists created in order to ameliorate citizens' participation in the community, and "ethos" suggested a moral regime for the individual in relationship to the community or polis. Though African masking traditions serve multiple purposes, generally their primary function is the same, especially if we expand the community to include those whom Soyinka called the living, the dead, and those to come.

African cinema might be viewed, like Achebe's literature, as subservient to a pedagogical telos, and we aren't surprised when Sembène calls African cinema

Africa's *école de nuit,* night school, even as he acknowledges that his efforts to reach out to an audience are determined by more than merely advocacy, but include the creation of works that appeal to the audience (Gadjigo).

Rancière's second regime of art is defined by mimesis and is termed "representation" since it stresses the artists' desire to create works whose value is to be measured by the technical ability of the artist to represent with fidelity and skill an actual object or set of objects in the world, and whose audience, one with cultivated taste, would be trained to appreciate the skills of the artist. This regime assumes predominance in the west with the rise of Renaissance art, that is, with the notion of the fine arts, "les beaux arts," and it continues as dominant until modernism comes into its own in European culture in the mid-nineteenth century with writers like Stendahl and with poets and artists of the Impressionist period. This period of "the arts," as opposed to that of ethos, gives rise to western notions of high culture and beauty associated with artistic skills and cultivated audiences. Chopin and Rembrandt, not the Beatles and graffiti; Senghor and Césaire, not Fela and Nollywood.

These two regimes, those of ethos and representation, have obvious parallels to the developments of African culture and arts in the twentieth century, where the telos of African literature and cinema in Europhone languages has been built on solid foundations of responding to western racism and colonial domination. Anticolonial discourses were at the heart of Negritude as well as Achebe's project of providing teaching tools to counter western misconstructions of African people and culture; and when he uses the metaphor of seeing through a clear window onto African worlds, he is evoking the second regime of representation, with mimesis as the underlying assumption.[5] We can see that Diawara's frequently cited division of African cinema into "narratives" that focus on "social realism," "colonial confrontation," and tradition, which he calls "return to the source," are all based on a representational imperative. The demands of Ferid Boughedir and Teshome Gabriel that African cinema be politically committed are also predicated on the same notion that fidelity to the revolutionary struggle could be represented accurately by demonstrating what was the basis of the oppression. Classic examples might include Sembène's early films or *The Battle of Algiers* (1966). The prevalent modes were variants of realism—socialist and social realism, and neorealism. Faith in representation prevailed.

When twentieth-century modernism entered the scene, it brought a skepticism about mimesis and the feasibility of the project of representation, and the creation of works based on verisimilitude. Modernism arose from the crisis of representation, and the project of the regime of representation began to collapse on two levels. The first was self-awareness of artists whose works were not transparent but became visible by virtual of the appearance or foregrounding of the artists' technique. The second was a turning away from subject matter identified by higher or lower social rank in favor of subjects from any social class, of any ontological standing—with indifference toward hierarchies of class, even of beauty, dignity, honor, and so forth. Rancière likes to cite the example of Stendahl for his attention to the word over the image, to the equality of descriptive terms over the inequality of figures of representation, and finally to the charter of language over the fidelity to reality or the capacity to create the ideals of beauty or skillful figuration. "Far from demonstrating the independence of aesthetic attitudes, Stendahl testifies to the aesthetic regime in which the distinction between those things that belong to art and those that belong to ordinary life is blurred" (2009a: 5).

As Rancière opens his discussion of the aesthetic regime, he returns to the issue of aesthetics itself occupying a separate regime from politics, each having its own specificity, its own elements by which we recognize something as art as opposed to politics. Even "political" art, like Goya's "The Third of May," is seen to be a painting before it is recognized as having a political message; and even a street demonstration with dramatizations or masks is recognized as protest before its aesthetic qualities are considered in identifying it. Each regime has its own sensibilities, its own framing and tangible elements.

Following the regimes of ethics and representation, the "regime of aesthetics" is that by which art in its singularity is identified and encountered as such. Each regime has a relationship to what is shared *(partagé)*, what is held in common, what people viewing the art hold in common. What links art to the common is the construction, "at once material and symbolic, of a specific space-time, of a suspension with respect to the ordinary forms of sensory experience" (2009a: 23). The emphasis in the modern period shifts away from the art object, with its intrinsic qualities or its relationship to a larger body of objects or former objects deemed art, to the viewer's experience of the object. For Rancière, art is not political "because of the messages and sentiments it conveys conveying the state of the world." And it is not political "because of the manner in which it might choose to represent society's structures, or social groups, their conflicts or identities." Most significantly, "*It is political because of the very distance it takes with respect to those functions, because of the type of space and time that it institutes, and the manner in which it frames this time and peoples this space. . . .* The specificity of art consists in bringing about a reframing of material and symbolic space. And it is in this way that art bears upon politics" (2009a: 23; my emphasis). In the narrow sense, we can talk about content as delivering the political message of the film. But what if that message, say one calling for an equitable social order, is contradicted by the way the work constructs its spaces, its hierarchical articulations?

When we consider the multiple ways in which symbolic and material space are configured in the representation of the political in African cinema, it become clear how a range of expectations have been set up. A political rally, outside of cinema, might be reconstructed within the film, and the street rally might have its own choreography, yet each remains within its own specific domain. No scene choreographs the great mass movement of revolution more than the magnificent ending of *The Battle of Algiers.* Yet above and beyond its depiction of the passage to action on the part of the masses, larger formal questions concerning the relationship between the ululations, the haze, the long shots, and the effects of distance and proximity need to be worked through if we are to assay their relationship to hierarchical versus egalitarian models. In *Xala,* the opening shots of the Chamber of Commerce (viewed as the Chamber of the Ruling Party) create for the viewer a formal space that mimetically represents the Senegalese public space and the subordination of its government. In contrast, the scene at the end of the film in the private home of Awa and El Hadj functions as a metaphorically political space of class redressment. Similarly, the principal setting in *Bamako* (2006) is placed within the compound where Mele and Chaka live and functions as an obviously formal public and politicized space while also absurdly functioning as the site for the staging of the mock trial with its judges placed on high and the audience below. The audience can partially establish the political quality of the space and, within its narrow symbolic function, address the specific and thus narrowly defined political issues at stake: who is guilty, who has power, who abused power, who is victim of the power, what must be done. None of these questions changes the opening of a cinematic space itself as a contested construct grounded in broader assumptions about how to frame basic elements of a distribution of the sensible. Yet it is there, and only there, that the politics evoked in cinema is ultimately played out since the pre-text, the pre-framing of the space, of the issues, defines the kinds of understandings at stake: "Politics, indeed, is not the exercise of, or struggle for, power. *It is the configuration of a specific space,* the framing of a specific sphere of experience, of objects posited as common and as pertaining to a common decision, of subjects recognized as capable of designating these objects and putting forward arguments about them" (2009a: 24; my emphasis). This framing of cinematic (or artistic) space outside of specific political agendas is dubbed metapolitics by Rancière, and it is the exclusion of the metapolitical that has led to the reduction of political analysis of African cinema to purely ideological content analysis.

Without defining narrowly what "politics" means, Rancière focuses on what we hold in common, what we consider of public concern, what is subject to public discourse. It isn't simply a question of setting an agenda for preconceived concepts of the common or the public sphere, but of staging the setting of the agenda, of the pre-agenda politics of the staging that is constructed word by word, image by image, into that which gives coherence to the settings of common concern. What is to be the brick that counts, the word attended to, the image of value to the concerns in question—versus those elements to be discarded, that are expendable, that are of no worth, that are holes in the fabric of the argument. In the past, we debated which terms mattered: the Fanonian terms, the Marxist terms, the Freudian terms. Now it becomes simpler: what do we perceive as piecing together the fabric of the world that we experience in common, what comes to constitute the *"sensible,"* that is, the world of what is apprehended by our senses, the material words and things that together create a familiar regime. In the process, whose voices are heard and whose presence is attended to? What is the sensibility of those lacking the voices and limbs? "Politics occurs when those who 'have no' time take the time necessary to front up as inhabitants of a common space and demonstrate that their mouths really do emit speech capable of making pronouncements on the common which cannot be reduced to voices signaling pain" (2009a: 24). Leaving the speech to these trashy figures was the great discovery Césaire made in the course of the *Retour*. He had to humble himself in order be freed of the pretentiousness of calling himself a mouthpiece. Trinh T. Minh-Ha's "speaking next to" was an attempt to arrive at the same point (*Reassemblage* [1983], *Woman, Native, Other* [1989]). Both efforts were too limited, though moving in the right direction—not because of a newfound confidence in the vox populi, but in opening the possibilities of framing a new regime beyond that which had resolved itself into some hierarchical structure. Here is the essential point that Rancière makes in this revision of our notion of the political: "This distribution and redistribution of places and identities, this apportioning and reapportioning of spaces and times, of the visible and invisible, and of noise and speech constitutes what I call the distribution of the sensible. *Politics consists in reconfiguring the distribution of the sensible which defines the common of a community, to introduce into it new subjects and objects, to render visible what had not been, and to make heard as speakers those who had been perceived as noisy animals*" (2009a: 25; my emphasis).[6]

Rancière seeks more than changes in perception per se, arguing that disruption in the dominant political economic order addresses the agreements, the consensus, that make that order perceptible and therefore sustainable, enabling it to reproduce itself.[7] The disruption is termed "dissensus," and rather than dismissing aesthetics as irrelevant or marginal to dissensus, he views its role, through the erection of a regime of the sensible that no longer relies on exclusionary hierarchies, as necessary to effecting change. Not all disruptions are dissensual. "Creating dissensus informs an aesthetics of politics that operates at a complete remove from the forms of staging power and mass mobilization which Benjamin referred to as the 'aestheticization of politics'" (2009a: 25). Here Rancière's target is the choreography of fascist power politics targeted by Benjamin in his assessment of fascist aesthetics.

A new "aesthetics of politics" does more than effect change in perception per se or reorder the bricks of normalized understandings, be they of art or of power. It is closer to movements like that called Set Setal, or Clean It Up, in Dakar in 1992, when the youth sought to address the phenomenon of garbage strewn in the streets of Dakar. It grew to confront the garbage politics of Abdou Diouf's regime and the "proper" dispensations of "ordered" society, "orderly" protest, "orderly" politics in the mono-regime Senegal had known since independence. The opening for public art had existed for a long time in Senegal, and in Dakar in particular, where it has long been the custom for adherents of the Mourid or Tijani orders to plaster the external walls of their homes, trucks, car-rapides, or shops with images of their serigne, or signs of their orders (Roberts and Roberts). From there to graffiti art as political protest required the intermediary step of moving beyond the Senghorian notions of public order, beyond the staid politics of Diouf, to the opposition represented for years by Abdoulaye Wade. Youths covered walls along the street, buildings, whatever external surfaces they could find, with slogans about Set and ultimately stimulated the radical political art of Papisto Boy who created an enormous mural in the Belaire industrial zone of Dakar (Roberts and Roberts 285–88). The mural contained a range of images of political radicals, from rastas to American civil rights heroes, and it made use of public space and objects recovered from the trash dumps (see figure 2.1).[8] They bridged the gap between detritus in the form of actual garbage sites and images, people, and politics, opening the way for commercial usages to follow. *Récupéré* art—recuperation[9]—ultimately became chic, with objects composed of combs, computer parts, metal scraps, and so forth refashioned into birds and other forms that sold in the prestigious French Cultural Center as well as along city streets or on Goree to the tourists. The regime of the sensible had changed—the artists' ways of doing and making, the audience's ways of perceiving and making sense had changed. Yet soon enough the cooptation of the change followed, with its various forms of commodification in tourist art. Like all movements there was a sense of a mass mobilization, of youth changing the landscape, and then, with time, the settling in of a new consensus, a comfortable established body of orderly thinking, aligned with the forces of well-ordered society—the ensemble creating what Rancière means by the police[10]—that is, those regulatory mechanisms that function like unwritten laws, regulating and normalizing the distribution of roles in society and their social customs and practices. Police versus dissensus—that which disturbs or challenges the established hierarchies that give definition to the distribution of the sensible—define the borders of politics, political action, as well as the spaces addressed by art, the spaces of art's address and reception. As this address encompasses a public space of viewing and participating in the experience of art, the politics of policing and dissenting, of completing the orderly or disrupting and renewing the order, come into play as giving definition to the symbolic spaces of art. Art's specificity, its need for public address, is thus aligned with "a certain way of being of the community" (2009a: 25) Thus, "art and politics do not constitute two permanent, separate realities whereby the issue is to know whether or not they *ought* to be set in relation. They are two forms of distribution of the sensible, both of which are dependent on a specific regime of identification" (2009a: 26).

If "police" is that which accounts for those who are seen and heard, or excluded from the community, the opposite of police is what Rancière calls "politics," namely that which disrupts the police(d) order, which disrupts the distribution of the sensible, which provides the context for those who have no part, no voice, no image within the community to disrupt that which prevents their being seen, heard, or participating. What the disruption accomplishes is not, like revolution, a change in the ruling body, but a change in the dominant structures that account for a way of seeing the world that excludes those with no part.[11]

The politics of Rancière represents an approach to community and citizenship that precedes a political orientation on a left-right axis. It turns on belonging and exclusions and thus being part of a community constructed on authority and power, or being excluded, not being counted, and thus becoming simply the people, *le commun;* as such it relates to aesthetics as well as society in that the same issues of hierarchy and commonality or equality function in both domains. In both domains, preceding any consideration of specific aesthetic or political qualities, there is the question of what structures an order, what polices or maintains it, and what disrupts it, especially as the question of maintenance or disruption turns on those who belong versus those who have no part. The group that is constituted by the *commun* is "the people," as in the Greek notion of the *demos* and an African sense of the community. The community is viewed in two ways. When the community is exclusionary, it is termed the *ochlos,* the "throng of people" (2009b: 88). Those who are excluded from the community, from the dominant distribution of the sensible, are the demos, *le peuple,* "the people," those unaccounted for in the established or policed order (2009b: 88). The "African community," when viewed as those who had been in revolt against colonialism, were termed *le peuple,* especially in leftist discourses, as in the grounding of revolt in "the people." When the community is portrayed in a text like *Things Fall Apart* (1958), it is closest to the *ochlos* as we see in the unified voice of those responding to the call "Umuofia Kwenu," the call-and-response of a congregation whose members belong. The silenced, excluded ones, like the *Osu,* would be closer to those occupying the site of dissensus. The conversion of the *Osu* might be viewed as a redistribution of the sensible, a challenge to the community's consensus. In every sense, every revision of the community's shared vision is challenged by this dissensus that renames the evil forest, the place of twins, or the distribution of titles, not as a "falling apart" but a new dispensation.

Reconfiguring the distribution of the sensible so as to encompass the political subjectivization of the excluded is what provides the conditions of democracy. What defines dissent, or *mésentente* (disagreement, as well as dissensus) is not a question of conflicting arguments over values as such, or conflicting discourses, as much as a contestation over a given distribution of the sensible and what remains outside it (2009b: 4). Dissensus entails the provocation in the given "policed" order, the given consensus, thus seeking to inscribe those whose voices aren't heard or whose presence is not seen—the part of those without a part—so as to reconfigure that which sustains the "sensible": "The dissensus by which the invisible equality subtending social distinction is made visible, and the inaudible speech of those rejected into the obscure night of silence audible, thereby enacts a different *sharing* of the sensible" (editor's introduction, 2010a: 7). The sharing of a perspective on what is real, how this reality is divided up, who belongs and who does not, who should be heard or not, whom we see or do not—this "sharing" is what gives substance to the "distribution of the sensible," while the perceptible features of the order of society, of the arts, prior to the disruptions of dissensus, form the key dimensions by which we understand a world to belong to the consensual realm of the political or of the aesthetic. Dissensus speaks to redress those orders on the basis of a need for equality.

Like the Set Setal movement in Senegal, Fela and his Afrobeat musical performances provoked the Nigerian government and Lagosian order with his politics, seen in his club at the Afrika Shrine, his home at the "Kalakuta Republic," his twenty-seven wives, and his vocal and provocative verbal dissensus (Olaniyan).

The separation between art and politics was not ever presented as an issue in the performances of Youssou Ndour or Fela, but in their assumptions about political action and performance, they were unable to forge a new regime of sensibility. Abacha and Wade, the successors of the old order, not only reproduced the same structures of power and wealth but elicited the same discourses about those structures, the same visions of what put the structures in order, the same bases for understandings, and thus the same failures of opposition forces to mount or sustain dissensus. Fela and Youssou Ndour's professed goals express, however, much of the egalitarian impulses found in Rancière's work where he defines dissensus as that which disrupts the agreements that ensure the "power of 'form' over 'matter,' . . . the power of the class of intelligence over men of nature" (2009a: 31).

In celebrating free play and free appearance, following Kant, Rancière calls for the founding of a "new community" that stands for the "refutation, within the sensible, of this opposition between intelligent form and sensible matter . . . the difference between two humanities" (31). Order and "police" constrain free play: "Play's freedom is contrasted with the servitude of work" whereas "free appearance is contrasted to the constraint that relates appearance to reality" (31). Free play, identified ordinarily with postmodernism, takes two forms in Rancière's analysis. In one direction, following Lyotard, there is the coming to grips with that which exceeds the possibility of accessing it, the sublime, which Kant defined as not susceptible to representation. The abstract work of art that strives to generate the effect of a flash encounter with the indefinable evokes only the impossibility of resolving itself into a comprehensible articulation, thus eliciting "the irreducible gap between the idea and the sensible." Despite Senghor's resistance to modernist art, the revolt of the artists of the late 1970s in Dakar moved precisely in this direction, challenging the dominant norms of Negritude forms of representation.[12] In cinema, the closest to that gap came in Djibril

Diop Mambety's auteurist *Touki Bouki* (1974), made around the same time that Sembène made *Xala* (1974), his masterpiece of realist political satire. In both films, at extreme ends of representation, the elements of an incommensurable gap or void can be seen just as they both gesture toward a political orientation around similar issues.

In the order of African cinema, free play was long associated with western decadence, or its derivatives, eventually vilified as postmodernism. Djibril Diop Mambety's free spirits, from the marginalized figures in *Badou Boy* (1970) to Anta and Mory in *Touki Bouki,* engendered confusion and rejection in African audiences[13] until the powerful return of Diop Mambéty with his decidedly less "experimental" *Hyènes* (1992). The constraints on our thinking about aesthetics, that is, the presuppositions inherent in an established distribution of the sensible, tie us here in our limited approach to freedom no less than to politics. Rancière's adherence to egalitarianism doesn't suffice to broaden our understandings or to permit a new viewing of Bekolo's *Saignantes* (2005) or the unstated politics lying behind, underneath, around Sissako's films. The trial in *Bamako* (2006) tells us that we have to look not only at what occurs on the level of the mise-en-scène, at the location of the staging of the trial, not only in the overlong discourses of the public advocates for the people, but beyond the logic of the trial in *Bamako,* in the locations that are to be found elsewhere and do not proclaim their presence, like the reddish waters dying the ground beneath the dripping cloth, details of life seen from below, views from the trash landscape that don't figure in the Fanonian liberationist schemata. "What they in fact describe are the *forms of domination and of equality* operative within the very tissue of ordinary sensory experience" (2009a: 31; my emphasis). The call here is not to end the opposition to domination—this the easiest ground for dismissing postmodern playfulness—but to avoid replicating the epistemological foundations for an order that calls for its police in the most effective location, in the understanding of the ordering of the real. Whereas Sissako addresses directly the policies of the World Bank, of the neoliberal economic order, of the western imperium and its global order, Rancière reserves his critique for another level or order of experience, that which accounts for hierarchies, for exclusions, written on the structures of the aesthetic practices or on the consensual social order. Instead of the call for justice and punishment that we hear in the trial scenes in *Bamako,* Rancière's approach would call for the exposure of the underlying hierarchies that account for the exclusions, hierarchies manifest in the very power of the word ("mythos" or story) over the image, of the idea over the material, of the well-formed shots that construct the well-made play or description, over the marginal moments of anti-Art, the trashed-out locations where detritus is conveyed not in its literal embodiment but in that next order of expression that comes after or to the side of representation, after the rule of mimesis. Detritus as dissensus. Here I would cite the melodramatic effects rather than the formal attributes of the court scene in *Bamako;* the sensational and spectacular exhibitionism of the scenes of death in the desert rather than the testimony that provides those scenes with their meanings. Reading back from the lowest forms deflates an order of higher ideation, so that instead of the colonized fighting back, writing back, it refuses the colonial or postcolonial order of higher and lower altogether and posits a place in the spectacle for those denied entry into the courtyard of justice by the guardian of the door.

In the regime of the aesthetic, we have a rapprochement between the ordinary and the artistic, the mixing of the abstract and the figurative, the hodgepodge of installations that play on "the indiscernibility between works of art and objects or icons of commerce," this marking the "nihilistic accomplishment of aesthetic utopia" (2009a: 20). At every stage of the invasion of trash into the interstices of the ordinary, there is some dimension that exceeds or dodges the idea of the truth. We want to ignore the ugly little piles of dirt and get on to the clean, pure nature of the truth being revealed. Sweeping away the detritus, however, leads us back to the "déchets humains" whose débarrassement" (elimination) El Hadj requested of the president. They return across the dunes, and even before they speak we are invited to accompany them on their relentless, helpless journey, their return, their stubborn rejection of the abjection.

Their tie into the politics of aesthetics, the "metapolitics" of the aesthetic regime, lies in the reconfiguration of elements within the aesthetic realm that disturb the previous hierarchical arrangements. These elements vary according to the particular branch of the arts—that is, the elements taken to be part of the world of art as such. Thus, in the representative realm, the separation of the idea, the form, the rational order from the base material, the feeling or emotion— that is, between the privileging of logos over pathos—is disturbed as mimesis loses its primary function: paintings that have no clear message, no clear social readings, no higher ideals, inaugurate an appreciation of qualities of color per se, of feeling per se, of linguistic sensibilities and words per se—of people per se. Whereas mimesis depends in fiction on the plot or story, and in film on the diegesis as the location to establish meaning in a hermeneutic analysis, in the post-mimetic modern order, destabilization of the hierarchy of living speech and action over depicted images forms an analogy with the deconstructions of the hierarchies of the social and political order (2009b: 17). Rancière lists a range of hierarchical elements in which the aesthetic order undoes the hierarchies of the representative: the privileging of narration or story over description and language crumbles, along with the primacy of speech over image. In *Fable Cinématographique* (2001), he signals the reversal of the old Aristotelian hierarchy that privileged mythos (the rational structure of the plot) over opsis (the emotive effects of the spectacle) (8–9). More broadly, the reversal of the hierarchy of genres, of serious over light fiction or film, is inaugurated; the hierarchies of high style, high culture, high thought over base styles and so on, are undone. Literary or cinematic subjects, like those objects of solemn Renaissance portraits, are opened to the inclusion of the clowns, the rubbish of society, to the point of excluding high society. Where the objects of art once stood in a passive relationship to the subjects that created and viewed them, now the relationship between them was equalized as the factors that accounted for the domination were supplanted by new means of making and viewing art, new forms of creating, new positions of spectatorship. Whereas the arts had their own order of privileged categories, now there is art as a singular category, no longer subject to the hierarchy of higher or low art forms. The fine arts tradition, bound to the training of the talented creative figure of the artists, with his or her "way of doing," yields to the emergence of the common object, placed in a relation to other objects, or to the spectator, so as to end the Privileges of Art. Duchamp and a urinal signed by R. Mutt made its statement. And in Senegal, without the dadaists' imprimatur, Amadou Bamba's image appears on the bumpers and in the windows of *cars rapides* in Dakar—his eyes engaging the passengers as they enter the rickety vehicles under his benediction. With the question "Is it art?" comes the apprehension of the object shifting ground, undoing the previous criteria of art "appreciation." The presentation and apprehension of the experience of art are now freed, and as they appeal to *le commun,* the sensorium that lent itself to the hierarchy and its modes of domination is freed as well.

The *commun* is both the site for a community of the people, the demos; and for its equivalent in status, the material, which since Plato was designated as lower than the idea, the ideal, the form and its formal properties. With the aesthetic regime, logos over pathos goes the way of the sensorium of the hierarchy and its privileges. The power of form over matter had paralleled that of "the power of the class of intelligence over the class of sensation, of men of culture over men of nature. If aesthetic 'play' and 'appearance' found a new community, then this is because they stand for the refutation, within the sensible, of this opposition between intelligent form and sensible matter which, properly speaking, is a difference between two humanities" (2009a: 31). How does this aesthetic metapolitics bear on the reality of politics itself? Rancière talks of parallel structures, modes of thinking that "correlate," modes of apprehension that are "consubstantial" with each other, as if the apprehension of the distribution of the sensible of the one is inscribed on the other. In both cases, a major change in the distribution of the sensible had begun with the new political thinking and aesthetics in the eighteenth century, culminating with the ascension of modernism and postmodernism. The provinces of art and of politics had come to be marked by adherence to a "sensorium different to that of domination" (2009b: 30). That may mean that there is not much more than an echoing of the one regime in the other, rather than any real kind of causation linking them. But liberation, emancipation, domination, and free play do not occur in a vacuum, and if the kind of making sense that works in one realm is echoed, is "consubstantial with," is "correlated to," the other, that would be no stranger than seeing the war protests of the 1960s linked to the liberationist countercultural moment. We saw this in the symbolic joining of "'68" in France, and in Europe, with "'68" in Africa, the period marking increasing student unrest from Senegal to Ethiopia. Freedom, claims Rancière, following Kant, is the sign of play in the realm of aesthetics, in contrast to the constraint of the servitude of work. Similarly, free appearance is in contrast to the constraints of the mimetic order, and what joins these factors, appearance, play, and work, is that they turn on domination as set against equality, which are "operative within the very tissue of ordinary sensory experience" (2009b: 31).

What signals domination in art and in politics is very different—on the surface. But if a consubstantial evocation of these qualities can be derived from the underlying features of each realm, where domination and equality mark the fundamental relations of each realm—relations that are prior to any ontological formulations that emerge from the distribution of the elements into a sensibility—then the metapolitics of each will share similar features. This is quite different from a reading of each based upon the significations of the contents. The question of where to start in a determination of the degrees of domination or equality can begin with the Bataillean notion that a perspective from below, and an aesthetic identified with/as trash, would be indispensible in making such a determination of hierarchy versus commonality, domination versus equality—and especially dissensus, the prerequisite for freedom. From that initial moment, it becomes possible to determine the power of an elite to establish whose higher taste, whose active roles, and ultimately whose intelligence will prevail over base sensation and crudity of tastes (2009a: 31). The revolution's politics, which entailed far-reaching contestations between Reigns of Law, of Terror, and of emancipation, echoed the contemporary revolution in art, leading Rancière to make this central claim: "The aesthetic suspension of the supremacy of form over matter and of activity over passivity makes itself thus into the principle of a more profound revolution, a revolution of sensible existence itself and no longer only of the forms of the State" (2009a: 32).

Sembène pulls up short in this revolution in the "sensible": his dogma always maintained the constitution of the sensible along lines that continued to make sense in a sensorium scarcely different from what preceded him. From the outset, Mambety constructed a distribution of the sensible that would fit more comfortably into a world of Godard films than those of Pontecorvo. Sembène took the direction that social realism had carved out, and Mambety inclined toward the edges of a New Wave surrealism that gave freedom a possibility for African cinema. This shift in African aesthetics, which these two creators sketched out—twenty years before Ben Okri broke the representational codes of fiction, before Jean-Pierre Bekolo imported his satirical disjunctive MTV style with *Quartier Mozart* (1992)—adumbrated the move toward an aesthetic regime that spoke to the needs of an emancipation appropriate to the younger generation in Flora Gomes's *Blue Eyes of Yonta* (1992), the postrevolutionary generation attuned more to pop music and soccer than to the revolutionary state that the older generation had created. The style and discourse of the youth were liberated from the revolutionary burdens of the past. The two generations were joined, but not seamlessly into one African world. Rather, they had dissimilar visions of the future; they represented an old and new distribution of the sensible, held different perspectives on what was possible to imagine for their lives, to the point that Yonta thought that she had a real relationship with Vicente while he was still communing with the spirits of the ancestors, his spirit ensconced in the world of the past, as he tried to establish a successful business. The abiku child of Ben Okri was able to see the spirits that populated the New Age; the visions of the older generation in Madame Koto's Bar stopped at the line drawn by the powers of the state. Two relatively distinct sensoriums, one built on a regime of mimesis and representation and another on the impossibility of conveying the sublime, and simultaneously the compulsion to convey the banality of virtual figures caught in a situationist's dérive,[14] a relationalist tableau vivant, or a neobaroque spectacle.

Toward the end of *Faat Kine* (2000), Sembène invests his faith in the new generation led by Pres, the son who has no father, but whose future has been prepared by the work of his mother and grandmother. Sembène stops at this point, as he does in *Moolade* (2004), with the familiar configuration of the progressive movement and its committed actors. Rancière argues that the politics of the aesthetic regime moves us beyond the logics of progress, which bring us closer to a mimetic regime with its certainties and truths. Instead he argues for a metapolitics that shifts location from the public contestation over power with the state as the target and ultimate prize. He presents the contemporary scene of the struggle for freedom as the "infra-scene of underground movements and the concrete energies that comprise them" (2009a: 33). The African equivalent for what he is envisioning, "a revolution within the very idea of revolution" (2009a: 33), can be identified in the work of a new generation of filmmakers who have relocated the underground to the spaces previously passed by because of their detritus: the space of the prosthesis sought by the ironically named hero Vitorio; fields of trash and plastic bags in *Daratt* (2006) and *Le Franc* (1994); the desert that the emigrants sought to cross in *Bamako* (2006); the sea lying between Nouadhibou and Spain in *Heremakhono* (2002)—spaces that would reestablish our ties to the materiality of existence in the current terrain, where "the idea of a revolution of the forms of sensible existence [are] opposed to a revolution of state forms" (33–34). Dissensus takes shape on this terrain.

Paradoxically, Rancière argues it is art "as long as it is also non-art, or is something other than art" (46). As a political equivalent of dissensus, that which is grounded in equality and the struggle for inclusion on the part of those without a part, it attains an emancipatory status in its autonomy or solitude as a work of art in which he sees the seeds for "a new humanity": "The aesthetic regime of art institutes the relation between the forms of identification of art and the forms of political community in such a way as to challenge in advance every opposition between autonomous art and heteronomous art, art for art's sake and art in the service of politics, museum art and street art. For aesthetic autonomy is not that autonomy of artistic 'making' celebrated by modernism. It is the autonomy of a form of sensory experience. And it is that experience which appears as the germ of a new humanity, of a new form of individual and collective life" (32). That solitude "carries a promise of emancipation" that is fulfilled as the categories on which its status is based blur in the face of a dissensual approach. That is, the emergence of politics, through dissensus, in the reading of the categories of art and politics, challenges the policing of the categories. Art's solitude is grounded in the promise of emancipation thanks to the dissensual reading of its status, which entails its "elimination of art as a separate reality, its transformation into a form of life" (2009a: 36).

This is the central conundrum of the truly *engagé* film, that it both is and is not art. We study Sembène's films in film studies, accept his "mégotage," and work at a new distribution of the sensible, attempting to see from a site that is below before it is co-opted into joining a new place located above—like the acceptance of the graffiti artists into the gallery, where it loses touch with the very *commun* that had given the space below and outside their definition.

Sembène's or Cissé's or Ouédraogo's solidarity is in the service of a collective emancipation. However, with the passing of the grand Fanonian narrative, the new aesthetic regime now solicits in vain the inexpressible features of the sublime, and with the free play of the ordinary in graffiti art or in the telenovela series situated in everyday life, calls forth a different experience of the community. The sarcastic dismissals of failed communities and superannuated patriarchies in Mambety's *Hyènes* (1992), Teno's *Afrique, je te plumerai* (1992), Bekolo's *Saignantes* (2005), and Bassek ba Kobhio's *Sango Malo* (1990) render old-fashioned the sensibilities tied to past models of *engagement* for an African cinema now into its third generation.

In *Bamako,* Sissako critiques and mocks the old-style film audience who watch the mock-Western film. We could set them against three groups of spectators: those watching Mele in her club appearance, those in the audience at the trial, and those participating in the church service. In all cases, one could ask when active participation overtakes passive submission to the experience of the performance/trial/service, when the *commun* speaks to a new ethical imperative no longer subservient to the hierarchies implicit in the grand narratives of the past—"creating situations apt to modify our gazes and our attitudes with respect to our collective environment" (2009a: 21). The old models of spectator or political communities have now morphed into enthusiastic church congregations, mesmerized club audiences, or rapt critics of global systems of injustice. Spectator communities subject to dominant rhetorics of education, metapolitics of pedagogy, or entertainment setups requiring passive audience submission to spectacle might be set against potential modes of spectatorship, like those of Debord's situationist viewings (1967), where relations of domination are suspended and transformed into "generative principle[s] for a world without domination" (2009b: 36–37). Rather than a regime of art governed by positive political values, which reproduces the framing, even the assumptions of that which it opposes,[15] the aesthetic regime bridges the art-politics binary.

As it is an African aesthetic, in the end, that concerns us, one place to look for the new form of the response to the image would be in the Mourids' response to the image of Amadou Bamba. Starting with the creator of the iconic images figured in the shops that bear his image so widely through Senegal, we would begin with the understanding that for the viewer/believer, we are not placing before our eyes the object of our gaze but rather are ourselves the object of the gaze of the figure being portrayed. The passivity of the subject is transformed, reversed, as the supplicant is now identified with the gazer. And with his gaze, Bamba's *baraka*—the power of the blessing—is bestowed. The reversal of the representational or mimetic order is accomplished on several levels. Instead of the artist controlling the process of creating the image, it is the subject of the painting who creates in the artist the power to create the image, that power being identified specifically with the *baraka* or spiritual blessing of the Saint. In this regard, the act of viewing is a two-way encounter. The Senegalese Mourid artist Mor Gueye creates paintings as works of devotion that reverse, if anything, the conventional notion that it is the work of an artist that actively creates the painting as a passive object. Roberts and Roberts put another perspective on this relationship between painting and artist:

> Mor Gueye states that his compositions come to him through divine intervention, and some artists state more explicitly that it is Bamba himself who guides their hands as they paint (Roberts and Roberts 102). . . .
>
> When paintings like Mor Gueye's are discussed by Mourides, their narratives and underlying narrativity are directly activated by the Saint himself (103).
>
> As a "friend of God" (wali Allah), Bamba possessed and possesses *Baraka,* or blessed energy, that he offers those who 'remember' him through spoken and visual arts. *Baraka* is a *transformative* forces that Mourides find available to them through images of the Saint. The "participation" of Senegalese in the reverse-glass paintings they are viewing. . . . is achieved through Bamba's *Baraka.* For Mourides, images of the Saint are not passive illustrations and instead dynamically provide "visual piety" . . . The images are icons, empowered by the Saint's *Baraka*" (103).
>
> [W]hen I see his portrait it helps me overcome all obstacles. It gives me force, it gives me courage. . . . [E]very time you see this image, something goes into you and something comes out of you. (Papisto Boy, cited in Roberts and Roberts 60–61)[16]

Similarly, when the Senegalese artists sought autonomy in their creation, they needed to come out from under the burden of Senghor's state-sponsored Negritude. In the Senegalese Laboratoire Agit-Arts's bold push for artistic emancipation at the height of the "Independences" of African state art, the emphasis fell on the movement away from official state art. Harney describes the Village des Arts and in particular its Laboratoire Art-Agit movement as "a multimedia performance group comprise of artists, cultural workers and intellectuals whose main agenda was to liberate artists from dependence on the state. Artists such as Issa Samb, Babacar Traoré, and Youssouf John staged impromptu demonstrations and performances outside of official gallery and theater openings, bringing art back to people in the streets and calling into question the authenticity of invented traditions of the Negritude movement" (75.) They deployed improvisation and audience participation against a notion of officially sanctioned art. Rancière comes to similar conclusions concerning the political project of the regime of aesthetics in which a contrast is made between "the dead mechanism of state and the living power of the community nourished by the sensible embodiment of its idea" (2009a: 37). Two notions of politics occur here: one tied to the community that is evoked in the aesthetic regime and another in the political realm. The former retains its emancipatory promise to the extent that it releases any claims to a "consensual" community, that is, not only one that shares an agreement on the meaning of the experience but, more to the point, whose consent is built around the common responses to the sensibilities being evoked. On the one hand, there is a political program that would seek to overcome class domination and to enlighten its spectators as to the truth of their condition of oppression, a truth whose emancipatory force has long been spent; on the other, a "sensible" response that would be grounded in the "living tissue of experiences and common beliefs in which both the elite and the people share" (2009a: 37). The former calls for action and change predicated upon an audience's class readings of their situation, or that of their parents' generation; the latter for a commonality that precedes class identifications and responses. That "'aesthetic' programme" is defined here as metapolitical, seeking to accomplish a political task in "truth and the sensible order" that politics seeks to realize in terms of "appearance and form" (2009a: 37).

It is crucial that this move to a new sensibility not be taken as a dismissal of the old politics. Rather, it is an attempt to reconstitute politics, like art, in a location that stands apart from that constructed by the old order's terms. As we are considering the bricks on which the notions of art and politics themselves are constructed, and are looking for new understandings of both based on a reconsideration of the bricks themselves rather than the edifice they proclaim themselves to be, we consider that both the mansions of great art and great political houses are viewed by the lowly *déchets humains* as weighty artifices of power.

The metapolitics arising from the regime of aesthetics are not informed by a rhetoric of emancipation: "What aesthetic education and experience do not promise is to support the cause of political emancipation with forms of art. Their politics is a politics that is peculiar to them, a politics that opposes its own forms to those constructed by the dissensual interventions of political subjects."

Rancière calls metapolitics a form of thinking that passes from "the appearance of democracy and of the forms of the State to the infra-scene of underground movements and the concrete energies that comprise them" (2009a: 33).[17] Here Rancière expresses perfectly the opposition between the first twenty or so minutes of *Xala* and *Les Saignantes*. The former takes place on the steps of what appears to be the palace of government for the newly independent nation of Senegal, with its newly elected "president" and executive board, as the change-over of power is enacted before the spectators' gaze, both diegetically and in the sight of the viewing audience. (In fact, it is the Chambre de Commerce, but the scene is staged, and the discourses framed, so as to create the misimpression.) Power is on display, with police deployments, instruments of rule, rhetorics of "power pass power," as Sojaboy would have it, represented in visual and spoken terms.

In contrast, *Les Saignantes* begins in the private quarters of the call girl who is dangling her wares over the government minister. The old man is ludicrously stretched out on the bed, played out and finally broken before the erotic charge. The girl is in a harness, dangling sexually in triumph over his impotent lasciviousness, his ridiculous pretensions to being up to her, and ultimately his final dosage of xala. Perhaps this is to be viewed as a passage of power from the moribund old man to the young hot Saignante; but more, it illustrates the change from the old pedagogically illuminating scenes of oppression and redress to the new, noir versions of free women, with their clitoral or Mevoundou powers, their nighttime haunts, their vulgar displays of legs spread open so as to piss drunkenly on the images of men who would still dream they could have the Saignantes for themselves.

The location for literal politics in *Saignantes* gets displaced onto billboards whose messages intertextually proclaim Bekolo's truths about repressive Cameroonian regimes for which we have waited far too long for change, about the powers of women centered on their sexuality, on the mystical force and dark cinematic image of beautiful young and vibrant women, on the biting humor they share. Until the evil minister comes onto the scene, and in grotesque allegory tries to evoke male power, we are ensconced in Bekolo's new regime of "Mevoundou"—one that is not sustained till the end but that writes a script for the new location of power. The inscriptions mark the attempt to pass from the power of the images and their vulgar disruptions of the male order to the logos of political action and engagement—thus conveying continuity with the older representative order of the arts. The two orders of the sensible in the arts, that is, the representative and the aesthetic, are received in totally different manners, opening up the space for disruption envisioned by Rancière as the location where the subordinated, here the women, the eroticized named in blood as "saignantes," impose their images on the formal loci for death and control, the mortuary and the minister's office, the sites of male power. The clitoral order, ridiculous, erotic, drunken, sets in place its opposition. Dissensus enters through Mevoundou and the trashy women.

Dissensus with the excess, the wilding, the torture and fearfulness that underlie the action in Teno's *Clando* (1996), Marie's mockery of de Gaulle in the unforgettable scene of her entry into the French Culture Center in Yaounde in *Afrique, je te plumerai* (1992); the moment in *Chef* (1999) where the thief has been apprehended and is about to be beaten or lynched, when the screen abruptly goes black; and finally, the madness of the retired functionary in *Lieux sacrés* (2009), who has been reduced to scribbling pithy, incomprehensible messages on the walls of buildings in the quartier in Ouaga where the video parlor exhibits popular action films for the youth and unemployed. The rationality of the representative order and its commitment to progressive politics strain under the impress of the new regime of aesthetics that strives to establish its politics in a new configuration of *le commun,* in a new space for exhibition, given definition by the quartier setting. Teno conveys this political space in total eloquence and grace in *Lieux sacrés* with the gatherings around the drummer who offers his friends *thé à la menthe* along with his powerful djembe performances.

There was never anything in the old lineaments of power susceptible to the kinds of analysis needed to uncover these twin features: Teno's commitment to the documentary attestations, and Bekolo's evocation of Mevoundou and the devouring mothers' phallic powers, the states of exception, the destitution of those with no part. Rather we are addressing a sensibility in which the werewolf, the vampire, and the witch have taken hold. Just like the unrefined graffiti images of the genocidal crimes that decorate the walls of the rebel's buildings in *Nuit,* the nightmarish *mère dévorante* imposes herself upon the viewer who, confronted with her gaze, like that of the saint-marabout, is seized in her imagination, frozen it in its hold. We are enmeshed in the same struggle between the rational logos of the surviving women in *La Nuit de la vérité* (2004) who now teach the children about proper ways, and the deathly pathos of the figure of Edna whose disruptions attack the comforting genre of film as night school.

This is an aesthetic revolution that proposes to "transform aesthetics' suspension of the relations of domination into the generative principle for a world without domination" (2009a: 36–37). Aesthetic free play reaches to a space beyond politics as we know it: it "becomes the principle of a new freedom, *capable of surpassing the antinomies of political liberty.* In a nutshell, it becomes the principle of a politics, or, more exactly, of a metapolitics, which, against the upheavals of state forms, proposes a *revolution of the forms of the lived sensory world*" (99; my emphasis).

We now have the prolegomena for trash. More than a positioning within the same old frame of above and below, the wealthy and powerful versus the poor and dispossessed, the dissensus imposes a new relationship to the lived sensory world expressed through the immediate material environment, resolved into *images,* like those of the beggars of *Xala* across the sand dunes slogging their way back to the city, making a revolution in our visual space with their spittle and coarse laughter, their well-defined odor that reaches our senses along with their missing limbs, their crutches and cracked teeth, their beggarly appearance as *déchets*. Images we can't stand, were never meant to stand; images once in our faces but now much more of our faces; images of ourselves, which we perceive in their gazes upon us, as in the return of the gaze of the Mourid saint. What is needed is clearly not a new politics: the stench of trash, like Trafigura's dumping, cannot be hidden. There is a new African cinema that brings together the everyday object with the artistic setting so as to put in motion a new way of seeing the ordinary world, of leveling and democratizing its displays.

In *Aristotle's Plot,* the character of Cinema is joined at the wrist to the Cineaste E.T., and life and death frame the debate that the narrator presents: "we don't want to produce our cinema outside of life. Because when it is out of life, it is dead. Like a difficult childbirth, which do we choose, the mother or child? Life or cinema? Because when cinema becomes your life you are dead, it is dead. We are all dead." At this point, Art has become non-Art, and Politics another feature of the Plot. This is Bekolo's promise of emancipation: not through engagé cinema but through the work's solitude yielding its autonomy to life, to heteronomy, its "promise of emancipation" eliminating art as a separate category while celebrating its transformation "into a form of life" (2009a: 36). As art and politics cease to be what they were, forcing us to choose between their mother or the new child, we are compelled to establish the understanding of the new politics of emancipation through vectors we never had to consider before. Being dead is now the only way to see the functioning of the regime of sensibility that governs the range of films from Nollywoodian necropolitics to the festival circuit films that are currently endowed with the children of melodrama. It may have always been there all along, the tie to the gross and the emotional, the shock of the unexpected encounter, the trauma suffered by Wend Kuuni at the outset of his journey and again at the end. We always sought to reason with it before, rather than to engage the trashy frisson it evoked, to stay within the regime of logos and resist the pathos. Now it is in the frisson that the new politics of egalitarianism is to be found. But not without resistance from the aediles of celluloid film culture who cannot conceive of a rule that states that when cinema becomes your life, you are dead.

We need a definition of trash that will sustain a Rancière reading, one that will serve as a trope for the politics of emancipation and egalitarianism that he sees in the art installations that deploy in new ways the most ordinary, old hat sorts of objects—just as we would look to an art of recuperation and graffiti as the appropriate expression for movements like Set Setal. Trash can be tied to its material base in terms of its utility or use value, which is ostensibly none at all or worse, since it costs to have trash picked up—expenditure with expenses, excrement with cleanup charges; used water fees. Trash that cannot go, stains that remain, stubbornly, at a cost. "When cinema becomes your life, you are dead, it is dead, we are all dead." Cinema trash is devoid of any use value in the political sense. It has value as entertainment, but not in sociopolitical terms for which use entails more than expenditure; its detritus remains after the ninety-minute diversion, with empty popcorn containers, sullied aisles and seats in theaters whose chairs have become threadbare. If there is exchange value, commodity value, even that is devoid of life-giving usefulness: its adherents, like Cinema and the other tsotsis, have left productive activities behind so as to consume useless images that distract them from their lives. They are dead, and we are watching them too, as they enter into Hollywood fantasies of endless life, endless series of simulacra deaths that are undone with each new episode. The art becomes the site of death and uselessness, of the necropolitics, when measured against politics as the site of common actions undertaken for the common good. Without the trash, E.T. could continue to show his films and celebrate the usefulness of African culture, what the African American spectator in *Aristotle's Plot* calls his roots. The beautiful technical arrangements of cinema art would find their natural audience and home, and there would be an end to the colonial civilizations, but for the discontents. The avant-garde's struggle against mass culture would be accomplished, without cost or expenditure.

Unfortunately, there would remain the *objet a,* the stain, to remind us of what we were trying to forget during the showing. Modern art denounces capitalism and its division of work, its commodity consumerism, but at the price of the work being "even more mechanical, more 'inhuman' than the products of mass capitalist consumption. But, in its turn, this inhumanity causes the stain of the repressed to appear, thus disturbing the autonomous work's beautiful technical arrangement by recalling that which founds it: the capitalist separation of work and enjoyment" (2009a: 41). Autonomy comes at a price, that of maintaining the gap between "the dissensual form of the work and the forms of ordinary experience" (41). Without exhausting the dissensus, our definition of trash as that which lacks usefulness, nonproductive work and enjoyment without the sublime to provide value, bears the mark of its foundation, the stain of the repressed or forgotten, of what is discarded, even in a moment of distraction. The old furniture of the mind marks all commodity cultures that require new turnovers constantly. And in their recuperation, they turn from useful work to useless art. The object that has become obsolete, unfit for consumption, can become available for artists' use, "as a disinterested object of satisfaction, as a body ciphering a story, or as a witness to an inassimilable strangeness" (50). Though the products of art become commodities, in an age of commodities they leave their use values behind to become "either hieroglyphs bearing their history on their bodies or disused, silent objects bearing the splendor of that which no longer supports any project, any will" (50).

The creator of the kind of cinema of such objects that have crossed over the border of usefulness and value is undoubtedly Abderrahmane Sissako whose *Heremakono* (2002) turns on the useless light bulb, the dead bodies that wash up onto the beach, the used tires, the languid figures of those who are waiting for happiness without hope, as the children continue to learn their trades, sing their songs, and carry on life. *La Vie sur terre* (1999) is a hymn to those old objects of marginal use, the radios, telephones, cameras, that barely work—objects so outdated as to be quaint in the eyes of the viewer—the telespectator whose own cell phone has supplanted virtually all those outmoded technologies. The post office telephones, the photographer's studio camera and sets, implements of quaintness that still require one to pose, to speak loudly and quickly, to listen to the voice of the other while sitting around in the shade, shooting the breeze. The discovery of their splendor is the source of Sissako's art, and in effect he succeeds in turning the entire town of Sokolo into a piece of installation art whose value is not given in terms of work, usefulness, or political meaning or power. In terms of the capital, Sokolo is a small corner of nowhere, without importance, even if bearing the signs of its history on its body—an autonomous splendor.

By itself, Sokolo might be taken as the idyll of nostalgic pastoralism. When situated along the currents that flow from the metropole to its margins, it bears the trace of what global commodity cultures produce, a shock that reveals "one world hidden beneath another" (2009a: 51). Rancière's reading of capitalist violence is that it lies beneath the happiness of consumption: "and commercial interests and violence of class struggle [remain] beneath the serene appearances of art" (51). This violence attests to the state mechanisms and domination of the market that quash the potentialities of critique. As Dramane leaves Europe, in the beginning shots of *La Vie sur terre,* he stops in the supermarket to buy some last presents, and the camera catches him before the displays of butter and dairy products extending the full length of a long aisle. When he gets to Sokolo, we encounter two villagers disputing the likelihood of there being such a thing as an escalator. The heteronomous elements of modernity and its dependencies are caught in the art of the camera that reveals one world tied to the other, just as the words of Césaire reach us across time and distance to bring out the call for an action, any action, that would redress the inequality of the situation in which the black man finds himself. "Il faut partir . . . gardez-vous de croiser les bras en l'attitude *stérile du spectateur"* (It is necessary to leave . . . beware of crossing your arms in the sterile posture of a spectator. 32; my emphasis). With Sissako, the aching nostalgia attached to the poet's words functions not as a renewal of their mandate but rather as a discovery of a splendor whose price is the same as the useless furniture. Even in *Bamako,* where the cries for redress are endless, the complaints against useless cowboy movies reiterated in deeply ironic forms, we still return to images of pure materiality with the lengthy shots of the dyed fabric and the dye water runoff. A cinema of the purely material reaches for an aesthetic of trash more than a politics of revolt, and it is in the former that a metapolitics must take form, rather than in any return to the latter.

The metapolitics of a reconfigured material world of discarded objects matches Lyotard's claim that the commodity culture generates a meaningless equality of value for objects since "everything is good for consumption" (cited in Rancière 2009a: 95). For this study, our notion of a trash aesthetics is based on the claim that "everything is good for expenditure." With the former, "taste" becomes the method of discerning value as it relates to any commodity and its desirability. The result for Lyotard is an abasement and general leveling: "This taste is no taste." This marks the transition to postmodernism for Lyotard and the end of representative realism. Similarly, for E.T. in *Bamako*, the movies consumed by the tsotsis were "shit," worthless entertainment. For Lyotard, "What are called upon by eclecticism are the habits of magazine readers"—we would say, the habits of inveterate movie watchers, faithful viewers of soaps, addicted consumers of Nollywood films—the needs of the consumer of standard industrial products that he identifies with "the spirit of the supermarket shopper" (cited in 2009a: 95). Lyotard sees in this the source of the pressure being placed on the postmodern artist and those who distribute his or her art, thus "deresponsibilizing the artists with respect to the question of the unpresentable" (2009a: 95)—the key question of importance for Lyotard for the coming century.

Bearing that responsibility in mind, never letting go of the import of a meta-politics that reinvests responsibility on the level of the reframing of a material, sensory world presented as a new regime, we must take up the gage Lyotard throws down and assume the responsibility as critics of the "inadequate," "up-and-coming," or decisively trashy films being produced in Africa. Rancière takes up our challenge, albeit unwittingly since for him there is no Africa in sight when he states of Lyotard, as he might have done of Sembène, "Lyotard upholds the tradition of that Marxism which, notably in Adorno or Clement Greenberg, tied art in its radical autonomy to the promise of social and political emancipation" (2009a: 96). This tradition has always defended, against the conventional oppositions of art for art's sake and politically engaged art, a different idea of art's politicity: "namely, that art is political provided that it *is* art. And an art is only such if it produces objects that, both in texture and the way we experience them, have a radically different status to the objects of consumption" (2009a: 96). A political representation, within the diegesis, becomes something other than a political act on the street: the former remains subordinate to the hierarchies that govern the image and that which vehicles it through effects of genre, narration, mise-en-scène, and conditions of exhibition. The latter takes on its meaning within another context, one in which the hard conditions of privilege and power are contested.

What the absence of an Africa in the above debate between Rancière and the Frankfort school philosopher and modernist critic of high art leaves out is the relativity of the notion of consumption, of objects of consumption, not to mention the historical resonances of social and political emancipation. A Mudimbe would be right to point out that every term in this credo is culturally relative; that the very notion of social and political emancipation in the west turns on its dismissal of the African Otherness as the sites for repression or domination, and that the emancipation from consumerism, from the shackles of being forced to choose among hundreds of varieties of butter weigh down the consumer in the metropole so very differently from the consumer in Sokolo.[18] But it announces the revolution in the sensorium that is at the core of the change in politics we are evoking. "This is a revolution in the forms of sensory existence, instead of a simple upheaval of the forms of the state; a revolution that is no mere displacement of power, but a neutralization of the very forms by which power is exercised, overturning other powers and having themselves overturned. Aesthetic free play—or neutralization—defines a novel mode of experience that bears within it a new form of 'sensible' universality and equality" (2009a: 99). This revolution was precisely what Fanta Nacro backed away from at the end of her long Walpurgisnacht scene in *Nuit de la liberté*. As with Sembène, in his farewell performance of *Moolade*, liberal humanist values come to prevail at the end as the repressive old guard is overturned. The realm of the sensory for both, and its hierarchies, thus remains untroubled.

For Rancière, there is another scene to which we must refer besides the restoration of an order that comforts us in our expectations of progress, and this is the scene that "serves to ground both art's autonomy and the promise of an emancipated humanity in the experience of the sensorium of exception, *where the activity/passivity and form/matter oppositions governing the other forms of sensory experience are cancelled out*" (2009a: 99; my emphasis). I would call this the moment of the Red Cloth in *Bamako* when Sissako bravely holds the image of the red dyed cloth before our eyes, completely filling the screen with it for seven seconds. This is a new aesthetic, an "aesthetic 'free play'" that is more than simply an intermediary between high culture and simple nature, or a stage of the moral subject's self-discovery. "Instead it becomes *the principle of a new freedom*, capable of surpassing the antinomies of political liberty. In a nutshell, it becomes the principle of a politics or, more exactly, of a metapolitics, which, against the upheavals of state forms, proposes a revolution in the forms of the lived sensory world" (2009a: 99).

We will seek the lineaments of that revolution in the new forms of African cinema that have emerged in the past two decades. In part, most obviously, we must attend to the radical sensorium of Nollywood. But the melodramatic, neobaroque, commercial cinema that has taken off in Nigeria and Ghana in the 1990s and 2000s is not alone in evoking the extravagant, unworldly, overdone fittings of the material realm. There is a point where we have to address more than the contours of the commodity and its comforts, more than the emotional, more than the dramatic, unexpected coincidences that mark the melodramatic, and ask more pointedly what is there that shapes what we are expected to see and to feel. And in that sensorium, we will find that "Nollywood" is everywhere, has always been there and is only different because it is so unabashed about evoking desire and feeling, about presenting the desirable and its opposites in

Figure 2.1. Mural of Amadou Bamba over junkyard.

their fullness, as embodiments familiar to the popular screen. At that point, we can gesture toward the new metapolitics of African cinema.

Metapolitics are and are not the simple location of politics; they are not reducible to a unified or totalized space. The move to repudiate dogma will not lead us to do away with a politics of resistance. Ultimately we are setting about to redefine an approach that will yield the contours of an African metapolitics in light of an African metapoetics. The impossibility of arriving at a broad, totalizing "Africanness" will be finessed by our choice of films that define the spaces for the new aesthetics to be viewed.

3   The Out-of-Place
Scene of Trash

> *Parergon:* neither work (*ergon*) nor outside the work (*hors d'oeuvre*),
> neither inside nor outside, neither above nor below, it disconcerts any
> opposition but does not remain indeterminate and it *gives rise* to the work.
>
> —Jacques Derrida, *The Truth in Painting*

What is worthless? Who is trash? Following Bataille, we can locate the site for trash in the mud, or more generally, "below." Down in the dirt where the "big toe" (Bataille 20)[1] can dig in and soil itself. With Rancière, trash can be identified with those outside the community when the community is seen as being constituted as those who "count" when determining the sum of its parts ("Who Is the Subject of the Rights of Man"). Those outside the count, when the parts are counted—the part of those who have no part—become the subject "deprived of any right." At its limit, we can glimpse trash in the Agamben figure of the human reduced to "bare life" in the state of exception. Trashy people are those whose voices are not counted as they do not count and thus cannot be heard. Rancière quotes Hannah Arendt concerning those who had lost everything after World War I and whose rights as mere human beings, apart from nation or property, were abstract, essentially meaningless for them, "the mere derision of right"—the rights of those effectively excluded from the political sphere, not accorded a place, and therefore not having a voice, resulting in "a life entrapped in its 'idiocy,' as opposed to a life of public action, speech, and appearance."[2]

So these are the worthless people, trashy people, when measured by a community conception of value. There are structures that incorporate into their order a measure of value that permits us to make a distinction between what Sembène has called *déchets humains* (human trash) in *Xala* (1974) and those subjects whose value is clearly educed from their wealth or access to political and economic agency. In *Homo Sacer*, Agamben assigns the term "people" to "the poor, the disinherited, and the excluded" (1998: 176), where their exclusion is from the political realm. At once "ordinary people," but in the parlance of anticolonial rhetoric, the disinherited are "les damnés de la terre."

The familiar scene of committed African cinema takes this definition of people who are dominated, revolting against colonialism, from *La Bataille d'Alger* (1966) and applies it to the resistance to neocolonial authorities in the independent

African states, especially when those states are repressive. Sembène depicts this in almost all his films, including those that represent the oppressive order in its formation in the past (*Ceddo* [1976]), those oppressed under colonialism (*Emitai* [1971]), and those still engaged in their combat in the present, as in his last film (*Moolaade* 2004). In its most pathetic formulation we find children, exploited and exposed to grave dangers. In Dangarembga's *Everyone's Child* (1996), AIDS carries off the parents and the orphaned son winds up in Harare, sniffing glue, stealing, running through the streets, crying in the alleys—playing out the role of the valued child now reduced to trash. Meanwhile, his sister, back in the village, has to sell herself to the shopkeeper in order to acquire the basic necessities of life.

Trashy people count less and less, until they are lost in the count. In an unforgettable scene in *O Heroi* (2004), we see the people of Luanda appealing to those who are watching television to help them locate their lost relatives, while Vitorio, the film's ironically named protagonist, tries to acquire a prosthetic limb to replace what was lost when he stepped on a landmine. Lost children, lost sisters, lost fathers, all constitute a horde of ghosts, like the sensation of phantom limbs generated by the memory of missing parts—absent presences whose former value can only be remembered and who exist only as long as the memory is not dissipated.

Trash engages in a series of modifications of value that involve memory, loss, and ultimately a transformation that is made possible by the act of recycling. This is the etiology of trash: it begins with value; it loses its value; it teeters on the edge of total loss, its identity precariously retained despite the loss; and then, like the car in *Divine carcasse* (1998), is recovered before being totally dissembled. The god's devotees pass by the wreck and recognize its innate qualities; a blacksmith rehabilitates it before the loss becomes permanent. It is recovered, reconstituted, and transformed into a Fon god Agbo. Ghosts in the bush, with life still, waiting to return through the anthills.

Is the loss complete or only partial? Is the return a resurrection or, still more, a divinization? Today, on the streets of Dakar, one finds vendors of *récupérés*, sculptures constituted from objects ostensibly culled from the trash heap: parts of computers, combs, tin cans, sublated by an iron poker in the fire, readied for their apotheosis when they are to be finally danced with the whole community—or sold to the tourists.

Or is it more of the secular, banal treatment of waste that we are seeing? Trashy people, dead drunk, robbed of their prostheses, miserable, self-pitying, consigned to a final rubbish heap—heroes no more, their medals a farce. Trashy second wives, with their grasping, unappreciative brats, Oumi piling up the furniture in the truck and moving out once the money is gone; money as filth, excrement as Freud would have it; El Hadj's stolen money that bought her, the money that runs the entire machinery of capitalist, bourgeois marriages. The predictability of Sembène's portrayal of the greedy, modern second wife in *Xala* is radically altered in Nacro's farcical dismissal of Salif, the unfaithful husband, at the end of *Puk Nini* (1995) while Fatou, the slutty Senegalese lady of high fashion, joins sides with the betrayed wife Ada, redeeming her status after having prostituted herself with the worthless Salif.

After the earlier generations of African cinema, the figures of loss morph and are no longer *le peuple*, source of the original revolution, no longer outcasts, cursed and oppressed, but now have become recycled, transformed after the loss of victimization into the triumphal status of the victors, at least temporarily. Ramatou, the rejected girl-lover in *Hyènes* (1992), returning as Linguère Rama tou, queen, creature of prosthestic gold parts, now fabulously rich, powerful, and vengeful—recycled from poor village trash to absolute ruler over wealth and death. One step away from the neo-feminist mystique that we can now trace through the capitalist resurrection of Faat Kine to the women who are dancing at the end of *Moolaade* (2004), to Bekolo's Saignantes (2005), the black-belt warrior women, to the Carmen figures in Ramaka's *Karmen Gei* (2001) and Dornford-Mays *U-Carmen eKhayelitsha* (2005), to Nacro's wives in her short films *Puk Nini* (1995) and *Le Truc de Konaté* (1998)—women who establish their superior moral position over their philandering husbands, who can stand up and insist on their use of a condom. We are far from the trussed-up Fili, circumcised victim in Sissoko's *Finzan* (1992), but only a step on the path of "liberation."

However, from Fili to the "fillies" of Nollywood, a thousand generations of African cinema as we knew it would not have been able to make the leap. Fili's losses experienced as a victim of village patriarchy, as portrayed over and over in the films of Sissoko, Ouédraogo, Kabore, and Cissé, do not seem of a piece with those that transpire in the urbane scene of neoliberal globalization. Fili and her world come from the other side of the great divide between modernist social critique and postmodernist cultural indeterminateness, and now the post-postmodern commercial revolution, which depends on a leveling of all in the face of money. In the Nollywood classic *Osuafia in London* (2004), the gold digger has become a corrupt, trashy white Brit who has already seduced Osuafia's brother and connived with the assimilated barrister after the death of Osuafia's brother, her original Nigerian lover. With the arrival of Osuafia in London to settle his brother's estate, she seduces and marries "our Osuafia," the village bumpkin. With Nollywood's endless series of poisonings, magical love potions, and devious dealings of death and betrayal, the status of the woman-in-revolt-against-patriarchy, as has been seen in many of the films from the 1970s to the 1990s, is now frequently lowered to that of the bought goods, sold off and discarded bodies, or those abandoned to display their final decline into the ultimate status of trashiness. The Nollywoodian *Without Shame* (2005) parades an endless number of such figures.

At this juncture, with the passage into the crassness of the purely commercial cinema, we have the option of reading the proliferation of eroticized or domineering feminine roles as marking a transvaluation of loss into some version of John Waters's "Divine," camp queens of marginalization crowned within the framing of Trash Aesthetics. Alternatively, the "phallic mothers" could be seen as constituting dark figures of monstrous sovereignty, beyond ordinary cognition, asymptotically approaching the sublime, as in *Beyonce* (2006), *Blood Sisters* (2003), or in the final scene of *La Nuit de la vérité* (2004) with Edna, as she passes from grief and insanity into the status of Queen of the Night, if not *mère dévorante*. This trajectory culminates not with the queer triumph of death, as in Waters's classic camp film *Female Trouble* (1974), when Divine is electrocuted in her joyful assumption of her role as notorious killer, but with the return to normalcy where the violated Fatou becomes the schoolteacher for the next generation of children in the new world of peace based on liberal values of decency and normalcy.

It is the premise of this study that we cannot appreciate the central role of the trope of trash in African cinema without considering its relationship to the materialization of the trope in its various configurations as actual "rubbish," "garbage," "waste," designated by a series of terms used to signify that which has lost its value, and that is susceptible either to total disappearance or to some version of recycling, of returning. Jonathan Culler (1988) turns to the binary configuration of "transient" objects that are susceptible to decay and partial or total loss, and "durable" objects that retain their value and are preserved. The former might include a steak that is consumed, passing from food to ingested matter, to energy and fecal waste. If it is recovered as shit, there, we learn in the *History of Shit* (2002), it may be used as fertilizer, as perfume or beauty unguent, or collected and "treated" so as to be converted into a "clean" form.[3] In its transformation from dirty to clean, from impure to pure, from trash to valuable, the transient object undergoes changes intended to restore value to that which has lost it. The "durable" object, like a painting of trash, a recycled *récupéré* piece of art, a painting of the Virgin using elephant dung, is memorialized, museumified, remembered so as to be preserved in its original state as an object of value.

The contours of these stages might be seen in the work of Mary Douglas (2002) and Michael Thompson (1979), two of the doyens in the theorizing of trash. We will first establish the cycles they propound and then relate the status to which they assign trash. Douglas famously defines dirt, after William James, as "matter out of place." The definition fits with Douglas's propensity to read the aspects of society in structural binary terms like order and disorder. Thus James's "matter out of place" becomes, for her, matter that conforms to "a set of ordered relations" and "a contravention of that order" (Douglas 44). Dirt and order oppose each other, and as such constitute a larger order; the system they construct is defined in terms of their relative placement: "where there is dirt there is system" (44). What dirt provides is the location outside of the ordered space of the proper (*le propre*) wherein purity, goodness, and value can be located. As dirt is located out of that space, a margin or border must exist to enable us to differentiate between the two. Dirt interests us because its exclusion renders it, or reduces it, to "inappropriate elements" (*l'impropre*) to be rejected from the proper system, the proper locations. The border interests us because it must assert itself with sufficient force to protect what is proper, to keep out what is undesirable. Precisely as Kristeva's abject must pass through a semipermeable membrane to permit the clean self or ego to exist (*Powers of Horror: An Essay on Abjection,* 1982), so the dirt that is situated outside the ordered site of proper relations must exist outside of, but be present to, the order from which it has been expelled, thus sustaining their difference.

The passage from the one side of the border to the other implies that the relations are not permanent. Cleanliness is a state established by the expulsion of dirt, not a condition that is permanent. Nonetheless, brahmins are born into an upper class; Osu are born as the bottom sector of Igbo society; castes are inherited, and the disinherited are often far from ever being the heirs of the earth. The border is reiterated to keep the undesirables, the untouchables, out; to keep those on top in their "proper" place (*propre* in French). For Douglas, this broad understanding applies both to those she terms "moderns" and to "primitives" (50), another antedated, we might say "inappropriate" set of terms designated to keep the border between them permanent despite the experience of pollution shared by both groups. "Primitives" are excluded from the order of "moderns," yet, ironically, they are the favorite objects of anthropological scrutiny for Douglas and her generation since they exhibit all the more clearly the patterns discovered by the anthropologists, the order with its border and its others. "In the primitive culture the rule of patterning works with greater force and more total comprehensiveness. With the moderns it applies to disjointed, separate areas of existence" (50). Douglas cannot bring herself to let go of the distinction that gave rise to her field, presenting us with the irony of seeing her deploy her 1960s notions of dirt in a postcolonial age where her categories of order have turned against her discipline and imposed on its former lights an evaluation of something approaching pollution, or otherness.

The notion of the passage of dirt from worthless to valuable depended on the anthropologist-discoverer who gave us the meaning of dirt and the understanding of those outside the "disjointed, separate area of existence" inhabited by those living in the modern space. Yet Nollywood shifts our vision of the modern "disjointed, separate area of existence." In the blink of an eye, Osuafia takes a plane from Nigeria and passes from one area of existence into the other, arguably infiltrating both with the dirt from each space, returning with the gold-digging Samantha to his compound in Africa and bringing his ridiculous notions of proper walking and greeting people to London. The global film postulates a modern-primitive binary that is always already polluted, there being no moment of discovery of the one by the other.[4]

Dirt must undergo the passage from valueless to valuable again, just as the initiate must pass from the ill-defined ontological place of not-yet man or woman to member of society. The passage across the border is motivated by the same impulse that drives the cinematic narrative forward: it is the impulse for a change of value, that which supplies the system with its dynamic ability to prevail, and for the dominant features of the hierarchy to be sustained. The change brings its dangers, just as consumption brings its exigencies for expenditure and excretion, followed by renewal or recyclage. Recycling of generations, of sexual fertility, of used up material: dead skins, dead motherboards, dead car engines. All regurgitated, expelled, reconstituted, cleansed, renewed, and so forth. The cycle of an earth struggling against ultimate extinction: this is the meaning of the anthropologist's reading of the poor, primitive, dark child who is not yet prepared for the airplane and the scholarship that will carry him to the dark and cold north, but who is enacting a passage, what they call the rite of passage, across a fundamental divide—the anthropologist's epistemological night of truth. "The theme of death and rebirth, of course, has other symbolic functions: the initiates die to their old life and are reborn to their new" (Douglas 120). What a wonderful normalizing move that "of course" conveys—what we had always already known about the primitive and his cycle: the purity of the order before the modern discoverer had come and polluted it. There, in that anthropologically defined space outside the complexity of history, in obedience to its structures, was the border experienced purely by the primitive, the child-man figure. Here was the true site of danger: "To have been in the margins is to have been in contact with danger, to have been at a source of power. It is consistent . . . to treat initiands coming out of seclusion as if they were themselves charged with power, hot dangerous, requiring insulation and a time for cooling down. *Dirt, obscenity and lawlessness* are as relevant symbolically to the rites of seclusion as other ritual expressions of their condition" (120–21; my emphasis).

Derrida's question of whether the frame belongs to the inside or the outside goes ignored in this structuralist reading of the margin.[5] To the anthropologist, the space of order is well-defined: the space outside is clearly different, and the margin performs its work well as long as we can perceive the order that is being preserved. Clarity of what is "*le propre*" is sustained in the triple structure of society, outside-border-inside, defined in cinematic realist terms as faithful to the genre as mimetic fiction: "The idea of a society is a powerful *image*," an image with well-defined form: "it has external boundaries, margins, internal structure" (Douglas 141; my emphasis). With dirt excluded, the margins empowered, and the center protected, each element is in its place, in its order—nothing is out of place, not even dirt. The system holds structure in place, making change on the metasystemic level impossible. Dirt's power is contained, dirt constrained, trash under control.

But the system itself must be renewed, just as the initiate must pass through the powerful sifter to emerge from the sacred wood and return into the village. The amorphous ontological state of the children is resolved into clear identities marked by clear genders. From their state of confusion, passage, and re-entry comes the renewal of the community: from dirt and the passage through the border stage, the initiates emerge cleansed, and into their final passage and death they will go trailing clouds of identity, until, with time, eventually even their names will be forgotten and they will become the dirt from which the new members will find their originary substance. Dirt's cycle for the anthropologist is complete: "First they are recognizably out of place, a threat to good order, and so are regarded as objectionable" (197). But as a bit of dirt, instead of a totally amorphous element, they retain the specificity accorded their partial identity. They must rot until "all identity is gone" (197), and enter into the "mass of common rubbish" (197). Finally, as all identity disappears, their appurtenance to an in-between state also disappears, leaving us only with the rubbish heap. At that point, the "cycle has been completed" (198), the dirt is now without name, without specific place, located in the rubbish heap, which for the anthropologist becomes formless, undifferentiated. Terminal. Until called upon to start the cycle all over again, saving us from the lapidary fate of an unchanging purity by the insistence of this originating dirt that it return.

There is no question about what is the beginning, what the end; where the locations for above and below are situated; what the outcome must be; what the rules must perform. The complicated space of those who have no place, who are not assigned a place in the order, and who are therefore not endowed with the right to participate in the story, does not emerge to trouble these waters. The flood will come; the Osu will run, convert to somebody else's religion; the study of Okonkwo's death will be completed, written up, and published. Dirt will have completed its work, and the order within which it will be inscribed will prevail. Every attempt to read this dirt back into some system must be completed on the grounds that the cycle has order, at whatever level it is understood.

Yet the logic of the supplement cannot so easily be dismissed. William James gropes toward the supplementary nature of a dirt that refuses this incorporation back into the rubbish heap, or rather, that remains with some troubling identity despite all efforts to amalgamate it: "Here we have the interesting notion . . . of there being elements of the universe which may make no rational whole in conjunction with the other elements, and which, from the point of view of any system which those elements make up, can only be considered so much irrelevance and accident—so much 'dirt' as it were, and matter out of place" (cited in Douglas 203).

We need a human image of that figure that resists the call of recycling, that remains an element of bare trash existence, as it were. This we can find in the thinly disguised reggae star Jimmy Cliff in *The Harder They Come* (1972), playing the village bumpkin, come to town to make his fortune. After spending the night with his mother in the poor neighborhood called the Dungle, he is cast out on his own, barred from entry into the orderly, well-to-do parts of town. Thrown up onto the Tip, Kingston's garbage heap, down on his luck, starving, he must discard his last vestiges of false pride and dig in the muck for his supper alongside the other garbage diggers. He stands on the edge of the garbage dump and intones the words that describe his condition in the song "Many Rivers to Cross":

> Many rivers to cross
> But I can't seem to find my way over
> Wandering, I am lost
> As I travel along the white cliffs of dover
>
> Many rivers to cross
> And it's only my will that keeps me alive
> I've been licked, washed up for years
> And I merely survive because of my pride[6]

At this point, Cliff's character Ivan Martin has been told by his mother to return home to the country, that there is nothing for him in town. He has met the neighborhood dealers and sharks, and after a night on the town is left totally destitute. He spends the day begging for work from the rich, hoping for a break with Mr. Hilton, the local music producer, soliciting any kind of work on a building site, or gardening in the wealthy suburbs. In all instances he is turned away, just like others waiting on lines seeking a job, an entry into the economy. "Many rivers to cross"—having come from the poor countryside, where his grandmother had just died, with no money, no movies, no images, no hopes for a future, to the town where the new rivers to cross now stop him. Once in Kingston, as he passes from the Dungle and his mother's ramshackle lodgings, the windy streets and slums, to the Tip, the city dump, the flow of images takes him down to his lowest point. We see the women standing in the middle of the trash as the words of the song intone, "it's such a drag to be on your own." One woman with a colorful stovepipe hat is standing up, arms akimbo, back to the camera. Around her, women are going through boxes, looking for food, some of which has just been dumped. A child has found three eggs. Other children are dumping barrels of trash. The lyrics, "and I guess I'll have to cry." The tracking shot crosses to a tree, a sapling with someone holding it. The camera continues crossing to the right, revealing a hand holding on, an arm, a yellow shirt, a young man with a trilby, back to us, looking over the Tip (see figures 3.1–3.) From the Dungle to the Tip: Jimmy Cliff contemplating his fate, weak now with hunger. "Licked, washed up": the crossing hard, with the river of trash before him, and the common people of this city to which he has just come.[7] "Wandering, I am lost," the soundtrack of the Cliff song.

There is a space between the aesthetic capturing of this moment in the camera's traveling across the scene and the music's richly textured tonality, like gospel, marking both despair and commonality, as well as hope, beginning with "merely surviving" and "pride." The image is at once "ostensive," advertising its aesthetic qualities with the shot of the poor trash pickers of Kingston, and "metamorphic," inscribed in an order of social commentary (Rancière 2009c: 22–25). We are reading these images of trash, trash pickers, and our protagonist-not-yet-famous, not-yet-cinema-hero, though launched and soon to be en route to the conventional goal of "finding my way" through the movements of the genre that will be surely carrying us over those "many rivers to cross. . . ."

For this key first image of trash, it is important that we see the conjunction of extreme poverty and wealth not as inscribed in an inscrutable system whose features are immutable but as shores on the opposing sides of rivers to be crossed. One crossing we will come to, through the church, will be Joe Hill's challenge to the preachers who proclaim every Sunday that one great day, after this life's travails, the flock will find their reward above. The socialist Joe Hill's lyrics do not take long to define the persona Jimmy Cliff will assume as Ivan the Outlaw, who fights as hero of the common people of the Dungle for his share of "what's mine," instead of hoping for the "pie in the sky / waiting for me when I die."

The trash in the Kingston Tip will either be gathered up by the trash pickers and recycled back into their stomachs, enter their stomachs, cycling again from useful to discarded, almost completely losing its value only to be restored as food within another system of value—or it will be amalgamated into the mass, become indiscernible, undesirable, unresurrected matter. The people will eventually die, and either their bodies will molder and disintegrate down to the bones in their graves, merging with the dark earth, or return, rise up, and have their pie in the sky having crossed the Jordan River. The image of the destitute picking through the detritus situates trash in its synecdochal relationship to trashy people; it situates the social meliorism that crosses one dimension of Henzell's film against the material actuality protruding from the ideological impress, concretized in the image of the film's star, Ivan the Outlaw, Jimmy Cliff as simultaneously reggae star and down-and-out trash picker whose failure is already being transformed into lyrics with "I can't seem to find my way over / wandering I am lost." Lost, but already re-mediated into the image of the hero-to-be, the rebel-to-be, the people's savior-to-be, that is, the movie star and popular singer. The popular singer crosses inside and outside the diegesis: Ivan becomes what Jimmy Cliff is, like Elvis in an Elvis film; like Belafonte or Poitier in a Belafonte or Poitier film—heroes of the poor within the porous borders of the diegesis, stars for the ghetto, with everyone else watching and listening outside. The figure of the Western movie hero, appearing in scenes at the outset of his adventure and at the end, merely echoes this image of the film's hero as popular singer, whose need to linger briefly in the rinds of the smelly Bottom will quickly morph with his transformation into ganja-dealing outlaw and then social rebel, ready to fulfill the prophecy of the lyrics "the harder they come, the harder they fall, one and all."

This is the resurrection of another sort, the media metamorphosis, that joins the human protagonist to the material detritus, whose fate is not to disappear among the mass, losing all identity or ontological status, but rather to return in the higher stage of that which is recuperated: the true *récupéré*. The recuperated objet d'art, like the resurrected figure, participates in three economies. We will call these economies market, art, and memory (Assman 2002: 81), and their three stages—so as to return to the figuration of those objects as cinematic images that will return the gaze to us in three forms—the naked, ostensive, and metamorphic.[8]

The economies engaged by the artist-filmmaker who chooses rubbish (like cigarette butts) as his or her medium begin with the market.[9] Objects are valued initially according to their use value. As they become enmeshed in a market economy based on the sale of commodities, their use value yields to exchange value, and their life span of usefulness is correspondingly reduced. Discarded because of being used up, emptied of their use, they are either gathered into the dumpster and eliminated, or saved by the dumpster diver who revives their value by turning them into objects with a new identity, like a sculpture or door stop. The emptied object might be considered obsolete, like a car that has passed out of fashion, whose old engine does not work with unleaded gas. The newly discovered object then enters the economy under a new aegis, a new economy.

Ivan Martin (Jimmy Cliff) the villager never had much use value as "country boy," and his screen time as such is confined to the opening scenes. But as Ivan Martin (Jimmy Cliff), he returns with star qualities and commands the central position in the story till the end. There is in this three-part pattern of originary state, decline, and resurrection a transition period, one with the greatest dangers, which in this case would have been for Ivan Martin (Jimmy Cliff) to have lost all potentiality of usefulness as star, and never to acquire any exchange value. That is the risk of becoming like all those who accept the Preacher's way: working for petty wages, accepting the restrictions against taking the Preacher's girl, drowning his hopes to be a famous musician, cleaving to the straight and narrow, and disappearing into the masses, thus losing his cinematic identity as Someone Special, that is, the star or hero. This dangerous space of the intermediary stage, according to Douglas, poses a threat to good order to the extent that it doesn't succeed in keeping out that which disrupts the order. But which order is at stake, the order of the "film," that is, the imaginary that is realized in the cowboy film within the film, or the outlaw film constituting the film's diegesis, which requires the bad boy to emerge into his own, parallel to the magic of the film star emerging from the Dungle? The latter requires the fateful intervention of the hero's aura or charisma within the narrative to effect his transformation and emergence from the intermediary position that risks stifling that star quality. The good Ivan who follows the orders of the Preacher is the waste material for the popular "film" into which he is ultimately to be inscribed. In short, he is out of place when most docile in his acceptance of the dominant social order in Jamaica—the order that has ganja dealers paying off the police, that has singers controlled by Mr. Hilton (or just "Hilton" as he is occasionally called in the film) and the disc jockeys, that has the music, the poor, and the Tip under control. But that control is precisely the border that must be crossed, the river with the pie on the other side, for the miracle of the movies, for the Great Singer to transgress, in short, for Jimmy Cliff to appear. Only then can he play at the drama of the rebel, enter into the imaginary of the film-within-the-film's diegesis, cross over the river of the Symbolic Order, and acquire an exchange value of great worth.

This is no longer the market economy by itself since it involves cinematic value, not merely market value. The cinematic value, with its own economy, has its own groundings: "truth, beauty, and meaning" (Assman 81), or, we might say in postmodernist terms, "transgression, ugliness, and ambiguity." John Waters has given us all three in the cross-dressing, transgendered figure of Divine whose sublime embodiment of all three values, from *Female Trouble* (1974) to *Hairspray* (1988), from most to least transgressive, confers increasing degrees of market value just as it veers increasingly away from the sources of its Trash Aesthetic value.

After the market and art, the last economy of trash, according to Aleida Assman, is that of memory. Here the identity of the object is enmeshed in personal and cultural memory, where it retains what is relevant for being remembered or forgotten as long the mechanisms that permit the recalling of the lost person, or object, are retained. As the constraints of time diminish memory, following the pattern of entropy, the resurrection of those previously deemed paltry or worthless into new positions of visibility counters those forces of oblivion, returning John Donne to us after T. S. Eliot rediscovers his poetry, reviving Shakespeare from his weak status in the nineteenth century. After Ivan Dixon dies, with his mother gone, who will remember him? But after he becomes "Jimmy Cliff" playing Ivan the Revolutionary, he will have become the figure for a song that marks his own passage into his persona: "The Harder They Come" performs his transformation into a "free man in my grave."

Assman sums up the relationship between the three economies of market, art, and memory by showing how the passage through one signals an entry into the other: "Industry and art . . . both operate on a principle of innovation, have a common boundary with the possibility of a transference: what has become old in the system of the market may be recovered as new in the system of art" (81). Memory's relationship to art is less well-defined as artists who find their inspiration in dumpster diving relate to memory in a manner that is different from normal by "stress[ing] the possibility of counter-memories and a new vision of culture. In the totalitarian context, the dump becomes the emblem of a subversive counter-memory that cannot be controlled by the institutions of political power, figuring as a perpetual resources of creative energy" (81). Cultural counter-memory becomes the "refuge for the forgotten and rejected," and as such opposes the memorial art of the establishment with the "ars oblivionales" of recalling the lost ones, the forgotten ones (81)—what Buñuel called "Los Olvidados." At the end of *Los Olvidados* (1950), we have one of the unforgettable images of cinema, with Pedro's body dumped off a donkey into a ditch. At the end of *The Harder They Come* (1972), the hero dies in the film-within-the-film's shootout, having passed in Ivan's dying imagination into an imaginary realm that triumphs over the symbolic order. Whether it is a "counter-memory" or a commodification of hero depends on where the viewer/consumer places value—on the act of transgression or on its being tamed into the popular song.

At the end of Douglas's excursus through the role, place, and function of dirt, she claims that value is tied to order and its borders, establishing a binary structure with the border separating that which is in place from that which is out of place. In Michael Thompson's study of rubbish, *Rubbish Theory* (1979), he marks the passage of artifacts through an itinerary of value, not based on their role in sustaining order but on the manner in which value is acquired in dynamic systems. Artifacts initially have a use value that is "transient" and that decreases over time. Unlike Douglas, who focuses on loss as occupying an intermediary space, he identifies the loss of an object's values as resulting in it becoming "rubbish." However, it is still in a state of transience, and the object acquires an aesthetic, museological, or historical value, which marks the passage from transience to permanence. Interestingly, the value of the object in this third stage might well considerably exceed the initial value (Moser 2002: 93).

Moser illustrates his arguments with examples of objects that passed from the second stage of worthless objects, like cracked coffee pots, to becoming collectibles. Culler cites British "Stevengraphs," commonplace scenes ("Dick Turpin's Ride to York on his Bonny Black Bess") that became valued Victorian memorabilia for wealthy American tourists and collectors (2002: 172). We might cite those bubble-gum baseball cards or comics we wish we had kept. The gum we spit out might seem to have lost all possible worth until we remember how the rubbish archeologists, the garbologists of today, now turn their attention from all kinds of figurative to literal shit, as described in *The History of Shit* (2002) to reconstitute the past, remember a society whose detritus gives life to what was "lost to history" or "lost to memory."

All these examples presuppose the existence of a culture, an order in which innumerable new forms of memory and knowledge could be attached to lost artifacts and that disposes of sufficient surplus value to reattach it to forgotten objects so as to inform them with new worth.[10] Resurrection or recreation of value? Recycling, or a recuperation, with a seemingly infinite supply of "mass"— not yet rubbish, with fragments of identity still attached; not yet rubble in which all elements of identity, except for the chemical substratum, are lost.[11] Until the final station is reached: bare bones, reduced to that last bare ontic dimension of being without properties, without name.

This is Agamben's *bios* turned into *zoe*. To be precise, it is the stage at which a life marked by identity and distinctions, by a relationship to an order (whether as part of or excluded from that order), becomes a fragment no longer defined in any relationship. Dead meat, like the body parts of the government minister in *Les Saignantes* (2005), who is pieced together any old way since his identity was never really individuated or socialized, in life or in death. Parts of bodies floating down a river—signifiers of genocide, from Rwanda's history to Fanta Nacro's *La Nuit de la vérité* (2004). The shocking proposition from Agamben is that what modern society in the west has wrought, so perfectly illustrated in the concentration camps, is that the decline of people to bare meat, what he calls the bare life of zoe, has passed from being an exceptional circumstance to becoming the fundamental normalized basis for establishing political, ethical, and ontological difference:

> The decisive fact is that, together with the process by which the exception everywhere becomes the rule, the realm of bare life—which is originally situated at the margins of the political order—gradually begins to coincide with the political realm, and exclusion and inclusion, outside and inside, bios and zoe, right and fact, enter into a zone of irreducible indistinction. At once excluding bare life from and capturing it within the political order, *the state of exception actually constituted, in its very separateness, the hidden foundation on which the entire political system rested.* When its borders begin to be blurred, the bare life that dwelt there frees itself in the city and becomes both subject and object of the conflicts of the political order, the one place for both the organization of State power and emancipation from it. Everything happens as if, along with the disciplinary process by which State power makes man as a living being into its own specific object, another process is set in motion that in large measure corresponds to the birth of modern democracy, in which man as a living being presents himself no longer as an *object* but as the *subject* of political power. (1998: 9; my emphasis)

This crucial passage defines for us the foundation for Thompson's middle stage of that which is worthless, to which he attaches his rubbish-in-transition. Culler's examples of the cute Stevengraphs, Thompson's examples of a cracked piece of pottery or faience, are set off by the horrors of the Holocaust, where great value and great loss asymptomatically approach the Armageddon of the sublime. We need to read these figurations in terms of African imagery, not to free ourselves of their frame but to recalibrate their western epistemologies so as to accommodate African viewpoints and realities. The state in this refocusing ceases to be that entity that determines an individual's relationship to power and society by limiting the degree of individual freedom. Rather, we are confronting images drawn from Mbembe's necropolis, like those of Nigerian gangsters in *District 9* (2009), conjured from an imaginary born from the state of anomy fostered by fear.

Social disintegration now provides the familiar landscape of child soldier films like *Ezra* (2007), or those that furnish corresponding visions of genocidal wars like *Blood Diamonds* (2006). And in a plethora of documentary or docudramatic films, that same vision of genocide returns in naked images that evoke the Holocaust, such as the road filled with corpses over which the truck bumps in *Hotel Rwanda* (2004) or in more sinister terms, the image of the hateful "devil" in Dallaire's *Shake Hands with the Devil* (2007), where Conrad's *Heart of Darkness* has returned full blown, now under the guise of the "poor Canadian general" represented as the psychological victim of what he witnessed and could not stop!

Jimmy Cliff singing about hard times on the edge of the Tip now seems like child's play. Chris Abani's *Song for Night* (2007) corrects Ivan the down-and-out villager's sense of loss with an absolute encounter with death as My Luck (the child protagonist) rides down the river on a corpse under the aegis of the Necropolis.

We rehearse these configurations of empty value not because they have some exclusively dark, pessimistic relationship to the African state but because they have become markers of the location of trash within the larger global economic order in which fragile African societies now find themselves. Beginning with the dumping of toxic waste by Trafigura, we need to come to terms with the figures of bare life and nullified existence, from Abani to Nacro to Sissako to Adichie, in order to place *les déchets humains* in their proper place. Thompson might see his rubbish returning in the form of collectibles; we will see them return in the form of graffiti in Nacro's *Nuit* and not in the comforting ending of the rehabilitated Fatou. There is no simple passage from zoe to bios, from stage two valueless to stage three invaluable—no dialectic motion, no sublation. The stages must be read simultaneously if we are to escape from the forlorn sense of loss incurred by a liberal humanist order that has proved itself totally helpless before the vicious onslaught of the neoliberal economic order.

We can see something of the simultaneity of the valued and valueless when considering the injunction to the scientist and garbologist to make mere matter talk. Not only electrons and protons enjoined to speak about the irregularities of the quantum or dark hole but the garbage as well, interpellated by the archeologist to provide its evidence, mute trash no longer having the right to remain silent: "Waste thus becomes the synecdoche for a whole complex sociocultural situation. It falls to the researcher to develop the necessary rhetoric to make it speak, to make it tell all it knows. It is then a matter of articulating not so much a discourse of waste, but rather the discourse *of* waste itself" (Moser 99). Like Prospero teaching Caliban to speak, we end up with Pozzo in *Godot* forcing his thing, Lucky, to recite, unleashing the logorrhea of words that subsequently flow out, flooding us. What the archeologist never expected, like the anthropologist before him, was that the thing itself could talk back in a language of relentless accusation. Like Caliban, the garbage spoke its truth to power, in the matter of waste: "waste does not lie; it is the most truthful language a society holds with respect to itself" (Moser 99).

From this, Moser concludes that waste cannot be avoided: "Waste is permanent and unavoidable" (102), and yet at the same time is "unstable and evanescent," like the colonialist discourse that tries to freeze the colonial figure into an immutable identity, only to be undone by the instability of the signifier. The images of waste are markers of this instability, for as they identify the conditions of bare life under the sign of waste, simultaneously they cause it to speak in the tones of the naked image, the need, the demand of those who have no part because they have no voice in the order (Rancière, *Politics of the Aesthetic* and *Future of the Image*). The images as naked images are the demanding part, seen from the outside as unavoidable; sensed in the odors and vermin they inevitably must carry; insistent on being heard by Mr. Hilton in his Mercedes who decides which voices will be recorded and played on air, and which will not be heard.[12]

They are not put on air, yet also not totally silenced, since we, the audience on the other side of the diegetic divide, hear and witness the scene: we see the attempts of a quartet of street singers to solicit the attention of Hilton, the wealthy and powerful representative of an order that simultaneously lives off their surplus labor while driving the prices of labor down, skimming off the profits while paying the talented a pittance. Ivan tries to market his recording of "The Harder They Come" on his own after refusing Hilton's paltry offer of $20 for the song, and is blackballed by the DJs. When Ivan later becomes the Rebel, the Star, the Hero, his popular song can't be stopped and surges to the top of the charts.

Here the waste succeeds in making itself heard and, while still ensconced in a policed order that considers it bare life, hunts it down, and kills it: it provides value and profit to the recording industry. It vacillates before it can be killed off. It moves into sight, though now as a cinematic image, not as a real man; it moves outside the immediate material frame of the diegesis as Ivan hallucinates his shoot-out at the end, enacting his escape from the entanglement of the real world with the reggae community, the drugs, the sick child, and Pedro the Rasta dealer who betrays him. Together with his memory of the film first seen with José the cowardly dealer from the Dungle, the trashy streets and their cruel drivers all create a dialogue between Ivan and Jimmy that attests to the instability of the status of trash. Trash "leads from the one without ever fully reaching the other, for as it tends toward the second term [of loss of value], the category of waste must decay and become nullified. It is that unstable position in which purity seesaws with impurity, value with nonvalue, memory with forgetting. The movement it describes, however, is never entirely accomplished. Were it to reach this limit point, it would cease to be conceivable and, therefore, knowable" (102). Moser concludes that it is both "systemic menace and regenerator" (102).

In this regard, Moser arrives at the same position as Larry Summers who calculates the cost-benefit value for the impoverished African state to accept the dumping of European waste, toxic in all its forms of signification, for a good price. The link that ties colonialism to totalitarianism, that Hannah Arendt traces from the genocide of the Herero to the Nazi concentration camps, also joins the ascension of the ideals of western democracy to the extension of western dominion over the colonized territories seized by the Europeans in the nineteenth century. As the human hovers, under the sign of the necropolis, between zoe and bios, Agamben asks why "democracy, at the very moment in which it seemed to have finally triumphed over its adversaries and reached its greatest height, proved itself incapable of saving zoe, to whose happiness it had dedicated all its efforts, from unprecedented ruin" (1998: 10). The infamous Summers memo charts democracy's path of privileging the more "valuable" zoes of the countries with greater longevity by adding to the risk of those whose lives "barely" enabled them to share civilization's more permanent values of long life, health, liberty, and happiness.[13] Agamben presents this paradox of the democracy turned toward Guantanamo-type exceptions, expanding into totalitarian entities in the form of the aporia caused by the figure of the "sacred man," the "bare man," whose life "cannot be sacrificed yet may, nevertheless, be killed" (10). Such a figure is the complement of the "sovereign power" that precedes any social contract, forms the basis for the state, and exercises its control over the body in the manner of Foucault's biopower.

Two images that evoke this "double sovereignty"[14] are those of Nacro's colonel, leader of the opposition, reduced on the grill to a reddish, marinated figure of burnt meat—zoe as bare existence turned into bare flesh to be eaten by the dogs and birds, as Homer put it—and Vitorio, hero reduced to the status of a homeless man without a leg or prosthesis, begging for jobs like Ivan Martin. "Today politics knows no value (and consequently, no non-value) other than life, and until the contradictions that this fact implies are dissolved, Nazism and fascism—which transformed the decision on bare life into the supreme political principle—will remain stubbornly with us" (Agamben 10), with necropolis (Mbembe 2003: 20). These two images convey the parameters of non-value for human trash: the body of the one turned into grilled meat, the subjectivity of the other defined by the absence of a body part. Both are subject to the state through biopolitics: notions of rights are superseded by issues of control over the body. The abstract quality of the notion of civil rights when confronted with the actualization of their bodies into images redefines their place within the spectacle of the cinema. The ideational yields to the effect of the material on the image as we are focused on the surfaces of their bodies.

We are at the zero point for trash, now, as zoe in the state of exception corresponds to Rancière's demos, those who have "no share in the communal distribution of the sensible" (2009b: 84). The demos is defined as those that disrupt that governing body, the community (ochlos) that defines itself by the exclusion of others, here the demos. It isn't simply le peuple as such, now, but all those excluded by a community whose members' inclusion is always at the price of the exclusion of some others.

Those living on the borders outside the nation could be designated in descending order of value as foreigners, immigrants, illegal immigrants—or ultimately, in some politicized jargon, riffraff, trash, the homeless, street people, and so on—those dubbed *les déchets humains* by Sembène, *les damnés* by Fanon. For us, the ultimate cinematic image that captures this excluded community is that of the beggars and handicapped struggling to return to Dakar after having been expelled from in front of El Hadj's shop in *Xala* (see figures 3.4–6). They will be the images enabling us to enter into the space defined by Agamben as the state of exception for those whose lives are characterized as possessing only existence, zoe—bare life—those with no part. For Sembène, they are the victims of capitalist theft. While not excluding that definition, we must go beyond it, just as the denizens of the concentration camps or of the genocidal conflicts of recent years in Africa were not simply the proletariat or lumpenproletariat, but also wealthy capitalists, educated and cultivated members of society, political opponents, Tutsis but also moderate Hutus, now all lumped together in one heap, ultimately fated to have their bones put on display in the genocide museums of the world.

Although the demos in these shots from *Xala* (1974) constitutes the detritus of society in the broader sense that Rancière employs it, the demos is all those people excluded from participation in the running of the state. Those who have no part are not without qualities, except in the division of society into the haves and have-nots. "Haves" might mean having the right ethnicity, religion, connections, as well as property; "have-nots" meaning those not counted, according to whatever system of counting is being employed. In modern capitalist societies, value is usually understood as the property of capital, financial or symbolic. In an African society like Senegal, for example, symbolic capital might consist of being a Mourid or a Wolof, or a Wolof speaker. In Rwanda, lacking such capital might mean being a Twa, or, more importantly, being on the side of those accused of "divisionism" or of "promoting genocide ideology"—that is, those considered to be in opposition to the government. These are the qualifications for not being counted, for not being a subject with a political identity, for not having a political subjectivity. Without a bios or location in the scheme of the state, one is reduced to exclusion, the status of zoe. Without qualification, one is like rubbish that is undifferentiated, that is, with no value. Trash. And it is in the totality of those who are both counted and uncounted that democracy is defined by Rancière:

> Democracy is the power of those who have no specific qualification for ruling, except the fact of having no qualification. As I interpret it, the demos—the political subject as such—has to be identified with the totality made by those who have no "qualification." I call it the count of the uncounted—or the part of those who have no part. It does not mean the population of the poor; it means the supplementary part, an empty part that separates the political community from the count of the parts of the population. (2004: 305)

What makes this supplementary part "political subjects" rests upon Rancière's reading of politics as the product of dissensus as opposed to consensus that is directed by the exclusionary ruling figures.

The image of the *déchets humains* coming over the hill, back into town, asserting their place, their part in a community that refuses to hear or see them unless forced to do so—the beggars returning from the expulsion from town by the "Cerebes," the police who maintain the order with its rules for determining those who count and who are not to be counted—this image conveys the dissensus on the part of those defined by El Hadj and the president of the Chamber of Commerce as human trash. It is an image of those who limp, who have to be carried at times but are also put down so they can continue to return on their own. Beggars who sit down together, deciding what is right or wrong in what they have been subjected to and determining how to right the wrong by their actions. Those defined by Rancière as the ones who give definition to humanitarian rights.

Still, granting rights to them would appear to be meaningless unless they can take possession of their rights. Otherwise they remain "the victims of the absolute denial of right": "the rights of those who have no rights, the rights of bare human beings subjected to inhuman repression and inhuman conditions of existence. They become humanitarian rights, the rights of those who cannot enact them, the victims of the absolute denial of right" (Rancière 2004: 307).

With "bare human beings," Rancière gestures toward Agamben who famously defines human life in the "state of exception" as "bare life." We can work backwards from these terms in order to understand my claim, now, that bare life in the state of exception is like that of human trash. Not trash in the spectacular sense of "trash" when famously displayed by Waters's Divine, or even with Bataille's fleshy toe ensconced in the mud. That is trash that flaunts its extravagance and makes of exclusion a privilege. Divine trashes bourgeois culture in Baltimore, or rather "bourgeois" culture, since the stereotyped figures of her parents, for instance, or any of the other figures set up to represent the social norm, are really stock types, stiffly constructed so as to set off the over-the-top gestures and movements, both physical and verbal, of our "heroine" Divine.

With bare life we are returning to the original sense of trash, the more literal, immediate sense that resists the playful ambiguity of a postmodern performance. No one could laugh at the victims of a genocide. Fascism and totalitarianism themselves are easy targets for the popular culture to parody—both before the Holocaust, with Chaplin's Great Dictator, and after with Mel Brooks's "Springtime for Hitler" (1968), or the recent burlesquing of *Mein Fuhrer: The Truly Truest Truth about Adolf Hitler* (Dani Levy, 2007), which depicts the dictator as a clown. But the *déchets humains,* and before them the image of "La Noire de" lying bloodied in the bathtub, belong to another domain of representation, ethical in its demand and representational, in Rancière's sense of faithful to a mimetic conception of reality. Bare life belongs to this realm of art where the mise-en-scène of the state of exception begins with a notion of "sovereign power," power without check, without a preexistent social contract or dominion of law, a power that creates the possibility for a polis or a state to come into existence. The flip side of the figure of this sovereign without check is the desolate human being who has no "part" in the state whose other members are assigned their own proper parts; one who has no place in a community that is guaranteed by a legal framework in which he or she would be situated. The best figure to represent this "homo sacer," as Agamben names him or her, is the figure of the exile who is placed apart, or excluded, from the normal life of members of society by virtue of being under a ban. One thinks of *Wend Kuuni* (Kabore, 1982) where the child's mother is accused of witchcraft and ostracized from the village, as an example. Banished into the wilderness, she dies alone. Yaaba is another such figure.

There might be many ways to describe the ban. One would seem to be that placed on Cain; a figure apart; a figure doomed to wander; a figure who is excluded and marked as different. But most importantly, Cain cannot be placed in a situation in which his death might be taken as a sacrifice because he has forfeited everything that would make a sacrifice possible. He is the opposite of the innocent Isaac. He acted, unlike Isaac, who waited to be told what to do, what to think. Cain's banishment meant that his risk of death was ever present, but only inasmuch as he wore the marker of the sacred in his death: whoever killed him would also bear that mark, although that didn't protect him from such a fate. Cain's lament was that he was made into a "fugitive and a wanderer" in the earth, a fate later assumed by the attribution of "wanderers" to the Jewish people in their Diaspora.[15]

The compulsion of the Nazis created one kind of bare life for Jews, Gypsies, homosexuals, and Communists, making it seem that such terms as "parasitic vermin" would inevitably denote an extreme state of oppression, not just "exception." But "déchets humains" are not always subject to a final solution, and their exclusion is not always confinement or expulsion. To be under the ban, as Agamben conceives it, is to be subject to "sovereign power," and that power is viewed by him as logically prior to the creation of the juridical-political state as such. Those placed outside that community, under a ban of one sort or another, remain subject to the sovereign power that is limited in its control of the members of the community once the state is formed. *Ostrakismos*, exclusion from life in the polis, was worse than death for Socrates, who chose death over bare life. But he wasn't merely an artisan or a member of the demos or mass of the people. He had a voice. Bare life meant a life of speaking without being heard, in a place where there was nothing to say, under an authority that remained deaf to the cries. Bare life is the life of trash, precisely in Mary Douglas's sense of an object with a mere fragment of identity clinging to it but without any worth. A piece of dirt.

If we could bring that being down to its nadir, to the fate of waste that goes through an amalgamation as mere matter combined with other matter, undifferentiated like the hair taken from the heads of Jewish women, the skin made into the lampshades, the gold teeth melted down, the bodies boiled into new matter, we might then see the ominous fate of this recycling also as part of the cycles of life and death, and understand how Bataille could turn to de Sade as a model for thinking through the ultimate destiny for human morality. But the state of exception, like the fate of Cain, lies in between the harsh beginning and the brutal end of the bodies.

These examples are limit cases. In their ordinary lives, Africans, after all, are still figures with identities, marked by names, ethnicities, countries, and continent, are not "bare lives" and are well integrated into the system that conveys value to the dominant classes according to neoliberal structures of wealth. But for those on the margins, living in the state of exception, the camps for refugees and exiles, the inhabitants of conflict zones, and the homeless who live on the streets, today's "Osu" and Twa, at times of crisis,[16] *déchets humains* becomes the designation of those whose existence is closer to the pure physical state of the body in a location where the sovereign's power rules without check, unlike the exercise of power that is carefully calibrated with respect to the members of the community.

Being outside that community is not like being totally apart. Rather, those who are excluded can only be considered so in relation to the system that banishes them. To be ostracized is to be excluded in relation to that which is included; it is to be included within the system that defines outside and inside. It is, thus, to be included and excluded, in an indefinite state, an ambiguous state—trash before it loses its identity.

There is one other quality of the figure of bare life, conveyed at least in part by "bare," in the sense of denuded, stripped of qualities. Agamben makes the distinction between bios, a life that is specific to the person to whom we can ascribe subjectivity, and zoe, life as plain existence, as is common to any living thing. Bare life is one such denuded existence, one marked by its complete immersion in the realm of the material world as physical being. Bare life brings us back to human trash in the sense of the material, and especially of "this too too solid flesh"—bare life as bare flesh. We can expect to encounter this bare figure in Lear under the elements, exposed to his madness and loss of station, loss of sense of himself. But more pertinent to the bare life of the flesh in the state of exception is the treatment of the Jewish people subjected to Nazi medical experiments. There the *homo sacer,* the being who existed in some existential state outside of the norm, the exceptional figure, like the sacred man, like Cain in his life outside of all other social beings, like the ostracized figure living under banishment, under the ban, that figure whom Agamben describes over and over as susceptible to being killed but not sacrificed—a nothing figure because of being reduced to bare life—might well be killed without his or her death being called a homicide: "a life that may be killed without the commission of a homicide" (159). For it to be called a homicide, he or she would have to be of some worth, be worth something more than trash. How could this have happened, asked Agamben? "Precisely because they were lacking almost all the rights and expectations that we customarily attribute to human existence, and yet were still biologically alive, they came to be situated in a limit zone between life and death, inside and outside, in which they were no longer anything but bare life" (1998: 159). They lived in a no-man's-zone, as they were "no men," in an interval "between death sentence and execution delimit[ing] an extratemporal and extraterritorial threshold in which the human body is separated from its normal political status and abandoned, in a state of exception, to the most extreme misfortunes" (159). Following Foucault, Agamben traces the biopolitics of modernity that makes possible this existence where now the sovereign ruler, who in the past could act without constraint, has been replaced by the doctor and scientist who can explore the limits of medical experimentation in the name of preserving those other bodies of normal people (those with bios) whose health counts, whose lives matter.

And that means not trash. The counting of lives that matter now is measured in biological years, years where longevity has a meaning, where health can be paid for and preserved, where the financial outlay can be justified. And this is precisely the reasoning followed by Larry Summers when, as head of the World Bank, he sent his infamous memo concerning the dumping of toxic waste in Africa:

> The measurements of the costs of health impairing pollution depends on the foregone earnings from increased morbidity and mortality. From this point of view a given amount of health impairing pollution should be done in the country with the lowest cost, which will be the country with the lowest wages. I think the economic logic behind dumping a load of toxic waste in the lowest wage country is impeccable and we should face up to that. . . . I've always thought that under-populated countries in Africa are vastly UNDER-polluted, their air quality is probably vastly inefficiently low compared to Los Angeles or Mexico City. . . . The concern over an agent that causes a one in a million chance in the odds of prostate cancer is obviously going to be much higher in a country where people survive to get prostate cancer than in a country where under 5 mortality is 200 per thousand. (http://www.whirledbank.org/ourwords /summers.html)

Summers employs a logic not unlike that of the Nazis whose purpose in exposing Jewish bodies to freezing temperatures was to develop mechanisms that would help sustain the lives that mattered, those fighting in the cause of the superior race. His cost-benefit analysis appears to be so heartless because it is based on a rhetorical denigration and reduction of those Africans subject to poisonous elements to figures of bare life, beings who would not be victims of a homicide if they died in greater numbers as a result of the dumping because they were already nothing but bodies to be measured in statistics that compare "people who survive to get prostate cancer" with those whose chances of surviving childhood are one in five.

Agamben asks how it was that experiments undertaken in the United States on African American men who were subjected to infection with syphilis or other diseases could have also taken place, why it was that it wasn't only totalitarian states who committed such crimes against humanity. His answer is that the state today exercises its sovereignty over the body, controlling the life and death of those under its sway when those bodies are "separated from [their] normal political status and abandoned, in a state of exception, to the utmost misfortunes" (159). Those who were sentenced to death, or detained in a camp, fit that description. But to be more precise, those who were consigned to the state of exception fit that description.

Which takes us to the limit case of today. When the genocide in Rwanda broke out and spread from Kigali south to Butare and beyond, to wherever the Interahamwe and the Rwanda rump state maintained their sovereignty, the state of exception for those considered vermin was to be found. Tutsis came to be designated as objects to be "shortened," "sent back" by river, up north "where they came from." The killings that extended throughout the country were made possible by the sovereign's power to broaden the state of exception over the regions where the Rwandan government extended its rule. More than warfare and violence, it was the breakdown of a normal state where the rules of the social contract obtained. There was Force, as in the Force of Law, without the contents of the law itself. Those who were victims of the killing were treated as so much waste, to be collected and dumped, at times by bulldozers, into ditches or churches and left to rot.

For Agamben, such exceptional situations are more and more applicable to the social realm under modernity, especially as the rule of the biopolitical exigency now assumes the status of sovereign power. However, he does not really consider how the onslaught of such modernity in Africa was conditioned by the frame of colonialism where terms similar to *inyenzi*,[17] like dirty nigger, *sale nègre,* functioned similarly to reduce those beings under imperial rule to *homines sacres,* lives that could be killed or bodies that could be mutilated without the commission of a crime. Lives that could not be sacrificed.

Historically we can trace these dehumanizing attitudes back to the slave trade, and then to colonial rule, especially as it depended on the collection of cash crops like rubber or ivory. Infamous accounts of cutting off the hands of those resisting orders to collect ivory or rubber have been documented in works like *King Leopold's Ghost* (1998). In Cameroon, I have heard similar accounts of physical punishment for those who failed to bring in their quotas of rubber or cacao during World War II. In *Emitai* (1971), Sembène presents similar abuses by the French forces during the war.

But perhaps Sembène's most shocking historicization of the state of exception is in the story of a camp, one in appearance not unlike that of a concentration camp, where similar injustices occurred—his *Camp de Thiaroye* (1987). Again, African needs were made to seem incommensurate with Europeans, so that the decommissioned African soldiers who were gathered in the camp at the end of their tour of duty in World War II were told not only that they were to be paid half of the normal wages, half the wages their European counterparts were to be paid, but that it didn't matter because their needs were certainly less than those of the Europeans (this argument prefiguring Larry Summers's logic). One of those in the camp is a man called Pays who had been held prisoners by the Nazis; when the barbed wire and manned towers appear, Pays reacts as though he were back in that prison camp. At the end of the film, when the rebellious soldiers are mowed down, the images of the black bodies are rendered as so many figures of detritus: we get glimpses of who they are, but no longer as speaking figures with voices that count. Rather they are rabble being turned into rubbish whose elements of identity are assimilated into rubble.

There are always going to be protest films, scenes of oppression and violence and of struggle. What is striking here is how these scenes are figured in the reduction of the "naked image," as Rancière would have it, to that of the figure of bare life. Bare life as trash begins in this chapter with the destitute Ivan Martin standing on the edge of the city garbage heap, emerging from the Dungle with nothing. By the end he will complete the passage from villager to urban trash to outlaw and finally hero, "Jimmy Cliff." But the cycle often stops before recuperation, before the image of the poor villager can be transformed into something better, as we see in *La Vie est belle* (1987) or *Osuafia* (2004). Instead, we will slow down the reel to focus on those moments when the possibility of perceiving the naked image of bare life can be seen. Those are moments that occur under the state of exception, or rather, within the film's diegesis, *in* the state of exception where we must bring to a halt the flow of the narrative and place before our gaze the full barrenness of the *homo sacer.*

One such site occurs at the end of *Daratt* (2006), when Atim has led Nassara out to the desert where the Grandfather, the Force of Law, awaits the moment when his son's death will be avenged. Nassara is stripped, lies stretched out on the ground as Atim holds the gun to his head. In that moment, before another regime besides that based on biopolitics is asserted, we are prepared for the death of this body to be enacted. Instead it is reenacted. Atim simulates the murder, and his blind grandfather is led off contented in his misapprehension of what had just occurred.

Heremakono (2002) figures the body of an immigrant washed up on the shore, unidentified to the police because those who knew him are unwilling to take the risk of providing the police with his name. Djadjam's *Frontières* (2002) and Sissako's *Bamako* (2006) contain similar images of such victims.

Figures 3.1–3.2. Jimmy Cliff at tip.

Figure 3.3. Jimmy Cliff at tip.

Figure 3.4. Xala *déchets humains* returning.

Figures 3.5–3.6. Xala *déchets humains* returning.

Agamben assimilates their state to a combination of holiness and dirtiness (76), forms of exclusion for those who stand apart from the ordinary lives of people with proper places in a normal society. As such they are thus sacred (sacer) and trash (dirt), excluded and yet contained within a system that accounts for them, but only in their exclusion. Excluded-included: this is the status of trash, produced within a society that must deal with it because the pollution is an inevitable product of its own consumption.

Appropriation is always followed by expenditure, but the stages are actually cyclical and thus, when considered within the overall system, are simultaneous inasmuch as they are present to each other. Sembène's *déchets humains* park themselves outside El Hadj's shop because their space and lives are defined in relationship to his life and his business. They return, not only as the oppressed but more as his *damnés*, reduced to their lowly state because of his thievery and betrayal. Holy figures of revenge, normally cast into the background of the "gritty streets" of the urbane necropolis in Africa, they turn their status as trash into that of the artisans of the future as they spit on El Hadj to cure him of his *xala*. If *xala* literally means the curse of impotency, figuratively it is the cur(s)e of trash, since that is what it makes of its victim in a phallocentric and neocolonial state. The film ends before we see the cure effected: the figure of El Hadj remains frozen, his body covered in spit, and as the screen goes dark, the sound of the spitting continues. Thus does the filmmaker take his revenge on the anthropologist for whom this "interesting moment" conveys an ethnic truth. Sembène is closer here to the reporters who identified the infractions in the dumping of Trafigura, seeking not to reveal an ancient cure but rather a modern crime.

4 Globalization's Dumping Ground: The Case of Trafigura

"Trafigura" might be the name for toxic dumping in Africa, for Europe's disparagement of African soil, blood, and tears, for Summers's coarse remarks about toxic dumping that matter only in that they reveal the perspective of the global north toward the global south. It is a relationship grounded first and foremost in financial calculations, where hundreds of years of disparate relations of power, from the time of the slave trade, and then especially of colonialism, until the contemporary phases of neocolonialism followed by globalization have all taken the form of toxic dumping.

In Bataille's terms, the west has been the site of appropriation and Africa of expenditure. In grosser terms, the global north has been the locus of commodity capitalism, recently taking neoliberalism as its model, and Africa the site where the excretion or waste of that consumerism has been dumped. We can see this in the flow north of raw materials—agricultural products, fish, oil, minerals, and human labor—while the detritus of that flow, the slag created by producing goods for consumption up north, has remained in the south to foul the lands. There are innumerable examples, of which I will mention only the most salient, to focus eventually on the notorious case of Trafigura.

Where there are minerals of highest value, the conditions created for their extraction have often resulted in crimes against humanity. In South Africa, the extraction of gold and diamonds enabled the injustices of apartheid to be established in the nineteenth century. The labor, especially of miners from the Bantustans or neighboring southern Rhodesia and Mozambique, was extracted often at the cost of the miners' lives, not to mention of the social fabric of their homes. The colonial pattern was not confined to South Africa: the use of taxation as a whip to drive Africans to labor on European farms became widespread, and settler colonies like Mozambique, southern Rhodesia, and Kenya saw a high percentage of the best lands occupied by white farmers or corporations. Black farmers were driven to work there under conditions of thinly disguised enslavement. The same was true when colonial governments used forced labor to build roads and railroads, to collect rubber or ivory. The practices in King Leopold's Congo Free State were not an aberration; they were the norm in Central Africa.[1] The removal of Leopold's authority over the Congo in 1908 ended only one instance marked by the grossest of excesses, but not the system of expropriation that underlay the pattern. To a greater or lesser degree, from the very outset, the introduction of capitalist economies under colonialism was intended to insure European control and profit and eliminate African competition, as in Sir George Goldie's early twentieth-century conquest of the Niger River region and imposition of a trade monopoly for the Royal Niger Company. The march of colonial power coincided with the subjugation of the peoples and territories and their eventual incorporation into single states, as in the case of Nigeria under Lugard, which he formed into one colony in 1914. As with the march of French traders up the Senegal River, native or métis traders were supplanted by Europeans as colonialism took hold. Goldie simply imposed taxation on African traders that they couldn't afford. When they revolted, they were massacred (Falola and Heaton, *A History of Nigeria,* 2008).

Each act of subordinating labor and lands turned colonial occupation into a pattern of expropriation tied to consumption, appropriation, and expenditure. Rubber, diamonds, gold, ivory, cocoa, tea, coffee, peanuts, cotton: these were some of the raw materials extracted, shipped up north, turned into commodities to be sold on the world market, and consumed in wealthy European households. Some small portion of the Nestlé chocolates, Nescafé coffee, teabags, candy bars, soft drinks, and processed foods were shipped back to Africa for consumption by those able to afford the items, while the siftings of the ores, trees, or animals were left to rot on the side of the mines or fields, the corpses of elephants crisscrossing their former grazing lands. Even the images were taken, processed, and returned: images of big game hunters, standing over their prey, raw materials turned into cinematic models; images of bare-breasted "native women" turned into postcards (Malek Alloula, *The Colonial Harem,* 1986)— all of which can function as metaphors of the horrific conditions that colonialism imposed throughout the continent. The patterns they established have continued even after Independence. Mining conditions in the eastern Congo region, for example, have been described in Amnesty International reports as virtual killing grounds. Armed guards surrounding the large gold, coltan, diamond, and tin mines require bribes for workers to enter.[2] The miners are exposed to dangerous working conditions, and are subject to brutal methods of surveillance to insure they do not steal any of the minerals. In some instances, they labor as virtual slaves in a system that requires them to risk their lives extracting minerals, most of whose value is seized by others: by those who control the transport of the minerals from the mines to the centers of collection, from the centers to the companies buying the minerals, from those companies to the officials in neighboring states through which they pass, to the countries where the raw materials are converted into usable metals or jewels, until they finally make their way onto the world market. As the arms trade makes these exchanges possible and profitable, arms dealers complete the circuit, sending in weapons to those able to control the territories. Nation-states, the initial predators, have struggled and increasingly failed to maintain their monopolies over these trading patterns: as the wealth they generate is so considerable, conflicts ensued, and it has been difficult for national armies to maintain their control over the affected regions. The older monopolies of trade created during neo-colonial days morphed in the 1980s into global neoliberal patterns of exchange where local militias proved too strong for national police or armies to maintain their control, from Sierra Leone and Liberia to the Democratic Republic of the Congo, Somalia, and Darfur.

The trash of the trade came to be constituted by the residues of the armed forces: child soldiers, women subject to brutal violence, victims of ethnic cleansing, and above all, the detritus of an economy driven to the limits by monetary incentives. For instance, the recruitment of Hutu or Tutsi young men or children into militias in Burundi and the Democratic Republic of the Congo after the fighting had largely ended in 2009 resumed in 2010 as the returning soldiers found themselves unemployed and were lured back to the militias by the prospects of good wages. It reached the point where the recruits would self-identify as whatever ethnicity the recruiters were seeking: the economies of Burundi and the DRC could not provide work for the young men who had previously been trained as child soldiers, and thus had no place for them after their demobilizations when they were facing difficult economic conditions. They became virtual mercenaries, serving a market that used their labor while the great profits went elsewhere.

The contemporary example of the Congo merely highlights patterns of appropriation, consumption, expenditure, and excretion that have been in place for much of the period during which exchanges between Europe and Africa have occurred, during which they set the stage for current conditions. They help to define the way a notion of global trash might be understood, so that it is not viewed simply as the creation of recent economic exchanges. It attests to the nature of a system generated by unequal relations of power, exacerbated under colonialism, and now under neoliberal globalization. It made it seem feasible to those operating on the margins of this system that any kind of exchange, even the most outlandish act of dumping, could become possible.

Mbembe sums up this twenty-first-century conjuncture in terms that bring together Bataille's vision of excess with the troubling portrait of an Africa fettered in a state of exception that recalls much of the nightmare conditions of twentieth-century conflicts, in the global north as well as the south. A regime determined by biopolitical power, the power to dispose of death and thus dispense with life, marks the dark vision of Mbembe's African "necropolis." However, in "On Politics as a Form of Expenditure" (2006), he turns directly to Bataille's terminology to argue that war and death dominate the current landscape. "*The giving of death* has become *a prime means of creating* the world" (Mbembe 2006: 299). He traces two "logics of expenditure," using a declension that conforms to Bataille's trajectory of appropriation-expenditure, but also Douglas's and Thompson's itinerary for the passage of trash from object having value to one that has lost it, only to return in forms of excess that mark the cultural landscape of poverty and authoritarian sovereignty: "The first kind of expenditure has to do with the capacity of combatants completely to invest in—and intensely sublimate—objects, resources, and even human persons; then to release an extraordinary amount of energy which functions to ensure their repetitive destruction—a destruction that results in a relative pleasure" (Mbembe 299). He assigns to this destruction as an "exclusionary act," and although he associates this, and the eroticism that accompanies it, with Bataille, it is no less my contention that Agamben's bare life, and Rancière's demos, are equally marked by exclusion, if not violence.

For Mbembe, as for this study, trash figures first and foremost as a material manifestation. Thus when we are considering the global economy into which twenty-first-century Africa is inserted, it is initially in terms of the production of trash that can be associated with Bataille's concrete physical descriptions of appropriation and expenditure. Mbembe calls this pattern "the work of destruction" and describes the extraction of mineral resources as also having the three-part structure of "extraction/consumption/excretion." If this produces the equivalent of bare life on one level, on the other it is the "giving of death" that he associates with the "spectacular manifestation of absolute and sovereign power" (299–300). In all events, he returns to figures of biopolitics, as the logic of cruelty and excess is "linked to the status of human flesh" (300). The sovereign's willingness to risk his life and to cause the death of the other completes Mbembe's portrayal of the logic of excess. Here he departs from Agamben's depiction of the *homo sacer* whose denuded existence is reduced to its lowly status precisely because there is nothing left to sacrifice. The denizen of the camp is reduced to the zero level of trash because there is no cost in ending its life: bareness is barren life, life that doesn't count, cannot count, and therefore counts for nothing in any sacrificial act. We are not enmeshed in a Hegelian dialectic in which death would move us upward or forward, unless we were to assign a positive value to the erotic charge accompanying the use of force. In the example of global exchanges and, in particular, global dumping, there might be acts of recycling but not without a larger loss accompanying it as the children who recover the rare metals from the scrap are at grave risk of being poisoned. This is both trope and reality in the case of cash crop trading as well as the disposal of toxic waste on the continent.

The neoliberal market system is governed by World Bank injunctions against tariffs or protectionism and has exposed African producers to conditions of dumping that make it impossible for them to survive. A case in point is cotton. A crop initially introduced by the colonial powers as a cash crop, it created a technology and source of revenue upon which farmers in the Sahel depended to make a living. As the United States and Europe pay generous subsidies for cotton, soy, corn, or other farm products, those commodities sold on the world market undersell those locally produced. Africans cannot erect tariff barriers because of IMF loan conditions. If they, or the fishermen of Senegal, or the rice growers or others can no longer harvest their fish, sell their crops, and earn enough to support their families, the only solution would seem to be emigration. "Illegal emigration," spectacular flights and dangerous crossings led to many dying en route, and many films like *Heremakono* (2002), *Bamako* (2006) or *Frontières* (2001) thematized the situation. On the emigrants' arrival in Europe, they found themselves desperate, willing to accept any kind of labor.

From these conditions have emerged increasing penury on the continent and desperate attempts at emigration. This has resulted in the erection of fortress barriers, walls of symbolic violence, with trash left at the foot of the closed doors. There are innumerable instances of this production of African trash. A few include the following paradigmatic examples.

In "Melilla: Europe's Dirty Secret," a story datelined April 17, 2010, published in the *Guardian*, Nick Davies wrote about an eleven-year-old boy who was discovered by a Spanish resident of Melilla who "noticed something strange was happening each night to the dustbin in front of his house." He discovered a boy removing garbage from the bin so that he could sleep in it. "The idea of the child being reduced to the status of trash was worrying but not entirely surprising to Palazon, who was used to the sight of migrants sleeping rough on the streets of his city" (Davies 46).

Davies explains that Melilla was a way station for emigrants seeking to gain access to Europe since it remains legally Spanish, though the enclave is surrounded by Morocco. Palazon, the man who discovered the child, tried to create an agency to help the children, but "they didn't want to help the children, as that would encourage more to come to Melilla." The reporter, Davies, continues his "analysis": "And that is the problem behind the simplistic calls for British jobs for British workers—if you treat migrants well, give them the kind of human rights Europeans demand for themselves, you only encourage them to keep coming."

The reporter's connection to this story begins with this perspective, that of the British living in a location that has been attractive to emigrants. He makes no effort to understand the motivation of the emigrants beyond that, or the way they have been produced as the expenditure of Europe's system of production joined to the extraction of resources from Africa. Nonetheless, he is clearly sympathetic to the plight of the emigrants, and his story has all the trappings of humanitarian aid to those who are made victims by the very economic structures that sustain the *Guardian*, a liberal journal one would expect to carry such stories. The frame of this story turns on the larger conditions that obtain with consumption in the north and expenditure in the global south. The images that sell this story contain the very figure that defines the outcome of the process, trash:

When Palazon found the boy in his bin, in the late 90s, this could be pretty crude. The Council of Europe's committee for the prevention of torture uncovered evidence that Africans who made it into Melilla were held in farm buildings where conditions were so bad, some took refuge in abandoned cars on a nearby rubbish dump. They were then likely to be given by the police a drink of water containing a tranquilliser, after which they could be wrapped in adhesive tape covering almost all of their body, including their mouth, for easy delivery by military plane to their country of origin where, in some cases, reports emerged of them being ill-treated and even killed by local law officers. (http://www.guardian.co.uk/world/2010/apr/17/melilla-migrants-eu-spain-morocco)

More ominously, reports of desperate people throwing themselves on the barbed wire surrounding Melilla emerged along with accounts of Africans taken by the Moroccan police and then dumped in the desert. Thus the pair appropriation-expenditure was turned into an obverse Kafkaeque Castle-Village, or Fortress-Prison, with the state of exception turned from the interior of the camp into everything on the outside: "The city erected an intimidating new barrier: two parallel 4m wire fences, topped with razor wire and with a tarmac strip running between patrolled by the Spanish Guardia Civil, all of it monitored by 106 video cameras, infrared surveillance, a microphone cable and helicopters. In Melilla, a man who had worked on the fence told me he would arrive at work in the morning to find his ladder covered in blood, where migrants had tried to use it to climb into the city and had become victims of the razor wire."

The report continues, building the portrait of a large-scale nightmare, with ten thousand people trapped in a no-man's-land, thrown into the desert between Morocco and Algeria, with those escaping subsequently caught by the Algerians and returned to Morocco only to be abused by Spanish or Moroccan guards, "dumped in the desert" again and again like flotsam on the surface of an endless ocean. Details emerged from Médecins sans Frontières reports, Amnesty International and Human Rights Watch reports, all indicating violations of conventions against torture, against human rights, against rights enjoyed by citizens in the north, and theoretically for all people everywhere but inoperative under these conditions of guarding the frontier of the fortress.

Bare life in which human rights were guaranteed by the international conventions of the United Nations lay exposed as unprotected life. Rancière mocks the hollowness of assigning rights to "clandestine immigrants in the zones of transit of our countries or the populations in the camps of refugees" when denied access to the means to articulate them in the public forum where they might be heard and acted upon ("Who Is the Subject of the Rights of Man" 2004: 304). As the *Guardian* reporter hedges his criticism of the north by evoking European international organizations and instruments intended to protect those rights, lacing his account with a humanitarian perspective, Rancière reads such humanitarianism as a form of charity that proves empty. Without a political state in which to act, the voices of those being violated will not be heard or count, will have no part in the political policies that determine where the razor wire will be erected and guarded.

> Ultimately, those rights appear actually empty. They seem to be of no use. And when they are of no use, you do the same as charitable persons do with their old clothes. You give them to the poor. Those rights that appear to be useless in their place are sent abroad, along with medicine and clothes, to people deprived of medicine and clothes, and rights. It is in this way, as the result of this process, that the Rights of Man become the rights of those who have no rights, the rights of bare human beings, subjected to inhuman repression and inhuman conditions of existence. They become humanitarian rights, the rights of those who cannot enact them, the victims of the absolute denial of right. (Rancière 2004: 306)

Along with medicine, clothes, rights, and subsidized crops, Europeans also sent their trash. As a business deal it seemed, à la Summers, a no-brainer. Ghanaian officials were convinced that they could accept Europe's garbage for its own welfare. The *Accra Chronicle* reported in 2008 that the deputy minister of local government, science, and environment had decided that Ghana would import garbage because of the needs of the "new technology of transforming waste to energy" that required large quantities of waste material. The Canadian company EITI Limited was overseeing the project, and had determined that "since the waste in the country was insufficient to provide the company with the requisite quantity, which is needed to commence operations with modern technology, the government is making the necessary arrangements with other countries, to import junk to the country for the commencement of the project" (posted on GHanaweb, Nov 25, 2008; cited on USAAFRICADIALOGUE@ googlegroups.com, accessed Nov 26, 2008).

In 2009, Sky News, the *Guardian*, and the *Independent* all produced reports of toxic dumping in Africa. Sky News's Catherine Jacob reported on "dangerous electronic waste" shipped from the U.K. "over to Africa" (http://news.sky.com /skynews/Home/UK-News/Sky-Probe-Reveals-Recycling-Scandal-As-Broken -TVs-Are-Shipped-Over-to-West-Africa, Feb. 18, 2009; accessed also as http:// news.sky.com/home/uk-news/article/15224628). Sky News reporters followed a broken TV with a tracking device hidden inside from the BJ Electronics warehouse in Walthamstow to a shipping container that eventually dumped it in Lagos. Once in Lagos, the reporters followed the trail of dumped electronics to scrap heaps where children scavenged the copper wire and motherboards. The plastics were burned off, the metal extracted, and the carcinogenic dioxin fumes inhaled as the recycling led to the recuperation of value.

A similar story in the *Independent* (February 18, 2009) alluded to the same itinerary from Tilbury Docks in Essex to the giant Alaba electronics market in Lagos "where up to 15 shipping containers of discarded electronics from Europe and Asia arrive every day" (http://license.icopyright.net/user/viewFreeUse .act?fuid=MjczMjQ2Nw%3D%3D). The story discusses the quantities of recycled electronic goods being produced in the U.K., the laws intended to regulate them, and the final shocking result of "hazardous waste" being "illegally exported as part of a wider e-waste market worth 'tens of millions of pounds.'"

The *Guardian*'s Environment blog carried a similar story as Sky News, reporting that Ghana and Nigeria were infamous dumping grounds for "toxic European electronic waste," disguised as secondhand goods. The story reports that an MP, Maria Miller, had raised concerns about the dumping the previous year, apparently with no consequences.

Thus when the BBC reported in September 2009 about the scandal of Trafigura's massive dumping of toxic waste in Côte d'Ivoire, it was far from the first account to be headline news. Its scale, however, generated comparisons with Bhopal, as upwards of 100,000 people appeared to have been affected.

The Trafigura story has its own detective fiction aura. As the BBC put it, "The chemical waste came from a ship called Probo Koala and in August 2006 truckload after truckload of it was illegally fly-tipped at 15 locations around Abidjan, the biggest city in Ivory Coast. In the weeks that followed the dumping, tens of thousands of people reported a range of similar symptoms, including breathing problems, sickness and diarrhoea" (http://news.bbc.co.uk/2/hi /programmes/newsnight/8417913.stm).

Apparently in 2005, an oil refinery in Mexico, owned by the state company Pemex, or PMI, inadvertently produced an impure form of gasoline that they were unable to refine. Trafigura purchased the oil at a bargain rate and shipped it to the coast of Gibraltar where it was treated with caustic acid, a process that generates enormously dangerous waste. The process is widely banned, and produces such dangerous materials that they are practically impossible to dispose of . . . legally. When Trafigura attempted to offload the waste in the Netherlands, the odor proved so strong that the authorities were able to detect it. Trafigura was trapped in a situation where it would have to pay a great deal to neutralize the material or load it back on the ship. They chose to do the latter, and shipped it off to Côte d'Ivoire. There they found a local contractor, one Solomon Ugburogbu, the owner of a company named Tommy, who accepted to handle the hazardous waste despite not having the facilities to do so. Tens of thousands of people eventually suffered the consequences of the dumping, and Ugburogbu was sentenced to twenty years in prison. On July 23, 2010, Trafigura was finally found guilty of illegally exporting toxic waste and was fined a million euros (http://www.bbc.co.uk/news/world-africa-10735255) for having harmed thousands of people in 2006. As the BBC later reported, the Ukrainian captain who concealed the nature of the waste was handed a five-month suspended sentence, and Trafigura lost in its attempts to prevent the *Guardian* from reporting on the proceedings against the company to Parliament.

Thus the context for Larry Summers's offhand remark about the cost-benefit analysis of Africans accepting toxic waste extends from Mexico's PMI to the transnational corporation identified on its website by the following text, adjacent to the smiling face of a young, attractive Indian woman:

> Established in 1993 as a private company, Trafigura is the world's third largest independent oil trader and the second largest independent trader in the non-ferrous concentrates market. It has access to approximately US$24 billion in credit facilities, with investments in industrial assets around the world of more than US$1.9 billion.
>
> Trafigura handles every element involved in the sourcing and trading of crude oil, petroleum products, renewable energies, metals, metal ores, coal and concentrates for industrial consumers.
>
> 4,000 of our people operate in 67 offices across the globe, to provide the local knowledge that enables us to anticipate and respond to variations in global supply and demand. (http://www.trafigura.com/about_us.aspx)

According to the website, Trafigura represents a global enterprise whose reach is worldwide: "In the metals and minerals sector, Trafigura currently owns and operates concentrate storage facilities in South America, Africa and China and one mine in Peru. Additionally, Trafigura has expanded its mining investment activities incorporating projects in South America, Africa and Europe, and is a significant stakeholder in various publicly listed mining entities." It boasts of having a "turnover" of $79.2 billion in 2010. Its website displays spanking new cargo ships ready to cross the oceans.

Starting with Joe Hill's socialist mantra about pie in the sky, our excursus through the philosophical and political dimensions of the trope of trash has led to the virtual web-reality of corporate global wealth, against which the concerns of *déchets humains* would seem petty indeed. Yet the trajectory that leads from the pollution of Abidjan to the trial in *Bamako* (2006) is the same as the one that leads directly from *homo sacer* to sovereign power. It can be traced back from the bare lives of the Ivoirians now excluded from any of the processes that led to their poisoning to the Trafigura ship anchored off the coast of Gibraltar, awaiting the decision from the corporation's sovereign power about where to dump its residual waste. Despite the court settlement, Kafka's man "Before the Law," would seem still to be waiting. The headline of the *New York Times* of November 5, 2009 reads, "Payments in Ivory Coast Dumping Case at Risk, Lawyer Says" (A9). As in Bhopal, there is little likelihood that the settlement would have managed to pass through the gates to reach the destination of justice sought by the "man from the country" as he waited for the gatekeeper to admit him. At the end of his life he is told, "Here no one else can gain entry, since this entrance was assigned only to you. I'm going to close it now."[3] Left stranded, he echoes the words of Jimmy Cliff, "Many rivers to cross / But I can't seem to find my way."

5 Agency and the Mosquito: Mitchell and Chakrabarty

Mosquitoes don't decide, they just [do] act.

Women as trash
Garbage, detritus, debris, residuum, waste, rubbish.
Déchets humains, homeless bums, worthless scum, street
people, street children, child soldiers,
handicapped, crippled, maimed, wounded
foreigners, immigrants, *immigration clandéstine*,
others, Others, gays, poor, unemployed, deviants,
perverts, criminals, condemned, sick, deranged, stupid,
worthless.
"Débarrassez-moi de ces déchets humains"
Trash
Slums, *bidonvilles*
Ubiquitous graffiti
Recycled, récupérés
Renewed, whitewashed, washed, scrubbed clean,
sterilized, inoculated, purified, restored, recovered, reused,
used up, rejected, *rejetté*, thrown away, trashed

Trash that needs to be thrown out. Where does the need come from if there is no agency? Where does the need to establish a boundary, to separate clean and pure from dangerous, different, other, come from if not by a choice?

For Freud, the production of babies is equated in the unconscious with that of money, excrement, the penis, all that which is detachable and joined to self-pleasure.[1] The messy joining of the terms disrupts the rational and conscious explanations for their production, for their locations in places assigned by the unconscious mind to images of insalubriousness.

Direction and purpose mark motion; clarity is disrupted by indirection, by a multiplicity of uncertain purposes. What if the motion of the mosquito corresponded to other motions, like those of love and war, and the practices of building construction, so that the processes of producing and therefore of producing trash were symbiotically enabled, along with those of expenditure—a process of life that meets that of producing death, as Bataille would have it. Mosquitoes move, men move; the motions of the one produce an impact on the motion of the other, but the relationship between them is not always reducible to cause and effect. Neither does death have to follow life like the effect of a cause, but it may be viewed as part of a process or system that functions in symbiosis, apart from causation and intention. The logic that looks for causation and intention will always impose it on the phenomena it explores, but what if trash is produced by bodies and represented in films because *both* bodies and representation require trash to be produced? In each case, their production is attended by a by-product, an unintended consequence. Intention and production get decoupled from the by-products.

Let's begin with unpurified trash, that is, unmotivated trash that can't be reduced to an effect of a system, of a grand narrative that has to produce explanations that account for the trash. Though trash is amorphous, and easily lends itself to notions of hybridity or oppression or power differentials, I want to try to take it for what it is—that is, a trope for what is worthless and needs to be discarded.

So the questions arise: why the need to discard it, from where does the need arise, and what purpose does it serve? Unlike an ideological analysis, here we refrain from asking what lies behind the fetish and its repressed motivation. We could begin by asking why there is a need to purify, but I want to resist the constructions of order, as given by Mary Douglas, or of the ego, as given by Julia Kristeva. My goal is not to fit trash or abjection to purity by explaining the establishment of the boundary between the two, or to clarify the need for individuals or societies to establish borders. Rather, we will consider trash as a part of a physical body, of a material realm, of materiality, and to the compulsion to see it, smell it, and then to put it out on the curb for the garbage man to take away. A material world marked by trash, by the trope of the night-soil man, by the nightwalkers coming out every night with their trashy, glittering clothes. Trash is a word that is marked by discarding and slumming.

Does a materialist theoretical approach require an actor, like capital, without agency? Similarly one could ask whether the role of the unconscious in psychoanalysis removes agency from the subject; whether the trope as source of meaning for a text removes agency and thus meaningful motivation from the character or narrator in a narrative. In all these cases, the nonhuman actor—the capital, the repressed desire, the trope, requires the human agent to be activated. Capital must move, must be exchanged, must "seek" growth to fulfill its role in the economy. The unconscious must "act out," must seek to discharge itself through conscious decisions and actions. If it is a mistake to think that the consciously expressed motivation alone can "speak" the character, can really express what is the basis for the character's actions, it is equally a mistake to think we can ignore the role of consciously spoken words in accomplishing the analysis. If dreams are the royal road to the unconscious, there would be no road if the dreams were not remembered, narrated, and then analyzed. And the analysis takes us to dreamwork, which functions exactly like tropes where meaning is embedded in the turn from one signifier to another. One seems open, the other hidden. The tendency to search for the hidden as if it were the source of true meaning, the only key for meaning, is to lose track of the agency involved in the very concept of meaning itself that we impose on the process of analysis, like the social scientist in Mitchell's "Can the Mosquito Speak" who imposes a sociological question on his data so as to derive a sociological answer. The nature of the answer, which is predetermined in this respect, lies in the attempt to find agency in the actor at levels that are not visible on the surface. The trope is like that: a surface appearance that provides clues for an investigation that will result in answers that lie only beneath the surface.

So the trope and the character, the performance of language and the performer of speech, each creates a dependency on the other for agency to work.

Where is the agency in all the stories involving trash? In *Rule of Experts: Egypt, Techo-Politics, Modernity* (2002), Timothy Mitchell describes how sociologists can answer all the questions they put to themselves because they've already decided at the outset who is an agent and how an agent would act. If "agent" means causative factor, and if mosquitoes aren't agents who decide but just do (act), then they can't be understood in the same way as people with intentionality. Mitchell brilliantly ties together the mosquitoes' migration north in Egypt during the time of the fighting in World War I to show how the course of history was affected by an action without a clear rational agent. Further, he demonstrates how the movement of capitalism and modernity into twentieth-century Egypt was determined by what seemed to be equally aleatoric events that defied explanations in terms of rational scientific or technological systems, those grand narratives that satisfied the need of the social scientists of the nineteenth century to explain the course of history.

In the chapter coyly titled "Can the Mosquito Speak," Mitchell evokes the agents of history generally credited with the introduction of the modern capitalist economy and political structures, explanations in which the "limited number of actors" fails to include the mosquito: "There are the British, manipulating Egyptian politics while resisting the incipient postwar usurpation of their role by Americans; there are the national elites—the monarchy and the small landed aristocracy—losing their power to a more dynamic class of commercial landowners, entrepreneurs, and military offices and now and again, there are the subaltern communities—the rural population, the urban working classes, women—making up the rest of the social order. The mosquito, on the other hand, is said to belong to nature. It cannot speak" (50). In Rancière's terms, the mosquito doesn't count, has no part in the social order. And yet, it played its role in the framing of the new order.

For us, the list of descending powers, from the high colonial rulers, the British, to the lowest rank of *le peuple,* ending with the women, takes us from the most valuable (factors, actors) to the least; from the elite to the trash. How to give voice to the mosquito, coming after the women, turns on our understanding of the actor and agency. What Mitchell does is establish the factors that led technological development in a certain direction (need for eradication of malaria transmitted by these newly arrived mosquitoes, need to create irrigation projects, need to develop mechanized weapons). These needs were met by programs and campaigns that "manufactured a world that appeared as natural resources versus technology, bodies versus hygiene, men versus machines, the river versus human ingenuity" (51). Yet every one of these campaigns came to be joined to other events that bore only indirectly on the iteration of binary patterns, human versus nature, active agent versus passive object. "Although technological development portrayed the world as passive, as nature to be overcome or material resources to be developed, the relations of science and development came into being only by working with such forces" as the chance factors that made it possible for technology to be envisaged as applying to the situation at hand (51). For example, the development of DDT, which came to be applied to the infestations of mosquitoes, came about by a series of circuitous events that had nothing to do with the crisis at hand, and were as much "agents" as the intentional use of the chemical.

Like the mosquitoes, capitalism in Egypt developed in ways that were susceptible to Mitchell's analyses. It depended not only on choices directly inspired by capital and the drive to accumulate, but also on the social structures and a combination of local and international forces involving "family networks, the properties of sugar and nitrates, the labor of those harvesting cane, imperial connections, and the shortages of war" (51). When "capitalist development" is evoked, it encompasses a broad range of agencies, with "logics, chain reactions, and contingent interactions, among which the specific circuits and relations of capital formed only a part" (51). Between "human intention and the world of experience," a series of events intervened that participated in both aspects of the binary in contingent fashion. But the events came to be framed afterwards as though there were an active apodictic necessity driving the movement of history toward a determined conclusion. That is the illusion driven by the social sciences that understand explanatory systems in terms of monolithic historical rationality.

This is the cautionary note we gather from Thomas Mitchell's account of the mosquito making its way up the Nile in the early twentieth century. He makes sense of its progress by demonstrating the seemingly inevitable sets of linkages that enter into the initial story. A mosquito, as he playfully asserts, cannot speak, and yet this progressive pattern of the mosquito entering into the region of the upper Nile was the result of a chain of events that its presence set off, and was due to conditions that made it possible for the mosquito to advance north. Some of these involved the expenditure of capital, as in the building of the Aswan Dam that changed the patterns of the flow of water and of transportation, of irrigation and ultimately fertilization of the lands, and of disease and the efforts to end malaria by the invention and implementation of DDT. Other factors included World War I, high finance, the changes of political power and rule, and so on. The underlying question posed by the social scientist trying understand the historical conjuncture of these events is, how can one account for it? The "it" is, of course, unidentified here because there is no single "it," nor even finite set of "its" to account for the conjuncture. We have to delimit the contours of the event, and every attempt to do so—to account for the impact of the dam, the biological factors in the spread of disease, the flow of capital, the shift in power in Egyptian history, the development of anticolonial forces—all these attempts return to a master narrative to give an account for the important event under question. In short, we find ourselves confronted with an infinite series of chaotic moments and a finite event with a conclusive explanation, both of which require the other to be completed.

On one level, the need for the explanation can be found in the association between the active agent that causes events to occur, and passive matter that is acted upon. If we view trash as a phase in the history of material existence, which is always transient, then the opposition of active and passive becomes a temporary, internal aspect of a larger external process that is irreducible to determinant agency, producing moments when the mosquito can come to be seen as "speaking back" against the explanations that had silenced it. The placement of the trashy woman on the bottom of list of power brokers, as with her silenced voice, begins to shift uncomfortably, in unexpected ways, as she finds her voice,[2] like the transformation of the devalued chipped vase into a sought-after collectible. As the series of explanations multiplies, motion and direction seem to be determined of their own accord, and the figure of the pilot disappears; a nonteleological actualizing nature combines a multiplicity of elements into what appears, ex post facto, to be causative: "What is called nature or the material world moves, like the plasmodium, in and out of human forms, or occurs as arrangements, like the river Nile, that are social as well as natural, technical as well as material" (52). Similarly, the dominant position of the idea over the material is challenged, permitting a Bataillean erection of the acephalus man in place of the Platonic idea, his heterogeneous impurity over the homogeneous purity (1989: xvii). The result in Mitchell is not a simple reversal of position but a deconstruction of logocentrism. In terms of African trash, it is not a decolonization but a true postcolonization that permits, finally, an opening onto transgressive figures that are not always already compromised by having to fit into the scheme of that which they are transgressing against. Mitchell's contention is that any straightforward rationalization of order cannot be sustained: "The world out of which techno-politics emerged was an unresolved and prior combination of reason, force, imagination and resources. Ideas and technology did not precede this mixture as pure forms of thought brought to bear upon the messy world of reality. They emerged from the mixture and were manufactured in the processes themselves" (52). He demonstrates the ex post facto reasoning that followed these processes that functioned, like Rancière's "police," to sustain a system of categories that reinforce the notion that the components of the social order are not constructed but natural. This is the power of the "police," that is, the ordering forces in society: they determine who and what go where, and what does not fit in: they determine the consensus, oppose the dissensus. For Mitchell, the social sciences are this kind of "police": "By relating particular events to a universal reason and by treating human agency as given," he claims that social science "mimics this form of power." Social science analytical methods reproduce the naturalization that sustains a kind of power that is "*taken in by the effects it generates*." In this way, social science formats a world "resolved into this binary order" and helps to "constitute and solidify the experience of agency and expertise" (52; my emphasis). He goes on to conclude that despite these claims, we cannot reify agency, causation, and knowledge into the straightforward fixed categories that provide answers already supplied in advance: power and agency are made into "questions," not "answers known in advance" (53), arising from what he calls an "unresolvable tension, the inseparable mixture, the impossible multiplicity, out of which intention and expertise must emerge. It requires acknowledging that *human agency*, like capital, is a technical body, *is something made*" (53; my emphasis).

The "inseparable mixture," the impurity of a tension without resolution, a text without closure, a multiplicity that gives rise to intention, all disrupt the rationality of the ordered place that is structured so as to enable a border to be erected and the dirt to be removed. The sciences that give rise to technology must simultaneously expel the heterogeneous knowledges that fail to conform to their "policed" order, their *ratio*. On the global scale, the global north provides the site for such dominant knowledges and their agencies to be validated. More than a geophysical location, the "global north" is the psychic location of modernism and its *ratio*.

We can return to agency when exploring the major motifs of *Karmen Gei* (2001) and *La Nuit de la vérité* (2004) by posing the question of where agency is to be located in the dramatizations of love and war, the free bird in the former, the ruptured bits of bodies in the latter. In questioning agency in love and war, we would find the natural order positing the same binaries Mitchell discovered in his reading of Egypt's mosquitoes, that is, the active, dominant position accorded the truth-making mechanisms of the social sciences, and the passive material, the earthly ground on which the ideas of science work. By a similar logic, love divides the couple into a strong, active, dominant male riding over the softer, more passive female. Her accordance, given all too easily, requires her accommodation to his advances to be made proper; her resistance, given all too reluctantly, falls within the expectations of norms. The sense of normalcy and naturalness frame the couple, building the very system that joined them initially. Love becomes a trained couple, not a free bird. This is the political realm against which the transgressions in both films are aimed.

War functions in the same way as the regime of love. The master-slave dialectic, the friend-enemy state relations, the power assumed by the superior actor, all are deployed in the conflict whose reasons are clearly established so as to make wars appear necessary and conquest desirable, even inevitable—manifest and determined. Whatever the scenario, the pattern in conflict resolves itself into a warrior's logic that equates the justifications for the conflict with its supposed reasons and seeks resolution in the sensible coupling of conqueror-conquered. The very posture of the one over the other, in war and love, is one of active over passive. The master remains in the superior position, the slave in the inferior one, the position to which the terms of inferiority are also frequently assigned. The man, in his triumph and excesses, may be indulgently designated as "womanizer"; the woman who strays, who is too easy, who lets herself be taken, is judged as trashy.

But that set of designations also falls within the presuppositions of a binary ideological structuring of gender and conflict, and requires more than a reversal of the positions to accomplish the goals of the garbologist-archeologist to trouble the waters. For this, the excessive immersion in the illicit flight of the figure, in disordered fashion, would be needed. Trash without intentionality, dispersed across a range of signifiers; trash, the end product of consumption and the beginning point for appropriation.

Bataille's notions of consumption and excretion, production and expenditure, provide the link between scatological and libidinal physical acts and the trope of trash, permitting us to define one facet of the trope as positioning the material against ideation. Ideation and value mark each set of objects and practices that make consumption possible, whereas the lowlife of the material, its end results of trash and excretion, are joined in their oppositional, excluded, belated position. Contemplating trash in this fashion generates a messy set of possible figures that resist all attempts at a master foundational narrative. This is all the more the case if we circle trash around, recycling so that what was expended is *then* consumed, troubling the finality of a binary structure that places production of commodities before consumption and the subsequent disposal of the end products. Trash has no end when viewed from the perspective situated below. We need Bataille here to challenge the Platonic urge to place the idea in the superior, logocentric position and also to disturb the tendency to return to a simple binary that sets trash against valued objects in a permanent state, apart from any act of agency.

Situated below we can ask, if the material body automatically and naturally produces excrement from food that is consumed, if society does the same with the wealth it consumes, what agency can account for it; what agency does nature itself embody? Mitchell's answer is that we need to interrogate our notions of agency, if not causality, to include the inert agency attributed to nature, to natural causes, as if they acted differently from those initiated through human intentionality. When he begins with the meeting of the mosquito and the first world war, both of which arrived in upper Egypt in the first quarter of the twentieth century, it is in order to explore interactions that neither had "predicted." The occurrence of the malaria epidemic in the south might have caused debilitating psychological effects in the north where the British were busy trying to contain Rommel at al-Alamein. They could not spare troops from the battlefront to confront the epidemic in the south, and so the mosquito was able to advance. The accounting of this advance had to do with complex factors, such as the type of mosquito, the weakness of the human population before the onslaught of the disease, the modes of transportation afforded the mosquito by changing patterns of travel on the river, by the incursion of boats, trains, and cars into the region. All this is to explain the figure of speech that joins the radically different locations of event, the nation, and the cell: "The chemistry of the epidemic operated at the level of the nation and of the cell" (25). This formulation repositions intentionality and agency as they enter into the immediate operations of the medical emergency.

For Mitchell, the conventional way of thinking about natural causation is not to attribute to it the intentionality of human agency, as though it were passive, external, incapable of bearing the responsibility of events. Yet the mosquito carries the malarial plasmodium, which itself "multiplies" under the right circumstances, or is prevented from doing so under others, as when DDT infiltrates its environment. Seeking agency just in terms of human intentionality is to define both the event and its causes ahead of time, before the event: it is to frame, and thus to limit, the possibilities of extending agency beyond the disciplinary borders of the master narrative—to delimit dependency and relevancy to a set of parameters with their own restricted scope of answers. This scope excludes the one factor we would want to privilege in this study, that is, the result of those processes that typically are taken to place valued commodities above excretion, trash, expenditure, and its waste products.

That is where film comes in. It isn't simply what is represented as trash, or who is represented as trash, not what values are trashed in the film, or what trashiness the film embraces that matters; but what accounts can be given for these values preceding the analysis of the film—what values frame the analysis and thus oblige the film to respond according to those postulations. Just as Žižek had the audacity to imagine that the characters in films were looking back at the viewers,[3] occupying a location of agency normally attributed only to the spectator, so too do we want to perversely attribute an agency to the very materiality of the film, as to trash in whatever forms it comes to occupy.

This would parallel Mitchell's sets of explanations for the wealth and power ʿAbbud acquired during this period of the first half of the twentieth century, when he profited from the dam, became a large landowner and produced cotton and nitrates, acquired banks, and so on. ʿAbbud's role in Egyptian history became central as Mitchell explored its role in the war, in the passage of Egypt to an independent state, in the state's acquiescence in modernist projects that involved health, science, economics, and eventually political power. In all this, we can say that figures like ʿAbbud, in their manipulations of the system, in their wealth and power, were able to define the shape of Egyptian history. However, at another level, that of the movement of bugs, there has not been a lot of thought given to their power to move history forward until Mitchell came to challenge the notions of history and of what constitutes it, of motion and of what and who defines it, of what attributes of progress and modernity are assumed, of what is caused and not merely who causes this or that.

In film, it would be the same. A series of ostensible causes are set out to account for the final product, The Film. First one looks to the director to ask who made the film and filled it with his or her intentions; next who financed the film; then who permitted it to be shown, and under what circumstances; and finally who was viewing it, and how they would be expected to receive it. In each case, there is a limitation placed on agency: that the director's choices might have included a multitude of factors known or unknown to him or her; that the conditions of production and exhibition could not be reduced to a simple schemata to be dubbed neocolonial or global, and so on. The process of freeing ourselves from the harnesses of agency thinking has to begin where least expected—in the spaces, gaps, borders and gutters between the frames, the unobserved as well as the unintended, that make a film something other than a result of a planned text.

Mitchell then asks about the successes of ʿAbbud: "what arrangements (of law, property, political economy, engineering, irrigation, and much more) made such a calculation [of what accounted for his success] possible, or what agencies kept those arrangements in place?" (33). Was it capital and its flows, or his decisions at any given moment—or, to enlarge the scope of the question, a multitude of factors that made both his choices and the flow of capital possible, that made the very question of a process that obeyed the laws of nature, or the laws of psychology and choice, possible? Mitchell concluded that certain effects were always produced that "went beyond the calculations, certain forces that exceeded human intention. Scientific expertise and national politics were produced out of this tension" (38). Trash is the trope for that which is excluded from the sensible explanation, that exceeds the rational intention.

Part of what generates the tensions of accounting for trash are viewed as cultural. For instance, when the American Embassy in Egypt sought to aid the peasants in ameliorating their construction of homes, they sought to change the means of manufacturing mud bricks and subsequently treating their surfaces. For the Americans, Egyptian houses were "dirty" and thus incapable of resistance to deterioration: "The peasant's house 'is never clean,' the embassy reported to Washington. 'The very nature of the mud brick promotes dust rather than cleanliness. Its surface is porous and will not readily take whitewash and paint'" (41). Mitchell takes some pleasure in dismantling this perverse desire on the part of the modern American diplomat to validate a change in home-building practices that dated back centuries: "Villages in Egypt already had a straightforward method of plastering over mud brick, using particular local clays mixed with straw, employed whenever a house needed smoother or more impressive walls. But existing practice, like the old knowledge of irrigation, involved an expertise that was too widely dispersed to provide a means for building imperial power—or the profits of a Boston consulting firm" (41).

The American diplomats had a need to find the peasant's house dirty, a need embedded in the social relations that marked the colonial rule from its inception. These were the needs that were served by the tools of vision, of evaluation, that saw in those other, different forms of houses, streets, cities the location of dirt, filth, and trash that the residents themselves did not observe. This is how Chakrabarty explains the first reaction of the British to the Indian subcontinent's cities. He cites a certain M. A. Sherring who in 1868 described Banaras as "foul" and "disgusting," where the "stagnant cesspools, accumulated refuse and dead bodies of animals" become legible to Sherring as a result of Sherring's "particular way of seeing" ("Of Garbage, Modernity and the Citizen's Gaze," 2002: 66). Like Mitchell, Chakrabarty recognizes the grounding of this "way of seeing" in a cultural bias or, to be more precise, in the epistemology on which the authorized perspective asserts its claims to correctness. That claim is presented in the global north as scientific, and in this case is based on social science, which validates the distance between its high status and the ignorance and prejudices of those occupying low status: "the nonbourgeois subaltern citizen is always already condemned in our social science, however sympathetic the stance of our ethnography. As social scientists, we align ourselves with those who want to build citizen cultures" (2002: 65). In part that means that the educated, disciplined social scientist can now perceive dirt where the native cannot, but the border established between clean and dirty when, say, the native housekeeper sweeps her courtyard's debris into the street is seen differently by the western observer than by the housekeeper. The housekeeper, thinking to cleanse her space, moves it out there where the nonnative has to step around or through it: the nonnative sees dirt, sees neglect, and ultimately translates that dirt into the threatening signifier "disease," an all-too-inauspicious transformation: "the outsider [or in our example, native housekeeper] always carries 'substances' that threaten one's [that is, the nonnative's] well-being" (70). Difference translates here into dangerousness and is communicated through threatening substances, dirt and disease, linked to the "inauspicious": "All forms of inauspiciousness are said to originate in entities and events that are 'different' and 'distant' from the person or other afflicted entity . . . they are alien" (70). The native's cleansing, then, is auspicious if it protects from malevolent influences and, in sweeping out the rubbish, creates a distance between the threat and the self: "The everyday practice of classifying certain things as household rubbish marks the boundary of this enclosure," and thus production involves marking off space, generating a border between what is enclosed and what is excluded. Rubbish is not simply the by-product of consumption or expenditure but is necessary to the creation of the boundary and the enclosure. This is the process of abjection, as Kristeva delineated it—necessary for the border of the self or ego to establish itself as separate from the other. This is Douglas's model too of the enclosed order with its clean space, the border, and the excluded places for dirt.

When Chakrabarty asks what constitutes the rubbish, that which is swept outside the enclosure, he turns to the bazaar—we would say in Africa the market, *le marché*—for an answer. Here the outsider and the familiar meet, with the accompanying dangers of an encounter that exists on the border of the regulated or disciplined. The mosquito, in Mitchell's paradigm, migrates north, and those previously unexposed to the risks it carries are vulnerable to its dangers. The site of the meeting between familiar and stranger, the crossroads where Eshu is to be found playing his tricks on the unsuspecting, retains for Chakrabarty an "ambiguous character": "It is exposed, and therefore malevolent. It is not subject to a single set of (enclosing) rules and rituals defining a community. It is where miscegenation occurs. All that does not belong to the inside (family/kinship/community) lie there, cheek by jowl, in an unasserted collection, violating rules of mixing: from *feces to prostitutes*. It is, in other words, a place against which one needs protection" (73–74; my emphasis).

In our paradigms from African cinema, we can locate a number of instances that fit this description of the bazaar, of the meeting between familiar and strange, where dangers lurk. Perhaps most powerfully, we have the scene in *Karmen Gei* (2001) in which Karmen has gone with Massigi to the cloth market HLM where he enters surrounded with his entourage. Here Massigi is feted by the women merchants as he sings in celebration of the end of one millennium and the start of another, "L'an deux mille." Karmen enters with greater uncertainty, examining the fabrics indifferently as the women call on her to buy their wares. Then she senses a presence following her and picks up her pace, glancing over her shoulder. She runs down a stairway, escaping into a dark enclosure, a dingy space out of the way, only to be confronted by her stalker. They meet in a space on the borders of the market, just as she later dies in a space that lies between the stage and the world outside.

Chakrabarty goes on to capture what is alluring about the market, inadvertently explaining why it is in Africa that this space is so often dominated by women,[4] and, as Tanella Boni demonstrated in her *Une Vie de crabe* (1990), why sexuality, death, and disease lurk in the imaginary that constructs out of the market an unregulated space of danger. "Ambiguity and risk are, thus, inherent to the excitement of the bazaar," as Chakrabarty explains. "It provides a venue for linkage across communities (linkages with strangers)" (74). The threat of such strangers has long been captured in the familiar West African tales of the "handsome gentleman," in which a handsome stranger arrives at the market and the inexperienced, incautious, beautiful young virgin, who has yet to know a man, will be exposed to seduction and disgrace if she falls for his blandishments (Garritano 2000). He is an evil spirit in disguise, and she is at risk because she has not heeded her parents' warnings. The market offers pleasures joined to dangers, like all stranger experiences: "The place is still pregnant with possibility. And such pleasures are, by nature, transgressive because they are pleasures of the inherently risky outside" (Chakrabarty 75). Following our paradigm, the risks entail not only death but "dirtying" one's reputation, losing one's value.

Chakrabarty sums up this description of the market and the Europeans' encounter with its space in predictable colonial terms. Its "dirt" engenders the European desire to "clean" it up, to discipline it. In recent years in parts of West Africa, a similar push to "modernize" the economy has led governments to attempt to rationalize capital exchanges by leveling the marché so as to end its undisciplined financial transactions and bring the processes of exchange under the authority of the city or state. Garbage is produced by this western epistemology in order that it be cleaned up. Chakrabarty neatly joins this perspective of the dominant ruling class to its production of that which it seeks to control, and that is thus defined as garbage:

> structurally speaking, the space that collects garbage is the one that is not subject to a single set of communal rules. It is the space that produces both malevolence and exchange between communities and, hence, needs to be tamed through the continual, and contextual, deployment of a certain dichotomy between the inside and the outside. This need to be tamed is what makes the outside exciting, albeit in unpredictable and dangerous ways.
>
> Both the colonialists and the nationalists were repelled by what they saw as the two predominant aspects of open space in India: dirt and disorder. (76)

As Chakarbarty concludes that the solution to this problem, the desire to clean up the space, is to level the bazaar and create the supermarket, one cannot but reflect on Sissako's opening scene in La Vie sur terre (1999), set in a huge Parisian supermarket, where seemingly hundreds of brands of butter are displayed in their cold, formal shelves along the aisle. "The thrills of the bazaar are exchanged for the convenience of the sterile supermarket" (77), and thus the constructions of the healthy body, the healthy site of exchanges between inside and outside, and ultimately the healthy nation are effected. The production of the colonized subject morphs into that of the modern subject, as Mitchell recognizes, along a wide range of registers—those entailing "modern knowledge," or science; modern institutions, modern spaces, modern economies, and modern rules, creating "long life, good health, more money, small families, and modern science," all appearing so "natural and God given" (Chakrabarty 79).

This pattern of the exportation of the west's most formidable product, modernity, or more precisely, the distribution of the sensibility of modernity, was replicated across the world in the nineteenth and twentieth centuries. In Colo-

nial Pathologies: American Tropical Medicine, Race, and Hygiene in the Philippines (2006), Warwick Anderson describes a similar process in the Philippines where American colonization brought hygienic practices that could be summed up in one word, the toilet. He quotes Toni Morrison's *Tar Baby* (1981), where she captures perfectly the perspective of the colonialist, the modernizer, the civilizer:

> Although they called it architecture it was in fact elaborately built toilets, decorated toilets, toilets surrounded with and by business and enterprise in order to have something to do in between defecations since waste was the order of the day and the ordering principle of the universe. . . . That was the sole lesson of their world: how to make waste, how to make machines that made more waste, how to make wasteful products, how to talk waste, how to study waste, how to design waste, how to cure people who were sickened by waste so they could be well enough to endure it, how to mobilize waste, legalize waste and how to despise the culture that lived in cloth houses and shit on the ground far away from where they ate. (175)

Reading this across the continental divides of colonialism, Morrison perceives waste, as Chakrabarty, Anderson, and Mitchell confirm, as lying in the eye of the beholder, and thus being projected, not innocently but in the service of a dominant order. Morrison ends *The Bluest Eye* (1970) on this note:

> All of our waste which we dumped on her and which she absorbed. And all of our beauty, which was hers first and which she gave to us. All of us—all who knew her—felt so wholesome after we cleaned ourselves on her. We were so beautiful when we stood astride her ugliness. Her simplicity decorated us, her guilt sanctified us, her pain made us glow with health, her awkwardness made us think we had a sense of humor. Her inarticulateness made us believe we were eloquent. Her poverty kept us generous. Even her waking dreams we used—to silence our own nightmares. And she let us, and thereby deserved our contempt. We honed our egos on her, padded our characters with her frailty, and yawned in the fantasy of our own strength.
>
> And fantasy it was, for we were not strong, only aggressive; we were not free, merely licensed. (205)

The licensing signals the epistemic revolution brought about by the transposition of modernity to the colonized world—the rereading or rearrangement of that world along lines by which the mosquito—or as Spivak would have it, the subaltern—is denied its agency, its speech. The project of modernity, along its technical lines of power/knowledge, established a world in which "science was opposed to nature and technical expertise claimed to overcome the obstacles to social improvement" (Mitchell 51). In speaking of the malaria campaign, the Aswan Dam project alongside the campaign at al-Alamein where "technicized warfare" got its start with the use of tanks and mines, a world was "manufactured" (51) that defines the modern man. And although in each case there appears a term embodying techno-agency, like technology, hygiene, machine, and ingenuity, each aspect of that modernity was produced by its nontechnical, subordinated term, like nature, bodies, or natural resources, dissipating any assignation of agency. For Mitchell, the lesson is that one cannot separate human intention from "the world of experience," what Rancière terms "le partage du sensible." He demonstrates how techno-politics "emerged [from] an unresolved and prior combination of reason, force, imagination, and resources. Ideas and technology did not precede this mixture as pure forms of thought brought to bear upon the messy world of reality. They emerged from the mixture and were manufactured as processes themselves" (52). The social sciences unwittingly duplicate these technological processes and their rationalizations in constructing their own ways of producing knowledge, and thus, like all ideologies, obscuring their play of power in the process. Mitchell would have "this play of power and agency left a question, instead of an answer known in advance" (52).

Our own issues with trash would indicate a concern less with the institutions of the production of knowledge, Mudimbe (1988) having well sorted out their Eurocentric dimensions. Rather, we would seek to reverse the argument, following the chain of reasoning established by Morrison when she identifies the fantasies of the dominant colonial subject as constructed by the workings of their "license." For if the European feeling of repulsion before the tableau of waste is experienced as natural, it is because the training that gave rise to the European sensibility was concomitant with the licensing of propriety as well as property—of the *propre*. If the social scientist concerns him or herself with the social construction, trash requires us to attend to the improprieties of the material, thus enabling us to join a perspective from below, a location from which to talk not only about "the 'social construction' of things" in terms of technics, but of "things clearly more than social" (Mitchell 52).

6 Trashy Women: *Karmen Gei,* l'Oiseau Rebelle

From the California Newsreel blurb about Joseph Gaye Ramaka's film:

> *Karmen Gei* is an adaptation of Bizet's *Carmen.* Joseph Gaï Ramaka writes, "Carmen is a myth but what does Carmen represent today? Where do Carmen's love and freedom stand at the onset of the 21st Century? Therein lies my film's intent, a black Carmen, plunged in the magical and chaotic urbanity of an African city." Here Karmen transgresses every convention. Like every Carmen, *Karmen Gei* is about the conflict between infinite desire for freedom and the laws, conventions and human limitations that constrain the desire. (http://newsreel.org /nav/title.asp?tc=CN0134)

The first thing one notices about this version of Carmen is that the music is original, largely consisting of jazz tracks and Wolof music, nothing like that of Bizet. But the plot is closer to that of the opera, and some of its best-known lyrics do follow those of the opera, including the well-known habanera. Our Karmen first appears in prison where she dances for the inmates and especially the female warden, Angelique. Angelique cannot resist Karmen's charms, and after a sexually charged rendezvous between the two, Karmen leaves the prison. There the plot loosely follows that of the Bizet version. She seduces the army corporal charged with imprisoning her, enlists him in her gang, and carries out drug deals and break-ins. He is turned away from his former life as officer headed for social success to that of an outlaw, lost to the wiles of Karmen. What ensues is a series of episodes in which Karmen establishes her independence from all men, asserting her adherence to the famous habanera line "love is a bird that cannot be tamed." In the end, in defiance of the threat of death, she remains true to her ideal of freedom and is killed by the jealous corporal Lamine.

L'amour est un oiseau rebelle	[love is a rebellious bird]
que nul ne peut apprivoiser,	[that no one can tame]
et c'est bien en vain qu'on l'appelle,	[it is in vain that you call him]
s'il lui convient de refuser.	[if he feels like refusing]

The French operatic version designates love as a rebellious bird, and in defining it in terms of its negation (something "that no one can tame"), it is also marked by its obstinancy ("s'il lui convient de refuser")—a definition marked by a series of negatives (can't tame, in vain, refuse).

In the same vein, the lyrics continue:

Rien n'y fait, menace ou prière,	[nothing works, threat or prayer]
l'un parle bien, l'autre se tait:	[one person speaks well, the other is silent]
Et c'est l'autre que je préfère,	[and it is the other than I prefer]
Il n'a rien dit mais il me plaît.	[he said nothing but he pleases me]

(http://classicalmusic.about.com/od/opera/qt/habaneralyrics.htm)

The perverseness is emphasized here: I chose him, the quiet one, not the one who speaks well; and the lines repeat, "he said nothing but he pleases me."

Her perverseness, more than stubbornness, signals Carmen's insistence on having it her way, and as that way runs counter not simply to the other, but to the Other, she is *willfully transgressive*. All these traits and figures are incorporated in the Ramaka adaptation.

These are two terms of significance in this attitude I want to emphasize. Her willfulness is promoted in virtually all versions of Carmen as an indication of her character. Though she is, in the original, a gypsy, a *tsigane*,[1] an outsider, a minority figure of nomadic unconventionality, hers is not a condition she has passively inherited but an indication of her personality and especially of her agency: she chooses *this*, not *that*; she makes herself the subject, refuses to be the object—especially the object of the other's desire. If she is an outlaw, it is not fate or circumstance but her choice to be "rebelle" and refusal to be subjugated. Yet her perverseness cannot help but be perversion since she can only define her transgressive acts in terms of what they are not, what rules they insist on breaking. She is thus included within the very system she seeks to rebel against since she has no other frame of action. She is a creature of those around her whose expectations and sense of conventional normalcy provide her with the measurements by which to construct her oppositionality. The rebellious bird needs that which it rebels against to define itself as rebellious.

Her rebellion is in many senses tame and predictable, but also violently subversive. The tameness comes from the bohemian sensibility of the artist who flies freely, a trope for the *artiste* that has marked Senegalese culture for some time. Modernism came late to Senegal, only after a decade of independence under the guidance of Senegal's first president, Senghor. Senghor created a state ideology that supported modernist representations of Africans and blacks who exemplified the values of Negritude, of the black arts world images of black culture. With jazzy rhythms and tones, syncopation, signifying with motion and attitude, old-school hip and cool affects, the late Harlem Renaissance made its way to Dakar and came into its own with state-supported oil paintings and drawings, sculptures, and even tapestries.[2] These high culture artifacts celebrated the new nation's independence; but after a decade or more of this orientation, many artists grew restive and sought freer styles that were not beholden to Negritude.[3]

The abstract and collage figures that emerged were clearly within the boundaries of mid-twentieth-century modernism, and not really late modernism, the precursor to postmodernism. But they were precursors to montages that were increasingly abstract and constructed with recycled materials. A notable example was Moustapha Dimé, who employed found objects and local materials in his sculpture (Harney 2004: 79).

It was in that period, the 1970s and 1980s, that we saw take hold the figure of the artist-musician in Senegal as the bohemian, the outsider—the one who resisted both conformity to state art and to the straight and narrow path of the Muslim orders, the Tijanis and Mourids. It wasn't the radical rejection of nation and religion, however, that emerged—indeed, Mouridism inspired the mystical and liberationist tendencies of a number of artists like Papisto Boy whose amazing murals in Colobane include scenes of devotion to Amadou Bamba—but rather a vision of both that was unscripted, unimpeded, and of necessity unconventional. Free forms of jazz, paintings liberated from representational constraints, free compositions, with a range of found objects and materials that could evoke difference, insubordination, ultimately created receptivity to tendencies in installation and conceptual art being developed abroad—a sensibility freed from the need to be called Senegalese, in art, in music.

It is hard to credit bohemianism and modernism with subversion anymore; they have long since become mainstream. Yet when set within the frame established by Senghor's stale state-sponsored academic dictates, they did represent revolt. And when set against social conservatism, they have a pertinence that would no longer apply in the west.

This sketches the scene that had developed a generation before *Karmen Gei* was made in 2001. This was one year after the socialist government had its first regime change since independence, a change that proved to be far from liberating. We can consider two of the key terms used to define the figure of Karmen and this film: liberation and subversion. These are terms heavily laden with biopolitical implications for gender. Liberation first conjures the notion of the woman no longer subordinated to the order of patriarchy. Subversion might well be called transgression, the determination to violate the constraints of the dominant order. The perverseness of tying liberation to transgression emerges clearly in the verses of the habanera that follow those quoted above:

L'amour est enfant de Bohême,	[love is a Bohemian child]
il n'a jamais, jamais connu de loi;	[it has never never known any law]
si tu ne m'aimes pas, je t'aime	[if you do not love me, I love you]
si je t'aime, prends garde à toi!	[if I love you, watch out]
(Prends garde à toi!)	
Si tu ne m'aimes pas,	[if you don't love me]
Si tu ne m'aimes pas, je t'aime!	[if you don't love me, I will love you.
(Prends garde à toi!)	Watch out]

Mais, si je t'aime,	[but if I love you]
Si je t'aime, prends garde à toi!	[if I love you, watch out!]

Outside of the law, love, the bohemian child, warns that those who love Carmen, or love her not, will be subjugated to her desire: will they or not, she will determine, perversely, to love the one who doesn't love her and he, or she, will suffer as a result.

Love her or not, she will not be ruled by order. She will violate order, she will bring danger; *prends garde à toi,* watch out. There is danger from operating in the space outside the rules, their rules, the rules of those who are afraid, those incapable of loving freely. How beautiful this wild bird, this wild dancer called the habanera, the gypsy dancer!

If bohemianism gives us what now feels like an old-fashioned image of rebellion or unconventionality, placing transgression in a postcolonial frame will enable us to broaden our reading so as to encompass what Sumita Chakravarty sees as the allegorization of the national drama wherein "it is not the colonizing Western power that is being excoriated, but the split body of the nation, at once patriarchal and feminized" (2003: 79). Chakravarty's thesis is that male directors of non-western films "present the oppression of women and the tensions arising out of transgressive sexual desires as allegories of social or national history" (79). With this reading, transgression and order become gendered, in line with the dominant male need to punish violation and insubordination against the order as something that is female. The rebellious bird of the present must be punished for her betrayal of the masculinist ideals that ordered the good old days, "the past being the displaced site of the tensions, failures and anxieties of the present" (81).

The expression of that anxiety, that tension, is figured in the erotic, and thus in our figure of the trashy woman. The erotic captures "the force of that which is unspeakable and suppressed in history, but needs to be articulated to make some kind of redemption possible for the collectivity" (80). The woman who dares must be contained for the good of the male-ruled order. All the features would seem to be in place for our trope of Karmen as the wild side of trashiness, with the police order and Lamine's cohort of male officers set against Ma Penda and her club scene with its drinking reprobates and celebration the past heroines like Aline Sitoe, Mame Njare Njaw, and water goddess Kumba Kastel. Karmen leads us there after her breakout from prison and Gorée.

As the film opens, the drums introduce us to Karmen. She performs an erotic dance for Angelique, the prison warden, unleashing Angelique's desires and the excitement and exuberance of her fellow women inmates. Having won her freedom from prison, she proceeds to Lamine's wedding where she defies and insults the ranks of the ruling military officers for having corrupted the nation. Hers are insubordinant dances, dances that distance her from the tamed women, those social figures of stature who are attending the wedding party.

Karmen lifts her skirts, throws down her challenge to their society, to the bride, to the generals, to all who keep order. She dances in disorder, and as such crosses the line between respectable and unrespectable.[4]

Corporal Lamine, who did nothing to stop her, is stripped of his bars and ordered to throw her in prison, but she breaks down his resistance as well, freeing herself from his grip and running off, laughing. She establishes the benchmark for the unrespectable woman, and as such lives it out in the rest of the film: bathing naked in front of her male gang, commanding the men in her gang, throwing off lovers, seducing women, crossing lines between Christians and Muslims in their mourning dirges, between those whose art was tamed and those like Samba who taught her freedom and revolted against the policing of their lives. As an antiestablishment rebel, the only word to describe such types, in the eyes of the conformist society, is "trash," and she established the bellwether mark for trashiness.

Mary Douglas famously defines dirt as "matter out of place," meaning outside its ordered place or, more, outside of the place of order, as that which disrupts order. Following this, the transgressions in sexuality of *Karmen Gei* could be read as one side of a dirty movie, a trashy movie. This requires a propensity to see trash as either a stain on order or a feature of subversion of order. We can say "out of place" is where the values of the object or person are lost, be that value defined in terms of the market, art, or memory. But that leaves aside the question of whether that place is the woman's place; what if the trash is gendered, and consequently, the order as well? What if trash is female? The trashy woman then is the one who violates the dominant order, and in violating the order, perversely, the trashy women produce it as male. Films of women-in-revolt revise not only the order but the history and gender relations that grounded it. Speaking of *The Red Lantern* (1991), Chakravarty writes, "The film presents an interplay of (male) prohibitions and (female) transgression, those twin processes out of which human history emerges" (93). Here I would add to "history" the term "order," and add to "transgression" the term "trash." Chakravarty brings together feminist studies and trash studies in ways that complete the analysis of Karmen as an ideal "trashy woman."

Following Aleida Assman (2002), I will explore three economies of trash to which we can refer in analyzing this film: the market, art, and memory (81). The three economies are defined by value and by their relationship to each other. Within the frame of *Karmen Gei,* multiple economies function simultaneously, and as the film's narrative unfolds across time in a linear fashion, the changes in settings and characters will open the possibility of new economies coming to the fore. We will explore the three economies of market, art, and memory to determine their relationship to the characters and plot, but also to each other, with the thesis that Karmen passes from one to the other of these three economies in the course of her own story's unfolding even as the three remain in effect throughout the course of the film.

The Economy of the Market

Market value is typically defined in terms of exchange value, or more broadly the value inscribed in the relations of capital generated in a modern economy. In this case, it is the modern neoliberal globalized economy that has dominated African states for the past twenty or so years, and that has been ideologically dominant in Senegal since Wade came to power in 2000. Objects (or people) defined in the regime of the market usually have transient value attached to them. As they lose market value, they submit to the possibility of having a different value under a different economy. Typically an object whose use value depreciates over time loses exchange value, like a car or house. But the car can become an "antique car" whose market value increases as its use value decreases. It enters into a different economy from its original one. The economies of art, the market, and memory can move an object's value up together, as in a painting that appreciates over time as the artist becomes successful. Or the opposite might occur, where the memory of an artist, like those who created much African art, is lost while the object itself gains in market value.

An object may become increasingly worthless in market terms but become available for recycling into objects of greater value in other economies. Recycled art objects built of recuperated materials are one example. Objects to which nostalgia can be attached, either by individuals or cultures, can acquire great value as collectibles; as works of art they are transformed into objects whose value is no longer measured in relation to an original use value and whose new exchange value might be determined by a local or international art market, a local change in culture, or a number of other factors. A photograph of Amadou Bamba might become invaluable as Mouridism ascends and his mystical powers come to be widely accepted by millions of people. A photograph might be offensive and worthless in one frame and an important artifact in another: images of nude or seminude African women, transposed onto postcards, offer a typical, notorious example, especially under colonialism (Alloula 1986). In market terms, trash is perversely associated with money. We can attribute the value of drugs (or shit, in slang) to money, following Freud's reading of money as excrement.[5]

In one scene in the robbers' den, Karmen divides up the "dirty" money from their drug heist among the members of her gang. Then she gives her share to Lamine, paying him off and ending their relationship. In the order of cops-and-robbers, where money is king, the king is male. When they divide up the loot, the other members of the band are excited; she is indifferent. Her participation in the economy of the market, with its accumulation of commodities, the pursuit of wealth, and the translation of value into exchange value, is subordinated to the value she embodies in the regimes of art and memory.

Shortly after this scene that ends her relationship with Lamine, Karmen and Massigi go to the HLM cloth market, and he sings "L'An 2000" in celebration of the new millennium (see figure 6.1). The market setting of lavishness and wealth is set against Karmen's subsequent descent to a basement and her flight from death. When Massigi enters the market, he is surrounded by his entourage and is feted by the women cloth merchants as he sings of the end of one millennium and the start of another. Karmen enters with greater uncertainty, examining the fabrics indifferently as the women call on her to buy their wares. Then she senses a presence following her and picks up her pace, glancing over her shoulder. She runs down a stairway, escaping into a dark enclosure, a dingy out-of-the-way space, only to be confronted by her angry ex-lover Lamine. She berates him, now exposing her apprehension and anger at Lamine. In this scene, we can see all the economies of trash at work, albeit in fragments.

On initially entering the market, the exchange value of the goods is presented in terms of commodity fetishism. A plethora of bright variegated cloths are proffered by the sellers as signifiers of sumptuousness. The narrow corridor in the market is surrounded by women into whose world we enter. Massigi is their *coq*,[6] the rooster whom the women spoil, lavishing their wares, their luxuriousness on him. He glows, welcoming the New Age with the assurance of the wealthy, popular, successful singer. Here all is charged with opulence. As such, though it is not under the auspices of the patriarchy, it is still under the sign of the market, that is, of commodity exchange as that which designates value. This is the grand African market, where the women can enter into the economy and create a space less regulated than that of the mall, its modern competitor. It occupies a median location between the "modern" shopping mall and an old city marché, what Chakrabarty (2002) refers to as the bazaar where strangers meet other strangers, bringing together the exotic and the dangerous, and where value is magically produced under the auspices of some trickster-like deity. In *Things Fall Apart* (1958), Achebe's characters attribute this wealth to an old woman who stands on one leg; in the Fon or Yoruba culture, it is Legba or Eshu who rules the market, capriciously distributing the wealth (Pelton 1980). In Africa, this space is often dominated by women. For Tanella Boni, sexuality, death, and disease lurk in the imaginary that constructs out of the market an unregulated space of danger, *un autre univers,* another universe.[7]

It would have been tempting for Karmen to let herself go in the marché HLM scene, following Massigi, basking in the glow of his celebrity status, but she had already rejected the appeal of money when dispersing the illegally gotten drug money to her gang and gave away her share in the process of dismissing Lamine, the poor lover who was more inclined to grasp than to give. Thus Karmen goes off on her own, apart from Massigi and his claque of women. We can say she leaves Massigi's mise-en-scène, its parti-colored clothes draped over his shoulders, creating something of a fauvist painterly setting that holds the assemblage inside the spaces of the corridor between the shops. As Karmen leaves, her smile fading, her polite refusals altering the mood, she comes to an intersection where a dark shadow of a figure intrudes on the edges of the frame as ominous tones replace Massigi's fading gay singing. She glances over her shoulder, flees up a flight of stairs, turns down another corridor and then rushes down the stairs to a darkened level where she finally takes refuge in a dark room with trash on the ground. The figure she fears approaches, she glances up and then angrily springs at Lamine, shouting at him, Why are you following me? The scene ends abruptly.

This is her transition out of the market, and it sets the stage for her final performance and death.

The Economy of Art

Aesthetic value is attributed in *Karmen Gei* to many domains. Samba is a sculptor whose studio on the water evokes that of the innovative, brilliant Moustapha Dime (d. 1998). Like Samba, he was marginal to the mainland, to its ordered culture and reliance on tourist or state support. He worked in mixed materials, local materials, and struck strong political poses with his art. His studio on Gorée overlooked the sea, resembling that of Samba. Samba himself is always to be found somewhere on the margins of Cap Vert, in the lighthouse, on his island, at his studio. He is found sculpting a face in the rock in the final scene he has with the police when they beat him and leave him for dead. An *artiste maudit,* his crimes like his art make him marginal to society.

Karmen too plays the role of "artiste." Her lyrics define her as a Senegalese performer, and she introduces us to music and dance in the performances with the women in prison, in her dance at what was to be Lamine's wedding celebration, in her songs at Ma Penda's club and in response to Majiguene's appeal for Lamine, and especially in her final performance at the Sorano Theatre. Her singing seduces Lamine and induces him to set her free. Her performances are set against the spaces of the police order where male regulations prevail, where the dances are confined by prison walls or by the watchful eyes of the gendarmerie.

Prison establishes the site for protecting that order and is emblematic of that order, in Rancière's sense of maintaining the distribution of the roles in society. At the prison's gates and walls, there is a border that protects the social order, the *ochlos,* which is across the waters on the mainland from the antisocial disorderly *demos* within. On Gorée, the trashy women are held within the prison and the normal society is located at a distance, across the water, where we find the city of Dakar. The prison's gates, and the shores of the island surround the women, define the border as located in the space of the water that lies between the mainland and its regulated, "policed" order, and the trash on the island. The mainland is protected from the detritus of society represented by the lascivious and scandalous women. On this island of Gorée are to be found sexuality, lesbianism, Christian churches, and women in revolt—women dancing their revolt.

Karmen's opening dance, in which she seduces Angelique, is provocative, powerfully driven by the djembes, the squeals of the women inmates, and finally by Angelique's acquiescence. As the dance ends, the yard empties and the women are rapidly herded back into their cells. They are disorderly and raucous, barely submitting to the guards who push them toward their cells, clanging the doors behind them, shutting them in.

All is defined in terms of order/disorder, with the prison guards reestablishing exactly those enclosed spaces that replicate the patterning of the social order without. Chaos is contained, if barely; walls and gates become permeable borders through which excitement and noise passes. Beyond, the protected social order cleanses itself of its detritus. Women in prison, as with Bessie Head's "treasures" (*Collector of Treasures* 1977), include women in revolt, willing to sing or dance so as to express their rebellion; women also in misery, in transition, and above all in transgression, willing to speak out, to write out, and to castrate the oppressive husband or lover who seeks to control his woman and possess her erotic charge. When Karmen enters her cell with the other women, they are jubilant—"she's got her!"—and Karmen happily distributes her garments among them apparently with her understanding that she will soon be leaving, and leaving the women renewed.

Karmen's tryst with Angelique is an openly lesbian scene, with jazz tones and naked bodies. It is difficult to imagine such a frankly erotic encounter between women in any African film before this one; its transgressive character occurs practically in the opening sequences of the film. They are completely joined to Karmen's dance in the opening scene and her sexual performance in the following scene. In short, transgression and performance are joined and gendered, giving definition to the regime of art. The reigning social order, the erotic order, and the libratory order of art are presented in gendered terms, permitting us to define trash in gendered terms as well. John Waters called it "Female Trouble" and used the term "trash aesthetics" to define his notions of subversion. They define the dangerous border spaces as well.

In between the mainland and the island, in the channel off the Cap Vert promontory, are the waters of Kumba Kastel. The waters are addressed in song by the blind woman on the beach at Ngor who sings of love. Love let loose, like desire, like sexuality, unhinges the order. Its medium is the water, its message is conveyed in the song. The waters of Kumba Kastel are dangerous: there Angelique, the prison warden, runs her search for Karmen in the prison patrol boat; there, in despair of losing Karmen's love, Angelique will drown herself. Those are the waters Karmen crosses, further up the cape, to reach Samba and his studio; there the drug deal is consummated. These waters are the border area defined by Mary Douglas as the dangerous intermediary space[8] between the controlled domain of order, over which the men, "the police," exercise their authority, and the exiled and controlled "state of exception" within which trashy women are confined, the prison of Kumba Kastel. But on the border between the two, as every adherent of Mammy Watta can attest, lie the dangerous waters of the goddess, she who reigns over love and women. This is the ultimate home for the goddess of trash, as viewed in the eyes of the respectable.

It is no wonder we will see Karmen buried on an island-cemetery, that of Joal, or that Linguere Ramatou will descend to her tomb on the edge of these same waters off Cap Vert in Mambety's *Hyènes* (1992). We see the *marginaux* Anta and Mori board the boat for Paris in the port of Dakar, facing these waters, in *Touki Bouki* (1973), and they make love on the cliff to the sound of the crashing waves of those waters.

We search for the trope of trash to materialize in these waters, trash as seen in the eyes of the lost souls, those transported to Gorée as slaves to be loaded onto slave ships setting out to cross the Atlantic. We come to that image in a sequence of three shots. First, Karmen at Ma Penda's with Massigi, singing with him, connecting to him, and offering him her red scarf, her gesture of taking him. Then a wreck of a ship, a scow half sunk in the water (see figure 6.2). Circling over the wreck are flocks of birds whose cries we hear. The camera fixates on this image to convey the trope of trash in the midst of the waters, trash surrounded by *les oiseaux rebelles*. Then, Angelique on a patrol boat scouring the waters of the channel in search of her love.

In the next scene, Karmen and Massigi are walking on the beach across from Gorée. Karmen looks over the waters, waving a red flag for her warden, her women. When Massigi says, "Tu es vraiment une drôle de femme" (You are really a strange woman), she responds, "Pas plus que les autres, Massigi. Seulement elles ne le montrent pas, pour ne pas faire des vagues" (No more than the others, Massigi. Only they don't show it so as not to make any waves).

These waters mark the space of the women's transgressive performances, setting them off from those of the ruling male order. Perhaps this explains why Karmen leaves Massigi's stage, the marché HLM, to go off on her own, and why instead of going onto the stage at the Sorano Theatre, she flees Lamine into the backstage corridors of its catwalks. The men's order of art has its official and semiofficial sites. Elsewhere the women, out of place, find their own stages for dancing and singing.

Later, in his realm of performance, Massigi, *le coq*, sings surrounded by the adoring cloth sellers of the marché HLM. An abundance of sounds, abundance of colors, the tracking shot as Massigi moves toward us: everything generates a mise-en-scène in which the stage of the musician is framed. However, as Karmen moves away from his scene, the movement changes from a Benjaminean flaneur window-shopping to a flight, from one mise-en-scène to another that is totally different. From the light of the market and its performance to the darkness below, with shadow, loss, and love turned downward—a dark hallway, fleeing, trapped. The value of the market and its transformed staging of the artist's performance is lost; now, danger lurks behind Karmen, whose frantic steps take her to a cul-de-sac where she at last stops and waits. Lamine, the rejected lover, follows—harassing her, destroying any pleasure in the music of the market, ending its exchanges and performances, imposing its dangerous nether side, the site for the meeting of the unknown.

I am reading the market space both literally as the scene for the economy of the market, where the decline in value is measured in terms of exchange value, and figuratively as the scene for Massigi's performance where he is seen not bargaining or purchasing but singing, performing. In that regard, it is not unlike the earlier wedding scene that provided the space for Karmen's performance, the place where the economy of art could supplant the original economy of the market under the control of dominant male powers. But the differences between the man's performance and hers as defiant woman are of major importance, especially when we place trash under the aegis of the economy of gender. The exchange in HLM involves cloth for money, and the market women are in control; the exchange in the wedding scene involves the ruling patriarchal families and their offspring, and insures the privileged role the powerful would continue to play in a male-ruled society. In the latter, Karmen disrupts the occasion, bringing chaos, undermining the orderly transformation of Lamine and Majiguene into a married couple. In the marché HLM, the dark shadow turns out to be the jealous male lover who cannot accept that his object of desire might escape his control. He ends the performance Massigi initiated on entering the market with Karmen, displacing the economy of art and its performative values with another economy that must entail the final passing of value through time, that of memory. And it is death that marks this transition between the two economies. Her flight from Lamine, and separation from Massigi, sets the stage for her final transition.

Before leaving the realm of art for the economy of memory, Karmen must leave Massigi's stage for her own. She seems poised to find this on the grandest stage in Senegal, the Sorano Theatre, the official site for major cultural performances in Dakar. The great site was inaugurated by Senghor in 1965 with its opening play *Lat Dior ou le chemin de l'honneur,* performed in Wolof and emblematic of his authorization of "les arts nègres" from the time of Negritude. It would seem to be her space because that is where dancers of her caliber are meant to perform. The great voice that prepares her entrance is one of Senegal's most renowned griot singers, Yandé Codou Sène, an impressive woman whose voice compellingly fills the theater as she calls on Karmen to perform. From the prison, to the scene of the wedding guests, to now, the stage of the Sorano, Karmen would seem to be progressing within the economy of art. It is clear she has her most commanding presence on these occasions as a performer, that is, as the figure we come to associate with the Carmen of Merimée and especially Bizet, the embodiment of a female love that rises above the pettiness of the men who seek to possess and contain her. In this, she carries onstage the aura of the great artist, an aura whose value is not, as Walter Benjamin has said, derived from the original regime of sculptors or carvings, which was that of cult objects, but rather from aesthetics where beauty or art is not obliged to serve any interest other than itself.

If the original regime for art, as for the value of its artifacts, was grounded in what Rancière defines, like Benjamin, as the ethical order (whose sculptures were made in the service of the cult), then Karmen, like all Carmens before her, gypsies, tramps, women of easy virtue and low birth, would have been regarded as a being of low value. Until she could translate her place into that of the performer within another order, she would have been there for men's enjoyment and dismissal—to be discarded after the pleasure, like trash after consumption. But the allure of the bohemian altered the place of the outlaw from one of low status to exotic and eventually desirable status as nineteenth-century art changed its subjects from the nobility to the bourgeoisie, and eventually to those in rebellion against bourgeois society. The world that is celebrated in late nineteenth-century opera is rightly caught by Puccini as that of bohemians in *La Bohème*, where the marginal becomes the locus for artistic value, even and especially as it distains crass market value. When Karmen first stands up in prison, takes center stage, and dances her erotic dance, she has already commanded value with her aura of the performer. The outlaw Bohème is not simply a figure for free love but more importantly for the artistic performance, which is exemplified in the griot's praises of Karmen.

Cult and art meet in conflicting scenes, as in the old vying with the new for dominance. "Works of art are received and valued on different planes. Two polar types stand out: with one, the accent is on the cult value; with the other, on the exhibition value of the work" (Benjamin 2008: 224). In photography, says Benjamin, "exhibition value begins to displace cult value all along the line" (225), but before yielding its value completely, the "cult of remembrance" offers a last refuge "for the cult value of the picture" (226). For the last time, in the photo of the beloved, something of the original is retained: its aura. "For the last time the aura emanates from the early photographs in the fleeting expression of a human face. This is what constitutes their melancholy, incomparable beauty" (226).

Cult survives, but it is eventually subordinated to the regime of art. Earlier in the film when Angelique, the prison warden, commits suicide, she is buried with full Catholic ritual and Karmen is silent at that occasion.[9] But as Karmen enters into the stage of performance, there, in true Benjaminian fashion, she asserts the primacy of art and projects the value of the original, the authentic, that cannot be reproduced in modern terms without destroying the aura that provides the value. When another woman in prison attempts to reproduce Karmen's performance, she fails to capture her aura, leaving Angelique in despair. But aura, like trash, like love for Karmen, is transitory. A rebellious bird, not a faithful Penelope. And most of all, as the figure of love she must undergo a transformation by entering into another regime, surpassing both cult and art, and that is memory—like Aline Sitoe, Mame Njare Njaw, and Kumba Kastel. All three function in the film, but with cult on its decline, art in the ascendancy, and memory incipient.

Karmen moves through these regimes and to do so must pass beyond the stage where her "uniqueness [as presenting] a work of art" (Benjamin 223) is to be displayed. We see her qualities as a performer throughout. She maintains the distance as a performer, and her aura places her above the ordinary object of desire. Most of all, her qualities are made available through the "exhibition" of her art: that is, her public performances. Even when she dances for Lamine in the intimacy of the bedroom, as this is a film the performance is before the camera. She is caught in the lens of an age of mechanical reproduction, performing the role of the well-rehearsed life of the gypsy lover. And in fact the whole of the nightclub is located right there, underneath the bedroom, as though sharing the space of her performance. The tradition and authenticity she exhibits is already transformed from the object of cult worship to one of aesthetic admiration. The price of this passage is the loss of the permanence attached to the cult. She becomes transitory—a bird in flight, never in repose.

Reproduced in the film, she comes to be associated with "transitoriness and reproducibility," like the Eurydice in Marcel Camus's *Black Orpheus* (1958) who will be reincarnated, after her death, in the young girl destined to take her place—a film version that was also made and remade. Similarly, this Karmen comes after her sisters who prepared her way—Carmen, Carmen Jones, and in another sense, Aline Sitoe and Kumba Kastel. This Karmen is ready for her performance on stage as the ultimate exhibit for an appreciative Senegalese audience. Karmen signals the departure of the cult: she is a bohemian and the figure of love as a rebel, but she is also part of the figures of the past who prepared the way for her role—figures of the stage and the screen, as well as those remembered in Senegalese history.

The Economy of Memory

From object of cult, and then art, and finally memory: Karmen achieves this ultimate transition in the most remarkable scene in the film where she is caught and trapped by Lamine on the catwalk, confronted with the choice of remaining the performer, always to perform her role of rebellious bird to be pursued by her jealous lover, or to challenge death and enter into its economy, the economy of memory. Her authenticity, her aura, her originality, and above all, the exhibition of her performance would have to end before this could happen. And thus it ends, not on stage before the waiting audience, within a staged play, but out of view, behind the space for performance, up in the walkway where the mechanical equipment is operated, where she sings for the last time her habanera in defiance of the threats of Lamine.

In the wings of the Sorano stage, waiting to go onstage, she glimpses the shadow of her pursuer and flees to the catwalk. There she becomes the performance, that is, performs herself—as a Carmen. She crosses the line between performer and performance ("O body swayed to music, O brightening glance / How can we tell the dancer from the dance?"), and as such moves into the realm of the third economy of trash and of value, that of memory where the remembered performance of Carmen's role overtakes her fate—when she must die as Carmen died, to become the free *oiseau rebelle*.

Becoming the performance doesn't mean achieving the transcendence of eternal art. It means passing into the realm of the economy where she will become someone to be remembered; and that which is to be remembered are her performances, culminating in this last one where she chooses Carmen's fate, so as to conclude her final performance with death. But a death not in flight, not on Lamine's terms where he would possess her, one way or another. In attempting to do so, he kills and loses her. But she leaves this last stage, that of the cultic myth of Carmen, not absorbed into the endless cycle of the rebellious women who must pay for their transgressions but rather as a Senegalese Kumba, a Senegalese Aline, who now will have created her own "site of memory," a memory that will enter onto an African stage marked by its own sites of enshrinement— Sorano, Gorée, Joal—all the markers for the national Senegalese memory to write its own tragedy of love, enslavement, and freedom.

Ramaka accomplishes this by moving to the twilight realm backstage that lies between the stage of the performance and the unseen location where the staging is created. Like the scene in the market, it begins with Karmen catching a glimpse of the shadow of her pursuer and fleeing. As she runs from the wings, she climbs the stairs that will carry her up high to the skeletal walkway framed by dangling cords and metal catwalks. A brief shot of djembes backstage, one on its side, abandoned. Lamine's shadow seen walking determinedly behind a curtain. She climbs up the metal stairway. As she leaves, we see and hear Yande Codou Sène's performance. Hidden from the view of the audience is the unseen flight.

Lamine follows her up another stairway, and they meet finally in the space that frames the definitive encounter. Yande Codou Sène's words and performance intercut Karmen's flight up to this final parapet. Karmen sees her pursuer—we do not. She backs away, behind her a large unlit spotlight (*projecteur* in French) pointing toward her antagonist (see figure 6.3).

What a powerful trope this mechanical spotlight presents: the "mechanical age of reproduction," now embodied in this somewhat old, perhaps discarded piece of stage equipment, its eye directly staring at the viewing cinematic audience, at the location ostensibly occupied by Lamine, who is about to end Karmen's last performance within the film's diegesis. The powerful eye of the spotlight stares blankly at us, mechanically. Its presence silently gestures toward her performance, and by inference the mechanical act that is recording it. Karmen stares forward, momentarily still, before taking flight once more up the iron stairs. For a moment, the two side by side: Karmen, the live performer; and the eye of the spotlight, the mechanical instrument. It is as though the world Karmen inhabits, its prisons, bars, and sovereign order, will be burst by her final scene, paving the way for the enslavement of the past to be ended.

Benjamin sees that end in dramatic terms that celebrate the advent of the new technology: "Our taverns and our metropolitan streets, our offices and furnished rooms, our railroad stations and our factories appeared to have us locked up hopelessly. Then came the film and burst this prison-world asunder by the dynamite of the tenth of a second, so that now, in the midst of its far-flung ruins and debris, we calmly and adventurously go traveling" (236). The new day he predicts is to arrive, but only after the violent end of the old order of art and its regimes of value are brought to their abrupt conclusion. With the transformation of art comes the accompanying change in the social order: "Evidently a different nature opens itself to the camera than opens to the naked eye . . . One of the foremost tasks of art has always been the creation of a demand which could be fully satisfied only later" (236–37). Karmen looks back to the past and signals the new age with her death. Is Karmen not the angel of history? Doesn't the griot's song, Massigi's songs of women past, along with the spooky evocation of the spirits of the dead slaves on Gorée, the scenes on the periphery of the prison walls, with the cannons facing outward, the business of slavery, the business of the markets, the business of the male establishment, the business of those who own, who consume, and who expend, doesn't this order generate its debris that the angel cannot help but contemplate as she is blown forward into the future? This will be Karmen's last gift to Lamine, the words of this angel cited by Benjamin: "My wing is ready for flight / I would like to turn back" (257). The angel sees "one single catastrophe which keeps piling wreckage upon wreckage, and hurls it in front of [her] feet. The angel would like to stay, awaken the dead, and make whole what was smashed. But a storm is blowing from Paradise; it has got caught in [her] wings with such violence that the angel can no longer close them. This storm irresistibly propels [her] into the future to which [her] back is turned, while the pile of debris before [her] grows skyward" (257). For Benjamin, this storm is modern progress, the power of a capitalist order to destroy all that came before. But Karmen's path is not arrested by the accumulation of debris because she doesn't remain immobilized in the realm in which Lamine seeks to hold her, nor in the realm of art within which her performance on the Sorano boards would have held her. In the film, she continues through the stages of transformation that takes its trash, its mud, and transposes it to diamonds ("une de ces diamonds . . . voir un diamant et mourir" [one of these diamonds . . . to see a diamond and to die] Boni 17–18).

So she turns and ascends still higher. Lamine peers through the vertical iron rods as though behind bars; all is dark and frightening. They meet on the high catwalk, at opposite ends, staring at each other. Karmen is dressed in red, the color we glimpsed at the beginning beneath her black dress, now in full display. She has finished running. She sings, "Love is a rebellious bird, and no one can tame it." You can't force it, you can't tame it, and "You can't buy it." She takes off her scarf and flings it to the floor. Earlier she had given her scarf to Lamine as a favor, to Majiguene's fury, and then later, to Massigi. Now she tells Lamine, "Love isn't a business deal. If you want to kill me, do it quickly," as he walks toward her. And then, her last words, "Tomorrow's another day." He stabs her and Yande recommences her chant. Karmen falls to the floor. The music continues.

The staging of the market, of art, and now of death have come together. As the griot's song continues, the moment of her death moves behind us, the camera taking us across to Gorée to pan the features of those mourning the dead, those of the past, yesterday's debris, the slaves gone by, the business deal and its sordid value to be remembered and then supplanted. And throughout all this, to the end, the powerful voice of the griot continues, carrying the body of Karmen to her grave on Joal.

The value Benjamin attaches to this new regime of art in today's age of mechanical reproduction derives precisely from the fact that she is now no longer an authentic original performer but "emancipated" like the work of art that no longer "parasitical[ly] dependent on ritual" (224). First in the economy of art and then in memory, she has become a figure whose life will be held up as a model alongside her former sister rebels—having acquired that value Benjamin calls political, as it will be received on a plane where the viewers will take away more than the beauty of the rebellious bird but also her pain as the price to be paid for a certain freedom.

Karmen is now the figure to be remembered, not in performance but in death. What was there before was transient and is now lost, like Samba's ability to have sex with her in the past, like Karmen's past love for him and for Angelique—yesterday's performances, remembered differently after the death of Karmen. The women celebrated in Massigi's song were heroines of the past that led ultimately to a militaristic police state dominated by patriarchs. From the police's point of view, these women were all criminals: Karmen, Aline Sitoe, Kumba, and even Ma Penda who harbors Karmen and Lamine when they were fugitives and thieves. For the police, the past is over, and the contemporary order is that of an established regime: Rancière's policed order, its conventional distribution of roles, each in his proper place, trash put out, over the border. Karmen is now disruptive only in the theater, only in memory, no longer the threat to order.

But trash is never static, even when it is dead. It follows the trajectory toward loss, loss in value, loss in status: it is transient, impermanent. It moves toward a stage in which it is either forgotten, at the last stage of memory, or it is transformed, that is, recovered like something *récupéré*, incorporated into art, into music and song, into poetry—like Aline Sitoe, like Kumba Kastel, and like Carmen.

In the market scene, Massigi looks forward to the new year, the new millennium. He is insouciant, untroubled, pampered, gay like the gay cock. Karmen enters this space of the HLM market following her troubled sense of the loss of Angelique, of love that she can't quite attain, of freedom that seems to be dissipated with each profitable yet pointless consequence of her acts. The scene of gain and profit with the cloth sellers provides pleasure only as long as the movements of the buyers are contained within their sphere. But Karmen turns away from them and their economy, pursued by the jealous corporal who seems incapable of shedding his infatuation with Carmen. She finds herself in a scene that has been reenacted many times over—another scene from another stage. This is not the habanera, not the dance of the free woman, but the male conquest of the fleeing lover, the entrapment and destruction of the free spirit. Karmen might have had an inkling of what was coming. The famous scene where she sees her fate in the cards of the fortune reader has already been reenacted with Samba and her gang members; she already has been warned, already has read danger, already has declared her indifference to what comes, already had lived the encounter with death. Already rehearsed the lines for this final performance.

Now she has entered into the space that all trash must come to, the space between the organization and the disintegration of order. Between the two, the space of transformation, of death and renewal, lies the ultimate danger for the performer: the drums no longer are sounding her dance rhythm, her time is slipping away. In between, borderland of life and death, memory of the old starts to fade away with the arrival of the new year, the new millennium, for the one can only take place with the ending of the other.

I prefer to read this memory extradiegetically: this film is a readaptation, a revision of the familiar tale, the familiar opera, and after many film versions now it is the familiar film of the loose woman who earns her comeuppance at the end. Carmen Jones, strangled by the maddened Harry Belafonte. And Carmen, with a C, comes to realize that this is what will be set out for her. Karmen confronts not only Lamine here, but the ur-Carmen persona, her birdlike predecessor whose fate is awaiting her. That old story has long since faded. Carmen is an old opera, sung many times in many versions. Carmen, Euridice, Persephone— Hades awaits your end.

Karmen struggles with becoming the transcendental figure of art, now: lost in life to Lamine's knife, she will become, as Shakespeare assured his lover of the sonnets, as Donne assured his lover in "The Canonization," immortalized through her transformation into the poetic figure. The trashy woman will die; the aesthetic image of Carmen will live.

Karmen becomes "Carmen," that is, a new Carmen, even a Wolof Carmen (now Karmen) and a gay Carmen, as in Karmen "Gei" when spoken, punningly, in French (*gei* and *gai* are homonyms). Existing between French and Wolof, the two languages she speaks in the film, she undergoes the transformation from the liberated figure at the beginning, whose song and dance give

The year 2000, the year 2000.

Figure 6.1. Karmen, Massigi, and Karmen entering HLM.

Figure 6.2. Scow half sunk.

liberation philosophy to the incarcerated women, to the doomed figure at the end where she faces the ultimate liberation—from fear of death, that is, from the limits of her status as a mere human. She chooses to face death in the face of Lamine's feelings of love that are possessive and refuse her freedom, his male love that is condemned by Samba for being badly done ("Lamine, tu aime mal" [Lamine, you love poorly])—thus setting a higher value on freedom over life.

Figure 6.3. Karmen and projector.

The music carries her after that stabbing, from the griot's voice to her burial, joining her now to the women who had come before, Kumba Kastel, Aline Sitoe, and Carmen.

The value lost in the market was exchange value. Now it is recuperated and returns with a new use, the use value of art, as she becomes Carmen, the rebellious figure, the rebellious bird in literature and opera. Finally that too is released as she chooses death over performance, and she becomes like Aline Sitoe, the Senegalese heroine whose sacrifice saves the dishonorable present by enshrining the memory of a courageous figure from a revolutionary past. Her liberation becomes political, in Benjamin's sense, and becomes more than a performance, or rather, something to be performed in memory because it was enacted in her choice to be free.

7   Trashy Women, Fallen Men: Fanta Nacro's "Puk Nini" and *La Nuit de la vérité*

Trashy women were there from the start, and their appearance was often predictable. Although there is ambiguity about Borom Sarret's wife who goes off to get food for the family—as Borom Sarret says to himself, where is she going?—Sembène is more direct with the model of the trashy woman in a conventional Marxist depiction of Oumi, the bourgeois, Frenchified wife who sells herself for her husband's money. When that is gone, so is she, and the kids and the TV (*Xala*, 1974). The trashy woman, in the eyes of many male directors, had two qualities for which she had to be punished (Chakravarty). She was erotic and she had power. Even if she had only one of these qualities, it was enough for her to be judged and to merit punishment. For Chakravarty, this punishment was an allegorization of the betrayal of the past, whereby true African society (or Indian, or other postcolonial societies) representing precolonial times had been betrayed when the colonizers came and conquered the land, and then took the minds of the women, "liberating" them with modern ideas about womanhood. When Oumi, wife of El Hadj Abdou Kader Beye, adopts the French language, wigs, Evian bottled water, French cuisine, European mannerisms, and expressions ("chéri, chéri"), she comes to define the image of the bourgeois prostitute in the form of the trashy woman. She is shown as sexually demanding, as bossing her husband around, as mercenary, and especially as being in contrast with the quiet, subdued, and dignified Adja Astou, El Hadj's first wife. The contrast foregrounds the decline of the African woman, though she has not yet fallen to the point of becoming merely attractive flesh for her husband, that being the status of El Hadj's third wife Ngoné, now silenced, naked, objectified for the camera and merely a marker for her husband's sexual deficiencies. Simultaneously, her aunt the Badian embodies the other fearful side of women for the patriarchy, the bossy or powerful, if unerotic, figure of the maternal woman.

Trashy women are dangerous because they are "fallen" women whose eroticism threatens male power and control, threatening the men's lives. There have been innumerable representations of Mammy Watta in African literature and cinema. A key early example is Flora Nwapa's Efuru (*Efuru* 1966). Henri Duparc creates a wonderful example of the Mammy Watta figure in his *Caramel* (2005). By the time Sembène gets around to *Faat Kine* (2000), the sexually dominant

women characters have reached the point where they are seen as having emasculated or symbolically castrated their husbands, threatening their virility by
insisting on the use of condoms, or by the refusal to have sex with them (see
Kine's friend Amie whose husband's "thing" goes from twelve o'clock to six
o'clock when she pulls out the condom, or Djenaba's husband in Nacro's short
film "Le Truc de Konaté" [1998] who refuses to use a condom and beats her
when she balks at having unprotected sex with him). The promise and anger
of Dikeledi's act of castration in Bessie Head's "Collector of Treasures" (1977)
is realized in these films. In Sembène's last film, *Moolaade* (2004), the women
come to be divided clearly into two camps: those who refuse to circumcise their
daughters and are shown to be victims of the patriarchy, and those who accept
the patriarchal rule. Those who refuse eventually move from being victims to
becoming menaces to the patriarchy.

If women were trashy at the beginning because they threatened male hegemony, by the end of *Moolade* their value has risen precisely because of that
reason, and they become tropes for revolt—women in revolt rather than women
in submission (d'Almeida, *Francophone African Women Writers: Destroying the
Emptiness of Silence* [1994]; Cazenave, *Femmes Rebelles: Naissance d'un Nouveau
Roman Africain au Féminin* [1996]).

Women filmmakers do not see things in quite those terms. In "Puk Nini"
(1995), in a remarkable reversal, Fanta Nacro presents the erotic Astou, a sexually arousing prostitute, in a positive light. At first she appears in a familiar guise
as selling herself to men, especially to Salif, cynically exploiting his weakness for
her guiles. But if she had been old-school trash, she would have been punished
for wrecking Isa and Salif's marriage and home life. The couple have a young
daughter and are presented at the outset as the ideal middle-class family. However, instead of being punished, Astou joins forces with Isa and completes the
humiliation of the cheating husband, as both laugh him off the stage at the end.
Similarly, Nacro uses the condom in "Le Truc de Konaté" (1998) to show the
power of young women, young wives, in standing for sexual rights and progress.

Similar depictions of the young woman leading us forward can be found in
Safi Faye's important early film *Lettre paysanne* (1976) and the later *Mossane*
(1997), where sexual eroticism is no longer sanctioned, with "modern" women
representing the betrayal of the nation, but rather is affirmed as the location for
female agency.

In *La Nuit de la vérité* (2004), the story is more complex. Power is now divided, with the victimized Fatou ultimately saving the community as its new
teacher while the "devouring mother," or phallic mother, Edna is punished for
both her sexual libertinage and for exercising power over the men. However, if
she is a kind of Lady Macbeth, we also have the colonel's wife Soumari, a Lady
Macduff who works for consensus over against Edna's *dissensus,* Rancière's term
for the political process that cannot be resolved by the conventional social order
and its judicial apparatuses, but that confronts the consensual ways of seeing

the world, the "established framework for perception, thought, and action" with what cannot be accommodated by the dominant order, that is, with the "inadmissible" (2009b: 85). For Rancière, it is only through this dissensus that politics can be effected, that a meaningful challenge to the dominant order can be mounted. Without dissensus, there can be no politics in his sense of a society grounded in equality: "Equality is actually the condition required for being able to think politics" (2009b: 52). Dissensus arises when there are disagreements ("mésententes") over what it means "to speak" and "to understand," and above all, over the "horizons of perception that distinguish the audible from the inaudible, the comprehensible from the incomprehensible, the visible from the invisible" (2009b: 84).[1] The mechanisms society constructs to maintain what is defined in terms of what can be seen, heard, and understood Rancière calls "the police"; and what makes sense, in terms of a policed society, is precisely what can be defined and understood in the terms used by the dominant guardians of the society. An obvious example might be the use of the term "terrorist" rather than "revolutionary," but more significant would be terms such as "art," or any other signifier that participates in the construction of an order of understanding, what he calls "la distribution du sensible."

The feminist agenda begins with dissensus: not simply in terms of an equality sought in a society whose terminology is ideologically infused with values that substantiate a patriarchy, that is, a way of seeing and ordering the world that is "normal," "sensible," "ordinary," and "natural," but an equality that arises from the resistance and refusal of an order whose "sensibility," both in terms of perception and value, is understood to be freighted. Rancière stresses what is visible and audible in his "distribution of the sensible," because these are what is most taken for granted, and thus most given to ideological hegemonical usages in the Gramscian sense of an unforced consensus. Dissensus begins with the notion that such a consensus is grounded in inclusions and exclusions, and our figure is that of the trashy woman, the excluded one who has no "part" in the spaces allotted to proper women in the dominant order. She is not demanding the part that was denied her because she was different, or uncontrolled by the patriarchy, or dangerous in her eroticism. She is not interested in sustaining the distribution of parts that made sense because of the distribution of the sensible. She seeks a new order where she can now be seen for what she is, be heard when she speaks, and finally accomplish a mission of equality that doesn't consist in joining a club that was already there but in reconfiguring the social order. She is trashy because it is only through passing through the trajectory of disintegration, of the diminution of value, through that border region between the old world and the new, that her goals can be reached.

Hélène Cixous and Cathérine Clément have called her the Newly Born Woman (1986), she who will be born by daring to write, to speak. It is in that spirit, and not in what seems a more old-fashioned women's liberation notion of equality, exemplified in the feminism of the old man Sembène, not to mention Cissé or

Ouédraogo, who persist in seeing women as victims of patriarchy, engaged in a struggle to achieve equality with men, that I am reaching for the more capacious notion of dissensus as a new politics of liberation. In one sense, what that means is that we need to strive for a space where the voices suppressed in the past can now be heard; but more, where these voices are not simply echoes of the voices of the past, not even echoes in reverse, but now speak in new accents that resist phallogocentrism as well as patriarchy.

The films of Nacro, especially *La Nuit de la vérité*, gesture toward this change. One key feature will be seen in the decline of the patriarchy; but the other is in the shift away from classical representation itself, so that we will have to attend to the melodramatic, the Imaginary, and especially to the genres amenable to graffiti-type images if we are not to duplicate the earlier scenes of oppression and liberation that have reached their limits to move us because they rely on the same old distributions of the sensible. New reaches of cinema, where Nollywood is not far from the "serious" models of Nacro's oppositional films, are emerging, and with them the familiar modes of African cinema, with their familiar fictional styles, now have to yield to those films that cross the lines between what had been the sensibility of documentary as opposed to fiction. Idrissa Mora Kpaï's *Si-Gueriki* (2002) and Carl Deal and Tina Lessen's *Trouble the Water* (2008) will further this pursuit of a new feminist sensibility along the fault lines established at the borders of the documentary film.

The theme of the women in power runs through all these films, and they therefore must begin as "trashy women."

6.1 *Puk Nini*: Où est l'homme?

"Où est l'homme?" [Where is the man?]
Central Motif: Fall of "l'homme"
Mode: Short film
Genre: Comedy; the Woman's Story; melodramatic elements
Last scene: Surprise, like punch line

Let the melodrama begin!

Isa and Salif: ideal Burkinabe modern couple, rich enough to have a car, which she drives. Salif offers Isa the washing machine her heart is set on. They admire washing machine in store display and kiss in broad daylight. People seeing this react. Astou, beautiful Senegalese woman, arrives by train. She sees Isa and Salif kissing and defends their open act to critical taximan. "C'est bon l'amour" (Love is good).

Later, home. Afternoon. Isa and Salif on couch. Despite her resistance, they kiss. Bintou, their daughter, comes home and sees them. They separate, embarrassed, especially Salif.

Salif invites Isa to go out for a fish dinner; she declines, too much work. Annoyed, he goes out on his own to meet friend at café. Astou shows up at café. All the men's heads turn. Salif and friend offer her a drink.

Cut to Astou's room. Astou massages Salif's toes. He expresses pleasure. Later that night, Salif seen sneaking into house, stripping down to red underwear and tiptoeing through living room. Salif into bed with Isa, putting his arm around her head. (Camera focuses on him, his naked body object of viewer's gaze, with him occupying position typically accorded naked woman; Salif effeminized.)

Next day. Salif as dentist drilling patient's tooth, again in role of "the man." Phone call, makes date. Lies to Isa about meeting. Rendezvous with Astou. Tells friend Isa won't ever find out. That night, Isa waiting up. Astou offers Salif cheb-ou-jen. They make love. Astou asks for money. Cut to Isa home with book in bed. Isa calls friend, discovers there was no meeting. Salif sneaks back, caught as Isa flips on light. Salif says, "meeting." Isa sees him in Astou's panties. Slaps him, calls him *menteur* (liar) and *salaud* (bastard). Salif embarrassed; passive. Isa, angry, goes back to bed and cries, pushing him out to sleep on his own in chair outside.

Next day. Salif heads out in car. Isa follows and sees him kissing Astou. Goes home and showers, cries. Salif reassures Astou that Isa doesn't know about her. Astou quips, "Qui aime les mets exotique ne doit pas craindre le piment" (He who likes exotic food shouldn't be afraid of pepper). Astou and Salif make love. Salif sucks on her aphrodisiac medicine. Drums beat. Salif sweats, torso and face worked up, looking repulsive. Astou laughs.

Next morning. Bintou watches video of her parents' wedding. Isa angrily rips out video, stomps out. Adé, Isa's friend comes to visit. In Isa's bedroom, Isa and Adé talk about mutual problems: Adé beaten by her husband again; Salif cheating. Adé advises they go see marabout (*moré*). Salif crouches outside bedroom door, listening in. Salif embarrassed at being caught in compromising position by Bintou. He cuts a foolish figure. Women discuss seeing *moré*. Isa says, "Why do you stay with him?" (after another beating). Adé responds, "I don't have the money to leave him." Adé tells Isa not to leave Salif because of a simple affair; she tells sad Isa to do something, to open her eyes. To beat him. To come with her to *moré*. "Il est très efficace" (he really works well). Isa is dubious: "*Moré*? Un voleur, ces coureurs de jupons?" (A thief, those skirt chasers?).

They visit *moré* who looks like a charlatan. *Moré* says he doesn't touch women, but when goes to "treat" Adé, it is in another room, away from Isa. Isa spies on them through keyhole. *Moré* has Adé spread her legs, and writes on her breast. Isa is now in male position of scopophiliac; *Moré* leans over Adé. Isa, looking disgusted, stomps out.

Market. Astou buys an aphrodisiac, thanks Mère Binta. Mère Binta says, "Qui aime les accras doit supporter le piment" (He who likes accra balls should be able to handle the pepper). A young man watching gathers some men to beat Astou, who is rescued by other women in market. Couple watching, laughs: "Où est passé la solidarité feminine?" (What happened to feminine solidarity?)

Astou returns home. Isa in Astou's courtyard, confronts her. Asks Astou what she did to have lost her husband. They chat, become friends. Boys sit on wall watching until woman chases boys away. Young girl brings Isa water, complains about beads she has to wear around waist. Astou says it is necessary for girl to learn to walk sexually and for her butt to become well formed. Astou speaks of the secret learned from their mothers and grandmothers, which is sex, but also food, smiling, caressing, massaging. They shake hands. Astou says she won't accept Salif anymore.

Middle shot of Salif showing up in car, singing, "Ce soir nous allons danser, sans chemise, sans pantalon" (Tonight we are going to dance, without shirt, without pants), positioned visually between the two women. Acts the strong male: "Qu'est-ce que tu fous là?" (What the hell are you doing there?). Isa pouts. Salif: "Allez monte. Monte je te dit. Je ne veux pas de scandale" (Go on, get in. Get in I tell you. I don't want any scandal here.) Astou stares at Salif. Isa looks off. Salif drives off in a huff. Astou and Isa laugh. Salif reduced to impotency.

Isa and Adé drive up to bar. Astou happens along, sees them. The three go off for breakfast and chat. Astou: "Ça va?" Isa: "Ça va, il est devenu sage maintenant. Il n'est pas passé depuis des mois?" "Non." (Astou: "How's it going?" Isa: "Okay. He's become well-behaved now. He hasn't come by for months?" "No.") Woman emerging from room in back, crying. Isa asks what is going on. Astou tells her they are rooms for making love *de passage* (on the quick). Women laugh as Isa gestures toward genitals. Salif emerges with white woman and stops in shock as they all see each other. White woman walks off. The women shake their heads. Caught in their sight, Salif is embarrassed, reduced to final foolish figure. They mock him as words of his song are repeated: "ce soir, nous allons danser, sans chemise, sans pantalon" (tonight, we are going to dance, without shirt, without pants).

The three women at end, like Faat Kine, Amy, and Mada in *Faat Kine* (2000), laugh about men and their needs. They laugh at the cock, like Massigi, "Monsieur le Coq" in *Karmen Gei* (2001). The three laugh at the male focus on his genitals and shake their heads at the foolish figure of Salif.

"Où est l'homme?" This refrain is echoed in films playing on the decline of the patriarchy, the mocking fall of the macho, the shrinking phallus, the dismissal of their "glorious" past, their fallen dignities, their former reigns. The relegation to the trash heap of the fathers of yesteryear—this is Sembène's motif in *Faat Kine* (2000), as in Kourouma's bitterly ironic *Soleils des indépendances* (1970) with the decline of the fathers of Independence, the fathers of the struggle, the fathers of the New Africa, already lost when it was new, already no longer the father figures. With the younger generation, in Bekolo's *Quartier Mozart* (1992), Mon Type, the neighborhood *chaud gars* (hot stud) is really a little girl curious about what functioned underneath it all. Mon Type could only play at being the *chaud gars*, because, as Atanga the tailor had already made clear, as the quipping Chef de Quartier made clear, as Samedi made clear, "Il n'y a pas de chauds gars dans ce quartier" (there are no hot studs in this neighborhood). As with Nganang's devastating attack on Paul Biya's corrupt rule in Cameroon in *Temps de chien* (2001) and *L'Invention du beau regard* (2005), it all ended up with a sad joke of a president nicknamed in *Le Messager* cartoons Popol (Popaul), the heir of the last of the Fathers of the Nation as the dictators, ironically dubbed by Mbembe *Le Commandement,* died off and the World Bank took control. *Où est l'homme?* asks, what man? With Bekolo's Saignantes, the entire panoply of the Law of the Father came to an end. Despite the pastoral idealizing of precolonial times as being under a gentle patriarchy (as in *Wend Kuuni* [1982]), it wasn't really colonialism that originated this decline: colonialism might have delayed it, even as it emasculated "the man" in the eyes of the old patriarchy. It wasn't modernism either, although that is the manifest target of those who wanted to set the return to the sources off by displaying the fall associated with assimilation or acculturation. We have passed to the second generation following through the long reigns of Soyinka and Sembène, with their barbed ridiculing of the gross figures of patriarchy and dictatorship. *Où est l'homme?* Was he ever there except as a placeholder for the lament for a loss whose compensatory acting out turned on new representations of the emperor or president for life, his mocked image caught with his pants down in an endless caricature of his phallic shame. "Ne bouge pas!" "Malchance" ("Don't move!" "Bad luck!"). Popaul caught, his pants down, about to shit? To rape? His victim, the "hallucinated subject," incorporates the dominating power figure and is ridden by him, trashed by him: "The hallucinated subject can then become the beast of burden of the 'thing' and his demon becomes his 'jester.'" Not knowing how to laugh and cry, the hallucinated subject turns to the cartoon that demonstrates his subordination, his *assujetissement* under the power of the autocrat: "The autocrat sits on his subject's back, harnesses him, and rides him. And makes him shit" (Mbembe 2001: 167; see figure 7.1).

Caught with his pants down—this is the location in which is situated our hapless dentist Salif, overseen crouching at the bedroom door so as to overhear his wife's conversation with Adé. The decline of patriarchy is not presented here as a gesture of defiance against a real menace but as a burlesque caught in panties, whose feeble excuses are made by Isa the New African Woman, who only temporarily retrogresses into the figure of the weeping betrayed wife. Her real visage, after having scornfully slapped, berated, and tsked her husband, after saying he now has learned his lesson, after his final silly appearance with the white girlfriend/prostitute, is that of the figure for whom the fight to establish equality has long since passed. The sign of that change is not the now familiar representation of the woman-as-man, as Fela scornfully calls "the Lady," but rather the ascendancy of the sentimental heroine in the drama and melodrama of Life. That is the location of a conception of equality of roles, of sentiment, where figures of importance and interest are defined not by their social stature but by their emotional attributes, their abilities to feel and weep, to generate those reactions in the audience, to merit the focalization and identifications that camera and narrative bestow on them. In short, as Rancière makes plain, we have to redefine our hierarchies and genres as participating in a world of making and doing—in this case of "Puk Nini" (1995), framed by a genre that has been increasingly marked by melodrama, by women's films that address the interior spaces of the home and heart.

The distribution of the sensible encompasses the reallocation of genres in the understanding of what constitutes African cinema. The distribution of the sensible engages the conditions for viewing and making sense that now accommodate those formerly marginalized spaces allocated to excessive, emotional charged drama that was expressed in the close-up spaces evocative of feeling and subjectivity. "Female Trouble." Trashy women, then and now, have become the vehicles not for questioning the betrayals brought by colonial conquest and modernism but for delineating the anxieties around the diminution of male authority, the falling off of patriarchy.

"Puk Nini" equivocates between this shift from past embodiments of the trashy and current redefinitions of empowerment, paving the way for a rapprochement with Nollywood. The trash here wavers between the figures of Isa and Salif in their fallen states of despair and indignity brought on by Salif's infidelity and demasculation. At the beginning of the film, Isa is shown driving the car as the couple takes off in quest of the family washing machine; but it was still Salif who decides about the purchase and generously offers it to her. He is the man seen in his office; but she becomes the driver of their relationship. As she spies on him in his rendezvous with Astou, she focalizes the gaze of the audience's prurient interest; and as he becomes the body to be viewed with desire, he shifts into the role normally accorded women. Throughout the film, he fills that role over and over: his body is displayed, he is captured and shamed, becomes passive and pathetic, becomes laughable and ridiculed by the women, exactly as in the comparable scene with the three women laughing at their men's foibles in *Faat Kine* five years later. Rather than Astou, it is he who becomes trash, typically the designation of the woman of easy virtue played by the Senegalese belle in Sahelian drama.

But we don't pass entirely into the world of melodramatic emotion, where the underlying "moral occult" is intended, conventionally, to reinforce the social norms[2]—in this case confusedly presented as a husband-wife couple undergoing mutation under the influence of modernism. Rather there is a conflict between the lessons we are learning about appropriate behavior given the temptation that the man cannot resist. The old lessons of initiation and entry into the community of adults—with control of emotion as a sign of the passage to manhood—compete with the newly mocked figure of manhood itself, as the female gaze has substituted the hot stud for the sexy whore.

Fanta Nacro loves her Astou, her playful, determined, sex-mom (Astou has four children back home in Senegal), but she is not going to be tragic over their separation, like Melé in *Bamako* who sings out her despair in the nightclub. Astou will laugh at it, at the pompous, self-important men who fall for her aphrodisiacal ways, and get her money. She will "beat" them, rather than be beaten;

but she is a model against which the beaten women, the charlatan marabout, and the cheating husband are set. Isa is plain and unappealing in comparison. In life as melodrama, we end with the punch line and laughter at Salif, but in the final shot of Isa we read disappointment and not humor on her face. Between the wife and the whore, it is the latter who gives the final lesson. And although she instructed Isa on how to keep her man, it didn't work, not simply because *Où est l'homme* has as its answer "nowhere," but because the answer to the question Where is the man? has become, look to the genre. In the emerging globalized cinema, genres of pay for play, pay for the pirated copies, and play on the registers of easy virtues and easy laughs, "the man" is now the figure for laughs, and the question will have to be not *cherchez la femme* but *cherchez the Nouvelle Femme*.

6.2 *La Nuit de la vérité:* Dissensus vs. Consensus

> Two households, both alike in dignity / . . . From ancient
> grudge, break to new mutiny / where civil blood makes civil
> hands unclean.

—*Romeo and Juliet* 1, 3–4

This time they are called the Nayaks and the Bonandés, and instead of being set in fair Verona, the action is set in some undefined West African country. Instead of star-crossed lovers, we have many people who lose their lives—children mutilated, women raped, fathers tortured, and others slaughtered under atrocious conditions. Fanta Nacro's *La Nuit de la vérité* (2004) doesn't pull any punches. We have an allegorical reiteration of the wars that have marred African soil in recent decades.

The moment of exhaustion having arrived, the leaders of the two camps negotiate a settlement and, on the night of truth, meet to sign a pact of reconciliation. However, there is too much bad blood between them—blood of the president's son, which his mother cannot forget; blood of the soldiers who died in the Bonandés' attempt to revolt against Nayak rule, blood of all the civilian relatives on both sides crying out for revenge. The Night of Truth turns into a Nightmare of Blood where the Bonandé leader Colonel Théo, who had led his people into the revolt and now into the reconciliation, is brutally murdered.

Nacro's film is filled with desperate macabre images that overwhelm any simple plot summary: it is the basic story of the African civil war, this time constructed in the mode of the post-Rwandan genocide film where the horrors must be told and seen in order that peace might be accomplished. The details of the plot might vary, but the basic trajectory of the story—the tension leading up to the killings, the acts of slaughter, and finally the aftermath of yet another "never again"—remains remarkably similar. It is a story marked so deeply by the recent military conflicts on the continent that it becomes difficult to read it other than as an allegory for real events.

In cinematic terms, *La Nuit de la vérité* is a mess. Can the mess be read productively, or does it fail to get beyond its flaws? It all depends on where we go to locate its politics, because it is a film that aspires to present itself as meaningfully political. The "mess" is relative to the aesthetics of "clean," as well as to the clean—that is, ostensible—political message, which vilifies the spate of conflicts in Africa occurring over the past two decades, including most notably in Rwanda and the DRC, but also West Africa, including Liberia, Sierra Leone, and Côte d'Ivoire. The film calls for reconciliation. It demonizes the figures of men at war as war dogs. It repeats the term "horror" or "devil" to evoke the situations involving atrocities and attempts to represent those events as such. Demonic, diabolic versus the sanctified rhetoric of the prophet Jeremiah who is evoked in the film with his call for peace: at the heart of its political sermonizing there exists a religious, evangelical spiritualism at work.

Alongside this, we have the conflict between "frères" Africans—Nayaks and Bonandés—who learn to become a unified people, a kind of hybrid that is no longer monstrous and evil, which is what the Nayak nationalist Tomoko, at the beginning of the film, calls Fatou, the daughter of a mixed marriage. Now the word signifying the combination of the two peoples, Bonandayak is like the name Burkina Faso—a combination of Moré and Dioula invented by Sankara— just like the film itself that employs dialogue in Moré, Dioula, and French. This represents that joining of two people, though they are not portrayed as really two separate people since they the share languages, understand the world in the same way, and are marked by only insignificant differences, as in the Nayak prohibition against eating caterpillars compared with the Bonandé prohibition against eating snake—and as all such taboos are seen as merely "cultural." With this paradigm, we are prepared for an ending that would look very much like that of *Romeo and Juliet* where the prince (here the president) chastises both houses with the goal of ending the meaningless and poisonous conflict between Capulets and Montagues. "All are punishèd."

Here there are all the ingredients of neobaroque tragedy: Sembènean *engagement,* Shakespearean wisdom, religious imagery and truths, figured in a range of scenes that include the inspired speeches by Colonel Théo, the acts of burying the hatchet and planting the tree of reconciliation, breaking bread in common, laying down of arms—in short, the dismantling of the drums of war (sounded at Govinda, the site of the film's major atrocities) that drove the men crazy with violence. In opposition to these tendencies, we have the president's wife Edna who fails to hold off the devilish spirit of revenge for her son who had died at Govinda when the colonel cut off his testicles and stuffed them into his mouth. Edna becomes a witch of revenge and death, a phallic mother who remains untouched by the colonel's sweet words, by the president's reasoning in favor of peace.

Similarly, as we leave the realm of conscious reason and enter into the kingdom of sleep, the colonel dreams of decomposed, dismembered bodies floating in red water, of a horrific-looking head floating next to a radio in the stream, of corpses like those that floated down the Nyabarongo and Akagera Rivers into Lake Victoria in the Rwandan genocide. Here the images of the symbolic and imaginary order begin to mix as the colonel's aunt leads women and children in creating a series of murals composed of cartoon stick figures armed with guns and knives, engaged in slaughtering children or raping women. At the height of this section of the film, we see a Walpurgisnacht scene, lit by fireworks scattering red, devilish hues of light marking and enthralling all except the Cassandra-like figure of Fatou, who had been traumatized by rape and witnessing the death of her family, and who now witnesses the braising of the guilt-ridden colonel as he turns bright red like the other meats being grilled.

In short, the film turns macabre and irrational at moments, creating a world marked by a cartoon-like figuration of monstrosity, while at the same time it preaches a peaceful coexistence, as with the colonel's religion-laced sermons and the president's exhortations to end the conflict. We understand that the true dogs of war are the soldiers turned mad by lust and violence, in contrast to female figures like Fatou who are their victims. On the other hand, though the colonel behaved like one of the male dogs of war when he castrated Edna's son Michel, he still begged her for forgiveness, felt guilt and atoned. Edna, though a woman, could not give him her pardon. That was the affair of God, she said, and instead she turned into a monstrous phallic mother, unconstrained by the Law of the Father as she implored the Nayak soldiers to return atrocity for atrocity, to turn away the efforts for reconciliation, and to bring forth Death and its nightmarish ghouls.

The two worlds between which *La Nuit de la vérité* clearly moves are the old ones of a cinema engagé whose goals of instruction are foregrounded and whose critique is based on the notion that it is possible to make sense of the world, and a new cinema completely indifferent to instruction, filled entirely with popular, subjective, imaginary images of a particular sort—images of magic, violent emotions, intense close-ups and family settings, radical change and intensity of visions—in short, everything the old guard of African cinema would judge inappropriate and that is now commonly found in Nollywood films.

We can say that Fanta Nacro has created a feminist cinema d'auteur where the woman's point of view is central and where women's concerns over social issues prevail. However, we can also discern another dimension marked by women's issues, that of a tradition of melodrama commonly associated with the popular cinema, as seen in the immensely popular telenovelas and series shown on African television. The "mess," the incoherence comes when the elements that normally compose the one genre conflict with those associated with the other, leaving the spectator unsure of how to respond or what to think. For a film that ends with the "prince's" speech to the community, and with a Fatou-turned-teacher giving the children a lesson on war and reconciliation, uncertainty over what to think can pose enormous problems.

Shakespeare was not unfamiliar with these problems, either. Though *Mac-Beth* or *Hamlet* or *Othello* might end with a sense of order being restored, what the audience retains are the figures of monstrous evil—Iago, Richard II, Lady Macbeth, figures like Nacro's Edna, jubilating as she braises the red, twisting colonel, laughing about the marinade (see figures 7.2 and 7.3). Between the politics of peace and that of the marinade—that is, the politics of serious commitment and the politics of trash—we need to rethink how the engagé film of today might be conceptualized, and how the input of women directors and women's issues play out in the New Africa represented in these films detailing genocide and crimes against humanity.

For Rancière, it makes more sense to see a politics emerge from the film rather than vice versa (2009b: 65): "It is up to the various forms of politics to appropriate, for their own proper use, the modes of presentation or the means of establishing explanatory sequences produced by artistic practices rather than the other way around" (65). That said, we must reverse our usual practice of reading a film as a statement of an ideology, and seek to see in *Nuit* a path toward a politics with its own peculiar heterologies—toward a new distribution of the sensible. The real advantage this provides is that it points toward the future, as it were; that is, toward a reading of the most studiously nonpolitical of African cinemas, Nollywood, indicating a new way to read "political," that is, to construct a politics that takes inspiration from the popular cinema, and, more important, a new way to elaborate the frame and horizon, the elements of our understanding on which to make sense of political overviews. In brief, we need to ask not what the politics of the president and colonel are, as they articulate them fairly directly, but rather inquire into the politics of the witch and her victims. As there are handicapped children lacking limbs in the film, we could as easily ask about the politics to be derived from their stories, their narrations, that are, like Edna's, equally gleeful and gloating and marked, physically, by the macabre—as with the boy who boasts that he didn't cry when they chopped off half his hand and who holds up his mutilated hand for us to see. Between these "naked images"[3] and the image of the marinated colonel, or those of the cartoon figures on the mural that would seem to denote a demented universe, we can well say we are within the orbit of *les déchets humains,* the trash who orient us not toward a politics from below but from sites marked by dementia and mutilation. This is the politics of what Rancière dubs the aesthetic regime of art, which he sets over against the representative regime of art[4]—or, in another binary, that of a politics of dissensus versus consensus, or what he terms "politics" versus the "police."[5] These terms all converge on a form of refusal of order, the "mess" in *Nuit,* which ultimately demands a new distribution of the sensible.

When Rancière uses the term "police," he employ two senses: a form of totalizing accomplished by making sense of such categories as good/bad or us/them, and totalizing in opposition to the formulation of community identities, although we must acknowledge that any community constructs itself in opposition to those who do not belong to it, as in the split between Nayak and Bonandé. At the lowest level, what Rancière calls "la basse police" effectuates a "distribution of the sensible," that is, a designation of categories that provide familiar identities: "terrorists," "good guys"; Nayak, Bonandé; colonized, colonizer. A figure like Birago Diop, who had a position of authority in the colonial regime, was both a *colonisé* and *colonisateur* and thus crossed over the categories, disturbing the distribution of the sensible as regulated by la basse police whose job was to maintain the borders between the categories.

In a crucial example of the porousness of these categories, we might consider the "monstrous" RUF under Charles Taylor, who hacked off limbs to terrorize the Sierra Leonean population into submission in the 1990s. In a brilliant essay on the RUF, Fabrice Weissman, a researcher for Doctors without Borders, analyzes their practices as obeying a certain rationality: "Contrary to a widely held view, the RUF was not a conglomeration of drunken, drugged fighters given free rein to their morbid impulses" (*In the Shadow of "Just Wars,"* 2004: 53). In this claim, Weissman directly counters the imagery of genocidal butchery in such films as *Shooting Dogs* (2005), *Ezra* (2007), *Hotel Rwanda* (2004), and *La Nuit de la vérité*. Weissman writes, "Their chain of command was far better structured than that of their Liberian (and even governmental) counterparts. . . . Backed by mining revenues and resources furnished by the Liberian president, the RUF's war economy was able to dispense with any popular support. Terror played a central role in organizing the rebel zones" (53–54). Although Weissman indicates the viciousness of the RUF, it was far from irrational. The organization of the territory was brutal, but calculated. Prisoners with needed skills, like doctors or mechanics, received privileged positions. The brutality visited on conquered territories served a specific purpose: "The aim of these practices was to drive away rural populations living on the fringes of rebel strongholds in order to create a protective no-man's-land. Further into government areas they sought to sap the confidence of Sierra Leoneans in a government that was unable to ensure their safety" (55). Weissman details the similarity of practices of all factions in the conflict, including the government forces, the Kamajors, and the ECOMOG forces who had been sent to end the conflict. As in Liberia, Weissman writes, ECOMOG was also involved in diamond trafficking.

In short, when the prince at the end of *Romeo and Juliet* indicts all the parties with his blanket judgment, "All are punishèd," it is apparent that the familiar scenarios that have policed the narratives about the conflicting forces in Africa's recent wars, dividing them into camps of victims and oppressors, fail to account for what has gone into the act of construction of the "distribution of the sensible" along the lines of those categories. The "sensible," our reductionist categories of understanding are disturbed when the woman who roasts the colonel is not depicted as an angel of peace but as a demented warmonger. To free us from the straightjackets of "la basse police" we need a means to chal-

lenge the "natural order," an order reconstructed for us over and over in genocide films like *Hotel Rwanda*. While Nollywood challenges the natural order,
be it symbolic, rational, or normative, by its images of extremity, while melodrama challenges the naturalizing constraints of realism or even naturalism by
its imposition of a regime of extreme emotionalism, for Rancière it is *dissensus*
that enables the notion of deviation from the patterns of order to function.

Rockhill's glossary of Rancière's terminology states this about dissensus: "It
is a political process that resists juridical litigation and creates a fissure in the
sensible order by confronting the established framework of perception, thought
and action *with the inadmissible*" (Rancière 2009b: 85; my emphasis). Dissensus destabilizes the social consensus that holds that "every part of a population,
along with all its specific problems, can be incorporated into a political order
and taken into account" (83). Edna is the figure who functions best as the destabilizing factor in the film—the "trash" factor.

The Dead Who Will Not Go

When one first encounters Edna, she is visiting the tomb of her son
Michel. She "sees" him running, speaks to him, mourns him, refuses to let him
go. She refuses to let the dead go, to move on and cease being a part of their
community. Later in the film, the dead continue to make their presence felt.
The soldiers, led by an older soldier Koudbi, decline to take part in the celebration and eat or drink because the dead are unhappy about going unrevenged,
about having died in vain. When the colonel's wife Soumina wishes to appease
the dead, she pours them libations, and only then shares her gourd of drink
with the soldiers on both sides. At the end of the film, in another encounter
with the dead, the "fou" Tomoko speaks to and hears the colonel when visiting his tomb. He shares his meal of caterpillars with him. All are "punishèd" as
the prince intones in *Romeo and Juliet*: all have their dead, not just Edna. Soumina's father was also tortured before being killed; Fatou lost her whole family
who were slaughtered before her eyes. The *nuit de la vérité* is also very much a
"Night of the Dead," and in its most macabre forms, a real Night of the Living
Dead. It may be that the dead, as Birago Diop famously put it, are not dead—
they are in the breath of the world. But unlike Birago's celebration of an African
spirituality that is fundamentally vitalist, here we have, from the opening scene
at the tomb with recurrent moments of spooky music and apocalyptic imagery,
a city of the dead that is morbid and life denying. With the sight of the colonel
roasting on the spit, with his body turning bright red and rigid in rigor mortis,
a marinated human-lamb, we regard the image of the dead presented before
our eyes as the meal offering for some crazed cannibal-queen who attempts to
invite and incite all to enter into her ghoulish realm.

Edna's refusal to let go of her son is part of a larger pattern of trauma, melancholy, and mourning that haunts all the major characters in the film, includ-

ing especially Fatou and the colonel as well as Edna. The familiar pattern we will delineate concerning psychological trauma will be joined to other major interpretive approaches: the role of memory and the archive, the fall of the patriarchy associated with the figure of the phallic mother; and the shift in Rancière's regime of representation to that of aesthetics, in which the privileging of speech is replaced by that of visibility. In terms of trash, this shift will correlate to the larger trajectory inscribed in the film in which the value attached to the Old will pass, as in the familiar pattern of the decline in exchange value of commodities, followed by the transformation and ascendancy of the New under a new regime of value.

The story of melancholy and mourning is well known; its link, through trauma, to the archive less so. In *The Ego and the Id* (1923), Freud develops the relationship between mourning and the formation of the ego. The loved one who is lost is incorporated into the structure of the ego. The loss of love is compensated by the loved one being sustained within the mourner who assumes the attributes of the other, even to the point of imitating the lost one. If one loses one's father, for instance, the incorporated father becomes part of the ego of the one who lost him, to the point where the mourner assumes the mannerisms, the voice of the lost parent.

But the relationship between a child, say, and his or her parent can be ambivalent. And in the case of trauma, the sense of loss might derive from the relationship with someone not necessarily loved but also hated. There is a kind of printing on the passive body of the one who survives, so that what is incorporated can now take an ambivalent form. As Judith Butler puts it, "In cases in which an ambivalent relationship is severed through loss, that ambivalence becomes internalized as a self-critical or self-debasing disposition in which the role of the other is now occupied and directed by the ego itself" (1990: 58).

I see internalization, then, taking three forms—forms that in a sense are identical. In the first case, the loss of the loved one is denied by taking him or her within, holding the person in loss through denial, refusing the loss, and, in the process, acknowledging that there is a loss to refuse by having to refuse it. There is already ambivalence in this refusal, which is sustained by the strength of the compensation for the loss that can be seen in the force of the denial. Edna denies the loss of her son to the point that she sees him running around when visiting his tomb, early in the film, and she speaks to him, to the distress of her husband.

When the loss is crossed by the ambivalence of a barred love, as in the incestuous feelings of a child toward a parent, the punishment for the barred feelings is also internalized, and the denial of the loss is accompanied by the guilt attached to the desire. To want and not to want is to be and not to be, and Hamlet's ambivalence toward his father is manifest in the split of the father into the loved and idealized Hamlet Sr. and the hated Claudius.

Since Hamlet identified with the very figure who managed to accomplish what Hamlet himself desired, to eliminate the father as rival, Hamlet's sense of guilt derived from that identification with Claudius. So he must have internalized the figure of the one he hated and killed, not just the one he admired and loved. This strikes me as similar to the effect of trauma, which is internalized and then later repeated (*nachträglichkeit,* which means the repetition of the feeling of the trauma at a later point, "nach" or after it occurs). The experience of the initial trauma is deferred, as *nachträglichkeit* means something like belatedness, and is usually rendered as deferred action. What is deferred in trauma is the response to the pain and violence visited on the victim. But all loss entails a response to pain, and when the loss entails confronting the situation of the loss, the fact of the loss, the image of the lost one, then the reaction to traumatic pain or loss can take a similar path as the reaction to the painful loss of a loved one—a loss that is recalled and rehearsed again, after the fact.

The complication or ambivalence can be experienced on many levels. Thus, if the one who is lost is a "tabooed object of desire," we learned that the response can be simultaneously denial along with affirmation of desire, whereby "it is the object which is denied, but not the modality of desire" (1990: 59–60), and the desire is simply displaced onto another object. In that case, we can say that the expression of the desire, originally marked by repression, is now made possible: the desire can be expressed, it can "speak." But when the desire cannot be expressed, when the prohibition and guilt remain within, when the loss of the other results in the punishment of oneself, mourning is not worked through but remains. It becomes the form of self-berating and internalization of guilt that remains, giving rise to "melancholy." Freud works this pattern out in "Mourning and Melancholia": "the self-reproaches are reproaches against a loved object which have been shifted onto the patient's own ego" (1976: 169).

The words Butler uses to describe this are crucial; summarizing Freud she writes, "The lost object is set up within the ego as a critical voice or agency" (61), and now that internalized voice "berates" the ego. So not only is the loss internalized but so is the blame: "In the act of internalization, that anger and blame, inevitably heightened by the loss itself, are turned inward and sustained: the ego changes place with the internalized object, thereby investing this internalized externality with moral agency and power" (62).

If the loss is acknowledged, the mourning can be worked through, as Abraham and Torok argue in distinguishing mourning from melancholy, and the loss can be expressed and resolved with time. But if the loss is "incorporated," resulting in melancholy, the grief is "sustained" in the body. Abraham and Torok define this internal space where the grief is sustained as an "*empty space,* literalized by the empty mouth which becomes the condition of speech and signification" (Butler 68). The crucial point now is that this loss can be resolved only when it can be articulated, *spoken,* rather than resting silently held within. And the speech must take the form of displacement, not simply reiteration of grief: "The successful displacement of the libido from the lost object is achieved through the formation of *words* which both signify and displace that object; this displacement from the original object is an essentially metaphorical activity in which words 'figure' the absence and surpass it" (68). Here a distinction is made between introjection, which is the work of mourning, and incorporation, which is that of melancholy. Introjection turns into speech, speech as trope, and thus "metaphorical signification," as in Rancière's "metamorphic" images that express meaning through figuration, through troping, rather than through imitation, mimesis. In contrast, incorporation is "antimetaphorical" since it maintains the loss as "radically unnameable." Melancholy, by refusing to acknowledge loss, refuses the mechanisms of speech that always entail turning repressed desire from the "empty space" within into a space from which words originate, and thus are turned into displaced terms. "But the refusal of this loss—melancholy—results in the failure to displace into words" (68), and the lost figure that is internalized remains "encrypted," that is, permanently residing within the body as a "dead and deadening part of the body" (68).

While the mechanisms of trauma might derive from the painful experience that one has gone through as well as the loss of the other, it is experienced as loss in both cases, and can result equally in the "empty space" within and the need for speech to both name it and to figure it. The naming and figuring, that is, the speaking of the trauma or the loss, is manifest in words and images that reiterate or repeat the experience. And this can occur over and over, after the fact, felt more painfully after the fact, as the deferment of the original experience.

The original experience can be immediate or more distant. For instance, in an article dealing with the Israeli withdrawal from Lebanon in the film *Beaufort*, Raz Josef (2011) describes the loss experienced by the soldiers as reflecting not only on the immediate sense of humiliation in the retreat but the longer-term loss attached to their sense of the nation as well as the trace of that national sentiment in the loss of patriarchy. Tracking back to the origin so as to establish the base for the memory of the trauma leads us to the relationship between that constructed narrative of the past we call history and that subjectively retained relationship called memory. The loss of national memory, as Pierra Nora puts it, corresponds to the need to compensate for the loss by the creation of *lieux de mémoire*, sites on which to tack the points of signification that define the nation to which its citizens belong. The loss of that sense of belonging, as in the trauma effected by loss of connection between the past and the present, gives rise to what Glissant called "originary" thinking, that form of a reconstructed past that locates identity in a fixed, idealized location, like Egypt for Afrocentrists, or the golden age of Greece for Eurocentrists, or the age of Muhammed for Islamocentrists. This religion of the past is secularized with the Enlightenment in the west, and reconstituted with moments like the French or American revolutions, with founding fathers, constitutions, glorious moments of revolt instantiated into statues, films, images, and idealized signi-fiers that are attached to nationalist identities and sentiments.

It is this point of beginning that Derrida calls the commencement for the ar-chive, a moment set into place by those authorizing bodies called archons, the founding rulers who disposed of the power of command, what Derrida terms commandment. On the basis of these twin features, a memory is constructed by the decision to preserve, in some designated public location, that which it is determined ought to be remembered, while that which ought to be forgotten, the trash of the past, is treated like trash and discarded in order to be forgotten. The war over what goes into the archive or into the trash bin is the site of what Derrida calls archive violence, and though that war might be repressed, it re-turns when the trash finds its voice to speak from out of the empty spaces, the excluded spaces, the exceptional spaces to which it was confined. If Karmen can sing after her death, speaking through the voice of the griot whose praises ac-company her to her grave, then the voices of the lost ones, incorporated within the grieving body, the traumatized body, should be able to speak again as well. This is the work of the archive being constructed in *La Nuit de la verité* by the women who had suffered the traumas of archival violence.

That violence will be repeated for two reasons. The first lies in the nature of trauma, or more, the work needed to give voice to the empty space within, and that is the work of mourning, of dealing with loss through acknowledgment, and thus repetition and speech. The second lies in the very basis of the drive to archive, which Derrida associates with the Freudian death drive, a drive to reduce the energy of life to stillness by evoking the violence in life, such as the destructiveness of the traumatic experience, causing one to act out without knowing why, to repeat oneself without remembering why, to become that me-chanical automaton that the repression of violence inaugurates. Freud attaches this automaton to the fetish object in his work on the fetish: it is the object that we want to deny because it is the sense of ourselves as figured in the reification of the object itself. Yosef sums up this point well when he states, "Time and again we return to the archive, to the memory of the past, in order to confirm and preserve it. Yet there is no repetition without the death drive, without violence, without the possibility of forgetting traumatic content that would sabotage the archive's desire to return to the absolute beginning, to return to the original past event" (77). In Judaism, this impulse to return to the original point precisely so as to deny it, to reject the traumatic content that must be forgotten, is ensconced in the apparently contradictory injunction to forget Amalek, the enemy who attacked the helpless women and children in the rear guard of the Israelites in their passage across the Sinai. Every year we are reminded of the necessity to forget Amalek, thus reiterating the incorporation of forgetting into the struc-tures of the archive of the past called the Torah.

This is the situation of the traumatized women and children who paint the graffiti murals and who retell the stories of their mutilation in the wars between

Nayak and Bonanté. Their stories and images rehearse the scene of the fall of the patriarch in the form of the naked image, which is silent, and the metamorphic image that speaks, as opposed to the representational image that sees. The images convey the strategies to convey the pain of trauma.

We see this figured in the scene of the crazed Edna, in whose "triumph" the rational Law of the Father has fallen, despite the efforts of the prince-president and teacher-Fatou at the end to inculcate a realm of reasonable moral order. Their police order cannot hold against the force of the images that are the most striking elements of the film. Of all the images of the film that belong to the genre of the horror film, there are three that stand out and that suggest an appurtenance to three different orders:

1. The colonel on the spit, as an example of the naked image.
2. The colonel's Rwanda-like dream of the dead floating in the waters. These are evocative of the naked images of historical news accounts of the Rwandan genocide, and could be viewed as ostensive.
3. The mural, belonging to the aesthetic order, in Rancière's sense of what he terms the aesthetic versus the order of representation.

In *The Future of the Image* (2009), Rancière presents us with these three kinds of images: the naked image, the ostensive image, and the metamorphic image. These images function in different regimes of art, most notably the representational regime and the aesthetic regime—the former lending itself to the formation of a policed order, and the latter to subverting that order.

The naked image makes indubitable, innate claims that cannot be subject to conflicting interpretations. Rancière's examples are drawn from well-known concentration camp photos. We have their equivalent in the photos of bodies floating down rivers in Rwanda during the genocide or more recently the Abu Ghraib photos of torture. On one hand, these images resist interpretation: there is something obscene about interpreting the camera angle or lighting when considering, face-to-face, something that speaks in terms of evidence, and evidence of an atrocity so horrible that words like genocide, holocaust, and the sublime intrude automatically on any attempt to reduce them to the stable order of ratiocination.

The signification of the naked image cannot be gainsaid without simultaneously denying its evidentiary qualities—to deny the image would be to deny the Holocaust, a crime of historical revisionism rather than a misinterpretation. However, not denying the Holocaust can be accomplished in more than one way; there are images that have become etched into the public consciousness through dint of repetition. They have become archived, and as such have gradually faded along with the memory of the Holocaust itself. Their value as naked image depends upon the memory of the event they evoke, and eventually their place in the archive will be more historical, and then purely historical, purely evidentiary. At that point, the film that depended upon them would be resurrecting archive images instead of exposing naked images to the shock of the audience. That was the work of Jean-Marie Teno's *Le Malentendu colonial* (2004), which commemorates the all-but-forgotten genocide of the Hereros and which depended upon the Lutheran archives in Germany to invoke the missionaries of the turn of the century who played a key role in the events. As *Nuit* depends on the familiar images of the Rwandan genocide, it places those naked images into a dream fantasy whose impact will gradually be shifting from historically evocative to something closer to the nightmarish scenes incorporated into horror films, and the audiences will no longer be able to engage the affect in its original formulations.

The ostensive image equally resists interpretation outside its aesthetic frame. Rancière refers to the image that states, here I am—see me, confront me as a being "without reason," with the "luminous power of a face-to-face" (23) engaging the affect or impact of the image on the spectator (2009c: 24). The "haeccity" of the image-object declaring, I am here, or we are here, requires us to adjust our reactions to the call of the image on its own aesthetic terms. In *Nuit*, the interpellation of the images of the decapitated head floating in the river or the colonel roasting on a spit is meant to elicit our shock, though the former is mediated for us through the colonel's guilty dreams and the latter through the evocation of a murderous Walpurgisnacht. Each tends to freeze our engagement—the naked image in the confrontation with the horrors it mimes, the ostensive with the sense of an art that speaks directly to the viewer. Its terms exclude the sentence, as Rancière would put it, which gives meaning to its expression. Rather, the expression gives fullness to the experience, in terms that can be read along lines that convey the "peculiarity of art faced with the media circulation of imagery, but also with the powers of meaning that alter this presence" (23). That meaning is centered in discourses and institutions that have developed aesthetics as a way of confronting presence, as a way of eliciting from the experience of art all those values and sensations whose meaning constitutes, and is constituted by, aesthetics.

But again, as aesthetics do not work in a vacuum but in a history of discourses and institutions, we come to the image, the film image, almost perversely, like a doctor who shuts off her emotions so as to better treat the patient. The beauty in the sublime might emerge from the sight of a cardinal sitting in a chair that suggests an electric chair as well as the famous painting from El Greco on which it is based. The works are isolated as we situate them in the space of aesthetics: "so many icons attesting to a singular mode of material presence, removed from the other ways in which ideas and intentions organize the data of experience" (23). No matter how the image presents itself, as the ostensive image it is infused with the "dissemblances of art" (24), checking our tendencies to read it outside those borders.

Only on the level of the third type, *the metamorphic image,* are we freed to engage the image with some degree of agency. The metamorphic image, unlike the other two, resists the appeal to a presence so limited as to isolate the "artistic operations and products from forms of circulation of social and commercial imagery and from operations interpreting this imagery" (24). Rancière uses the example of installation art for this third set of images, seeing in such works a "set of testimonies about a *shared history and the world*" (25; my emphasis), and claims that they no longer impose a reading of art as the discourses of aesthetics have generated but rather "possess no nature of their own that separates them in stable fashion from the negotiation of resemblances and the discursiveness of symptoms" (24). Rather, they lend themselves to "playing on the ambiguity of resemblances" and the "instability of dissemblances" that empower the artist to "play with the forms and products of imagery" (24). Again, that play will not occur in a vacuum, and the instability and playfulness will enable the viewer to engage the work on his or her own terms that resist any incorporation into the former worlds of aesthetics.

Of the three sets of images under our consideration from the film, the one that most exemplifies the world of shared histories is the colonel's dream sequence of body parts floating down the river (see figures 7.4 and 7.5). It is certainly marked by the untouchable quality of holocaust representations since we associate it so closely with the infamous reports and news photos of dead bodies floating down the Rwandan Nyabarongo and Abenga Rivers. But its function as a naked image is displaced to a hypodiegetic level since it appears through the colonel's dream rather than in the film's diegesis, or even in his memory. Of course the implication is that in his dream he is reliving a traumatic memory, and there is nothing to indicate whose bodies are floating in the river. However, they do not remain pure naked images: they not only lack the verisimilitude we would associate with such images, and as such the understated quality of naked testimonial imagary compared with the more dramatic images typically created out of the imagination to reflect these experiences, but they are mediated through the dream of a man whose mental stability is called into question in the course of the film (he collapses when he hears the drums that remind him of Govinda), and who passes from a subject in control of the action, as witnessed in the scene of reconciliation and its choreography, to one who is served up on a spit, red and ultimately rigid. We have a pastoral scene of goats being herded at the beginning; we see a herd freed by Tomoko at the end. However, the colonel's demise occurs at the height of the frenzied night when the murder—one might say, the ritual, scapegoat murder—is carried out, and he becomes the object of the ritual, not its subject, and no longer an agent. He is frozen into position like a statue, an object to be contemplated with horror.

For Edna, his death is in retribution for the castration, brutalization, and murder of her son. In that case, his life has value, and his death is the payment—he is not a *homo sacer*. Yet in killing him by grilling him alive, she reduces him from someone who is human to something that is a mere object, in fact, a simulacrum of meat, a dish to be consumed in violation of taboos, returning us to the Nayak-Bonandé division over eating taboos. The soldiers suffering the traumatic effects of war—not eating because of the echoing presences of their dead companions in battle—abstain from sharing the food of the feast of reconciliation, till persuaded to do so by Soumari. In grilling the colonel, Edna reverses Soumari's meal—the meal of reconciliation that is symbolically evocative of the Last Supper—and in its place recreates the Last Supper prior to the transubstantiation of the body of the sacrificed Lamb. She thus prevents his death from speaking, that is, from metaphoric displacement. She attempts to impose the empty space of her trauma onto the bodies of everyone around her, bringing them into the realm of the antimetaphoricity of trauma. When confronted with her husband's anguished "What have you done?" all she can do is laugh.

Similarly Colonel Theo was not able to let go of his trauma by mourning, and now, on the spit, has turned into the very image of the trauma—with his entire body having become that raw, burned expression of transgression figured in the castrated penis. Given his own melancholic obsessiveness throughout the film, one might question his dream's "reality," and in asking whether he is remembering a real event or dreaming a hallucination, we would subject the dream to an interpretation that is not admissible were it a naked image. The images of his dream are cast further into this no-man's-land because as the images appear, the soundtrack becomes mute; the images repeat themselves, and our attention is focused on body parts, especially detached heads, caught up in the current that is frequently depicted as red. There are moments where we see only the waterfalls, and they too have red currents flowing. Nature is marked by more than death here. The realization that these are body parts, that that is a head tumbling, that the radio, shoe, arm, torso once belonged to someone, once attested to ordinary life, and that they were brutally separated from that life, all this cannot help but compel us to recall the events staged around the Nyabarongo— the river intended by the Hutu genocidaires as the means of "sending the Tutsis back where they came from." Only at that point do we cease to accommodate the sequence of images into a narrative and freeze them into a realization: this is what genocide looks like, this is a genocide. For a moment, they seize us in their nakedness.

Then the colonel wakes up, the images cease, the forward movement of the narrative resumes, and the images return to the normal diegetic types used to move a narrative along. We pass on from a moment where a meaning is established to moments where a story is being told. But the story cannot be the same from here on out: the colonel dreamed of a genocide; he told his wife Soumari he had committed a crime; he is dreaming out of guilt. She cannot hear the confession. The words do not come; he cannot shake the nakedness of the image; the exchange with the Rwandan genocide cannot be dismissed. Sierra Leone, Liberia, Rwanda—and one could add to the list others that will haunt the night of truth. The image circulates among the histories and their accounts, adding not to their "truth" but to their insistence on remaining in our memories, like traumas, not to be exorcised but to return from their depths. The film moves between the desire to move on, to return the dead to their resting places and to give them peace, to give us peace, and the fascination with them, their fetishization into nightmarish images that are comprised of the detritus of the lives of the slaughtered. In Rwanda, we would say these are images for shrines, *lieux de memoire* that shore up a regime intent on representing itself as the one that brought the killings to the end. But the patriarchal return to order, the reinstallation of a prince on his steed, standing before the people to lecture them on their sinful nature, can work only if the mourning for the dead has been spoken—expressed. At night, the dreamwork of the trauma will not remain still: the drums return and the dance of death begins in the stillness of night itself.

The drums function as *Nachträglichkeit,* repeating incessantly a beat of guilt that cannot be spoken. As Colonel Theo attempts to confess to Soumari, she refuses to hear it, refuses his guilt, expostulates, "You are a warrior and you've fought fairly," preventing the empty space within to articulate its memories. He winds up not confessing, by making such broad and vague statements of guilt that we just assume he is a good man caught in a bad situation, one he is nobly attempting to resolve by seeking reconciliation with his enemy and reaching toward a broad national consensus. Of course the archive that would require this consensus to be achieved would also require him *not* to confess the full horrors of his actions, thus forcing him into the same situation as that of Edna whose incorporation of her son's body and melancholia is set against the mourning of all those determined to deal with their horrible experiences by confessing and articulating them. These include Fatou who immediately speaks of the horrors when she gets to the camp, the mutilated children who boast of their wounds, and especially those who paint the graffiti murals depicting the atrocities of war.

Colonel Theo has no one to listen to him, has boxed himself in to a position where speech is impossible, except to the one who cannot hear him and thus who cannot pardon him. In order for Edna to listen, she would have to dismiss the voice of guilt within her, which is the price she has to pay in order to maintain the presence of her dead son, the one she failed to protect, the one let down by her husband who has crossed over to the colonel's invitation for reconciliation rather than sharing her burden of guilt, hatred, and revenge. He is willing to let their son's death be mourned as well as to let the body be buried. But he has no control over her refusal to do so because with the end of the Day of the Patriarch they have now passed into the realm of the Queen of the Night, the phallic mother who has taken the place once reserved for the Name of the Father and imposed her own absolute law in his stead. Within the realm of the Law, the colonel can make his confession but there will be no metaphorical absolution. His words serve only to condemn him in the ears of his interlocutor.

Our images are inscribed into orders of cinematic sensibility. The colonel on a spit: the horror film, an image evoking the frisson between shock of recognition and the nervous laughter of denial. The dead bodies floating down the river: the horror dream with its nightmare image, held within an order intended to enable us to separate day from night, dream from reality, peace from war, man from woman, human from animal. The cinematic dream is always framed by the world experienced when one is awake, and conversely the world of being awake is circumscribed by the imminent possibility of the dream taking over. Both of these images undermine the patriarchy and its logos, its phallocentric order. In the case of the dream, the police order is disrupted; in the case of the colonel on the spit, the powerful Patriarch, and especially his regime of Truth, is demolished.

The third set of images, those of the mural, moves us onto an aesthetic regime, in Rancière's terms, where the Law of the Father is once again diminished through the regime of represented images, public murals and graffiti art whose informal presentation joins it to those public spaces of representation in much of Africa that provide the expression of the public's politics outside of those official events organized by the state. In terms of the regimes of trash, we move from the economy of art, which Rancière defines as the realm of representational art, to that of memory, enabling us to approach Rancière's realm of the aesthetic where the political meaning of the memory is evoked.

The murals define public and political art, as did the Set Setal movement in Senegal in the late 1980s (Roberts and Roberts). There the youth of Dakar generated a movement to "clean up" the politics, "clean up" the city literally and morally, and they drew posters on walls all around the city with the goal of conscientizing the populace. It was a movement of powerful activism with public spaces appropriated for political action and political speech. The tension revolved around the sensibility involved in the occupation and use of public space: the struggles over controlling the space engaged the policing of the public discourse. The murals in *Nuit* express the same sentiments.

In *Nuit,* we encounter the graffiti murals first when Fatou and Tomoko are rolling into town on a jeep. Tomoko had just come from the countryside where he encountered a convoy of soldiers and a corpse whose boots he had removed. Fatou, we are to learn, had just experienced the death of her family and rape, and was seeking refuge. The sight of the mural would hardly have comforted her as we see her as a traumatized victim now exposed to images of atrocities (see figures 7.5 and 7.6).

The first drawing is of someone shouting and decapitating his victim with a cleaver; there is blood, and the killer has ears that look like flames, like those of a devil. The second image moves by as the camera tracks along the wall and as the soundtrack gives us a background mélange of sounds conveying everyday life. Now a man, eyes and ear in flame shapes, killing a child, cutting its throat as blood spurts all over the wall. A row of three men, angry looking, with red berets, placed above and beside the child's head. The third panel presents a man whose hands are bound; behind him stand two soldiers, red berets, bodies outlined in white, eyes white and demonic, mouths open, shooting the man in the back of his head. The jeep rolls into the camp; soldiers are singing as they perform their exercises. The panels have passed from the edge of the road, with the jeep, into the camp. The images now haunt the soldiers' spaces: normal exercises and singing are framed by totally different figures: soldiers turned into demons. We understand the message of the murals and move on.

What space can these images occupy? They keep us within some frame of the horrible: we don't know who painted these images or why. We don't know how to take them, why the soldiers would have permitted them to be painted, what they are supposed to accomplish. Perhaps the demonic soldiers are simply the enemy, but there is no Nazi swastika or other insignia to mark them as Nayak. Indeed, their red berets mark them as Bonandé, not Nayak. They are points of entry into the macabre, images that complete some statement about the world created through the acts of soldiers and of the fall of that Great Man whose Name conferred authority and whose law that would justify the soldiers' acts, but who is lost. We have instead a *folle,* Fatou, the damaged goods whose gaze is marked by jangled tones as she walks past the soldiers. The handicapped children who then appear, and whose stories emerge, present a point of connection with the mural whose images, like Tomoko's story of chasing off fifty Nayak, are filled with bluster and exaggeration and yet attest to the trauma of war.

After Fatou settles in and the tears over her story are shed, we pass to the night and the colonel's dream of the bodies and the river. He wakes, the morning comes, cattle are driven off to pasture, and the images on the wall return (24:40), this time with women and children drawing figures of soldiers with guns shooting victims, with more blood splattered about. A woman sings in a defiant tone as we see more women drawing more demonic soldiers with red berets, more women with their hair standing on end, tears flowing; a child, its mouth open in horror recalling Picasso's *Guernica;* an animal, perhaps a goat or cow; more women drawing, one with a child slung on her back, another pregnant; and then the road, vehicles entering on the right of the frame, passing to the left—a motorcycle, a cart crossing the scene, and on the wall two soldiers holding down a woman, the one on the left spreading her legs. Public and private acts are placed on display. The camera holds the image of the rape, the woman now more than a stick figure, with her flesh colored in, her clothes in yellow and white boldly displayed—the shock of showing what is obscene sustained through the bold notes of the song. And finally, a woman alone, a complicated set of figures being drawn, a mural of violent acts with blood, stick figures of children being killed, a soldier with a helmet, another crying out. The wall of a house now more than an exterior space, bearing a message (see figures 7.7 and 7.8).

This is the third space of the image: the one that is least real in appearance, most violent in its actions and extent, bringing creators, figures, and viewers together into conjunction with the "normal" actions that precede and follow the camera's display. The goods on the wall speak only of killing and suffering, and they do so in demonstrating how the screens prepared by mural paintings across the urban landscapes, where the residents attest to their loyalty to this or that belief, this or that political agenda, this or that value, have prepared the way, framed the sensibility for this unknown woman artist to speak her mind through these figures.

If direct violence is too difficult an image to portray for Fanta Nacro, here in these three sets of images we are allowed to relate to them as naked, ostensive, and metamorphic. Of the three, it is this latter metamorphic set of mural figures that comes closest to the film's own representation of itself as communicating with the social and historical discourses about the wars of our times. The woman whose back is turned to us, later identified as the colonel's aunt, is painting, like Nacro, a world whose acquisition is made possible by the sensibilities framed in genocide. They are horror film sketches, rough frames for the storyboard whose creator moves within and outside the narrative of *Nuit*.

When we return to the sight of the mural, the children observe the painters and comment. They see the colonel, and then a "many-headed" woman with her children. She replaces the military man, the Mother who comes to ride over the scenes of carnage. This is followed by a mother and child walking off, in the background more women and children. This time the two principal figures have white eyes—the dead, no longer surrounded by blood or violence, in their own realm. The woman appears to have crutches, and the children attempt to enter the house to see more of the painted images. They recognize and identify the two dead figures before the woman artist turns and grabs for them. They flee, and we understand that she is probably not totally mentally balanced. The children tie us, through their reactions, to the images on the wall and the time within which they are caught. One comments on the black paint, explaining to another it is not marinade. The red marinade for the colonel is being prepared as a world of sensibility is also prepared and distributed by the murals. They do not create this world but the politics with which we frame the figures.

The central question for *La Nuit de la vérité*, posed by the atrocities committed in the death of Michel, Edna's son, the traumas experienced and recounted by Fatou, the violence directed against the children, the nightmare dreams of the colonel, and finally by these public murals, is how it is going to be possible to convey the world of the Nightfall in Africa, in an Africa marked by unimaginably painful conflicts and brutality. Not how people will recover; not how Africa will restore its image; not how these conflicts will come to an end, or how justice and peace will be restored, or how to avoid falling into the traps of Afropessimism. Not why these things happened, either. Trauma and violence are not unique to Africa; the play of global economic forces imposes conditions that eventually result in violent competition for control over resources along with the weakening or collapse of the nation-state incapable of maintaining sovereign power over its territories—these are not imponderables. The problem for the filmmaker is more direct: how can she turn this parable into images? Our three images address the question in three ways.

On the one hand, the dream sequence of the river, freed from the constraints of the symbolic order, can juxtapose fantasies of fearful and guilty scenes using images of what has been shown in newspapers or on television, images that are imagined, in combinations that take pieces and juxtapose them: dreamwork lends itself to the patterns of emotions, repressed and conscious, carrying us into realms of surrealism deployed by filmmakers for the better part of a century, especially since *Un Chien Andalou* (1928). By combining familiar images of the Rwandan genocide, not to mention those of Sierra Leone and Liberia, with the colonel's obsessions over his guilty participation in the slaughter at Govinda, Nacro moves us onto a familiar level of horror commonly deployed in "genre" films, and now exploding in Nollywood video films.

The culmination of the "genre" effect, the scene in which Edna grills the colonel on a spit during the "nuit de la vérité," moves the diegesis perilously close to the supernatural horror video film of ghouls and vampires. Edna now seems insane, with her last scenes marked by violent laughter and crazy motions, placing her on a precipice where the chariots of the gods might lift her, Medea-like, up into the skies or where the earth might open up with a roar as the demons that drive her now take full possession. The nighttime sky is lit up with violent explosions, fireworks ironically celebrating the peace, as the flip side of the world turns to the demonic. We are in full Nollywoodian display, although again, as with the dreams in the first example, we do not cross over completely to the Imaginary, to horror film's unreality, to surrealism's dreamworld. We remain within the conventions of a realist cinema in which the disruptive changes brought by the contemporary world to a formerly ordered society are now figured in the form of the woman, the sexually active or attractive woman, the woman whose illicit sexual behavior allegorically conveys the anxieties of society, typically the anxieties over change (Chakravarty), anxieties over modernism, and anxieties over memories and the past, so that until she is punished the tensions will continue to haunt us. She has to be killed by the patriarch, weak though he may be, weak as in the last scenes in Hitchcock's *Psycho* (1960), weak like Fortinbras or the successors of Macbeth. Weak and late. Peace and restoration seem small moments in the face of such violent upheavals that have shaken the Globe in its Nighttime frames.

Both the grilling of the colonel and the colonel's dreams are figured in diegetic images of the film that are directly linked to the action. They differ in this major way from the graffiti images on the walls, images that are given to us as representations of the violence, not the violence itself. And that takes us to the central question I posed above: how one is to represent these "unimaginable" horrors, how to represent what Rancière calls the "unrepresentable." Simultaneously, one must ask how to give voice to the contents of the empty box within, created by trauma; how to speak one's mourning so as not to fall into the silence of the melancholy?

How can one dare touch without defilement the scene and narrative of the victims of unspeakable violence? How can one dare make a film, an entertainment film to boot, of the Holocaust; how can one dare show images of dead bodies floating down the river? How can one enter into the state of exception and normalize the bare life of its prison-like world while showing that life as human? Isn't there too much ever to show, and aren't the means always too little for the task? These are the questions that Rancière gropes with, asking whether any such representation can be commensurate with its contents, and whether we have not approached the limits of what art is capable of doing (2009c: 110).

These are questions that take us increasingly away from aesthetics to ethics, since the underlying question is that of the victim who says, how dare you do this to me, after all I have suffered—how dare you make my story serve as someone else's entertainment or your profit. And there is also the flip side: please tell my story so it will be known, so its horrors will never again be perpetrated on others.

What are the tools of the artist before these contradictory pleas? The answer in *Nuit* lies in what the graffiti murals represent—not their content but their way of conveying the content. We have the artists, their scene, and those who see the images. And most of all, we have the images themselves that speak in their own particular way—a way already historically prepared by the graffiti artists in the Bronx who started staking out their claims for public art, their visions and styles continued by the artists of Set Setal (Roberts and Roberts 2003) and the expansion of the movement of public art throughout Africa, and finally, the articulations of those whose memoirs and accounts, in music, art, and literature, of the Holocaust and of its subsequent iterations, have prepared the ground for these murals.

The voice that will speak of the horrors will not depend upon artistic mastery to convey its memories or feelings, although any narrative it constructs, any language it uses, will ultimately be slotted into some storytelling tradition, some genre, some mode of narrative so that the account will make sense to the storyteller and the audience. There is no escape from the necessity to choose how to tell the story, even the story that has never been told before and that cannot be told.

Rancière postulates a choice of a style that he attributes to Plato, the "straightforward tale" that does not require the artist to tell it and that does not result in art—simply providing an account. He joins this possibility to a witnessing, a *témoignage* to the fact that it happened, that "there was," even if that which "there was" exceeds thought (2009c: 111). Lacan follows Kant in defining an expression that exceeds the symbolic as the sublime, that which records "the trace of the unthinkable" (cited in Rancière 2009c). The bare bones of the image that reaches toward this unattainable form, again called "simply images" by Rancière, are to be judged by how well they accomplish the task of relating to their origin ("Are they worthy of what they represent?") and their destination ("What effects do they produce on those who receive them?" [111]). Those are questions that are displaced to a second order in the film, since the events that are represented in the graffiti murals are imagined for the film, even if recognizably tied to recent conflicts in Africa, and the audience within the film's diegesis are stand-ins for the film's audience, whose reactions are focalized through the eyes of those who see and respond to the murals in the film.

The speaking of trauma or mourning in images involves more than an equivalency, which is what representation sets as its goal, but is a translation, even an imposition: "this is too much," or the cry of agony, in its ultimate form, exceeds the ability of the frame to contain it. Its excess becomes the site of the abject as something beyond the borders or limits. The example Rancière turns to is Oedipus's gouged-out eyes, which exceeded what French classical theatre could accept, and represented "the brutal imposition in the field of vision of something that exceeds the subordination of the visible to the making-visible of speech" (209C: 113). This is the key point, that the speaking of trauma means the making visible of what had been internalized because it was too painful to confront and express. It is incorporated like a pain that is too difficult to bear, and the expression repeats the sense of it being too painful again. "Speech makes visible, refers, summons the absent, reveals the hidden. But this making-visible in fact operates through its own failing, its own restraint" (113). One indication of the failure to accomplish this need of expression lies in the terminology used to convey it, the "sublime"—something that is inexpressively beautiful, inexpressively horrible. The other is the "grotesque"—too horrible again to be seen, so it is just glimpsed through that which gestures in the direction of the original—"I can't believe it," "it is so horrible," and so on. This limit of speech and seeing, of what is known and can't be accepted, and what is acceptable but not quite known, this is the order of interaction and interdiction expressed as "wanting to know, not wanting to say, saying without saying, and refusing to hear" (114). Between the neobaroque excesses of contemporary horror films, like Sam Raimi's *Evil Dead* (1981), with its banal or tongue-in-cheek dialogue and its violently shocking images, and the ultimate incoherence of the tortured confessions in Michael Winterbottom's *Guantanamo* (2006), we have two extremes of grotesque and telegraphic styles to which Nacro could make reference. She chooses the silent moments of shock in graffiti's anti-art style that works through plain gestures more than aesthetic elaboration. There is an equivalence in the literature of trauma and Holocaust literature, the expressions of the unrepresentational of which Rancière gives an example, Robert Antelma's *The Human Race*, which begins, "Je suis allé pisser; il faisait encore nuit" (I went to take a piss; it was still dark outside; cited in Rancière 125), and continues, in translation, "Besides me others were pissing too; nobody spoke. Behind the place where we pissed was the trench to shit in; other guys were sitting on the little wall above it, their pants down. . . . A steam floated above the urinals at all hours . . . Nights were calm at Buchenwald. The huge machine of the camp would go to sleep" (cited in Rancière 124). The placidity of the abject is matched by the flatness of the tone. Only such unadorned prose could convey the desolation of bare life, of life as trash, and of a state of exception that turns all light into its theme of the darkness of night. The stick figures of the mural, the curved back of the colonel's aunt who is painting, and the children seeking images of themselves in the simple lines of the mural, these are the points of identification that public art, as archive of the horrors of genocide in West Africa, Rwanda, and Congo, is able to record.

The genocide becomes, like the narratives of child soldiers, the limits that defined the end of the social order intended to be preserved by the archive and by the authority of the archons. It is the social order of an *ochlos* or community sure enough of its rights to exclude the Other, to establish its borders and define the places for those to be included or expelled into that state of exception. The authority above all authority, that of the sovereign, ruling over its counterparts in the *homines sacri,* is shown in these images to have lost its control, to have been displaced by the forces that only trauma can seek to express—the loss of its moral authority, expressed by the disorder of a non-policed state. The patriarchs had instituted the violence of the archive, and now in the conflicts that have followed the logic of their ordering, the demos, the expelled, are shown having to live with the consequences. The fall of the patriarch is no longer followed by a credible restoration, or even a weak one, but more by the fantasy of such a return to the normal. But the impact of the dominant images—the dream, the graffiti mural, the grilling—reaffirms the anxieties over the decline of the patriarchy.

In all cases in *Nuit de la vérité,* the fall of the police order, the fall of the Patriarch, the decline and loss of the Law of the Father is framed along gender lines:

1. Edna, who is basting the colonel while he roasts, is seen as a phallic mother.
2. In the images of killings and rape, it is men who are perceived as monsters when acting outside the Law of the Father.
3. In the mural, we are presented with the end of the symbolic order under the Law of the Father, as images of killing children, rape, and violence are painted by women and children who now, without the father, create a new distribution of the sensible by showing fathers as killers, in contrast to the figures of the colonel and president.

To these three indications of the indicting, condemning, and decline of the patriarchy, we have the further central image involving the death of Edna's son

Michel. This is seen more in fantasy and dream than in real time, but it evokes an imaginary order in which the indictment of the Fathers is figured in their castration of the sons, that is, the Father's attempt to suppress the son's rise and eventual replacement of the Father by killing/castrating him. With Michel's death and castration, he is prevented from assuming that Oedipal role. Rather than simply eliminating the son, however, the act reduces the authority of the father figure who is seen as the undisciplined, violent monster rather than as the calm, wise paternal figure. The colonel could be cast for such a positive role, but in his confession to Edna, he is reduced to the figure of the irrational, monstrous killer. The president could also be cast for the role, but in his ineffective exercise of authority over Edna, he is revealed as the castrated or weak father—a representation furthered by Edna's scorn for the use of the term "father" in reference to his paternity over Michel and her revelation that it is Yakoub, the soldier who refuses the terms of peace, who is Michel's real father. Further, in the dispute between the colonel's brother and Yakoub, the latter is accused of being a weak schoolboy, and in Yakoub's response, "we have the power and money," he is shown to be morally weak. In short, there is no father figure who escapes condemnation, who is not shown to be infirm, morally or psychologically weak, and ultimately unworthy of the place of the Name of the Father. The Father is in decline, lost to the sons and mothers who have now taken his place in the phallic regime, whence Edna's triumphalism.

At the end of Shakespeare's tragedies, we have typically a final scene in which the order—read patriarchal order—is restored. But the price of this restoration is often excessive—the blood that sets awash the stage in *Hamlet* or *Macbeth* overwhelms the audience's sensibilities, and the feeble attempt to restore a distribution of the sensible grounded in patriarchy flounders. The politics of uncertainty prevail at the end of *Nuit* despite the belated attempt to restore *auctoritas* to the president in the form of the prince's speech, despite the transformation of Fatou from hybrid Cassandra victim to Teacher of Truth, of daytime verities, to the children in the classroom at the end. The times of transition in England's seventeenth-century Renaissance were violent and brutal, especially for the lower classes who had experienced enormous displacement from the countryside to the city, losing their lands, forced into urban slums, moving into a naissant capitalist system that required their cheap labor, thus destabilizing older patriarchal pastoral social forms. Nostalgia, conflict, a yearning for the Old Guy—the days of Hamlet Sr., the time before Octavius Augustus Caesar when love was possible between Antony and Cleopatra—all this now just a manufactured dream, a false memory of someone Cleopatra's kind Roman captor Dolabella doubts ever existed. Cleopatra's description of Antony as the giant whose legs bestrode the ocean is met by Dolabella's dubious response:

Cleo: Think you there was or might be such a man
As this I dreamt of?

Dolabella: Gentle madam, no.
(*Antony and Cleopatra* V, ii, 93–95)

This is the response to Hamlet's own vision of his father, "He was a man, take him for all in all, / I shall not look upon his like again" (I, ii, 187).

The times that are described as out of joint in *Nuit* are much closer to the horror film version that establishes the dominant imaginary realm in *Nuit*, better suited not to the times of Hamlet Sr.'s reign, or that of Antony, but rather their fall, described best by the more pragmatic Horatio:

A little ere the mightiest Julius fell,
The graves stood tenantless, and the sheeted dead
Did squeak and gibber in the Roman streets;
As stars with trains of fire and dews of blood,
Disasters in the sun.
(I, i, 113–18)

Nuit begins with Michel running outside of his tomb; later Sargeant Koudbi and his soldiers refuse to eat because they are aware of the dead, and Koudbi tells Soumari that he knows how they feel, even if she cannot sense them. Edna speaks to her dead son, whom we can see though the president cannot. "Disasters in the sun" turn day into night, and the scene of the fireworks display, intercut with the macabre braising of the colonel, speaks to the undoing of the old order as the dead seem to rise up and overwhelm the living. The fall of an older aristocratic order in England has its parallels to the fall of an Old Africa in the grip of the globalized economic order and its ruthless predatory wars over resources and power.

The trajectory of trash, with the old value declining until the passage through the border finally occurs, it what makes it possible for the space of the new order of the Bonandayak to be formed. The Night of Truth, like the Walpurgisnacht or Kristelnacht, is a night of the slaughter of innocents, a night that the living must somehow pass through if they are to see a New Africa emerge. The fallen patriarchy pays the price for this transition, just as the passage from a feudal economy to a mercantilist capitalist economy had to pass through social disruption and violence. This reading is so tempting to us because the extreme images of death and dismemberment, from Sierra Leone and Liberia to Rwanda and East Congo, impose a narrative of programmatic violence, loss, and change on the literary imagination. But the "times [that] are out of joint" are also, and perhaps above all, the times for matter that is out of place, which we come to understand in the body of the text, here given as the cinematic text, as times subject to the broader patterns of decline that we associate with trash—as matter subject to the transformative effects of temporality.

Instead of reading forward from the social condition to the film, we can read for textual/social understanding from the film back to society. This would require us to move into the dialogue between the mural cartoon, the figure of the aunt-muralist, and the camera's eye that records this new form of cine-graffiti. That is the "Realm of the Aesthetic" that *Nuit* sets out to establish. Rancière says, "The aesthetic regime of the arts is first of all a new regime for relating to the past" (2009b: 25)—in this case the past being transcribed into the new archives under the Name of the Mother. That can be seen in the failure of the patriarchal *commandement* to express adequately its new order in the oratorical performances of the colonel and the president. As we have seen, the former moves into the new space of the evangelical preacher and the latter into Shakespeare's prince—both sites of truth (religious, western, classical) that the night school of Sembène and the Africanists of his generation, not to mention Bolakaza critics, would have found abhorrent.

Indeed, the policing of the boundaries that established that regime of old-school serious African cinema has now dissolved, not due to the horrors of civil wars and blood diamonds but due to the impress of new forms of commercial filmmaking that have led to the exponential growth of melodramatic video films and Nollywood styles. The "old" now is reborn in fantasmic terms, once shunned by Teshome Gabriel and Ferid Boughedir as representing lower inauthentic film practices. Fanta Nacro's "mess" is to be aligned with a new order beyond the old representative regime of art, one in which it has become possible to mobilize a range of violent, naked, and ultimately melodramatic, neobaroque images in the service of a doctrine that hopes to accomplish a new accommodation between warring factions—be they cinematic factions or armed men vying for power. In the eyes of the old order, that threatening new rival is commercial and trashy; in the eyes of the women—violent, victims, or traumatized though they may be—it is a new order, and despite the pain, it is giving birth to a new day, one long overdue. The men may have their consensus. The women have moved onto a new realm through the politics of dissensus. A sense of that new order can be gleaned in Kpaï's *Si-Gueriki* (2003).

6.3 *Si-Gueriki*: The Decline and Fall of the Patriarchal Order, Part 2

Si-gueriki means queen mother in Bariba. In Idrissou Mora Kpaï's film of the same name (2003), he recounts his return home to Beroubouay in Benin where he had planned to see his father, reminding us of Abderrahmane Sissako's return home in *La Vie sur terre* (1999). Kpaï had remained in Germany for twenty years completing his education, and as he was planning the return, his father died. We are told that his father was a Wasangari, a noble warrior of the type who ruled over the region of Borgu in the past. There is no image of colonialists in sight when we are shown pictures of the former noble cavalier. The turban, spear, horse all bespeak another era, and when Kpaï describes his youth, it was as a male child who spent all his time in the men's quarters. If ever he saw his mothers, it was to deliver a message from his father. He spent no time with the women's quarters, though the women were not sequestered and it was not a Muslim household. The men in his compound were under the aegis of the noble patriarchy, and the boys were raised to perpetuate that rule.

His passage to Germany was like that of many Africans who had gone abroad during the late colonial and postcolonial periods—an adventure in education that marked a change in mentality whose "ambiguity" could only be perceived on the return to an Africa now experienced as an alienated space, even if it were "Mother Africa"—perhaps especially if it were "Mother Africa." Kpaï tells us, at the end of the film, "As a child I was convinced only men could be Wasangari. I was immersed in the world of men and unaware of the situation in which my sisters and even my mother lived. I was proud of being Wasangari, to be noble, to have the father I had, and it stopped there [et ça s'arreta là]. I never associated nobility with my mother, and yet if my father were living today, tradition would oblige him to bow down to my mother."

When Camara Laye evokes his mother, her powers, her feelings, her role in his life, it is very much through the eyes of the African child whose experience he attempted to recapture in his memoir L'Enfant noir (1953). In most other African accounts of the mother's ascendancy to power, it was through her link to her father or husband, or through her connections to men who had passed on and had no male heirs to take their place. The mother's power was often depicted as being due to her control over the household, including that of the son, so that the adult Mawdo, in Une si longue lettre (1979), whose mother finagles his marriage with a young relative, appears ultimately incapable of resisting the mother's choice. The same might be said for the role of the Badian in Xala (1974), the aunt who plots and controls the fate of her niece and who retains her control over the domestic space even after the marriage. Rare is the instance in which we see that maternal reign extend beyond the family compound.

And yet we can find examples in the literature, as well as in the archive. Cheikh Hamidou Kane gives a political force to the person of La Grande Royale who stands over against the men, including those with mystical powers or those seen as collaborating with the colonial regime. Similarly Appiah's aunts, whom he describes in In My Father's House (1992), are seen to have power within the royal household in Kumasi, within the "traditional" Akan house of rule. In California Newsreel's notes for Si-Gueriki, compiled by Beverly Stoeltje and Edna Bay, we learn,

> The title of "queen mother" is misleading to Westerners since the si-gueriki is most typically not the mother but the aunt, niece or cousin of the king. From Ghana to Swaziland, legendary noblewomen have been praised for their prowess as military leaders. They have had their own palaces, feudal land holdings, retinues and, like the king, even enjoyed sexual freedom. They characteristically resolved disputes especially in the marketplace and in agriculture, two arenas controlled by women in most of Africa. The "queen mother" even could nominate the next king and serve as one of his counselors. As Prof. Beverly J. Stoeltje

has written: "A significant number of pre-colonial societies are structured on a dual gender principle, but the changes resulting from colonialization and modernization have weakened the role of female authority considerably." (http://www.newsreel.org/nav/title.asp?tc=CN0154 accessed September 8, 2009)

In Kpaï's film, the queen mother continues residing in her old compound along with her remaining co-wife Bona, even after her ascension to the position of si-gueriki. There is nothing regal about their surroundings, about their lives, other than those occasions when royalty is called upon to perform its social roles. Otherwise she sells salt and potash, raises her adoptive daughters, and lives in a modest compound exactly like those of her neighbors. She exercises no visible powers, no rule, has no visible domain. Unlike the president's wife in *La Nuit de la verité*, there is no conveying of the abject or monstrous, no images of excess that transgress the phallocentric order. To the contrary, she has come into her position to perpetuate that order, indicating that the phallic power of the Name and of the Law is independent of the performance of gender as royal powers of rule are seen as transcendental and not dependent on the individual inhabiting the position of king or queen. Thus, says Kpaï, "if my father were living today, tradition would oblige him to bow down to my mother."

Si-Gueriki is a film that demonstrates perfectly the way in which a feminist agenda can function so as to simultaneously embrace the contradictory impulses embedded in women's liberation and in a phallocentric order. If we recognize that the phallus embodies the dominant social and psychological values associated with patriarchy, we can see that the call for women's greater participation in the social order and her emancipation from the practices that limited her potentialities in the past can be commensurate with the continuance of the rationality of order itself that sustains the logic of hierarchical symbolic power. We see that power vested in the colonel and president in *Nuit*, and in the course of the Night of Truth, of the Night of Nightmares, of the Night of Walpurgis's tempest, order and rule are inverted and mocked. Here it is the opposite: the male Wasangari's order of male riders continues with the si-gueriki herself safely conveyed between the men in their bush taxi to the annual Ganni celebration of royal power.

The scene in which the si-gueriki's role is sprung on us, the viewers, is preceded by a number of scenes in which we see the filmmaker querying the system that excluded girls from secular education, that required girls to be raised away from home so that they would not be ensconced in too close emotional relations with their mothers, thus unduly softening them. Kpaï's mother Bougnon puts it best when she justifies this system of the removal of daughters from their households: if we had shown affection when the girls left, they would have fallen ill and the mothers would have too. "We prepare for death, that's why we don't fear separation." She rationalizes the emotional distance between parent and child by stating that that is what makes it possible to deal with hardship, and the shot of her face, from below, as she states this is meant to reinforce this embrace of practical reality, of hardening of the heart.

The voyage away from home for Kpaï was intended to complete his education, thus preparing him for life. And the scenes dealing with girls in today's village were also intended to contrast with the forgotten past when only boys received any kind of education, Qur'anic or secular. The progressivist side of the feminist agenda is clearly delineated:

> But modernity is finding its way into the Borgu lands. The filmmaker's sister, Adama, has divorced her husband and returned with her six children to support herself as a single mother selling cloth in the marketplace. A young woman employed by the government tries to convince the village mothers to send their daughters not just to Koranic school but to the state school where they can receive an education for the 21st century. With the current emphasis on the key role of women in development and on using traditional structures as the basis for progress, the role of the si-gueriki could become reinvigorated if she uses her authority to struggle for women's schooling, planned parenthood and AIDS education. (California Newsreel notes http://www.newsreel.org/nav /title.asp?tc=CN0154)

For Kpaï, this agenda serves life, not death. The path to education and development contrasts with the agenda of his father's Old Africa where the preparation for death, as it was taught by the Sufi Master in L'Aventure ambiguë (1961) as well, supplanted the material work of laying brick to brick to build the New Schools, New Lives, for the New Age. The path to this New Age lay through the separation from the Old, as Camara Laye had so poignantly reminded us in L'Enfant noir. For Kpaï this dilemma, where the preparation for separation entailed a preparation for death, and yet was also required for education, life, could not be separated from his repeated questions to his mother—embarrassing questions she laughed at but answered. I avoided sleeping with your father by irritating him, she said. Bougnon and Bona, the last remaining co-wives of the Wasangari father, laughed as they remembered not answering the father when they tired of him. As punishment, he avoided them for a month, exactly what they themselves desired. The laughed when remembering how they had found in each other not the rival but the mate whose presence mattered most to them, whose presence made life bearable. They laughed remembering how they manipulated the patriarch by deploying traditional social practices, and yet themselves returned to those same notions of tradition to justify their views and roles today.

The proprieties of the past were gone: Kpaï now spent all his time with the camera in his mothers' quarters. But the question that almost ended his interview with Bougnon, his genetic mother, was about why his father was noble. The question was so disingenuous she stated that she was going to leave, but Bona insisted on answering. He, the Wasangari, had the right to be buried in the compound, unlike other believers who belonged in the cemetery. He was noble; Si-Gueriki as well, though she wept when she learned that she had to be elevated to the role of queen mother, not wanting all that power, all those expenses.

The sound of the long horn called her to her role. The messenger came and prostrated himself before her. The ceremony began, and she assumed her proper position. And the son, recounting all this in French to his filmic audience, informed us of his pride in having seen his father among the riders, never imagining that someday it would be his mother before whom men would have to bow down—presumably including himself as well.

The tradition, like the one remaining male ruler, is king, and the si-gueriki herself comes to play the role that sustains the phallocentric order—even as the invisible state, the invisible colonialists, the invisible global order continue to undermine its foundations. *Si-Gueriki* is not a celebration of that order but rather a testimony to the dilemma embodied in the meeting of the two orders that see in themselves the two poles of tradition and modernity, the one involving the noble preparation for death and the other the practical preparation for life.

But when we read this film against the backdrop of *Nuit*, both tradition and modernity collapse on the borders of the rational during the night of the exploding fireworks. Both films were made in the new century, within a year of each other. Both present us with the African woman as strong and assuming positions normally occupied by men of power. But the *Nuit* subverts that order of normalcy, while *Si-Gueriki* celebrates its underpinnings even as it urges the transformation of its elements, opening places for the girls in the household, the school, and the government. Fanta Nacro's subtext is written out like the graffiti, exposing the remains of the humans as they floated down the river. Idrissou Mora Kpaï's subtext strains to accommodate the modernist agenda with those changes it knows tradition has always been able to accommodate. At the end of the film, he pushes us to embrace those changes at the limits of gender identity and homosociality when we learn of the devotion his two mothers held for each other.

Bougnon tells him that when she became queen, Bona wanted to leave because without Bougnon she wouldn't get along with anyone. Bougnon tells her son that it was the same with her: that she would be "uneasy" without Bona. Thus, though queen, she decided to stay in the village and not to live in the royal quarters at Nikki, center of the Borgu universe. "It was God's will that Bona and I became friends, that we see things the same way. Co-wives don't always get along. With Bona and me, only death will part us." These final words, that see in death the ultimate challenge not to life's ambitions and man's plans for the future, but to their relationship as women, suggest an order that goes beyond what the patriarchy had intended when it ordained that a man could take more than one wife.

"Don't move."
"Bad luck."

Figure 7.1. Image from *Le messager* of autocrat shitting.

Patriarchy is sustained. Despite Bougnon holding the highest position to which a woman could ascend within the traditional order, the mothers continue to embrace the traditionalist economy in the face of modernist pressures. However, most significantly, "only death will part us" were the final words delivered to the son by his mothers—not the word that celebrated his mother's regal position or fidelity to her task as wife of a Wasangari. It was on that note that he thanked his mothers and indicated his affection for what they had offered him.

At this point, we must reconfigure our understanding of the term "phallic mother." Deployed by Žižek as the figure of authority and power who functions outside of the order initiated by the castrating cut of the Father's Law, as the embodiment of abjection, what Marcia Ian calls "the conflation, compaction, concretion of all the most primitive fears and desires of hegemonic heterosexist white bourgeois patriarchy" (7), we must reinscribe the figure into the spaces delineated by Fanta Nacro and Idrissa Mora Kpaï, where the mothers who survive the roasting of the father and the death of the Wasangari now represent the two extremes of the New African Order. As this is an order engaged in the struggles initiated by the global economy, an order that is both post-traditional and postmodern at the same time, we are obliged to see in both the figure of the si-gueriki and Edna, the president's wife, the potential for new economies of subversion. In reading both films against each other, the phallic order that had enabled a certain vision of Africa to prevail has come undone: Edna will no longer respect her husband's attempts to comfort, or to squash, her emotions and powers; the two co-wives will no longer be bound to their husband's word in defining their relationship with each other, or with the camera wielded by their son.

Figure 7.2. Edna jubilant.

Figure 7.3. Colonel grilled.

The image that brings together these competing orders is the still photo of Kpaï's sister Adama as she recounts her memory of being taken as child from her home to her mother's older sister's compound, where she would be raised. Her mother, Kpaï's mother, the si-gueriki, had just finished telling him that her sister could not hurt Adama, her own niece. The story we get from Adama, now a newly independent wife who decides to live without a husband the better to raise the children she had had by different husbands, is at odds with that. At

Figure 7.4. Colonel's river dream.

the moment in the narrative in which Kpaï asks whether she remembers how old she was when she left home and she says she was too young to remember, we see her posed in a studio photo. The photographer used a typical modernist device of doubling the subject so that she would face her own image, here seen seated in a chair, her body facing her double as she looks at the camera (see figure 7.9). The image isn't very clear—it denotes a time past—but shows her wearing a short black shirt, a vest, and a checkered skirt, perhaps a pagne.

Figures 7.5–7.6. Graffiti mural images from *Nuit*.

The floor is checkered and the background a plain, unadorned wall. She is serious, not posing with an "attitude." The style brings us back to the early years of African photography when urban cool was captured in the style created by Seydou Keita's modern camera's lens, a history to which the contemporary filmmaker tips his hat as he discusses the more painful past with his favorite sister. Adama tells us she knew she had a mother somewhere else, not with the people with whom she lived, but didn't know her. When she returned home, she didn't recognize her mother. Her elder daughter, Adisa, now works in the

166 TRASH

Figures 7.7–7.8. Graffiti mural images from *Nuit*.

market. Like her mother, she was raised by another and was deprived of the opportunity to attend school, was beaten, was treated worse than her cousins. Now Adama is "modern" and Adisa independent. Yet the images we construct of them are doubled, like the photo. Modern and traditional sisters stare at each other like twins who have entered into a magic box where the time travel of the image holds them transfixed. We move away from Kpaï and his gentle questions about the emotions and pasts of his mothers, his sisters, his nieces, to engage the images of the women who have both asserted their presence and

Figure 7.9. *Si-Gueriki:* studio photo of Adama.

denied the men's requests. Adisa is not yet ready to marry. Her mother has left her husband to raise her own children. And Bougnon has chosen to live with Bona, not with the king's entourage. Every one of these decisions was something we can view, like the photo, as old-fashioned liberationist choices or as bold moves. The twinned images stare out at us, making their statement, outside the sweet voice-over of their brother/uncle/son that seeks to guide us in deciding how they are to be understood, and at every moment, as they laugh and decide to answer his question, they convey another reality on another level that eludes his grasp. The photo of a magical doubling is the moment where that look is best captured—that "regard," as in the French meaning of both gaze and appearance.

The final twinning really captures it best: the film is ultimately about the rediscovery not of just the one mother, Bougnon, but of the other as well, Bona, who doesn't speak up significantly until directly questioned about her work as a wife for the Wasangari husband she shared with Bougnon. She described their servitude and little "game," known only to the two of them, of refusing to answer him and saying to themselves "good" when he would punish them by refusing to call them. Their twin subterfuges as servants brought them together, living in the same "case" [house], sharing secrets from a husband who brought them nothing but one blanket a year to sleep on. They were women who shared a quiet revolt, knowing no love, except what each was able to give the other and that they could not give meaningful voice to. At the end, there is an understanding of what each meant to the other, and that was communicated to Kpaï who became, finally, their child.

If Edna had lost a child and found revenge, Bougnon and Bona would seem to have found their lost child whose idea for this film had been to rediscover his father and who discovered instead two mothers. The sequences that carry us through the generations down to the girls in school are meant to indicate how far the girls and women have come; instead, by the end, there is another discovery by the son, that his mothers had found love—not for his father but for each other. With that discovery, he rapidly brings the memoir to an end, drawing a line, as it were, at the revelations these two old women were willing to provide. At Bougnon's final word, with Bona and me only death will part us, he ends the interviews with the expression of the pious sentiment that he was enriched and hoped to develop closer relationships with his two mothers—"mes deux mamans"—before extending his good wishes to the viewer. If the aporia is not quite postmodern, neither is it to be located in the patriarchal silencing of the women: it is the son's flight from the night of truth that he could only skirt around, despite his twenty years in Germany—or perhaps because of them.

Though *Si-Gueriki* is completely different from *Nuit* on aesthetic terms, it is interesting that this quiet, modest film, as well as its noisier opposite, registers the decline of the patriarchy, the trashing of an order now generally relegated to the past. In its cycles, it offers an alternative to what Mambety called the present, the time of the hyenas. Instead, it is the time of the mothers.

8 Opening the Distribution of the Sensible: Kimberly Rivers and *Trouble the Water*

What does trash look like? It depends on where you stand when you are looking: the site of enunciation as site of subjectivity. If standpoint epistemology requires us to see the world through the eyes of oppressed women, what would a trashy epistemology look like?

Feminist standpoint epistemology calls for social change and activism based on seeing and understanding the world through the eyes and experiences of oppressed women—women treated like trash and called trashy. The common language focuses on what signifies the lack of value in material terms as well as figuratively.

Trash is what is discarded, what one averts one's gaze from, what repels and stinks, what is the last resort for people who have nothing, what animals scavenge through, what people who become scavengers rely upon as their last resort, so it is the last resort for those who are last. It is also collected and abjected to the edges of town, to the margins of society, to the borders of our consciousness. It is, in film, associated with melodrama and Nollywood, genres that persist in returning for popular audiences, for "common" taste, to commercial cinemas that refuse the rejections of the scions of culture.

In our lives, it is what steams, steaming stories, steaming, screaming, pornographic images that "should never have been published," much less studied. It is our feces, as well. Our urine and our urinary problems, aired outside the doctor's office; our blood and guts, the skin on the surface of boiled milk, as Kristeva has said—all that we wish to vomit up and move outside our line of sight, our smell, our touch.

How far can we go in rejecting the call of New Orleans, Hurricane Katrina, the squalor of the Convention Center, the shame of FEMA, of Brownie-you-are-doing-a-great-job, and worst of all, beyond all, the pettiness and distress over what was destroyed and who was responsible and who suffered and who really cares? Worst of all, the normalization of the word "Katrina" now as synonymous with failure and pity; failure of the government, pity for the victims. Trash, the melodrama; trash, the sentiments; trash, the manipulations and conventions of editing that direct us to their ends.

The epistemological standpoint that starts with "vision and knowledge of oppressed women" is completely familiar to Africanists whose academic institutions were created in the decades after World War II and "dedicated to the struggle for the liberation of African peoples everywhere." The African Literature Association's credo, as it appears on its official documentation, states, "The ALA as an organization affirms the primacy of the African peoples in shaping the future of African literature and actively supports the African peoples in their struggle for liberation" (JALA, back cover). That language, which dates back to the early 1970s when the ALA was formed, was intended to be inclusive of African peoples everywhere, including the Lower Ninth Ward of New Orleans. Its epistemological standpoint necessarily stands *above* as it proclaims sympathy for the victim, the oppressed women, the oppressed black people, the oppressed of the earth, *les damnés de la terre.* And if we were to stand below, *with* the oppressed, then the deployment of the term "with" places us "above." If we were to stand alongside the oppressed, as Trinh T. Minh-ha has urged (in *Reassemblage* [1983]), what is there in "alongside," in "with," in "in solidarity with," that does not posit the speaker of these prepositions from being positioned outside, that does not remove us from actually being the oppressed, because as every voice that speaks *au bout du petit matin,* who speaks for the "jew-man / Kaffir-man / Hindu-man-from-Calcutta / A Harlem-man-who-doesn't-vote / the famine-man, the insult-man, the torture-man you can grab anytime, beat up kill—no joke, kill—without having to account to anyone, without having to make excuses to anyone" (Césaire 1983: 11–12), inevitably winds up saying, "And if all I can do is speak, it is *for* you I shall speak" (13; my emphasis).

That is Césaire's starting point in his voyage home, not his final point of return. For that we have to move away from Senghor's high, parched hill, that vista point of Midi, and come down to boogie in the trash. There is no reconciliation of the eagle, the princes of Mali, of that Black Naked Woman, or of the Lion, the Bull, and the Tree that he sees on Harlem's streets. To speak for is already to be outside that which one is speaking for—to arrogate for oneself a position. For the advocates for trash not to become the advocates of the poor[1] requires first that we hear. For that, we need to go slumming on the streets of New Orleans, and that is where we are led in the opening footage of *Trouble the Water* (2008).

The establishing shot takes place in what looks like the outer corridors of a convention center. Kimberley Rivers and Scott Roberts walk in, intruding on an interview that a faceless cameraman and director are apparently setting up; they are told to return in fifteen minutes. From this point on we are compelled to ask who is doing the speaking, and who is doing the speaking for. Whose film is *Trouble the Water?*

As the voices intermingle, as the camera shots are edited and mixed, it becomes difficult, without slowing to a crawl, to differentiate whose shots we are viewing, Rivers's or those of the "producers and directors," Tia Lessin and Carl Deal. A contamination, but whose? The damned or the sympathizers for the devil? We can easily uncover the hypocrisies and gauche phrases of comfort Bush extended to the people whose needs he failed to meet. But the situation of Tia and Carl, and of Kim and Scott, is more convoluted as we learn that the latter dealt drugs in the ward, engaging in all means necessary to survive the storm, or indeed to survive conditions of life before the storm, and the former have no difficulty in positioning themselves as the political activists whose film this is. Yet Kim and Scott are our heroes in this film, and our devils, and the only way we can walk along with them is by approaching the standpoint epistemology of the street filled with the water and detritus of a hurricane. Lessin and Deal fail, repeatedly, to descend to that depth, as they insist on intercalating Truths at the appropriate moments—Truths intended to uncover the hypocrisies and failures of the authorities and their representatives, from Bush and Michael Brown down to the Navy personnel who denied succor to the hurricane's victims—and to expose the machinery of government that continued the policies of the past that enabled yet another flood and broken levee to visit destruction on the poor black population of the city. Lessin and Deal's is the familiar world of progressive reformers.

We begin the real entry into Kim's life with her own footage. She shot apparently using a simple Sony video camera, and as the hurricane was approaching the city, used her camera to interview her neighbors and folks on the street, asking them if they were afraid or intending to leave. The wind picked up, the rain began to come down; she catches us up in her moments with camera angles that wildly gyrate from the sky and ceiling to the pavement, floor, wall, window—introducing angles and motions articulating the rhythms and excesses. This is the grandchild of Espinosa's idealized vision of Imperfect Cinema—that is, truly a cinema of the people, untainted by the professionalism of the shots that appear on TV, warning the residents of the impending storm, or of the muckraking shots of Lessin and Deal, ironically disabusing us of the city and federal governments' admonitions.

The contrast between the two different sets of footage employed in the first twenty-five minutes or so is dramatic. Rivers is caught up in the storm: she is an amateur, a nonprofessional, a non-truth-teller. In contrast, the intercalated segments of Lessin and Deal are pointed versions of muckraking: Brown or Bush would make some straight government claim, like Brown saying everything that can be done is being done, or Bush saying that no one could have foreseen the inadequacies of the levees, or Rice saying that it is inconceivable that black people would be treated differently from white people. The footage that follows might include a TV announcer intoning how long the knowledge of the dangerously poor condition of the levees went unattended, or how inadequate the treatment of poor people was, given that there was no way for them to leave the city on their own, no buses having been provided, and so on. The juxtaposition of the two scenes invariably leaves us with the exposure of the administration's failings or lies, an exposure grounded in clear, unambiguous texts intended to present the Truth. This is Kino-Pravda documentary filmmaking, with voice-over, or intertitles that convey the Truth, especially intended to uncover the Truth, with the voice of *celui censé savoir,* that is, the One Who Knows. The Magisterial position of knowledge (*l'enseignement magistral*).

There is no postmodern gesture toward ambivalence here, nor toward self-reflection, not to mention any inflection of the Truth. The effect is not only to disabuse the viewers of the dominant ideology of the flailing administration but to convey an ideology that normalizes the filmmakers' view of events.

But which set are we to credit as the filmmakers? With the final credits, we learn that both producers' and directors' credits are given to Tia Lessin and Carl Deal. Kim Rivers Roberts is credited as one of two directors of photography. This distribution of credit—indeed, IMDB lists the filmmakers as Lessin and Deal—strips Rivers of her role in providing the film with her footage, her narratives that inform almost the entire film—indeed, her own life story on which the account in the film is based—and especially her voice. It is a real theft, but that is only the surface of how she is trashed. More significant, in terms of the ultimate politics of the film, is the unstated, that is, ideological, claim that the Truth provided in the film is articulated by the documentary filmmakers Lessin and Deal's intertitles and muckraking, whereas Rivers (which is the name she uses in presenting herself [2:30] when not introduced as Scott Roberts's wife)[2] can only provide the raw materials, or the base if you will, out of which Lessin and Deal are able to construct the superstructure. The Rivers footage is the *material base* in the sense of trash, of a cinema of *mégotage,*[3] constituted by the outtakes whose exclusion from the "real" film provides the space that makes possible the continuities of a linear narrative. The logical connections must be effected by removing the extraneous material. Here, however, the extraneous materiality is presented, represented actually, by the relation of Rivers's footage to the intercalated footage of Lessin and Deal's documentary. Rivers's footage is predominant at first; but as the crisis of their survival is transformed by their evacuation from the city, and then their return two weeks later that led to the meeting on September 14 with Lessin and Deal, so too is the film transformed into something we can call not their story but the story about them, with the images no longer shot on the small Sony video camera but with the professional camera of Lessin and Deal.

The superstructure is the documentary, that is, what is made of the film as a whole with the editing. It is a documentary in that it confers the rationality of a narrative intended to expose the conditions of the Lower Ninth Ward both during and after the hurricane. This is the work of classic realist documentary filmmaking, in the tradition of Grierson, whose goal was to expose the truth to the viewer. Following Grierson, Vertov leaned on Truth, or Kino-Pravda, that is, Cinema Truth, framed by socialist realist messages conveyed through a range of cinematic techniques that were specific to the camera, the lens, and not the unmediated reality being filmed. Here Lessin and Deal's use of Rivers's footage effects a radical separation of the classic documentary social realism from the untrained recordings of Rivers in the service of an overarching Kino-Pravda.

We are caught up in Kim's trapped condition: too poor to leave without wheels, determined to ride it out with the neighbors, and rapidly caught in the trap of her home, her attic, with a dozen others, waiting to be rescued. Twenty minutes into the film, we hear the chilling words of the 911 operator, that no rescue will be forthcoming. The storm has carried its wrath into the city, its trouble. By this point, it has become clear that the hurricane is carrying death into the Ninth Ward, and that the residents must meet it entirely on their own. The raw sewage of Rivers's camerawork constitutes the most compelling portion of the film, by far. Not only because it is shot "from below," in every technical, political, theoretical sense of the term, not only because it is a continual doubled echo of Spivak's subaltern speaking directly, not only because it is Rivers shooting and recording her own voice and perceptions, but her direct articulation of the situation is entirely centered in her immediate situation, one entirely captured in the interactions with and voices of her neighbors, family, and friends, who are facing imminent death.

The most spectacular, unforgettable moment of that confrontation occurs with Lessin and Deal's intercalated soundtrack of a 911 call of a woman with twelve children trapped in an attic with no way to get out (22:00). In contrast, Rivers and her family and neighbors are saved by Larry, a friend who shows up on a boxing bag that he uses to bring the people in her house out, two at a time, and lead them to higher ground. As we are caught in a limbo, a true state of exception, where survival was in question, before Larry's arrival, before the 911 call, Rivers records her own pedestrian presentation of her condition as though speaking to posterity: "Me and my neighbor Nicole don't know how long we're going to be in here, but doing the best we can." Lessin and Deal introject a backdrop of music pounding to a regular beat, signifying danger; they slip in an intertitle as the water rises, "The New Orleans levee system is failing" (16:24). The water rises, the images become chaotic as the inhabitants of the house head upward to the crawl space under the roof. We have to suffer through an intercalated scene of Michael Brown on television stating the readiness of FEMA to respond to anything before returning to the riposte Lessin and Deal have prepared, that is, the material immediacy of Rivers's own footage at that moment. We see the roof, with the water streaming in.

Uneven camera movements mark the panning across the faces of the people trapped in the crawl space, and then again, back to TV footage of a reporter down on the streets speaking to the national audience. Then the almost perfect sequence of shots that bring us into the moment, Rivers calming down and telling Moms, one of her older neighbors, that she can't leave the crawl space and descend for a smoke, and Rivers's shots as she moves us through the space out to the window, the ledge, her dogs perched on what appears to be a portion of some roofing, and then down into the flood below. A view of hellish water, troubled water, encased by shots of fragmented windows, walls, detritus and discombobulated spaces rendered in terms of light and speckled darkness. Without an ascent into the realm of art, here is the closest effect of the surreal edge of existence, the moment where survival peers at its opponent, uncertainly clinging on.

Of course, this is the moment Lessin and Deal choose to present Bush's idiotically smiling face, the moment they choose to dismantle a failed state's response to its poorest citizens, those soon to be represented by the Republican worldview as a cohort of thieves and drug addicts who are getting what they deserved.

Rivers's footage of the flooding, the breaking of the levee, and the timely arrival of Larry are recorded, along with Rivers's relief at his appearance and shock at the news of the levee breaking. Organ music (21:57) rises, and the voice-over of the 911 call for two minutes rivets us.

We can't help but be riveted. If the footage now were more professional, instead of purely commensurate with the flooded streets and the howling wind; if we were not shifted about by the movements of the camera, the voice of Rivers trapped in her crawl space, if we had not been told repeatedly what to think about this experience by the continual interventions of the "competent" professional editors, the directing hand of Lessin and Deal, we would perhaps not have been able to encounter this next moment with its full heteroglossia, its contaminated horror. Because what follows is a pure horror, encased in all the mixed trash of the documentary and the recordings, the Truth and its messy materiality, now reduced to a shocking voice that asks the disinterested operator, "You mean we gonna die?" The operator answers, the police aren't coming in the weather. "So I'm gonna die?" No answer. "Hello?" "Yeah"; the operator meaning, I can't do anything; meaning, what do you want me to say; meaning, that's the way it is; meaning, there is no help at this end why put the burden on me; but still there to hear and record the quiet, plaintive, not yet desperate voice say, "I can't get out." We never hear the outcome of this (17:24–24:02).

Rivers and her entourage are taken out; they struggle but manage to get themselves and thirty others out of the rotting city. We never learn about the woman caught in the attic with twelve children and uncounted others.

The impact of the editing, the voice they captured, the framing, all generate a new conception of hybrid cinema. Not grounded in ethnic mixing or cultural transplantations, not in a dialectic informed from the start by an idea toward which the editing directs us, not subordinated to an aesthetic of class or race, but a cinema of trash that eschews any reduction of the trash to a meaning. We get it, but we have to move on beyond the first or second or third message to the immediate moment of water rising and shit really happening, recorded for posterity.

Kimberley Rivers signs her name to this film for us; she fills it out with her life, her struggling determination that carries us along through the rest of the sequel to the hurricane experience. She lifts us with her rap song about her life, "Amazing," and it takes little for us to concede the adequacy of the attribution to this strong black woman. She seems far from the notion of the subaltern woman prevented from occupying a site of enunciation that would reach to those empowered to determine the shape of society and its dominant order. What she does do, however, is supply the images, words, and most of all presence that enable us to bear up when the words "So I'm gonna die" reach us, and stretch us to our limits in the desperate attempt to cross the unbearable barrier of being an audience that cannot save that anonymous woman and her twelve little children, despite our strongest desire to help. But helpless to do more, to do anything, we can only rail against those indicted in the film, Bush, Brown, Nagin, Rice, the Navy officers who drove the crowds seeking refuge away from their base, and finally the police who stop and frisk Rivers and her party when they are walking down the street after the storm, filming the debris left throughout their neighborhood.

Trash cinema begs us to go beyond the initial impulse of imperfect cinema to articulate a dialectic originating from below. It is difficult to imagine a notion of action alongside the mounds of trash that settled into place after the hurricane and flooding wrought so much trouble for the Lower Ninth Ward. That's why Rivers's footage and recording are so invaluable. They are the site for a newfound enunciation, one that must struggle not only against the hopelessly lost figure of Bush and his mouthpieces, but also, more especially, against the easy and obvious Truths generated by the mechanisms of Lessin and Deal that cannot enable any subalterns to speak, and that actually stifle them by speaking for them. More importantly, we must learn to look and listen in new ways if Rivers's footage is to open the distribution of the sensible (*partage du sensible*) to a dissensus on which a cinema of trash can be founded.

9 Abderrahmane Sissako's *Bamako* and the Image: Trash in Its Materiality

Individual and social processes correlate with broader patterns of consumption, what Bataille terms appropriation, and with its opposite, expenditure or excretion. With larger social systems, the quest for accumulation of capital is the measure of consumption, enabled by the exploitation of those whose labor and goods, lands and cultural possessions, are used and discarded, left in the dumping grounds for "eaters of leftovers," Olunde's scornful terms for his father in *Death and the King's Horseman* (1975). The leftovers are the garbage whose forms have multiplied in the global South since neocolonialism and globalization have imposed their orders: *les déchets humains, les damnés de la. terre, los olvidados,* the people associated with the waste products, the endpoint of processes of production and consumption in the north, the inhabitants of the dumping grounds where trash pickers live. The rubbish tip, abjected from the center of town, away from the wealthy quartiers up on the Plateau where the fresher air protects the colonizers from the miasmas of those down below. Treichville, the Medina, the Cape Flats versus the Plateau, Bastos, Cocody. The architecture of colonialism was built around this division, and in our analysis of *Bamako,* we take one aspect of this division, the split between idealism and materialism on which the Hegelian dialectic, the logocentric ideal, is based: that of the superiority of the idea over the material, of logos over physis. Further, we take the material substratum or base, no matter how necessary for the ideal superstructure, to be closer to the excremental, expended, projected, discarded, suppressed elements of the systems of production and consumption. In a sense, logos cannot function without this relation to physis: it is itself ideational only by virtue of its distance from, its height above, the material.

Bamako is a film, more than most, of ideas. The Grand Idea: that debt is crushing Africa as the result of World Bank policies that serve the interests of the wealthy powers and continue the exploitation of the continent. The "African Story": European imperialism, mutatis mutandis the global in its various formulations, now appearing with a series of key terms that mark this historical conjunction. In the case of Mali, these would include gold, and then cotton (elsewhere it is rice, coffee, cacao, along with diamonds, coltan, tin, lumber), as well as clandestine emigration, the failure of the state, corruption, privatization, and neoliberalism, and the consequential misery, low life expectancy, poor health and education, lack of decent water, food, and so on. This is not Sissako's usual set of terms for portraying Africa, as he has previously emphasized much that is beautiful, has dignity, and is to be admired, despite the shadow of unequal wealth distribution between Europe and Africa. In *La Vie sur terre* (1999), he sets the excesses and consumption of the North (specifically France) against the old-fashioned technologies of the South (here Mali), but France is distant, and the encounters between people pedaling on bicycles in the village of Sokolo in Mali are not marked by an envy for vehicles with more powerful engines. In fact, the slower pace of the bicycle ride and the evening stroll enable a connection with the landscape and with others to be made, evoking the beauty of Sissako's humanism. Sissako draws upon Césaire to guide his ideas about the splendor of his homeland and the people. Despite the material impoverishment and hardship, *La Vie sur terre* is celebratory in the way that Césaire's epic *Cahier* (1983) turns lyrical and celebratory of Negritude at the end of the poet's long trajectory home.

Heremakono (2002) offers more of a mixed message. But even there, despite the strong images of death, of illegal emigrants washed up on the beach of Nouadhibou, it is the figure of the young child Khatra that sustains us in the end with his certainty about making his way through life. And with the apprenticeships of the children, the girl learning music and the boy electrical repairs, our overwhelming impression is the opposite of stagnation.

Bamako is different. While there is still a young child, Ina, the daughter of Chaka and Melé, she is much more passive and vulnerable: she appears mostly in scenes in which her parents hover over her, apparently concerned about her fever or getting her to sleep. Chaka is primarily charged with her care, and at the end of the film he puts her to bed and goes off to commit suicide, perhaps because Melé is about to leave him or because he sees life in such desolate terms. Unlike *La vie sur terre* with its scenes of playful flirting, *Bamako* is more consistently bleak: it opens with the shot of Chaka walking at night, coming upon a dead dog. And toward the end, when he's committed suicide, a dog comes and sniffs at his body. In between, we are treated to a series of speeches, some lengthy, on the failures of the IMF and World Bank policies of development in Africa. To be sure, Melé is very beautiful and the sonorities of her voice are stressed—but in contrast to the singing at the end of *Heremakono*, her last performance is marked by her tears, and in the scene following Chaka's suicide, we see her wrapped in widow's weeds, now silenced and diminished as she appears not in the center of the screen in close-ups that set off her beauty but in a long shot that shows her in mourning, needing the assistance of another woman and reduced to the understated figure of sorrow.

Bamako is marked by a set of ideas that constitute a strong diatribe against neoliberalism and globalization, and by narratives and images that present the materiality of life and death in the quartier of Hamdallaye where the action is set. The two poles—the idea and the material: on the one hand, the trial, with its procedures, structure, and speeches; on the other, the everyday life of the people in and around the compound. The declaiming of ideas sets off the emotional drama of people's lives encased within their materiality, surrounded by the expressive material side of life that becomes the image for the camera. All this we can read in terms of the joint figure of what Rancière calls the sentence-image, a concept that allows us to highlight the contradictory and conflictual qualities of the material as the site of the struggle over appropriation and expulsion, and simultaneously to hold onto Sissako's insistence on the importance of the idea, his Césairean humanism, that sustains his notion of the community, an African community under duress.

The problem posed by *Bamako* is simple: if we take its dogma straight, that is, take the film for its message alone, we not only reduce all the nondiscursive qualities to dross, we fall into the trap of the message-film for which the work of hermeneutics subsumes all other cinematic, visual, and ultimately material dimensions. This ultimately results in the dismissal of the message itself as no longer necessary, no longer functional, no longer even audible. My interest does not lie in saving the message here, which in any event is not being called into question as such, as much as in opening up the experience of the film; and for that, the sentence-image serves as a device to enable me to do so.

Rancière writes of Vanessa Beecroft's video installation showing upright naked torsos of female bodies in such a way as to enable us to move on from a preoccupation with denouncing the link between artistic stereotypes and female stereotypes (2009c: 64). There is a point, writes Rancière, where the strangeness of the bodies "seems instead to suspend any such interpretation, to allow these presences their mystery" (64). He sees in this movement a shift from the "querying of perpetual stereotypes . . . towards a quite different interest in the uncertain boundaries between the familiar and the strange, the real and the symbolic" (64). I am interested in a similar shift in my reading of *Bamako*—not so as to eliminate our commitment to the idea that governs the film's discourse, but to look elsewhere so as to think otherwise (*penser autre*), as Khatibi would have had it. To do so, we have to lay out briefly what the sentence-image struggles against.

For Rancière, the conventional relationship between text and image in what he terms the "representative" regime (2009b: 91) conforms to a poiesis of mimesis that was dominant in western art until the twentieth century, and that has dominated African cinema since its inception. Generally speaking, the coherence of such works of art was "policed" by rules and conventions that determined values based upon common understandings of people's identities, the positive or negative roles they play in society, or more broadly, what is understood to be visible or invisible, audible or inaudible, sayable or unsayable (2009b: 89). The dominant position accorded the text in such an order derived from its communication of common values, what Rancière terms the "conceptual linking of actions" so that a coherent understanding might emerge (2009c: 46). This policing of our thinking provides a "totalizing account of the population by assigning everyone a title and role within the social edifice" (2009b: 89). Most importantly for us, the relationship between text and image entails the subordination of the latter to the former, in "the supplement of presence that imparted flesh and substance to it [the representative schema]" (2009c: 46).

The new functions of the "sentence" and image, in an age of a new aesthetic not bound by the strictures of the conventional representative regime, are now radically different as the age of contemporary art/film/literature no longer presents us with texts dependent on coherent structures of meaning, or "meaning" at all as understood in past centuries. A painting of white on white, like the Ghanaian-Nigerian El Anatsui's assemblages, great sheets of bottle tops,[1] does not inscribe meaning onto its surface as much as it evokes sensorial reactions tied to weariness with earlier regimes of value. The "sentence" still links the elements of a text, giving it flesh—but now joined to things lacking rationale: "the great passivity of *things* without any rationale" (2009c: 46; my emphasis). The image is no longer subservient, then, to a meaning-generating process, and it functions precisely to disrupt such processes, deploying the "active, disruptive power of the leap" (46) between the sensory orders of image and text. Rancière sees this joined signifier "*sentence-image*" as functioning between a fascist totalizing communality of meaning and a schizophrenic rejection of all meaning, with the "sentence" component offering continuities and coherence, and the image the power of rupture.

In the court scenes of *Bamako,* text still rules over image. Long takes of argumentation interspersed with breaks, marginal moments, all sustain the coherence of a trial in which an indictment is to be aired. In those scenes, the film's messages entail the subordination of the image and eventually of the materiality of the apparatus. The camera, its placement, its relationship to the spectator, the attention to the placement of the spectator before the screen, all become incorporated into an ideological function that is not only to be discerned and demystified, but ultimately subordinates all other reactions to the image. In the course of this analytical approach, to what we could call the process of listening and reflecting, we occlude what we see. The image becomes the vehicle for the word, or logos, and the logos for thought, perspective and value. The materiality disappears under the guise of ideology and its work. Following Williams's *Marxism and Literature* (1977), we need to imagine continuing to hold on to the material, not as base for a dialectical logos as such, but as immediate, what we can imagine as being unmediated. In short, we need to recognize both the conventional subordination of image to text or word, and the need to willfully subvert that order[2]—a need tied to the emancipation of African cinema from a heritage that has become a constraint on its need to flourish.

But neither word nor image can be taken as immediate without a consideration of their different permutations. Image can become immediate and material
only by a decision, that is, a choice not to prioritize the idea produced by hermeneutic interpretation, and to forebear placing that meaning in the forefront
of any reading/reaction. The meaning will not so easily let go. Even a naked
image's innate claims to our reactions adhere to meaning, albeit meaning that
cannot be subject to conflicting interpretation, or even to interpretation itself.
Rancière's examples are drawn from famous concentration camp photos. The
image is "never a simple reality" but rather is constituted as an operation that
establishes a relationship between what is said and what is seen (2009c: 6). What
is to be said in front of the image of the tortured man at Abu Ghraib is also being said for us. The logos hasn't disappeared but in a sense has submerged the
image by its force. In the relationship between the "sayable" and the "visible," the
image emerges (2009c: 7). "The visible can be arranged in meaningful tropes;
words deploy a visibility that can be blinding" (2009c: 7). But for the naked image, the mimetic function has been transformed into something more direct,
"the imprint of the thing, the naked identity of its alterity in place of its imitation," or, more importantly, "the wordless, senseless materiality of the visible instead of the figures of discourse" (2009c: 9). Such wordless, senseless materiality
would seem obscene in face of human catastrophe. But what is "obscene" was
originally too horrible to be represented, and thus for the Greeks was *ob-skene*,
off scene, and thus abjected from the stage, from the visible scene. The imprint
leaves its impression, like the memory on which Derrida claims the archive is
founded—an act and object simultaneously. Its naked and obscene character
lies in the nature of the archive it founds, grounded in what is authorized to
be remembered, and what is to be forgotten, remembered in its absence.

The "naked" image, as I have stated earlier, is distinguished from the ostensive image whose function is tied to artistic display, whose presence as such
affirms its being as image. This image is marked by presence that "interrupts"
history and discourses in the name of an immediate "face-to-face" experience,
a "being-there-without-reason,"[3] like an icon engaging the relationship between
"people and things" (24).

The crisis in Africa that Sissako addresses in *Bamako* gives specificity to the
catastrophic; as such it reads the image inevitably in relation to the African
Story, which is marked historically by the slave trade, European colonialism,
neocolonialism, and now globalization and its miseries. It imposes on the spectator a need to comment on the naked and to relate the presence of the ostensive image to the site of enunciation on which the image is built. The enunciation may address relations between people and things, but not as an icon whose
being-here suffices. It demands the larger scope, one provided by the "metamorphic image" that doesn't isolate art from "*forms of circulation of social and
commercial imagery* and from operations interpreting this imagery" (2009c: 24;

my emphasis). The "metamorphic" quality of the images enters into the equation with their relationship with history and its context, as well as with their interruption of that relationship, a break that leaves us without the words to present its meaning. This is absolutely necessary now for an African discourse whose familiar story has come to submerge all into the message of the catastrophe. Sissako's great accomplishment till *Bamako* has been precisely to avoid that reduction.[4]

The devices of contemporary art involve the play between ordinary, commercial, familiar urban scenes or objects, and disruptive, playful, ironic, allegorical readings. As modernity shifts into postmodernity, the play supplants the disruptive function, but we engage a familiar world that surrounds us, whether to disrupt it or to dance with it.[5] One has no choice but to read Africa in or around the crisis, whether by confronting or ignoring it: it haunts the future, like Derrida's specter of Marx, compelling our reading of the passage into the new millennium in *La Vie sur terre* and marking the aborted futures of the figures in *Bamako*.

With installation and public art, ordinary material objects acquire a new visibility, and this is because of the "metaphoric, unstable nature of images" (26). We can borrow this in our reading of the image, and especially the sentence-image in African cinema. This will be crucial to our argument, the instability of the image whose very properties of confronting the spectator require volatility in order not to become banal. For African cinema, the image often works to unsettle and also to join the spectator in a common purpose. In a crucial passage, Rancière evokes community when describing the *liberating power* of the image: "On the one hand, then, the image is valuable as a liberating power, pure form and pure *pathos* dismantling the classical order of organization of fictional action, of *stories*. On the other, it is valuable as the factor in a connection that constructs the figure of a common *history*. On the one hand, it is an incommensurable singularity; while on the other it is an *operation of communalization*" (2009c: 34; my emphasis). Every word in this description of image works for the African oral as well as cinematic performance: both singular and liberatory, even disruptive, as well as an operation of and with the community. The reduction of either pole reduces the oral performance to the dead word, often given as "The Word of the Griot," rather than as the living voice.

The image retains an "active, disruptive power," while the sentence enables the meaning to move forward, for the joining of word to word, brick to brick, to take place without passing into schizophrenia or consensus. The image "repels the great sleep of indifferent triteness or the great communal intoxication of bodies" (2009c: 46). Were African societies to be under the threat of totalitarian rulers, that intoxication might constitute a risk. But as the example of Popaul in Cameroon demonstrates, the brutal face of power is largely disdained or mocked, while the more ordinary face of a Wade or Yar'Adua evokes (or evoked) a sigh of disappointment. What the cineaste *most* confronts is the great sleep of the African Storyline that has lost its power.

We have to read *Bamako* through its images if we are not to be lost in an intoxication of the sentence[6] in which its driving logic tends to submerge every other function in the film. The "sentence" provides the backdrop against which the image can perform that function. The sentence enables the image to be the site of conflict, of clashing forces that alone can speak to the new order of discourse and dominance that articulate the African Story. Behind the familiar contours of the old tale lies the new Africa, the "gold of exploitation" that is masked by every platitude about building a new Africa, about African traditions, about African truths. The image is not the site of conflict simply because art must be renewed; it is the site of conflict because the underlying contours of African society are now constructed so as to benefit the wealthy to the point of intolerable inequities and destructiveness. Sissako is right about the current conditions, but it cannot be said anymore unless the image can be used to unsettle the complacency of the sentence.

The gold for arms trade in East Congo that has gone on since 1998 has resulted in some 5 million deaths. The following description of the global north, complacent over the inequities generated at a time of neoliberal globalization, applies as well to the complacencies in Africa, especially when African culture is read as a direct expression of a people's identity: "What is involved [in contemporary art] is [the attempt to reveal] one world behind another: the far-off conflict behind home comforts; the homeless expelled by urban renovation behind the new buildings and old emblems of the polity; the gold of exploitation behind the rhetoric of community or the sublimity of art; the community of capital behind all the separations of spheres and the class war behind all communities." When the art speaks to the current conditions, it involves "organizing a clash, presenting the strangeness of the familiar, in order to reveal a different order of measurement that is only uncovered by the violence of a conflict" (2009c: 56–57). In order to evoke that "other world" behind the appearance of ordinary life, the sentence must be compelled to yoke the elements of distance and of a "collision which reveals the secret of a world—that is, the other world whose writ runs behind its anodyne or glorious appearances" (2009c: 57). The function of the image is to compel the readings that emerge through the violence of conflict, the organization of the clash—that clash in the tension contained in the dash that holds together "sentence-image." Distant and close, foreign and familiar, dissembled and displayed—the clash becomes visible when the image is slowed to the level of the scene, the gesture, and eventually the single frame that holds the eye in a new grasp. The grasp is held in tension against the cinematic motion, the narrative motion, that compels us forward in order that the story can be told, that the sense can be put together into sentence.

There is only one way now to accomplish this in African cinema, and that is through the reinscription of the sentence-image so that the new is no longer hamstrung by the function of art, or by the plain sense of the sentence. With this "new" reading, this "new cinema," will come a realignment in the distribution of the sensible, a turn toward the political in the sense of dissensus that challenges the underlying principles of hierarchy that sustain the representative regime. This comes about as *logos* is not set against *pathos* but combined with it, ending the privileging of speech over visibility, along with the other hierarchies built into the representative regime, hierarchies of "the arts, their subject matter and their genres" (2009b: 81).

The unified forms of classical genres yield in *Bamako* to a heterogeneity that includes scenes like the trial, Melé and Chaka's relationship, the cowboy shootout, the funeral, Melé's performances, the testimonial recreations of memories from the past during the trial, and so forth. The sentence-image, as central to this reading in terms of the aesthetic regime, destabilizes the older hierarchical structures and values that relegated melodramatic and personal dimensions to the margins. For Rancière, there is a "global analogy" to the hierarchical ratio that underlies the representative regime, and that is in the hierarchy of "political and social occupations": "The representative primacy of action over characters or of narration over description, the hierarchy of genres according to the dignity of their subject matter, and the very primacy of the art of speaking, of speech in actuality, all of these elements figure into an analogy with a fully hierarchical vision of the community" (2009b: 22). In contrast, the aesthetic regime, by identifying art in the singular, "frees it from any specific rule, from any hierarchy of the arts, subject matter, and genres." It accomplishes this by "destroying the mimetic barrier that distinguished ways of doing and making affiliated with art from other ways of doing and making, a barrier that separated its rules from the order of social occupations" (2009b: 23). The aesthetic regime, like the reconstruction of the site of justice in *Bamako,* the staging of the mock trial in the midst of the courtyard, the locus for the staging of "African life" within the quartier of Hamdallaye, permits us to rethink the staging of the political itself, especially as the "distribution of the sensible . . . defines the common of a community" and works "to introduce into it new subjects and objects, to render visible what had not been, and to make heard as speakers those who had been perceived as mere noisy animals" (2009a: 25). Construed thus as "dissensus," an aesthetics of politics becomes possible—one specific to cinema in that "the practices and forms of visibility of art themselves intervene in the distribution of the sensible and its reconfiguration" (2009a: 25).

The tension between the trial and the love story of Chaka and Melé is rehearsed in *Bamako* as the struggle over the politics of the sentence and that of the image, the image in all its materiality. Given the long speeches at the trial, we are obliged to attend to the visible in ways to which we are not accustomed, in African cinematic criticism. We can attend to two exemplary scenes in order to explore this new approach.

The Red Cloth Scene

The first we can call the Red Cloth Scene. The first session of the trial has ended and the participants are taking a break. They leave the compound, past the gatekeeper, and the white lawyer for the World Bank, Maître Rappaport, is looking at sunglasses while the seller is trying to convince him that they are really Gucci. Yeah, yeah, Maître Rappaport says, that's what they all say ("Oui, oui, vous dîtes tous ça"). A bit of comic relief at his expense: the familiar attitude of the skeptical European buyer, his offhand dismissal and offensive words, and later his posture and fearful movements while speaking on his cell phone that mimic a goat that is tied up. His words in the court provide the occasion for the spokespersons for Africa, for the common people, to advance their cause. He is the scapegoat of the story, a man whose name causes the presiding judge to stumble. Rappaport argues with the seller over whether the sunglasses really are Gucci since there is no logo. African seller, European bargain hunter. Then the sounds of the city are interposed over their dialogue. Our eyes travel lazily in the courtyard outside the compound; a sick man given water by a child; a baby comforted by a child who hums Melé's song; a goat, the image of a man on a prayer mat; Chaka telling Falaï that the police suspect him of having stolen a policeman's gun. Then the participants drift back in as a new witness is sworn in. The sound of the gate closing as we see a deep red cloth hung on a line, outside the compound, where the dyers go about their tasks of producing those beautiful Malian cloths. Her back to the camera, rubber gloves on her hands, the woman who runs the enterprise, Saramba, drapes the cloth on the line to dry. It hangs down, a rich red, covering the upper half of the screen as we see the wet ground below it. Behind the cloth, a man passes, and we see only his feet as he crosses from right to left. These cut-off images, these motions of partially viewed people crossing the screen horizontally— signature shots of the day-to-day "reality effects" of Sissako's Africa[7]—establish a mise-en-scène that speaks metonymically in response to the portrait of Africa constructed by words at the trial. The deep red cloth is suspended before our eyes long enough for it not to be ignored or subordinated. We are held by and in its presence, made to be present to it as another object beside the "real" Gucci sunglasses (see figure 9.1).

Madou begins his testimony. He has gained entry to the courtyard despite earlier being denied by the gatekeeper, and his testimony will be the most riveting in the trial—the testimony of the emigrants who died in the desert in their efforts to reach Europe. The testimony crosses the news accounts that marked headline stories about "illegal immigration" at the time the film appeared and since, and they repeat the imagery of *Heremakono* (2002) where the body of one such emigrant is washed up on the shore. Madou speaks Bambara, not French, whence the need for the interpreter—and for the spectator to wonder at his daring in attempting to cross into a continent whose languages he presumably does not understand. As he recounts the desperate journey, we are taken into the Sahara where he and some thirty others were thrown, ejected from Oujda by the Moroccan police. He is somber and direct in his account; images of people outside the courtyard listening intently are intercut with those of close-ups of his face. A frontal shot of Madou, with close-cropped hair, green lighting on the forehead, red tones across his cheeks and nose creating a mask around his deep eyes; he looks downward while speaking about the treatment they received, the close encounter with death (see figure 9.2). The Story is being told, and it is embodied in a survivor who testifies before our eyes. We are engaged in the purposes of the film's idea as listeners, as he addresses the court and as we hear the translation. When we engage the narration with the listeners outside, the sound is mediated through the loudspeaker and becomes hollowed out. A woman holds onto the cloth over the clothesline, gazing intently (see figure 9.3); the gatekeeper's head is bowed behind her, out of focus. Her face holds us along with Madou's words. Another man peers at us through two cloths. The hanging cloths outside; Madou's account inside. We confront both, are brought into both, not through contrasting worlds but as one. The account in Bambara brings together the people of the quartier and the compound, as well as the presiding judge. For the European interlocutor, it is an African voice he or she is hearing, and that interlocutor's sympathies must be tinged by anger and guilt over the treatment ultimately accorded the emigrants at the hands of those in the service of the European fortress. An African witnessing the performance must be disturbed by seeing his brother dying in the desert as Madou repeats the words of one who said, "I can't go on. There's no sense in you waiting with me." In Senegal, as in Mali, those listening would have known of one or two families whose children might have been on such a voyage. Who might have died.

"There was a woman with us, a Ghanaian," says Madou. "We didn't know she was a woman. She was disguised as a boy." The familiar image from other films, like Djandjam's *Frontières* (2001) as well as *Heremakono*, melds into the exemplary story of the human trash moving across the landscape, desperation matching their initial movements of departure from home and family. Madou tells us she was exhausted, and nothing could be done for her. The fellow travelers in the desert were helpless. Cut to the image of the ground outside the courtyard where the runoff from the dyers' cloth mingles on the earth. The green hose separates the deep red liquid from a patch of yellow, and above the hose the light plays off a surface marked by frothy bubbles of yellow scum as the ground hisses with steam. The red might evoke blood, or dyed cloth, or the stain of liquid on the ground. It is free to flow, and as the frame is frozen by this viewer, it resolves the elements of the composition into an abstract pattern of light, color, and shapes that hold Madou's plaint in suspension.

The two parts of the sentence-image must struggle for dominion: either we insist on hearing the outcome of his tale or turn to the liquid composition on the ground—that is, on the screen. Madou had just finished saying, "We couldn't do anything," as he shook his head. As the scene unfolds before our eyes, after we release the frozen frame, we see mist steaming up from the ground, and the movement of the liquid retains the dead seriousness of the narration now as the backcloth to what our eyes alone can retain, the dyers' world. Reflected in the water, above the hose, two legs are seen as shaky poles—life in their movement, in contrast with the Ghanaian woman who must have lain still stretched out on the desert floor.

At 38:34 into the film, the screen is filled with the image of the red dyed cloth (see figure 9.4) as the torso figure of Saramba, the woman who owns the dying enterprise, crosses, horizontally, from right to left. Where is she headed? The narrative pauses as we see the red cloth now completely filling the screen with absolutely no voice, just the "real" sound effects of life filling the air. We wait in that transposed space for a full 7 seconds until the transition ends with a shot of the desert, again filling the screen without any horizon but with beetles scattered on the desert floor. The body of the Ghanaian woman is about to appear, but the red cloth still marks our eyes.

The idea would reduce that cloth to the shocking metaphor of her story, her despair and moments of death, all the more deplorable given the beetles surrounding her body. She is everyone's child, daughter, sister, in her last moments, and her image rivets the interlocutors of Madou's account. But there is another side to the account that tugs at our emotions, which is provided by the impact of the red cloth itself. It would be a travesty to call it aesthetic, although it would be no less of a loss to deny its production of an aesthetic. We are in the presence of the image that imposes an order of silence on the story. For Mulvey, the female body had that impact, and we can feminize this image only by acceding to an anti-phallocentric reading of its impact. It succeeds in joining sentence to image not as the surrealist shock or derive would have it, but by its sheerness, its haeccity, that stops the flow of words. We are poised on the tension where words can exist only as edges of thought. The red cloth, after all, has texture, weight, imposing dimensions and aspects that catch us completely in its gaze, hold us in its impact. We and it merge for an instant that stretches until the desert can appear, transposing us into the diegetic space of Madou's story, taking us magically away from the courtyard of the trial and the reaches of all but his voice that continues its account. Before he resumes, the swishing sound associated with the cloth and the dying continues, tying them into the joint of the sentence-image. Sissako chooses to bring into line, then, the emotion with the scene: we hear sad musical tones of a violin, the woman interlocutor rubbing her mouth, her eyes disbelieving, echoing the sadness of the account. Madou stares down, remembering; and at that instant we see what he remembers, a bottle of water placed next to the Ghanaian woman lying, apparently unmoving, on the desert floor (see figure 9.5). A sad moment taking us over, away from the stains of the red cloth. Her abandonment. Shots of the beetles and sounds of an African stringed instrument. Shots of men walking across the desert, music as voices catch the refrain, a solitary figure crossing the desert, the red cloth now raised to the upper half of the screen with the ground below, more shots of figures walking in the desert, and Madou's statement that thirty people started out but only ten survived. The rest, he says, lost in the Sahara. He doesn't know. The final shot of the desert, and then the return to the trial and questioning of Madou Keita about why he left, about how his country had not been able to provide for him.

Sissako chooses this moment to have Saramba, the woman proprietor, now explode in anger at those black lawyers sitting next to Maître Rappaport defending the World Bank. Fools! she says to the African defense lawyers, you will never be like him, as she points to the squirming scapegoat Rappaport. After berating him and being asked to stop by the presiding judge, she storms out, intoning, "Enough suffering!" She heightens the black-white divide, the us-them divide, returning us to the trial of the west and its instruments. The Story has resumed with the twist in the drama, relieving us of the somber scene of the desert with the body of an expiring woman and the beetles surrounding her. Red splotches can be seen in bits of cloth on the lines that are strung across the interior of the compound, in the bushes. The red can't be expunged, but is reduced to a backcloth as the scene returns us to its idea, that a trial must take place for justice to be served.

Nothing touches us as much as the image of the red screen. It is joined to the figure lying in the desert; it is joined to the women and men dying cloth outside the compound as they hear the live testimonies; it is joined to the long speeches whose inspiration reaches far beyond their cinematic purview to a larger politics of struggle that is inseparable from that fight against colonialism.

Yet it is not enough to rest with the sentence, the final sentence that demands an accountability from the World Bank, Paul Wolfowitz, Bush, and, proleptically one might say, a Sarkozy and even Obama—all those who continue to lay the blame for Africa's miseries on Africa itself. There is an image that confronts the spectator with a force that resists its assimilation into those sentences whose sententiousness and tendentiousness do nothing to disturb the "truthfulness" of the sentences. The film of struggle cannot work on the level of truth alone, not anymore; and only uneasily did it do so during the years of struggle. We have to rewrite our relationship to the image in African cinema, and Rancière offers as good a place as any to begin in his differentiation between the ostensive and the metamorphic images, which we now need to elaborate.

The ostensive image he associates with those art exhibitions typified by what he calls the "voici" moment. He associates this image with the power of its "sheer presence, without signification." The red sheet is nothing but such a presence, prior to its metamorphosis in the red screen. Presence by itself, something that is purely here, hanging before us, demanding that it occupy all the space before our eyes: this constitutes pure "haeccity" that attests to "a singular mode of material presence" (2009c: 23). And although Rancière breaks it down into the presence positing people and things (me voici), of things between themselves (nous voici), and people between themselves (vous voici), the voici moment remains a display of presence.

This voici is contrasted with the voilà moment of an exhibition of metamorphic images that takes into account the relationship between artistic operations and "forms of circulation of social and commercial imagery" (2009c: 24) so that we recognize that the circulation of images does not occur in an historical or discursive vacuum. They do not enjoy a status of pure art that sets them apart from the mechanisms that govern their circulation, and although the power of Art is dismantled by this operation, there is no particular critical orientation that automatically follows. What is displayed relates to the community's perceptions and histories, "a set of testimonies about a shared history and world" (2009c: 25) thus enabling community and communication to emerge, subject to the dismantling of complacency. History marks the community's sense of itself; subversion, its interruption of dominant discourses that would resist change, that resist disruption of the community itself. At its ultimate stage, metamorphic images such as those given in installation art or recuperated art pieces, in public art like graffiti, enable us to encounter objects rendered as images whose instability and transformative qualities mark their presence as images, doubled by being self-consciously pressed into the service of art, or, in this case, cinema. The witty postmodern west might see in the installation works of contemporary artists the possibility of interruption, fragmentation, and reconstitution (2009c: 26), and even if Sissako's red sheet might accomplish other purposes, in both cases there is the establishment of "new differences of potentiality between these unstable elements." Here Sissako's cinema is decidedly New African Cinema as the instability in the nature and production of its images is best captured in this figure of the red sheet.

Indeed, what is the red sheet? As it hangs down and fills the screen, held in place for 7 seconds, it becomes the red screen, or simply, a screen. The screen is the site onto which can now be projected the naked image, in which case the red is the surface of blood, like the pool of red liquid at the bottom of the screen. The screen is also the site of presentation, and thus of presence. The presence is face-to-face, like a Rothko painting, or an El Anatsui assemblage, where we don't look further or past the surface, below the surface, beyond the surface— the surface suffices for our reactions, reflections, lucubrations of any sort, from the religious to the hyperreal. But the red screen is also the site of a transformation because when Saramba crosses it, we enter into another space beside the surface of the screen to its virtual reality. That other space is measured by its relation to the screen, and the measurement affords us the communality or common reality given by Rancière's metamorphic image. This transformation and reinsertion into the third space behind or in front of the red screen occurs not only when the woman-dyer passes in front of the screen, but especially when the screen is lifted, when we see half the screen below what is now the red sheet, and where the reflection of the legs of a person can be seen in the water on the ground. It is still only a reflection, but it points to a reality to which the reflection is joined. That reality comes to us as reflections as well—that is, as reflections or images—metamorphic images—on a screen, and the screen can take several forms. When it is in the form of Madou's imaginary, the reflections of his memory of his experience, they are projected initially through his verbal testimony that is heard by all throughout the quartier and by us. As we see the tense reactions of those who are listening to his words, we enter into their sentiments, sharing a community's measurement of their horrifying import. This is not simply the issue of public services being sold off because of the demands of some abstract institution named the World Bank, but of a sister or daughter dying in the desert not so very far from Hamdallaye—and worse, thrust into the desert by other Africans who happen also to be Muslim.

The scene here doesn't separate audience and projector, but refashions the possibility for the community to hear and see together. This possibility is amplified as the screen of the red sheet passes directly, if imperceptibly—because it is a jump cut—into the screen of the yellow desert floor that fills the entire diegetic screen, becoming a newly transformed screen. Its black beetles crawling over it give its surface depth perspective and space onto which the body of the Ghanaian woman is to be cast, and finally onto which the thirty or so African emigrants are to be seen marching off into the distance.

This is the screen of Madou's imagination, a supplement to the main screen, which is the scene of the trial. Likewise, when the children crowd around the TV at night, we enter into another imaginary space whose screen now presents the images of the cowboy film. This memory-screen is filled with a mock episode of the shoot-out where well-known directors or actors play at farcical roles of the good guy or bad guy to the delight of the children. Such films were common when Sissako was a child but have long since disappeared from the world stage and its contemporary screens. The scene becomes a foil, like Madou's memory-screen, for a present whose metamorphic images are split between those projected on to the screen of the trial and those of the lives of the people who live in or around the compound and who are often seen listening to or crossing through the spaces of the trial. Central to these are the figures of Chaka and Melé, and his eventual suicide. The screen of this space encompasses the shots of the dead dog and the sounds of the passing train, the train that, we are told, entailed the emancipation of Africa. This is a screen of another kind of passing or transformation, a dying screen with its cast-off images of discarded waste—

runoff water, dead bodies, the site of death, and finally, with the photographing of Chaka's funeral, the total silence on the screen, when all sentences are to be inferred only through images.

Sound crosses these various screens: we hold the sounds of the present into the passage onto Madou's memory-screen, the voice connecting past actions with present testimony. Similarly, while these different scenes, whose space I am identifying as being cast onto these various screens, are played out, they sustain a relationship to the dominant diegesis, becoming hypo-and meta-diegetic moments. On the level of idea, they are subordinated: we understand the import of their actions with relation to the issues raised in the trial: they fall under the judgment of the trial and lose their local specificity to the meaning of the African story. Yet when we stop the flow of words, we can view them, if momentarily, for themselves and recover some of the discarded waste that is ejected when they become only supports for the idea. That ejected materiality is inseparable from a certain time and place we can call Africa, the location whose dignity and worth the trial itself is attempting to restore. It is a difficult act of restoration, one that requires us to leave that courtyard, the scene of the trial, with its central stage screen, not so as to reinscribe a marginal or supplementary reality but to be able to actually see and perceive the other worlds being subordinated by the main screen. That would entail, for a start, seeing a red sheet as filling the screen as something other than a metaphoric statement of an idea.

In order to subordinate the idea, we have to have moments of incoherence and silence. We really don't know why Chaka committed suicide. The moment of the gunshot, we are barely out of Ina's bedroom. The sound of a shot, a car screeches to a halt at night, a man gets out to see whether what he heard was the sounds of his tire exploding. Strange irony, as the body of Chaka now lies stretched in the foreground while we see the car's blinking signal light in the distance. Time passes. The car remains with its light blinking as daylight emerges, Chaka still on the ground. Why is the car still there if the blowout was an ironic mistake?

When Chaka's levée du corps takes place and Falaï films it, we enter into the new world of Falaï's images, now cast onto his screen, which is totally silent. Another displacement, like that of the sound coming through the loudspeaker after we are hearing it "normally" in the trial, seen on the main screen. The sound has to be suspended along with the flow of time, of images, of the narrative, for the freeze-frame of the image to emerge into its own. That always entails a conflict since the sentence would want to resolve all the elements, like the elements of the phrase, into the meaning that emerges, at the end, as determinate.

"Africa" can't be resolved into that determinate meaning, despite the strenuous efforts of its advocates, its professors, its defenders. There is always loss, waste, discarded material in the desert, on the ground underneath the dripping cloth, on the funeral bier, to remind us of loss and the abject. When it is written on the faces of the Others who look on, listening to Another Voice, we confront the conflict of the image that is tied only through struggle to the sentence.

This is the case of the testimony of Zegué Bamba, whose words are not translated into French or subtitled but whose impact is written on the faces of those Malians who are listening. The naked image, ostensive image, and metamorphic image all meet on this screen of the griot's performance. He rises after Maître Rappaport has made his case defending the World Bank, and, in a momentary break, Melé has left the compound and is accosted by the police detective to whom she says she knows nothing about the gun that has disappeared. We have heard all the testimony, seen what we need to have seen, and it is at this moment that the griot chooses to speak, not waiting anymore as he had been instructed to do at the outset of the trial. He approaches the witness stand singing and waving his elephant tail brush. Standing next to the French lawyer for the civil society, the blond Maître Bourdon, he chants in loud tones. A medium shot of the presiding judge's somber face conveys the seriousness of Zegué Bamba's words. The judge's imposing red robes, black gown underneath, white necktie, somber glasses, his fixed look: we are focalized through him to receive a torrent of words—words with meaning, but only for some, and thus words that divide the interlocutors into us and them, just as Saramba's diatribe earlier had done.

The previous long speeches in French, with two more still to come, are now matched by an African master of the word, emerging into his own space, creating his own image of protest. But what protest? We cannot find out till the last of the African lawyers, Madame Tall Sall, the advocate for African society, speaks. She translates for us perhaps the essence when she quotes Zegué Bamba as having asked, "Why don't I sow anymore? When I sow, why don't I reap? When I reap, why don't I eat?" We understand his words are also poetry, rhetoric, and ideas, as well as words that reach out to a Malian world since now the sick man looks up with understanding, the women leaning on the wall of the compound look on with interest instead of strolling across the courtyard. The judge no longer stops the flow: he recognizes the importance of the idea being sung, being performed, as the chanting elevates the interlocutor whether or not the words are understood.

The performance cannot but be touching, overwhelming, and the beauty of its effects are seen in the figures of the two attorneys representing African society, Madame Tall Sall and Maître Bourdon, the black woman who is looking on and white man looking down, caught together in the impact of the old man's words as they are positioned slightly behind him to his left. They too are a part of the audience, along with us, all realizing that we are in the presence of a statement that won't be silenced. Ironically, if not understood, the words are no less enunciations of the African Story—that is clear from the images of the interlocutors and the context. The sentence and image are joined, sentence-image, flowing in Bambara speech, griot and audience, from the naked image of a pain being recorded, a demand being heard, and finally, a broader world of interpretation aching to be admitted to the circle of those who understand. As the sound reaches an apogee, crossing through the loudspeaker outside the compound, we track down to the figure of one of the women seen as part of Hamdallaye, a beautiful woman biting her lips and gazing down in concern. Her hair is braided and hangs down in front of her face, across a broad black hairband. Her deep red dress hangs off her shoulders. She is the Listening Woman of the Griot's Complaint; an image completely conveyed as a figure of the Caring Beauty. We have not yet metamorphized the ordinary object into some striking new posture of alterity: she is what we want to see as the vehicle for our concern; we trust her response, and are attached to her as the figure for the people she clearly represents.

Zegué Bamba reaches not only the people of the quartier but the larger world that the metaphor of his listener itself conveys. And with that shot, Zegué Bamba stops. Ironically, as Maître Bourdon begins his final summary, he speaks of the world that suffers as always being silenced. His voice is heard in French, the voice of Zegué Bamba in Bambara having provided the setting for him to begin. He speaks of Africa being silenced in its suffering, as the voice that articulated its suffering still rings in the ears of the interlocutors, within and outside of the courtyard. We return, in short, to the main screen after having been lifted to some other space for the three minutes of Zegué Bamba's performance.

As long as that performance resonates, the formal discourse of Maître Bourdon will remain partial—that is, an alternate version of the cries of accusation and the call for justice that underlies this version of the African Story. But the maître continues for ten minutes, a long and eloquent speech, with as its apogee the statement that it is as though there were a curse being placed on Africa ("Il y a comme une malediction sur l'Afrique"), as a carefully composed shot of the handsome heads of two Malian men, à la Rubens, is seen in a pose of close listening. The Frenchman's speech is followed by a last plea by his fellow counselor, the attorney for African society, Aissata Tall Sall. Black and white lawyers fill the main screen. Zegué Bamba has now disappeared.

The images of two pleas, that of the griot and those of the lawyers, however much arguing along the same lines, could not be more different. They strain the eye and ear while the mind resolves them into one sentence, even without knowing the meaning of half of the words. We may need a translator for the words, but they translate themselves. Madame Tall Sall tells us what the Latin Americans say about the debt, it is *impagadero,* and then translates the words for us. Then she interprets their meaning—unpayable because it is "illegitimate," "violent," "untenable." She repeats/interprets the gist of Zegué Bamba's speech, resolving any lost words back into the sentence we already understood. She performs for us as well, summing up the final image of the trial on the main screen before the last acts of the film will be played out on the other screen, that of Chaka's suicide, death, and funeral rites. The listeners, interpreters, outsiders, native speakers, are all placed within the comprehension afforded us by her sentence.

Bamako is a film of rich colors: yellows, greens, reds paint the screens across which the figures of lawyers in formal robes gesticulate, with women going about their daily routines and work, men sitting and chatting, children playing—Hamdallaye living its public life as the quartier, the compound playing out its life dramas across the stage set for a trial. We can choose to look at the trial so as to understand it, or we can look at the screens onto which are projected the vibrant images of life that a master painter, a master cameraman, chooses to give us. Those images have long been the support for the Master Idea. And we have magisterial robes to remind us of the staging for such an instruction, along with a crisis of dramatic proportions to keep our attention focused on the message. But to fill out the world of Bamako and its people, we need to draw out a little more the material side of the moving image if we are to hear not only the beauty of Melé's singing, the griot's complaint, the other voices, and even their silences, but also to see them as standing on their own, as creating another screen for our viewing and comprehension, so that, in the long run, the Story won't be lost.

Kafka's Gate

The sentence-image gives the Story a place, a there-is, which is the commencement. And it does so within the scope of the Trial under the *commandement* of the judges, the archons, who sit on high and preside in a manner to which we are accustomed, wearing the familiar black robes and wigs we would expect such figures to wear. They silence some and authorize others to speak; they listen and judge. But in the end, they do not pronounce a judgment. When we stand outside the compound, in the everyday world of the inhabitants of the quartier, we can attend to the words or tune out—even turn off the loudspeaker. When we are inside, it is as though the world of the trial has taken over the space and sounds of the African Courtyard whose inhabitants attempt to go about their everyday life, their arguing, and even dying, in the presence of this Trial.

What then is the Trial if not the incomprehensible work of the creation of the African Archive, an archive whose authority is constructed on the screen of the familiar site for juridical performance, the stage of the European cinematic representation of a trial transposed to Africa, assimilated into an imitation of justice and of life.

The exclusions and inclusions of the memories and the words depend partly on the orders of the judges, especially the African chief judge Houmèye Founé Mahalmadane who directs the action from his podium on high—by being another stand-in for the director, like Sissako's alter-ego Rahmane in *La Vie sur terre*. Here he functions as an embodied archon whose gateway rulings function primarily so as to enable the voices to be heard, the imaginary screen of the memories to be illuminated, and the speeches recorded, so that the African archive can be created. The griot's long untranslated words complete the transformation of the archive into an African one, that is a Malian, even a Bamakan archive, as its specificity is marked by the dual language competencies of the inhabitants who attend to the testimonies in both French and Bambara.

If all the events recorded in this film enter into the archive, then they will be marked specifically as the testimonies heard and seen on the screen before the judges, staged for their imitation of authority in the mock trial of the World Bank, and in contrast to the real-life events of the people whose voices and lives appear marginal to the main stage appearances of the trial's witnesses as they are seen, heard, and translated. As the transcript of the trial, the final judgment, and the inscription of the impressions remain unseen, the trial appears ultimately as a kind of dream that permits the unheard voices and unseen events of the past crimes to be evoked, only to remain held in the more ephemeral spaces of the memory of the audience—the diegetic audience, and by inference us, the film's audience. But the film doesn't end with the completion of the trial. That is supplanted by the "real-life" suicide of Chaka and his funeral, the record of what, like the record of the trial, is to be filmed before our eyes, the eyes of those in the courtyard seeing Filaï, and of ours witnessing the scene silently unfolding and being filmed by Filaï.

On the screen, the other one, the trial fades away as the demands of everyday life impose themselves on the scene. The imitation trial and its archive versus the real-life ending and its shots. Two competing archives under two alternative authorities—the one of the black-robed judges, held in some exception space in a courtyard that establishes the scene "before the law"; and the other, under the eye of the filmmaker, the ones playing their roles, like the cowboys in the cowboy film being shown on the television, including as actors real-life directors and figures like the semi-employed Filaï who picks up his camera at the end. In other words, the scene of a virtual archive being created and a simulation of real life being offered at the margin of the virtual archive. These two scenes, generating two different memories, create the materials for the archiving of the African Story. The more the words of the one take primacy, the more they displace the images and music of the other.

Sissako places them both under the heading of "Bamako." Both are recorded for the archive depending on whether the reader of this account, the listener, the viewed, is French, francophone, Bambaraphone, or both. Chaka's death, like that of his namesake, marks the significance of a past whose lost figures, even the famous and great ones, survive as ghosts or phantoms, of a severely repressed or suppressed past.

At the end of the trial, as the lawyers make their final pleas, Maître Bourdon calls for a sentence, the only just one, a modest one: "les travaux d'intérêt général pour l'humanité à perpétuité" (community service for mankind for all eternity). Madame Tall Sall speaks in equally humanist terms: "c'est notre devoir de génération de provoquer et de précipiter l'avenir de ce jour" (it is our duty as a generation to bring about the advent of that day) "car il y va de l'équilibre du monde et de l'avenir de l'humanité" (for the balance of the world and of man's future is at stake). Both evoke a future in which the sentence will weigh on the condition of all mankind. Both depend on the trial's impression on the archive, the site constructed in the film to rehearse the humanistic values of justice, to precipitate that future—as though justice, the memories of what had been said and seen, the sentence and now the sentencing would enable the encounter with the specter of the World Bank to change the course set in place by globalization. But that vision was already there at the beginning of the trial; it depended upon an archive of the past based on the universal values of humanism and a revolutionary republican order written on the robes of the judges who are listening so intently to these summations. They will have nothing to say because they are already silenced by the archive to which this appeal is being made inasmuch as that archive has been ordered for them, in the past, by the authority of the archons who established it.

How could the archive of the justices contained within the courtyard on which is written not only Césaire's rhetoric ("for the balance of the world and of man's future is at stake"), but also Kafka's equally rhetorical "Before the Law," with its empowered gatekeeper and eternally deterred applicant, establish a new sentence? At a minimum, the sentence-image of the Red Cloth and of the Melé-Chaka drama must impose themselves on the new archive, *not* simply in order that the voices of those previously excluded be heard or their faces now seen on the screen; but that the archive itself be revised by the resurrection from the ashes of the past of the ghosts that have continued to haunt it.

Derrida sees in the question Yerushalmi puts to the ghost of Freud, "Please tell me, Professor. I promise I won't tell," asking in whose name Freud's daughter Anna Freud was speaking when she addressed the Hebrew University of Jerusalem, averring that the accusation made against psychoanalysis, against Freud, that it was a "Jewish science," was a charge that should rebound against the anti-Semitic accusers and "serve as a title of honor" (1996: 43–44). So too would the canvas of the Red Cloth, the accounts of the death of Chaka and the mourning of Melé redound in honor of the African Story rewritten as "Bamako." In such a form of rewriting, says Derrida, the concepts of both "Jewish" and "science" would be transformed (45). The trial by itself cannot transform the archive or the African Story. The addition to an already ordered archive, its mere expansion, changes nothing. But the complete sentence-image of *Bamako* could undertake that transformation.

We could read the new archival inscriptions of this sentence-image in many ways. One is to return to Kafka's "Before the Law" and to read that scene in terms of Agamben's state of exception. The courtyard trial in *Bamako* offers the model for exclusion. If the concentration camp, Agamben's original site for the state of exception, was marked by its isolation from "normal society" under the sovereign authority of the social contract, and by its containment and isolation of those marked by bare life, the courtyard would seem to offer a similarly isolated space, where the imposition of a mock trial would suggest the impotency of the social contract in Africa. But as the testimonies emerge, and as the gatekeeper keeps out those unauthorized to enter, it is clear that those outside the gates resemble more the *homines sacri,* those whose lives are marked by limited value, bare value, than those inside the gates. This sets up the parallel to Kafka's "Before the Law" where sovereign power is exercised by the gatekeeper, and bare life is evoked in the reduction of the supplicant's plea to enter to nothing but a helpless appeal, with no authority to his claim.

Agamben reads the Kafkaesque ending perversely: instead of the supplicant's appeal being denied arbitrarily and in perpetuity, the closing of the gate forever means that the arbitrariness of imposing an unarticulated sentence, the ultimate act of injustice, will be closed to future fruitless appeals. The supplicant is sacrificed to a future whose meaningless is closed off. At the end of *Bamako,* with the death of Chaka, the gate must now be opened, enabling the private world of the common people's lives outside to infiltrate the closed off space of the public trial—a trial with all the appearance of a legal exercise, with the *form* of a trial, and with loudspeakers proclaiming the Truth to the world outside.

All that had been determined by the ordering of the trial comes to a stop with Chaka's funeral. The filming of the trial is over, and sound itself stops as Filaï begins to shoot the funeral. This reverses the positioning of the state of exception, defined earlier in terms of the gate and its gatekeeper maintaining the border between the inside and outside of the compound.

For Agamben, the sovereign occupies an ambiguous space defined as both inside-outside, a state of inclusion-exclusion where the force of the sovereign rules, and where we have the *homo sacer.* The sovereign's subject, and in a sense counterpart, the *homo sacer,* is banned from the normal state and placed outside society based on a social contract. Who functions as sovereign in Bamako? Who is *homo sacer,* the person with bare life? The space of the mock trial in the courtyard, appearing to be excluded from the world of Bamako, Mali, Africa outside the compound, reverses the binary of concentration camp and normal society, with spaces like those depicted in *Camp de Thiaroye* (1987), whose walls Pays, the former concentration camp prisoner, took to be those of a concentration camp. In this quartier of Hamdallaye, however, the state of exception is everything outside the walls, while inside the miming of the performance of the trial constitutes the attempt to restore order to the polis. But the attempts by the chief magistrate to restore order in French prove futile (compare with Saramba who shouts at him, the griot who won't remain quiet, the gatekeeper who accepts bribes, and the larger futility of holding a mock trial before a court that lacks the jurisdiction and power to punish). The contrast is given greater weight as we see the threatening figures of the police questioning Chaka and Melé outside the compound, where unemployed men linger on the benches with no real plans to find work, in a civil order described by the witnesses as having failed them.

We almost forget this as the trial goes on because we are so ensconced in the social order with its forms of justice, and assumptions about justice, that we can't recognize a form of dissensus other than an appeal/complaint within a given order of Law.

If there is the figure of the villager who stands outside the court, like Kafka's supplicant, never to gain entry despite his best efforts (like Chaka trying to learn Hebrew), it must be Chaka who unaccountably stands to lose everything (with theft of gun, his liberty; with loss of Melé, his wife and family; with her departure and his despair, his life). There is a sovereign we never see that reduces Chaka to bare life, and that demotion destroys him. Who is that sovereign that we can't see, that imposes the state of exception on Chaka, imposes its ban on him like that of the bad guys in the movie? What sovereign force sustains the culture that presents a cowboy movie to the public *within* the walls of the compound if not the World Bank and Wolfowitz who, like Summers, impose the conditions of bare life on the people who cannot enter into the order (cannot find jobs or obtain a part for themselves)?

Wolfowitz is not present at the trial, though he is on trial, as is his sovereign order. He exists as a force of law, as Agamben would have it, without any specific identity or constituted authority. He embodies this force not as the product of a social or political agreement or compromise among citizens. Under his authority, Africa has no place, no voice, is excluded from his decision-making assembly, that is, his polis, his *policed order,* à la Rancière. There is no justice or order without his authority, which is why the whole scene of the trial in Bamako is a mock trial rather than a symbol or metaphor or allegory of capitalist domination.

If Wolfowitz, as the name embodying the World Bank in the film, is the real sovereign, who then are the judge and court? They are the exception to the state of exception outside the walls. Within the walls we have a simulacrum of normal life, of everyday order, that is, of life outside the camp, outside the state of exception. But the state of exception, that which occurs outside these walls, has become generalized, and Chaka's death—where he himself has now become the corpse to be sniffed by passing dogs—cannot be kept outside the walls because the attempt to impose a non–state of exception inside the walls is only a simulacrum.

At the end, the sovereign power remains in force, and the bare life of Chaka ends up imposing the truth of Africa's generalized state of exception upon the space of the trial. As the compound is opened to the funeral, the wall between inside and outside is permeated, and we see that generalization of what Agamben defines as the space under the sovereign's authority. The state of inclusion-exclusion, the state of exception, is where the power of the sovereign asserts its authority, and its presence transforms the courtyard and the space outside

Figure 9.1. Dyed cloth and feet.

it into an indistinguishable in-between space where only bare life exists. This is the opposite of *La Vie sur terre* where, in Césaire's famous words from the *Cahier*—"man is not a dancing bear, man is not a spectacle"—we hear the affirmation of the state of freedom accomplished by decolonization. In *Bamako* it is not freedom or decolonization, not a state in opposition to Europe, but a certain unfinished project of modernity called postcolonialism, with the state under the sign of the World Bank. With Chaka's death, there is no sacrifice (since it is bare life) or homicide (since it is bare life) but an apparent suicide. He doesn't die under the sign of tragedy, but of a biopolitical order. He is condemned by Summers's regime that dictates that what matters more than the lives or the quality of the lives of those who fail to get to Europe or to get jobs in Africa is the improvement of quality of life where it really counts—in Europe. Europe is evoked in the film through Rappaport and his cell phone call "outside," his claims to judge what is authentically Europe or not (the "Gucci" sunglasses and offhand comment about "these people"), a Europe that hovers over the scene, excluding Chaka, Madou, and the others who tried to get to it, and that reduces their deaths to a legitimate act of murder without it being homicide since they are not *homines,* but *homines sacri.*

How does this change the archive? With *homo sacer* there is no life to record, to make an impression on the archive. But with the screen of the Red Cloth, with its scene of life, with the scene of the expanse of the desert to which it is joined by the jump cut, the simulacrum of a normal order can be set over against the world of the trial, where a simulacrum of a just order appears to function. The "other" world on the outside is written and impressed on the screen "other-

Figure 9.2. Madou testifying.

Figure 9.3. Woman listening intently over sheet.

wise, reversing the hierarchy of the order of the trial, imposing its moments of messianicity" (Derrida 1996: 36) that break the temporality of the hierarchical order. We hear this break when the griot speaks in the language of the community, without translations being provided for the foreigners, transfixing those listening outside; when the baby wanders into the space of the judges, when a gunshot intrudes on the quiet of the child's bedroom, when the dog sniffs the

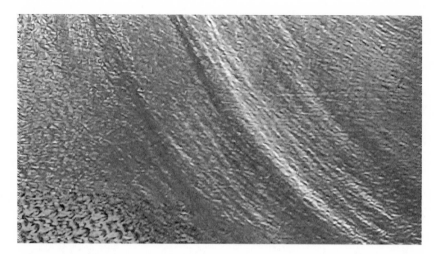

Figure 9.4. Red cloth.

Figure 9.5. Ghanaian woman in desert.

corpse, when the sounds of the train are heard and haunt the ear. All the detritus of that world, even that of the cowboy film *Death in Timbuktu* with the
scene of a woman and her child shot by the villains, all this simply accumu-
lates like the piles of trash that the angel of history views with dismay as she is
helplessly swept forward by the winds of Wolfowitz's progress. This postcolonial
archive is being written as we view it,[8] and is inscribed in and through the im-

ages of the excluded world outside the courtyard, "before the law," and in the sentence-image that is created by the fashioning of the trial within an exclusive space intended to differentiate what should be right and wrong, included and excluded. As the border between the two collapses at the end, as Chaka's funeral is staged before our eyes in pure and soundless space as a naked image, bare life arises in the echoes of Madame Sall Tall's summary words that were heard only over the loudspeaker outside the walls: "for the balance of the world and of man's future is at stake."

Her words record the commencement of another archive, one that begins with an attempt to put those responsible for the colonial archive on trial by the creation of a new, truly postcolonial archive. And its archons will no longer be sitting on high, on the podium, but in the audience with the griot whose authoritative voice refuses to be silenced and that insists on speaking in the language of the people.

10 The Counter-Archive for a New Postcolonial Order: *O Herói* and *Daratt*

The prosthesis that Vitorio needs in *O Herói* (2004) is meant to serve in place of his leg that was blown off by a land mine when he was serving as a soldier in the Angolan army. He returns to Luanda to find he cannot get work, but he is given a prosthetic leg at the hospital and later meets Judite, a prostitute, at a bar. Soon thereafter his prosthetic leg is stolen, and the bulk of the film is taken up with his attempt to recover it. The prosthesis moves from the hands of a malefic child gang leader named Caca, who sells it to a fence. Manu, a sad-faced boy who refuses to submit to Caca, and who has his own gang of street kids, steals a car radio that he exchanges at the same fence for the prosthesis. At the end, Manu's grandmother discovers Manu has the stolen prosthesis, and after Vitorio has made a national appeal for the return of his prosthetic limb, it passes again back to Vitorio. What is this prosthesis, what melodramatic or symbolic function does it perform? Why is it the central object in this symbolic system, this chain of substitutions and exchanges that seeks the impossible, to fill the hole left by the explosion of the land mine, to restore wholeness to the fragmented body of Angola caught in the throes of an endless war.

The question of the prosthesis can be read in several ways: as the supplement for the aporia at the center of all subjectivities, especially when presented as identities; as the device for rehabilitating a body that has lost its value, having become trash, having been trashed; and as the reiteration or copy of the original contents of the archive, a revision to a missing or absent original entry that reappears at a later time, thus permitting the revision of the order of the archive. The prosthesis represents a repetition or change of an original to another version, enabling us to establish the relationship to the Other, to establish the relationship of the original One to the Other. To establish that relationship, it is necessary to return to the original events in the past that we will seek in the archive, beginning with the first form of the postcolonial archive, with the first heir to the colonial archive.

From 1975 to 2002, the MPLA battled the FNLA and especially UNITA as Cold War proxies as the United States, China, Russia, Cuba, and South Africa lent support to the three different Angolan movements seeking to win power at the end of Portuguese colonial rule in 1975. As the civil war dragged on, with the MPLA taking control of the oil resources and UNITA the diamond mines near Zaire, both sides turned to brutal practices, forcing millions of Angolans to flee the countryside, killing upwards of 500,000 people, and strewing land mines throughout the land. Thousands of Angolans were killed or maimed by the land mines whose horrific effects also could be seen in wars throughout Asia and Africa during this period. In *O Herói*, as in Makhmalbaf's *Kandahar* (2001), it is the prosthetic leg that becomes the central fetish object of the film.[1] The prosthetic leg assumes an enormous value as one of the few objects whose exchange value comes to displace its original use value since increasingly large numbers of maimed victims of land mines seek to acquire one.

The major producers and users of land mines, the United States, China, and India, have still not signed the 1997 land mine treaty (as of this writing in 2012), despite the fact that more than a hundred other nations, including Angola and Afghanistan, have done so. Similarly, despite the blood diamond agreements of the 2003 Kimberley Process accords, large quantities of diamonds from conflict zones, like the east Congo, continue to flow through illegal channels into the mainstream markets in exchange for weapons that sustain the militias that control the trade. The trade in resources (gold, diamonds, coltan, tin, timber, and so forth) makes possible the continuation of conflicts and the brutal practices at the heart of the economic system with their conditions of exploitation and the corruption of the state. There is a process of production in this globalized economic system, one in which exchanges are produced that cannot ever be completed (Baudrillard, *Impossible Exchange*). They function like a number of human activities that entail an effort to bring completion or wholeness through a complex chain of substitutions that would seem never to reach an end.

This follows the logic of the supplement. The supplement replaces a lack and thus indicates the presence of the aporia that it supplements. This marks the incompleteness of the system in which this lack is produced. But as a supplement, it is also an addition to something that is already whole without the supplement. The supplement is both an addition and a substitution. It is indeterminate, and its indeterminacy, like writing itself, is generated around the lack that informs all totalizing systems.[2] Sarah Coffey cites Stiegler in drawing this comparison between prosthesis and supplement: "the double nature of prosthesis [appears] as extension and amputation when [Stiegler] writes, 'the supplement, marking the default of origin, does nothing but try and fill this default in; and yet, in doing so, it can only affirm it as necessary'" (260, cited in Coffey). Coffey describes the double meaning of prosthetics as "simultaneously supplementing a deficiency and signaling deficiency in the object to which it is supplied" (http://lucian.uchicago.edu/blogs/mediatheory/keywords/prosthesis/).

Just as the totalizing system of the body is supplemented by the prosthesis, so is the totalizing system of the national economy supplemented by the black market—by the activities of the people who cannot survive without trading in the black market, where stolen bicycle wheels can be exchanged for weapons or other stolen goods. The global neoliberal economy is supplemented by the local exchanges as it supplants local markets. Every person is marked by some missing part, some aporia that they continually seek to fill, as in the attempt to satisfy a desire whose object always appears through a substitute. The exchanges are impossible, as Baudrillard would say, because the lack generated by desire is implicated in a system in which no complete equivalency can be achieved. The prosthetic leg cannot give Vitorio the leg he once had when he was the complete, two-legged soldier. The black market cannot give society a just basis for exchanges that will sustain the ideals of the newly independent nation.

Similarly, Vitorio's relationship with Joana is marked by the supplement to the aporia that is due to their class relations. Joana is a teacher whose father is a successful businessman. Although she is presented in a positive light, her expensive apartment cannot give her the satisfaction she demands of life, as we see in her appeals to justice and humane treatment of others. But those appeals themselves are bound up in the system that enabled her father to obtain the luxurious apartment and that ultimately sustains the gap between the rich in their luxury flats and the poor in their favelas.

A third instance: Vitorio establishes a relationship with a prostitute, Judite, his central love interest in the film. Judite has lost her child in the war. When she encounters another vagrant child, Manu, who has lost his father in the war, she sees in him a substitute for her own lost child. But the love Judite seeks in place of her missing child cannot be replaced by Manu any more than Vitorio can replace Manu's missing father. The black market cannot replace the holes generated in a global economy in which commodity fetishism ultimately drives exchanges, especially those of the arms-for-resources trade.

Every exchange is based on the failure of these equivalencies because they are marked by the logic of the supplement that is itself marked by the lack it attempts to fill. For Lacan, such an object is called the other object, *l'objet a* or *autre*, which is the unattainable object that is always represented by substitutions. Whether a Marxist fetish commodity or a Lacanian *objet a*, the objects that mark our contemporary symbolic order are marked by a lack that is at the heart of our efforts to give them completion or wholeness. The lack is manifested, in one iteration, because the system in which a fetish object, or an object of desire, is made manifest works to conceal the very forces that made that manifestation possible. But for Baudrillard, there is a larger underlying, systemic explanation: the fullness of being can only be apprehended against a ground of that which is neither fullness nor being, what he calls Nothing:

> It is on the continuity and reciprocal exchange of the Nothing, of illusion, of absence, of non-value, that the continuity of Something is founded.
>
> Uncertainty in this sense becomes the very precondition for the divided nature of thought. Just as uncertainty in physics arises in the end from the fact that the object in its turn, analyses the subject, so the uncertainty of thought

comes from the fact that I am not alone in thinking the world—that the world, in its turn, thinks me.

The Nothing is only the ground—or background—against which we can apprehend existence. It is existence's potential of absence and nullity, but also of energy (there is an analogy here with the quantum void). In this sense, things only ever exist *ex nihilo*. Things only exist out of nothing.

The Nothing does not cease to exist as soon as there is something. The Nothing continues (not) to exist just beneath the surface of things. . . . Everything which exists continues, then, not to exist at the same time. (2001: 8–9)

In *O Herói*, Vitorio is given a medal as a hero because his leg was blown off. The medal is the first prosthetic substitute for the leg, but it cannot help him get a job; as the foreman says when he applies for work, only fit or whole men can be hired to do the kind of work needed in construction. He supplements his lost leg with the actual prosthetic leg, and as he cannot use it unaided initially, he supplements the prosthesis with a crutch and then a cane. When the prosthesis is stolen, he has to use two crutches, two supplements in place of the prosthesis. When it is finally recovered, he learns to walk with it, his handicapped gait a sign that the supplement cannot fill the lack but only indicate its presence.

There is a point where the critical question of land mines, wounds, maimed limbs, and even death cannot escape some kind of inevitable logic of the supplement, a deadly logic that evokes the limit point of reality where life has to engage the conditions of survival by confronting that which is missing. That point might be said to come in the film when the casualties of loss, those who have lost a child, a father, a husband, appear before the television cameras and microphones to make public and visible the face or visage of their lost ones. They seek to publicize the loss in the hopes that somewhere the lost one can be identified, found, relocated, so that they can rejoin their families.

The losses are proclaimed by the wretched petitioners who show their photos and tell their stories (48:25 to 51:44). In this scene, the style of the film, which has consistently flirted with melodrama, shifts to neorealism, or, more specifically, cinema verité.[3] The filming of the lines of people, whose ordinariness contrasts dramatically with the telegenic beauty of Judite, and whose plainness of discourse contrasts with her emotionally charged speech, suggest direct cinema's on-location unstaged shots. This would be the real at the core of the film, the site of loss enunciated, recorded, vocalized, and filmed by the television crews to be displayed throughout the country. Their loss, it would seem, cannot be filled nor reduced to a state of virtualness. It is an unmediated recording.

In contrast to the well-made melodrama of Vitorio and Judite's stories, their losses proclaim their stark reality, their bare lives. In contrast to a constructed fiction, their pleas proclaim a sincere announcement of truth. The scene is structured in the following way. It follows the touching sequence in which Vitorio and Judite are seen coming together, after her hard night working the johns in a bar. They are both tired; he is disturbed over the loss of his prosthetic leg, which we have just seen being used as a plaything by Manu and his gang, and she has had to deal with the abuses of the bar owner and a client. We cut directly to the next day and the line of petitioners being interviewed. The lines are long; the poor in their ordinariness recite their names and those of their lost ones, those for whom they are searching. Angola, ripped apart, now trying to refashion itself from the bits and pieces of people who still have a name but lack their loved ones. Judite and Vitorio are like those pieces arbitrarily joined for the moment. The camera pans to the TV cameras recording the scene; we focalize for a second through the gaze of Vitorio who is looking on, along with other spectators held behind a rope so as to allow the cameramen to work. "My name is Candida Jaõa. I am looking for my son, missing." The voices are plain, plaintive and repetitive; there is no background music to heighten the emotion. We see the backs of those reading the long lists of names tacked onto the walls, searching for their relatives so they can be reunited. The voices mingle, the "reality effect" powerful in its discretion.

The camera pans the faces, lines, and lists of names, and then passes to those watching the television screens on which this scene is being shown. The simulacrum of the staging of a virtual re-encountering of the lost ones enters into the moment as the viewing becomes another supplement to the broken relationships. We hear the voice of the petitioner as the camera pans the faces of those waiting patiently their turn in what seems an endless line: "My brother disappeared in 1995. I want to send him a message." Another: "His name is Zé and he left six months ago . . . I want to find my sister Maria and my brothers, Eduardo Pacheco and Aurélio . . ." And then, with something of a shock, Judite is there, her look broken, the implicit deep melodramatic emotion in the scene written on her features. She is lighter than the others, taller; she stands out. The coalescing of repressed feelings, the suppressed past, is now to repeat itself in her testimonial pleas. We move from the implicit, latest melodrama of the scene, the suppressed, but barely suppressed emotions of the suppliants, to the professional performative scene. The ordinary people become a backdrop and their real pleas now a reality-effect staging for the extraordinary figure that Judite makes, and we shift to adjust for what follows.

Up till now the scene doesn't seek the completion of a narrative nor the disguises of the narrative act that has to pretend that it is what it seems to be. And yet, the impossibility of its wholeness, like that of the exchange it seeks, must intrude. The very thought of its reality is external, supplementary, to its presence. The real appeal is read as real not by the petitioners but the audience. Yet the audience itself is already double: both the audience of the television recording within the diegesis, and our extradiegetic witnessing of the process of filming them.[4] We supplement the presence of the television audience, of the ones who create a reality effect, and impart to their reality the sense that they are engaging in the same act of staging a scene for the cameras that are recording their stories as this film stages the scene for the film in which they appear to our eyes. Their non-melodramatic nature has to be generated by our returning to them the very quality we see in their losses as negatives—the counter-images, so to speak, the reverse images that characterize the film's actual diegesis. We see them framed by the melodrama of Vitorio, the man who wears the prosthesis, and he and his fictional story become the prosthesis on which their realism depends, its crutch—its Nothingness.

To reinforce that point, the star of the lineup of the wretched is presented as the object of the camera's attention as Judite moves into the center of our vision. As her turn arrives and she testifies/recounts her sad story, a heartbreaking performance unfolds where she cries for the loss of her son, where she announces her sorrow as the *mater dolorosa*. She is the very image of sorrow, the figure of loss whose dramatic performance captures the essence of the stories of all the other non-actors who have given their unprofessional, undramatic, understated testimony before the lens of the camera (see figure 10.1). In short, her melodrama, the supplement to the real, is at the very foundation of that real, one that they need for their own stories to attain the tragic dimensions we wish to attribute to them. They need her to embody that tragedy, to give it life, to make it resonate as would resonate the cries and appeals for pity that mark melodrama. Their plain stage presence assumes the status of a perfectly inhabited ordinariness, made pathetic by the camerawork's construction of their loss. In a sense, they are the supplement to Judite's performance, without whom her dramatic reenactment would lose its effect. Between them lies the space of a difference that can only destabilize every effort to turn their effect, or her effect, into a unified presence that is sufficient unto itself. They relate as supplements to each other, and function as such in this supremely self-reflexive scene that mirrors the act of filming this film, thus ironically causing them to lose their moorings to a reality that would assure their role as the real reality and hers as the staged supplement.

The name of the location where they appear before the cameras is Punto del Reencontro, Santa Cruz. Needless to say, this *reencontro* is seen in what is filmed, in what is shot; it is not the encounter but its simulation; not the event but the virtual meeting. And that is what melodrama is intended to make visible by its deployment of overwrought emotional moments. The key moment of Judite's account is marked by the exchange between what is quietly normal and her manifestation of extreme sorrow: melodramatic grief. Female grief; women's tears, or weeping—the basis for "women's weepies." Though we are witnessing this scene in a public venue, it is her private internal feelings that now come to the fore. We learn she is not Judite the whore but is actually named Maria Bárbara Simões—the *mater dolorosa*, the bereft mother. Where we had taken her for the erotic object of our gaze, now she becomes the respected subject of her own tale of loss. Where we took the prosthesis to be a substitute for that loss, the losses to the nation in seemingly every family we encounter, every orphan or widow, she has now turned the prosthetic allegory into the site that is open for a transformation to occur, one that she drives forward with her own insistence on giving her own account. If Judite can become Maria Bárbara, and if she can bring Vitorio along into her account, her accounting, and fashion a vision of a new future for them after her melodramatic account of her suffering from the beatings of clients, despite his flaws and subsequent betrayals, then perhaps it will be possible to transform other prosthetic moments into a new future for the country.

"My name is Maria Bárbara Simões. I am thirty years old and I am looking for my twelve-year-old son." In a medium-close, frontal shot, her head, tilted to the side, fills most of the screen. We are ready to hear her story and to be moved. She confesses all, the birth, the separation, her need for him, her pain and tears. And then it is over. The nightclub scene and dancing, again, is now framed by Maria Bárbara Simões's story. This has entered the archive, competing for a space among all the others. Its claim to be measured against that of a lost father whose son both needs and rejects him. The tension between the two like that between the realism and the melodrama clambering for the recording camera's eye.

O Herói wants to end with the triumph of melodrama's moral basis,[5] one in which an already existent latent truth becomes manifest. "Judite" is replaced by the real "Maria Bárbara" whose maternal love is ready to embrace Manu; the victorious figure of the father will return to the home as the grandmother has invited the new couple, Vitorio and Maria Bárbara, to lunch with them in the sunshine of a new day. The hero can return home, even if he is not the real father, even if it is not his real home, even if Manu knows the moon cannot descend from the sky when he invokes it with the magic of the prosthesis. And Angola's war will finally be over as the new family has found itself together at last, in some sense, in some supplementary fashion.

We come to the prosthesis again, the key to this film. It is an object that supplements a loss, that fills a lacuna, that turns loss into recovery, that makes whole, and so on. But in this film, more than that, it is an object of exchange that passes from one person to another, and in so doing brings them together into a relationship. By tracking its movement, especially under the aegis of exchange, we can begin to see the importance not only of its role but, especially for this study, of the role of trash. To get to that point, we need to return to the regimes of exchange that I laid out in chapter 5 of my last book, *Postcolonial African Cinema: From Political Engagement to Postmodernism* (2007).

In that book I evoked Slavoj Žižek, who described three different systems in which objects of exchange played key roles, within clusters of objects/subjects/ socioeconomic systems. The first of the objects is described as the familiar Hitchcockian device, the "McGuffin," which is actually "'nothing at all,' an empty place, a pure pretext whose sole role is to set the story in motion" (1992: 6).[6] When the mystery of the McGuffin stands revealed, the desire would appear to be joined to an impossibly utopian vision, one in which any real hope of addressing an imperfect system and seeking to change it has been completely lost. If liberal capitalism and the autonomous subject are in play here, it would seem that their positive features that normalize western ideological values cannot easily be evoked, because the benefits and powers are inevitably bestowed on a subject who in the end is the wealthy other—be it the European or the Europeanized African bourgeois.

The second kind of object Žižek describes has a material form, and its function is to act as the object of exchange between characters whose relationship takes on a meaningful dimension as a result of that exchange. That relationship makes sense and motivates the action in the film in such a way as to account for meaning or sense—that is, to set up a symbolic order. Further, as Žižek states, here it is less the autonomous subject functioning in a liberal capitalist economy than the "heteronomous" subject functioning within a system of imperialistic state capitalism. If we focus on the diminished powers of the paternal figure, or Law of the Father, on whose authority is constructed the symbolic order, such figures have now been reduced to the burlesque "Popauls" of Mbembe's postcolony. Simultaneously, we see exacerbated the neocolonialism of the early period of independence as it passes into this far more debilitating condition of the failed state, of failed state capitalism and its far greater dependencies and incapacity.

The stages are not neat, like a step function, but often overlap—just as an economy functions simultaneously with multiple patterns of exchange, as in a cash economy and a bartering economy. In O Herói we have bartering exchanges and cash exchanges, sometimes in the same situation, as when Manu sells his stolen car radio for the prosthesis and cash. For the heteronomous subject, like the street children and their gangs, the losses that mark the subjectivities of the children relate to these objects in that they have no double, no counterpart, "as if [they are] in search of [their] proper place, lost from the very beginning" (1992: 6).

What Žižek refers to as "a little-bit-of-Real," a disruption, intrudes on their autonomous space, and they are forced to come into a relationship, a symbolic relationship marked by strife and disharmony, and by the creation of an environment in which negotiation becomes necessary. The "little-bit-of-Real" barely makes itself known to us: we get a glimpse of a lost father in a photo, a lost memory. Yet without it, there is no coalescing of peoples and issues around a central concern. This failure of the symbolic order to assert its presence without this object attests to the diminished presence of the "big Other," the figure on which the authority of the Name of the Father relies.

The third stage we will take up later, when considering Nollywood films, as it corresponds to a further loss of the Law of the Father, to the point where the typical subject has lost the nomos of the symbolic order. As Žižek puts it, "The father is absent, the paternal function (the function of the pacifying law, the Name-of-the-Father) is suspended" (1999: 99).[7] At this point, horrific subjects and enormous, monstrous objects dot the landscape, normalizing the abnormal, generalizing the state of trash, the state of exception, as it were. This condition is approached asymptotically at various points in *O Herói*, only to veer away from it at the end.

The key object in the film's narrative is the prosthesis. Initially it is given as a gift to Vitorio, although we can say it is also provided in exchange for his service. His claim is uncertain as it is not until he complains, and further specifies that he was a sergeant, not an ordinary soldier, that the doctor accedes to his request. Soon the prosthesis is stolen, and it enters into the black market economy that flourishes alongside the larger urban markets where Vitorio buys his clothes and Manu's grandmother sells her baked goods and buys her food. The black market shop is run by a dirty, unkempt man with a large belly. He buys stolen goods from the children gang leaders. Manu tries to buy a Kalashnikov, and failing that, manages to steal an enormous knife.

Eventually the stolen prosthesis winds up in that same shop, sold by the maleficent Caca who told his gang, when an albino member passed it to him, "This leg is worth a lot of dough." It is apparent that the value of the leg, like trash, is a function of the regime under which it appears. Initially, as a medical prosthesis it is invaluable. Vitorio cannot buy it but earns it with the sacrifice of his leg to the nation, to the war effort, to his commanders—ultimately to nothing, since neither nation nor war nor the military assume any responsibility for caring for him except by awarding him a useless medal and the ironically pointless title of "hero." We are told only one applicant out of 500 is given a prosthetic leg: the others have crutches, if they are lucky.

When the albino child steals it and gives it to Caca, it is with the idea of using it as a toy in the game of "Wooden Leg Pirate." The children's use of it mocks its original purpose so that its initial use value is lost. Caca does eventually sell it, but it is hard to imagine he received a lot since the black market owner lets Manu take it almost casually, bargaining for the stolen car radio and giving him $70, with the leg apparently a gift to sweeten the deal. "If you want a war souvenir, take it," he tells Manu. Manu too uses it for games with his gang.

Then it turns into a fetish object, what Manu calls a magic object, to which he alludes when he tells his grandmother, to her shock, that he knows a better way than God to get his father to return, and that is through magic. He holds the prosthesis up to the moon with both hands, like an offering, and evokes its powers. Twice in his dreams the moon descends, bringing a brighter day—turning into a basketball the second time, reversing the events in the opening scene in which he is hit inadvertently during a basketball game and cries. This time the bouncing basketball evokes a bright scene like those of the *Truman Show*, before the camera cuts to Joana as she wakes up—as though his dream had been exchanged for, or entered into, hers.

As she prepares a plan to publicize Vitorio's story so as to help him recover his prosthesis, Manu hides it under his bed prior to dreaming about the descent of the moon. There are several exchanges between these characters, but with the radio broadcast and the grandmother's discovery of the prosthesis under the bed, an order of right and wrong is reestablished. She spanks Manu and drags him to the radio station where Vitorio has just seen Joana kiss and leave with Pedro. The leg is restored; Vitorio goes back to the shanties and his shantytown wife, and all is well in heaven and on earth. In the final shots, when he has been given the job of chauffeur by the minister, he is walking without the cane, the prosthesis no longer visible, his limp barely noticeable.

When Vitorio was initially given the prosthesis, its function as a substitutive object, used to make up for the lack, would seem to work within a "normal" patriarchal order, one in which the Name of the Father, the father's function within the psychic order, was in its place. That function depends upon the son identifying with the father and giving up his rivalry with him. This identification begins a series of substitutions of the figure of the father, or more precisely the place for the function named by Lacan the Name of the Father, which the child incorporates. This is the prerequisite for the child's proper entry into the symbolic order as the internalizing and repressing of the Father's "No," his Law, establishing the basis not only for the superego but for the chain of substitutions by which the process of signification works.[8]

Manu has substitute figures for that Father as his own is missing: missing for so long Manu no longer remembers him. Manu misses him so painfully that he obsessively returns to the absent memory with such phrases as, "When my father returns," and so on; he misses him so deeply he immediately latches onto Vitorio, mistaking him for his father. The figure of grandmother fills that space of the absent father by assuming the role of the one with authority over Manu, and Joane, his teacher, does so partially as well. But the grandmother is tired, old, and weakening, and too absent during the day when Manu is mostly off by himself with his gang, away from her eye. When she takes Manu to church on Sunday, he doesn't join in the service with the others, doesn't pray or cross himself, and shocks his grandmother by telling her he has a better way to recover his father than praying in church with its God, and that is through the use of magic.

If there is a "normal," "natural," dominant symbolic order over which the Law of the Father rules, Manu has entered into it only partially. If Vitorio is the substitute father whose role is to sustain the order by his functioning as that Father, he too is only partially able to fulfill that role.

What we know of Vitorio is, first of all, that he is lacking, incomplete, and that he can never be made whole. He, too, was prevented from entering into the "normal" order of society by having been kidnapped by the army from the seminary when he was fifteen. We never see any evidence of the existence of his family, of his having a family, but only substitutes for it. For example, fairly early in their relationship he joins up with Judite, whose needs and lacks seem as great as his own, and accedes to her desire that they become a couple, a husband

and wife "forever." Although he betrays her soon after by attempting to seduce Joana, he immediately returns to Judite when Joana rejects him. As Joana subsequently turns to Pedro, the "natural" order is reestablished where the wealthy and powerful form couples with each other, and the poor and powerless do so as well.

If the basis for that order depends on the father sustaining his rule, by playing his "proper" role over family, property, and, symbolically, phallus, Vitorio's possession of these things is seen as tenuous from the outset. In place of his lost leg, he has a medal, but it is stolen by the child gang leader Caca. In place of the phallus, symbolically, the prosthesis is provided, but then stolen as well. Although he called upon his authority by insisting to the doctors that he was a sergeant, not a simple soldier, that doesn't guarantee his right to a prosthesis, and after it is lost, he has no more rights to one. Further, he lost it to a mere, weak, albino child. In place of home, wife, and family, he has the street and occasional stand-ins with the prostitutes; he has pity and charity from men who refuse to give him a job. To bathe, he must go to the public fountain where only the women are gathered, and he is hued off by them when he jumps the queue. When he saves Manu from being beaten, he does so with the very sign of his infirmity, of his "castration"—his crutch, which he used to beat Caca. Immediately thereafter, when Manu hugs him and calls him father, believing him to be his father who has returned, he denies that he is Manu's father. In short, if he is the support on which the symbolic order depends, it is in trouble.

The absence of the strong father figure in the symbolic order, the place accorded the Name of the Father on which the superego depends, is evident at the beginning of the film when the gangs of boys are seen roaming the city, stealing and fighting, abusing each other, out of control. Caca, the central such character, is leader of his gang and represents the failure of the paternal figure both in his own weaknesses and his abuse of his gang members. He enters the nightclub, obviously too small and young, and when one of his gang members tries to emulate him by stroking the buttocks of one of the streetwalkers, she is outraged and chases him off. When Vitorio enters the bar and sees his stolen medal on Caca's chest, he beats him and grabs back the medal. There are repeated scenes of these sons, these children acting out in some kind of insubmission to the absent father as when Manu and his friend steal the car radio and flee from the owner, a man who has gone off with his girlfriend. When the man is alerted to the theft, he runs after the boys but fails to catch them. The fathers have failed; the sons are out of control.

Vitorio is not the exception, then, as the weak paternal figure but representative of a world in which fathers are mostly absent, separated from their children, away at war, or missing and presumed dead. None of the men who appear in the film contradict this pattern. Joana's father lives in Portugal. The man in the bar with whom Vitorio shares a drink and who commiserates with him has lost his son to the war. In response to the man's optimism that things will get better, that at least Vitorio is alive, Vitorio recounts the following. When the soldiers were out on the field, at a particularly low point, a man approached them, offering his wife and daughters in exchange for food. The soldiers help themselves to the woman and girls, the youngest being only twelve. When they were done, the commander laughed and threw empty food tins at the man who wept and left. Vitorio concludes, war is shit. He doesn't exclude himself from this negative judgment. But it was more than that war was "fucking shit," it was the resulting situation in which the men were all absent from their families and homes—the absent fathers, the missing husbands and sons.

In this reading, the central scene in the film is the one at the Punto del Re-encontro, which emphasizes the separation of family members from each other. This is more than the fallout of a lengthy civil war, more than the allegory for a wounded nation, which is another figure for castration, but the staging of the weakened symbolic order itself.

In the first stage described above by Žižek, an autonomous subject integrated into liberal capitalist markets in which exchanges between people take place is sustained by a symbolic order that emerges as stable in the end; and the genre that lends itself to these traits is realism. In the case of *O Herói*, it might be psychological or social realism. But the dream, the imaginary intrudes as supplements to the simple truths of national allegories and their miseries. We come closer to the stark realism of war narratives in Vitorio's dream about the time he was walking with his platoon and stepped on a land mine. What he remembers of the past is largely reduced to the moment of his trauma, and what he retains of the past are the deferred reactions to that trauma that have not been resolved or worked through—not even expressed or cured—but which still leave him maimed. If the prosthesis, the substitute organ was intended to effect that cure as a technical supplement, it leaves him still in need of a cane and unable to retain it as a permanent solution. In social terms, it is as if the social order of exchanges daily taking place in the central market cannot function completely without the addition of the black market, which assumes a large, even dominant role in the economic order of the film. In the city market, Manu's grandmother works and procures what they need to eat. But when she sends Manu off to deliver her goods, he is robbed and beaten by Caca's gang from which he cannot escape. Buying and selling at the official market doesn't suffice to make the economic system of exchanges work. Manu is rescued by Vitorio with his crutch, but this is clearly not going to restore authority to the social order.

There are parallels to this situation of lack at every level in the film. The hospital where the prosthesis is provided cannot replace it when it is stolen. If the army was the real sovereign in the field, still it could not prevent Vitorio from losing his leg. If the political party, the MPLA, is the real sovereign ruling the nation, its government leaders are still seen as corrupt, cynical politicians. Pedro's uncle, the self-serving minister of the interior, has an expensive limousine and disdain for the common people who surround him when he emerges from the radio station. Other figures who have authority are equally abusive, like the bar bouncer who beats Vitorio and the bar owner who allows Judite to be beaten by a client. With the return of Pedro from abroad and his integration into the political system under the authority of his uncle, we see the reproduction of the corrupt ruling system with little prospect for change. In fact, if the decent and caring Joana represents that prospect, it would seem to be doomed to failure as she cleaves more to Pedro, one of her class, than to the maimed figure of Vitorio who is of the lower classes—despite the evident appeal he has for women, including her.

When Vitorio addresses the nation, as when he addressed Joana on the bench outside the hospital, the audience finds he speaks well, with feeling. He appeals to the heart in the name of the nation, an ideal Angola in which the losses would be restituted. He addresses the camera directly in these speeches—turning those moments into thinly disguised didactic instances of speechifying. He becomes the locus for the hope that when decency returns, a properly ordered ideal patriarchy would be reinstituted. He represents all those constructions of a nation that has experienced loss of the sort Pierra Nora attributed to the ideological function of sites of memory (*lieux de mémoire*). However, the object that performs that function is the prosthesis—the substitute for what was lost in the war, and not the real object on which that memory would be based, not the equivalent of the "milieu" of memory, or even the *devoir de mémoire,* or obligation to memory, on which a just social order would be founded. For that we would expect the returning soldiers, the returning expatriate fathers and sons, to fill in the aporias in the society and families. Instead, Joana's father remains absent and all she has of him is the apartment; and if Pedro returns, he seems more interested in Joana's body than her moral principles or her ideas. Finally, Vitorio returns and knits a relationship with Judite, only to fall for Joana on the first occasion of their meeting.

The order is fragile, at best; traumatized and wounded more than cured, despite the artificially happy ending—especially because the happy ending appears so incongruous with the landscape of the city. And the landscape finally and especially is marked by the one feature that distinguishes the films of our times that we have been studying here, and that is not one of order, but of matter and people out of place: trash. The striking scenes in this film are continually marked by the presence of trash. They include the remarkably heterogeneous interior of the black market shop: a kind of pawnshop mishmash with parts of cars, bicycles, weapons, tools, bric-a-brac scattered haphazardly on counters and in back rooms. Manu can emerge with an enormous knife or a broken toaster in exchange for the stolen tire or tools he brings in. The dealer seems to have no scruples, though he stops short of letting him take the Kalashnikov.

When Vitorio is homeless and sleeps on the street, the wall against which he puts his mat is marked by graffiti. The images do not function aesthetically, as in *La Nuit de la vérité* where the graffiti is integrated into the aesthetic and sentence-image of the film. Rather they are more of a backdrop, like the trash occasionally littering the streets or hillsides or the worksites where Vitorio looks for employment. At other times, especially when dealing with the two children's gangs, the sites are particularly notable as evoking the detritus of the modern urban landscape and of war. When Manu takes a shortcut to deliver his grandmother's baked goods to Joana, he passes by a hill littered with garbage (see figure 10.2), only to fall into the hands of Caca and his gang who are hiding in the shell of a disintegrating train car. They spy on him, attack him, using the train car as a kind of fort. It is warfare, gang-turf warfare, staged in the corners of the city where urban life is marked by abandonment (see figure 10.3). The image of the boys hiding in the train car is dramatically positioned along a long diagonal shot; they are crouching, peering out from the broken windows at their victim as he unsuspectingly walks by. The neorealism of location and action—grungy urban space, innocent child and dangerous gang, and so on—presents the familiar face of street children whose images date back to Buñuel's *Los Olvidados* (1950), where Manuel's street gang inhabited the abandoned back lots of Mexico City and attacked the paraplegic man who lived there. As the boys in *O Herói* chase Manu through the abandoned train yard, the handheld camera tilts and shakes: the boys are out of place, the trash out of place, the images equally atilt, disorienting. Trash creating a familiar scene of bullies attacking their victim. Unlike Buñuel, however, Gamboa does not tilt to the point of surrealism, does not put in weird musical sounds. We stay within the confines of neorealism. Like Vitorio's sad account of the man and his wife and daughters who were raped by the soldiers, the account is miserablist, with no one escaping the general condition of degeneration.

Thus it is no surprise that if Manu is a victim of Caca, "shit," and his gang, he himself turns to similar practices in similar locations. The prosthesis becomes a machine gun in his play with his gang before he takes it home and turns it into the fetish object. Shortly after Vitorio has had his prosthesis stolen, we see Manu and his mate playing at shooting in the shell of an airplane, with its broken windows. A man with a woman drives up and parks, evidently looking for a quiet place to have sex. As the woman objects to not going to a hotel, they walk away from the car where the boys will steal the radio. Here as in most of the other shots of the street, we can locate images that evoke urban blight, both moral and physical. As the man chases the boys downhill, they run through ravines marked by litter; the man slides in the dirt and gives up the chase. They have escaped into the city and will return to the black market dealer to sell their stolen radio after arguing about who will get the money. The street provides the moral frame; the landscape littered with broken cars, trains, airplanes; the street where a young boy gets hit at night by a car, Pedro's car. These provide the visual complement to the heterogeneous subjects and the heterogeneity of the social disorder that underlies their lives and the structures of the government that rules them.

The prevalence of trash on all levels prevents us from evaluating the people and the objects as being permanently worthless because the motility of trash lies in its being ensconced in systems where objects lose value over time, and at the same time enter into differing regimes of value. The three Hitchcockian orders of economy, with their subject-object relations that Žižek evokes, can all be seen as functioning in this film. The trash insures exchanges that move objects from one realm to another, and the prosthesis is the penultimate object presented in this fashion, from medical supplement to object of play, of worship, and ultimately to one of national pride. The movement is a result of the disruptive nature of trash since it is always in a state of change, losing and gaining value, shifting regimes, always in transition.

In *O Herói*, the fundamental transformation involves the social disruptions that twenty years of war imposed on the landscape, literally as well as figuratively. Angola suffered more from the ravages of land mines than any other country in history, preventing farmers from returning to their villages and fields, provoking massive migrations to cities incapable of handling the influx. The cities themselves are portrayed as dysfunctional: the lights go out, people complain about their lives, the ministers' drivers turn to pirate-taxi driving to supplement their incomes, the black market shop and the children's play display the material waste of the war machine. The state of disorder borders on the state of exception, as the absent *objet a* dissipates under conditions where the larger absence of the Name of the Father renders any repression or suppression inefficacious. The prosthesis cannot fill the hole, make the leg whole, end the trauma and its aftereffects, stop the limping, since the normal has deteriorated on all levels of the personal and the public.

Only the ending restores normalcy to the scene. A reversal so absolute as to suggest the happy illusionism of a Hollywood film, it presents a dream world in an instantaneous reversal of the conditions that preceded it on every level throughout the rest of the film.[9] There is no location in which to stabilize this new vision of a normal world, where Vitorio, now the minister's chauffeur, now the happy dad to the happy Manu takes him for a pleasant spin along the corniche, as the bouncy music carries them along. The real has lost its moorings, and this is because the cycles of trash, like the Nothingness that undergirds reality and value, provoke the disruption in this happy world in the manner of the obsession that disrupts the placid features of the fetish object. This disruption occurs because the counterpart of the "natural" and "normal" society evoked at the end, where family-society-object are presented in such harmonious fashion, is not the abnormal or disfigured, but the valueless object, person, or society—valueless in the figurative and literature terms of trash. The neatness and cleanliness, Manu washing after the beating, Judite washing her life: all depend on trash to be visible, to provide a place in the symbolic order, and to represent that order. Without trash, that order would be stable, and its ordering principles, its ordering archons, and therefore its hierarchies would remain in place. Trash functions to destabilize all those elements, and in this film it is the bare lives and states of exception that mark the landscape of Angola as a state "trashed" by war and corruption, that requires "trash" to effect change.

If we concur with Rancière in seeing the policing of the order and its hierarchy as inherently working in resistance to politics, which seeks to include the excluded and demonstrates its need for egalitarianism, then the naturalization of Vitorio working for the minister at the end undoes the work of the supplement to destabilize the unjust order. The restoration of order at the end is figured in Vitorio who is barely limping now, as though he no longer needed the prosthesis. As though the separations of the Punto del Reencontro were all resolved. But if we read that ending as the Hollywood fetish, seeing its production as occluding the sight of the poor, the trashy people and the trashy landscape, then it becomes like a work of installation art, one in which the discrepancy between the real context it evokes and its unreal representation creates a disjuncture, and eventually a dissensus because of the echo, the memory of the poor and handicapped figures that haunt the landscape. Their haunting is an echo of earlier scenes, the child brought into the emergency room at night when the nurse states there are not doctors until morning; the sight of the minister leaving the radio station, his car surrounded by the poor, the man in a wheelchair that blocks the car, the minister's instructions to the driver to take it easy and not hurt the people on leaving as that would damage his image, Vitorio splayed out drunk and defeated on the floor of the nightclub as the bouncer is about to throw him out and later beats him when he returns. Those images are cleaned up, too cleaned up at the end, like the final crane shots that pan over the city, starting with the corniche drive and then up over the neighborhoods, including the poor and the wealthy, seen from high above the ground, above the rooftops, distant, bouncing with the music, with the last images of Vitorio snapping his fingers to the beat, Manu nodding his head. This resembles Nollywood's prettifying of Lagos, which Haynes describes as a consequence of its commodity fetishism, with "establishing shots across Lagos Lagoon or Five Cowries Creek that, overlooking the squalor and chaos of this most unnerving of West African cities, [that] make Lagos look like any other international capital" (3).

Rancière gives us the ultimate judgment on trash when he claims that detritus is dissensus because dissensus creates the politics whereby the excluded can disrupt the order of hierarchy that relegated them to the invisible positions to which they are condemned, as in the final crane shots of Luanda: "The dissensus by which the invisible equality subtending social distinction is made visible, and the inaudible speech of those rejected into the obscure night of silence audible, thereby enacts a different *sharing* of the sensible" (editor's intro to *Dissensus*, 2010a: 7). The ordinary experience of a father driving his son down the corniche road renders invisible and inaudible all that preceded the ending. But the images and statements that constituted the archive of the disempowered up till that point haunts the final scene, disrupting its complacency. This disjunction, viewed by Rancière as the marker of installation art, is the cornerstone of the contemporary art movement he defines as the aesthetic stage, and its aesthetic revolution, its post-representative revolution. It is "one that proposes to transform [conventional] aesthetics' suspension of the relations of domination into the generative principle for a world without domination" (2009b: 36–7).

This scene represents the end of the logic of the supplement, as it has become the center of that which it was intended merely to complement. It is apparent that what it is filling in for is the aporia already there at the center. We walk into the final scenes of epiphany and joy with a strong sense of their unreality. The final shots of the car ride along the corniche and the smiles and bouncy music that replace the sad notes of earlier times complete this journey home. And the more we relax and allow ourselves to fall into the mood, the more we are nagged by the suspicion that the foot pushing on the gas is not real; that the medal doesn't signify anything of substance; that the limb will remain lost, whatever the substitutes; that Angola's corruption will continue unabated; that the poor, driven out of the city by brutal policies of relocation, will continue to struggle and remain a miserable lot. The war may have ended, the fighting is over and UNITA is finally gone; but the diamonds and oil are still there, still riding herd over a nation that may have begun to be integrated into the global order, but that is a long way from having achieved a just social order, especially because of the global order.

> The January 2007 Amnesty International Report, Angola: Lives in ruins: forced evictions continue, documents the forced evictions that has left thousands of families without homes since 2001. Thousands of families were forcibly evicted from various neighborhoods in the Angolan capital of Luanda in order to make room for public and private housing projects. These forced evictions were typically carried out without prior notification or consultation and without due process of law. Nearly all of the evictions were accompanied by excessive use of force. Officials specifically targeted the poorest families who had least access to the means of securing their tenure. Many victims watched as all their possessions were buried in a hole by a bulldozer. (http://www.amnestyusa.org/angola/reports/page.do?id=YCR0854005000E)

At the end of every story of bulldozed houses, there is the hole that is being covered over. We can take the search for Vitorio's prosthesis as the defining gesture of a certain "African Story." The turn toward the trope of the lack or missing limb speaks to the myriads of subjects in those countries that have experienced violent internal wars. Melodrama, the least realistic of genres attached to the real, would seem to serve that purpose of representing the experience. And the logic of the supplement, like the prosthesis, would seem best to enable us to deal with an excess that is being deployed so as to bulldoze over the unsightly detritus and holes caused by the dislocations of a globalized world order. The logic of the child soldier, the street children, the maimed victims of ethnic cleansing and of the violence of the wars over invaluable resources is that of a commodity fetishism that finds an absurd equivalency between a diamond and a gun, or a soldier's medal and his lost leg—trash within the economy of violence under globalization. A leg we can never really see, but that sets in motion a story about impossible exchanges and prosthetic parts. And that story cannot be rendered within the conventional frame of realism's logic, of empiricism's criteria for truth. Holes and prostheses demand the twin towers of prosthetic logic and deconstruction if we are not to repeat the fractured consequences of a global economic order written on the landscapes and bodies scarred by Africa's conflicts.

Daratt: The Deferred Obedience of the Son

"*Now might I do it* pat, now he is praying; And now I'll do't.
And so he goes to heaven; And so am I revenged. That would
be scann'd."
—(Hamlet III, iii, 73–75)

Chad's passage to independence in 1960 was quickly followed by one-party rule in 1962. The government of Tombalbaye was authoritarian and repressive. Thousands of opponents were imprisoned, and he discriminated against northern and central regions, fostered resentments and resistance. The first armed insurgency began in 1965, and continued despite the entry of French troops to support his rule. By 1975, the discontent became sufficiently widespread that the military rebelled and the gendarmerie killed him. Three years of military rule, followed by more civil strife. By 1980, Habré rebelled and successfully defeated the national army. Ten years of brutal military dictatorship; another rebellion, this time led by Déby, with the ouster of Habré. Chad, impoverished, largely sahel or desert, divided and immersed in armed rebellions for two generations. Corrupt and powerful leadership, still scarred by its past conflicts, with no real reconciliation having yet been achieved.

There will have to be a new archive. We can include the testimonies in the trial in *Bamako* in it; but better, we can include the stories of those not testifying at the time, like Chaka, Melé, Filaï, and those not asked to testify. It will begin with voices that have been silenced, like Zézé the griot's and Saramba the dyer's. It will continue to the voices and images before the camera at the Punto del Reencontro in *O Herói*. But simply adding new voices and stories is not enough. If the archive is already defined by the order of the archive that was originally instituted by the archons, with their originary impressions, with their institutional authority, the addition of subaltern figures will change nothing. In Derridean terms, we will have returned to an archive grounded in a metaphysics of presence, one that pretends to such ideals as truth and reality grounded in notions of unicity, wholeness, completeness, scientific thought, and rationality—in short, a monologue of truth and justice. It would have failed to take into account the logic of the supplement, what adds to or replaces a center marked by an aporia that it is intended to fill; the hole that creates an imitation of the whole, the center that simulates completeness by generating a simulacrum of that image, without any original. In short, it would have merely the attributes of discourse and what deconstructionists call writing (*écriture*).

This might be understood as the difference between the colonial archive, whose notion of "truth" constituted the colonial discourse, and a postcolonial archive, along the lines of what Mudimbe had in mind in seeking to unsettle the conventional European archive of knowledge in his novel *L'Ecart* (1979) and his essays *L'Odeur du père* (1982), *The Invention of Africa* (1988), and *African Gnosis* (1984).

Chaka's death in *Bamako* and its silences indicate the role of absence as well as presence. The hole, the simulacra, the aporias, and the melodrama of Chaka's failing marriage to Melé do the same. In *O Herói*, the neat ending provides closure to all the gaping wounds, not enabling the traumatic wounds to speak but rather answering them with its triumphalism. In contrast, the scene in the desert at the end of *Daratt* leaves ironically open the space between father and son, between the need for the father to be revenged and the son's trick in feigning it.

The ghost of the father demanding revenge, demanding a killing, reclaiming a lost limb, a lost authority, a lost penis, cannot be laid to rest in the new archive. There are two films of the weakened or absent name of the father, the diminished Law of the Father, that sets the stage for the new archive of trash—*Daratt* and *O Herói*—and films of the ascendant figures of women. In one, the phallic-mother-turned-clitoral-goddess Mevoundou (not Mammy Watta, with her return to the conventional social order after the appropriate sacrifices are made, but the new, urban *femmes*, what Bekolo calls bloodettes or "Saignantes," who combat the phallic king, the government minister). Others appeared in the spaces created by the melodrama of *La Nuit de la vérité* (2004), *O Herói*, and *Les Saignantes* (2005), quickly filling the desires of an audience avid for their emotional charge, and Nollywood stormed in to complete the passage from what was called in *Faat Kine* the "Old Africa" with its patriarchal rule to the "New Africa" under the aegis of the order of the triple mother-daughter-lover goddesses, now played by Genevieve Nnaji.[10]

With the decline of patriarchy signaled in *O Herói* and *Daratt*, we begin with the father-son relationship and the role of what Mbembe calls the "commandement." He evokes the tyranny under which a conquered Africa labored, its "*commandants*" or district officers functioning as laws unto themselves, as phallocratic autocrats:

In many ways, the form of domination imposed during both the slave trade and colonialism in Africa could be called phallic. During the colonial era and its aftermath, phallic domination has been all the more strategic in power relations, not only because it is based on a mobilization of the subjective foundations of masculinity and femininity but also because it has direct, close relations with the general economy of sexuality. In fact, the phallus has been the focus of ways of constructing masculinity and power. Male domination derives in large measure from the power and spectacle of the phallus—not so much from the threat to life during war as from the individual male's ability to demonstrate his virility at the expense of a woman and to obtain its validation from the subjugated woman herself. (Mbembe 2001:13)

Placing patriarchal dominance within the scope of colonial rule, Mbembe identifies three forms of violence with which colonial sovereignty was identified. His main point is that the postcolony is the heir of these forms of violence. The first, the "founding violence," was that of conquest, a series of military as well as social acts, summed up in the "cannon" and the "alphabet," as Cheikh Hamidou Kane put it in *Aventure ambiguë* (1972). As sovereign, it arrogated for itself alone the right to judge, to pass and execute the laws of the land. Secondly, to "give this order meaning," it created the justification for the "civilizing mission," producing an ideology that rationalized conquest thus providing self-authorization for its rule. Lastly, and most significantly, it extended rule from an initial force to an enduring hegemony, playing so central a role in "everyday life that it ended up constituting the central cultural *imaginary* that the state shared with society" (25).

The distant European white man became the pervasive colonial presence, the schoolmarm as well as the local shopkeeper, the trader, the political agent, the members of the social elite, the ideal figure for assimilationist emulation. Rule and power with comfort and luxury, enough to produce desire shaped by the phallic dimensions of *commandement*. By the time of the postcolony, it had morphed into "power pass power," in Ken Saro-Wiwa's phrase, a psychological impression driven home by the enormous disparity between the life of privilege lived in the European enclave and its opposite in the "native town."

Violence was joined to rule from the outset. The result was a division between the authority of the phallic ruler, the compliance of the "effeminized" ruled. "What distinguishes our age from previous ages, the breach over which there is apparently no going back, the absolute split of our times that breaks up the spirit and splits it into many, is again contingent, dispersed, and powerless existence: existence that is contingent, dispersed, and powerless but reveals itself in the guise of arbitrariness and the absolute power to give death any time, anywhere, by any means, and for any reason" (Mbembe 13).

The blow creates the trauma. The violence of the ruler, his system, the continuing struggle for power, and the sense of an endless conflict translate into heirs of *commandement* marked by the aftereffects of trauma. For the women, it forms part of the patterns of patriarchal domination instilled in the gender roles that accommodate phallocracy; for the men, part of the patterns of phallocracy demands of the heirs, the forms of necropolitics where the body has to translate subjectivity into subjugation, ultimately grounded in the rule over and dissemination of death.[11] Trauma and the body without rights; again bare of rights or protections; the state of exception with its first stamping grounds, the conquered, colonized lands of others; "*commandement* was based on a *régime d'exception*" (Mbembe 29). Within that regime, no blows were disbarred. At the beginning of *Daratt* lies the trauma. And the revenge.

Trauma and Revenge

Trauma is characterized by deferred reactions, as though the initial experience of the trauma were stored in the body to be evoked repeatedly at later points without being eliminated.[12] It is as though the cries and pain were based on the failure to express and thus eject, abject, the original wounds or blows. The body would seem to store the blows in a location that could not be healed, as though the memory of the past became the experience of the present. The memory is not stored as having passed, say, into an archive, but rather remains as though present, or even as though in the future—as if an anticipation of a blow already received was for a blow about to be received, or received again. The trauma becomes a like phantom limb that returns in the future to its loss in the past. It feels like a ghost of what isn't there, what isn't present, what has no presence, yet causes pain and anxiety. It creates what isn't real so as to experience real pain. The ghost (limb or lost person) becomes more real than the original being who can never match its imitation limb, its imitation tormenter, like a lost father whose injunction imposes its weight on the son to take revenge for the father's death.

The lost limb becomes Hamlet Sr., the trauma becomes his presence, the pain his orders. What is deferred is the obedience, obedience to a figure of *commandement* whose past presence and orders remain stored in the body's archive and create a ghost to whom the son must respond. In this play of substitutions, the prosthesis gives the absent limb the voice / the bodily presence it lacks, turning absence into presence, giving value to what was lost. If the son feels lost because of his failures, because of his lost limbs, his castrated and excised limbs, he is able to turn the loss to profit when placed under a new economy or order. Obedience becomes succession, where eventually it would no longer be the father who continued to command but the sons who had succeeded in eliminating the father.

The first elimination, that of the sons-as-rivals, gives rise to guilt and return of the order, one based on future submission and deferred obedience. If the order of Moses, in *Moses and Monotheism* (1939), means that the sons have internalized their parricide and its effects and now will have instantiated a new logos based on submission to the deferred *commandement,* then the archive of the patriarchy will have succeeded in establishing both its commencement and its commandment. The ghost of the archons will be indefinitely extended as the deferred obedience will guarantee.

If the order of submission is revised under the revolt of the daughters, if the Name of the Father becomes the Name of the Daughters, the possibility of a new archive will become real. There are then two steps to be taken: first that of the revolt of the sons who transform the deferred obedience into a strategically deferred revolt, and then the substitution of the father by the mother, into whose place the daughters can move. The first step is taken in *O Herói* (2004) and *Daratt* (2006), as well as *La Nuit de la vérité* (2004), *Faat Kine* (2000), and the second in *Les Saignantes* (2005) and *Arugba* (2010), the newest generation of African filmmakers.

The most visible play of deferred obedience occurs in *Daratt.* Atim bears the mark of his father's disappearance in his own name, which means "orphan." His father was presumably killed during the fighting that set the current government in place. As Hissene Habré was replaced in 1990 by Idrissa Déby, his former general, it was as though the parricidal mark of the archive, the archival violence, determined that the one in power had to be placed there at the expense of the one who preceded him—establishing a pattern that dictated the form of the archive, and of the deterred obedience that the son was to take when the father's ghost returned with his commandment.

For Freud, that returning figure is far more imposing than his original embodiment. "The dead father became stronger than the living one . . . in accordance with the psychological procedure so familiar to us in psychoanalysis under the name of 'deferred obedience'" (SE 13: 143). Perversely, the stronger the figure, the more conflicted the son, helpless to prevent his own act of interiorizing the figure of the father, helpless in his failure to carry out the commandment to take revenge, or, as the case may be, to kill the one who has taken the place of the father, his own father's killer: Uncle Claudius for Hamlet, or Laius, the simulacrum of Oedipus's father who, although actually Oedipus's real father, is not known to him as such since Polybus raised him as his own son. In *Sunjiata* (1974), the king Naré Maghan Konaté dies before Sundiata is grown. Against his father's wishes, Sundiata's elder brother takes the throne. The rightful ruler will have to prove his worthiness to become king by eliminating his rival, this time his elder brother who took his father's place.[13] Finally, we have *Daratt's* Atim, the orphan, raised by his grandfather Oumar Abatcha and virtually adopted by the man who killed his father, Nassara.

Nassara's power is like that of the figure of the Father, overwhelmingly powerful, supremely dangerous, armed to the teeth, and already having killed enough to have given him guilty memories—perhaps enough to account for his need, now, to pray at the mosque and to give alms to the poor children. He bakes bread and has a young wife, Aicha, with whom Atim falls in love.

Though Atim tries to carry out his mission of revenge, and even aims his pistol at Nassara at one point, he cannot bring himself to pull the trigger. Eventually he apprentices himself under Nassara, barely concealing his frustration and anger. Once, when massaging Nassara he squeezes his neck and brims over with fury, which Nassara cannot understand. Nonetheless, Nassara wants Atim to become his legal son. The father calls out to the son whose father he had killed; the son becomes his father's prosthetic cane, helping the helpless Nassara when his back spasms become too violent for him to walk; helping him when he gets drunk; helping him to make his bread and give it to the begging children. The son and father knit their relationship, even as Atim, like Hamlet, forges his plans for a revenge he cannot carry out.

The orphan of Déby's and Habré's wars seems to be the lost child of all those living in Chad whose state's rottenness would seem to echo that evoked in *Hamlet* about Denmark. The decent authority of the past is gone, and can only return behind the visor of the ghost who speaks only to evoke a lost commandment to remember.

Atim cannot help remembering, cannot flee the grandfather's order or lose the gun and also live with the obligation to take revenge; in Oedipal terms, as with Hamlet, he cannot kill his father, again, this time in the form of Nassara. The phantom limb has now become incorporated, like a trauma, into his body: "He identifies with him while interiorizing him like a phantom who speaks in him before him" (61). These words of Derrida in *Archive Fever*, representing Yerushalmi as a displacement of Freud, the latter himself a displacement of Moses, seem to apply directly to the conflicted Atim.[14] This figure of Atim returns along the well-trodden path already taken by other orphaned figures like Oedipus-Hamlet. Atim's has led him to the trash-strewn courtyard before the gate of the father figure, Nassara the baker. Like Hamlet, Atim's inaction is a case of deferred obedience.

We see Atim's conflict clearly after Nassara knocks Atim's cell phone out of his hand. Nassara retires to a rocking chair in the courtyard and falls asleep. Atim sees him and stares intently at him. Behind his back he is holding the pistol. A close-up of his hand, which is trembling and which he cannot control. Nassara awakens, stares intently, worriedly, at Atim who slips the gun into his pocket. ("Now might I do it pat. . . .") Nassara is distracted; the moment passes.

Nassara returns at a later point to find Atim chatting and laughing with Aicha, mocking his device for augmenting his damaged voicebox (yet another prosthesis). Nassara beats Aicha, and Atim is helpless to stop him. Atim repairs to the bakery, tearing up a baguette in frustration as he hears Aicha's cries. A bit later he comes to Nassara who is seated in the courtyard to tell him he has spoiled a lot of bread by forgetting to put in the yeast. Nassara tastes the bread, spitting it out in anger, stares at Atim, and wordlessly walks off, leaving Atim in the semi-obscurity. Cut to Atim, holding the pistol and pointing it at a mirror. His hand is not shaking; the figure at which the gun is pointed is the ghostly figure of himself. He holds the position for ten seconds before lowering his arm (see figure 10.4). Hearing a sound, he looks out the window. Nassara's back is to him; he points the gun, his hand trembles. Keeping the gun pointed at Nassara, he stares down, steeling himself. When he looks up again, Nassara is gone. All this proceeds without a word being expressed, without Atim able to comprehend what is happening.

The greater the frustration that Hamlet experienced, the greater the danger to all those placed between the "dragon and his wrath." Hamlet calmly and coldly sends Rosencrantz and Guildenstern to their deaths (they "go to't"), and Atim beats one soldier and fires his gun (or at least simulates firing) at another on the bridge at night.

The scene occurs after Atim emerges from a nightclub where a drunken soldier had fired his pistol in the air and then went out to urinate. Atim, who had earlier been threatened by that soldier when coming to town on a minivan and who had also been beaten by soldiers when urinating, himself, against a wall, picks up a stick and beats the soldier. Then he apparently takes the soldier's gun and walks off, coming to a bridge in the darkness. He walks partway across, stops, and stares over the handrail at the darkness before him (see figure 10.5). A voice interpellates him, asking for a cigarette. He complies. The figure of a soldier on crutches, missing a leg, becomes visible as he lights up and thanks Atim. Throughout the encounter, Atim has remained silent. The soldier then makes his way down the bridge. Atim turns, stares after him, and thinks (in voice-over), "I'm Adoum Abatch's son. Remember him." The camera presents his angry face in a direct mid-shot. As the words are repeated, Atim raises the gun and points it directly at the camera, in the direction of the soldier, menacingly (see figure 10.6). The words continue, mixing themselves up, as in a jump cut we now see Atim holding the gun in his other hand and facing the opposite direction of the bridge (see figure 10.7). The sounds and shot confuse the viewer. What has happened? Did he shift the gun to the other hand and point in the opposite direction, or did the jump cut correspond to his changing both his gun hand and his place 180 degrees, leaving him still pointing at the soldier? As the voices in his head reach a peak, he shoots and then looks in the opposite direction. Looking to see if the soldier reacted or whether anyone else had seen him? We cannot tell. He looks around. The sound of a motor, perhaps an airplane. He looks up.

Cut to the next day, Atim walking determinately to the entrance of Nassara's compound. It is locked. Frustrated, he kicks the door, walks about, and then sits, waiting. After some time has passed, Nassara and Aicha return, she in tears after the miscarriage of her child. The moment of revenge has passed. He can do nothing.

With Atim's failure to pull the trigger, a series of events lead him ever closer to Nassara and to Aicha, Nassara's young wife. Atim follows Nassara, even to the umma where Nassara asks him to pray. But Atim refuses. Atim is marked by the scars of his region, of his father's murder, of his revolt against his father, and places himself in the position of Safwan, the rearguard leader of Muhammed's forces who takes Aisha back to Muhammed after she lingers behind the main forces. Like Aisha, her namesake, Nassara's wife Aicha is beaten before being reconciled to her husband. In the Qur'an, Safwan disappears from the scene.

Haroun lards this account of Atim's deferred revenge with ghostly presences so that every figure would seem to gesture, intertextually, to that earlier moment in the desert, at the crossroads, where father and son meet in rivalry and love, provoking exchanges whose ultimate purpose would seem to be the eventual decline of the old and rise of the new, a new order that can't help but assume its rightful place assigned to it by the predecessor. If Atim's desire is a guilty one, his need for revenge repressed only to return against the surrogate figure of the father, he is not acting so much as obeying a deferred commandment that exceeds in strength that of the original injunction laid on him by his grandfather to take revenge for his father's death. After all, Nassara is there, alive, before him, occupying a place Atim comes to learn is his own: "The phantom thus makes the law—even, and more than ever, when one contests him. Like the father of Hamlet behind his visor, and by virtue of a *visor effect*, the specter sees without being seen. He thus reestablishes the heteronomy. He finds himself confirmed and repeated in the very protest one claims to oppose to him. He dictates even the words of the person who addresses him."[15]

This is the law of the archive, and Atim appears doomed to repeat the sins of the sons in their parricide of the father, both in his failing to avenge his own father, in failing to carry out the command of his grandfather—sinning against himself, his own patriarchal order that demands the justice denied it by the amnesty decision of the new regime, itself one that had supplanted its predecessor by a forceful coup d'état. And Atim sins against his surrogate father Nassara as he attempts to kill him repeatedly, assuming the guilt of an act he both desires and cannot commit. He lives in a state of conflict because the commandment of the archive is inscribed on him, not as an unconscious drive, but in the places marked by what is not repressed: "[Freud] had even stressed that what is most interesting in repression is what one does not manage to repress" (61).

In the structure of the confrontation between the son who failed to take revenge and the ghost of the father who returns to demand it, the son's need to create a space for himself cannot be answered. "The phantom does not respond" (62). This is the key moment for Derrida in his analysis of the son's attempt to speak to the ghost, to deal with the deferred command, and his own deferring of his obedience. The son asks for an accounting but gets no response. And of all the reasons Derrida gives for the phantom-father's failure to respond, refusal to respond, its retreat behind its visor, the most compelling is that the phantom, because it is a ghost, must remain heterogeneous to the son because as the returned figure it is now "other," and "the other will never again respond" (62).

To come to this point where the son can realize that his appeal, to be or not to be, will go unacknowledged, that all he will hear is the ghostly "remember me," Atim must lead Nassara into the wilderness where the site of the son's original encounter with the Law of the Father occurs. His grandfather has retreated to the desert, to the tree where God had once before come down to deal with his rebellious sons and put in place the order for those who obeyed. Atim tricks Nassara into coming with him there and fools the blind patriarch into thinking that his revenge was being carried out. Only by deceiving both can Atim presume to begin a new archive. As Derrida says, "to archive *otherwise*": "to repress the archive while archiving the repression" (64).

Here is the scene: Atim has led Nassara before his grandfather, as Nassara thinks he is going to meet Atim's parents and request their permission to adopt Atim. They come to the desert rendezvous. The blind grandfather stands erect, thinking Atim has brought Nassara before him so as to be killed. As the two approach the old man, Oumar Abatcha, he rises, standing above them on a small hill. The camera assumes his point of view, looking down at the two.

> Grandfather: He hasn't forgotten me, has he?
> *[Nassara looks behind him, light beginning to dawn on him about the situation he has come to. Grandfather chuckles. Atim looks back at Nassara.]*
> Grandfather: Ana Oumar Abatcha. *[I am Oumar Abatcha.]*
> *[He is seen in profile]:* May he suffer the same fate as my son.
> *[Midshots of Nassara, then Grandfather, standing thin and supremely antique, the patriarch in the desert, the god above, pronouncing his judgment. The economy of the desert scene is pure.]*
> "May he feel the same humiliation. Have him undress." *[The sightless god can issue commands all the more forcefully as he speaks, the only one to speak. The others respond mutely to his words.]*
> *[Nassara tries to run, stops as Atim clicks the gun and holds it to Nassara's head. No question of not being able to act now. Nassara strips, and Atim glances up at his grandfather, awaiting his orders. Nassara looks at Atim.]*
> "Execute him. What are you waiting for?" *[And at the pause, the last command.]* "Your hand must not tremble."
> *[Nassara mouths his last prayers. Atim shoves his body down, points the gun upward, and shoots. Atim holds Nassara's head down and stares at the grandfather, who speaks.]* Grandfather: "Finish him off" *[see figure 10.8].*
> *[Nassara moves his lips, we presume in prayer. Atim stares at his grandfather, and the camera cuts to his lower body, his hand holding the cane: the metonymy of the hard desert god-father. Atim points the pistol up in the air and fires. Nassara lies quietly under his hand, opens his eyes, realizing he has been spared. Atim holds his pistol pointing upward, to the sky that he has shot twice, looking down at the father figure lying in the sand. See figure 10.9]*

The parricide and the revenge have been completed, but in a new archive, necessarily ending the cycle that has now brought Nassara so low, that trashed his haughty place as the strong man he had been once.

[Atim looks up at his grandfather, who looks off, implacable, his orders having been carried out. Then Atim releases Nassara, goes up to his grandfather, takes his hand, and they walk off.]
> [Last words of the patriarch.] "Did your hand tremble?"
> Atim: No.
> Grandfather: Then you are a man, my son.
> *[They continue walking, and disappear over the hill.]*

Derrida's conclusions about the archive are both predictable and astounding. The predictable part is that every impression made onto the archive, every step recorded in the sand and then repeated as an impression to be remembered, recorded, and ultimately authorized by the archonic—"Then you are a man, my son"—repeats the basic structure of the archive itself as the repository whose *arkhe*, grounded as a commencement and a commandment, rests upon the instantiation of an order whose absoluteness is divided by the "substrate,"[16] the foundation on which the contents rest. The archival space is not an internal space but an external one whose contents are to be copied, marked by the obsessive quality of repetition, which is itself an indication of the violence of the archive[17]—a violence that excludes for every entry it includes, that burns to ashes as it simultaneously records for posterity, for the sons to come. It looks continually to the future, and that is the astounding part, that in recording the past on the basis of an act of authority, it opens itself to a future that is spectral, if not simply uncertain—spectral as in the repetition of the commandment of an authority that is already dead.

The commandment to take revenge turns against itself as Atim refuses to be the son, the grandson, or the adopted son of the three fathers who tried to claim him. Nassara, who killed his father, had become the one who most merited that claim because he had relinquished his rights as the one who gives, who orders, who dispenses charity to those lesser than he, when he begged Atim to become his son and eventual heir. But he had forgotten quite who this Atim, with his tribal marks, might have been; forgot those whom he had killed in the past; forgot his place in the archive of the patriarchs who still ruled in the desert. So his prayers at the mosque meant little, as the order he attempted to put in place would have merely reversed the position of those who ruled, and not its basic foundation. He remained under the rule of the One, as in the *Chadaha: La ilaha illa lah*—there is no god but Allah.

He had forgotten the original order, and so repeated it in his household with Aicha and tried to repeat it by adopting Atim, the orphan boy who was really an angel of vengeance. Between his forgetting and the injunction of revenge, of remembering, and more particularly, the ghost's injunction to remember not to forget—"Do not forget. This visitation is but to whet thy almost blunted purpose" (III, iv, 112)—we come to the core of the work of the archive: "As if God had inscribed only one thing into the memory of one *single people* and of an *entire people*: in the future, remember to remember the future" (76), this being Derrida's reading of the Jewish covenant with God.[18]

"Remember to remember the future," the work of the covenant in the past, like Atim's fidelity to his father's death and grandfather's commandment: it is from this work of remembrance that the foundation of the archive as a locus for both duty and justice arise. The duty arises as "duty of memory," the phrase on which the Rwandan genocide memory project was built—being not only the duty of the survivors but especially of those of the special people singled out for their obligation to the divine injunction. But as such, the Jews to whom Derrida refers would be different from the others, would be not chosen because of their qualities but rather their singularity. And as singular, different—other. The passage from archon to other is completed by Derrida in this declension: "Here situates the place of all violence. Because if it is just to remember the future and the injunction to remember, namely the archontic injunction to guard and to gather the archive, it is no less just to remember the others, the other others, and the others in oneself" (77). Otherness, exclusion, matter or people out of place—the trash that is Atim, the orphan boy lost in the city, the Hamlet who could not take proper revenge, the one who stands aside as the faithful complete their prayers—the other, now is both outside as well as inside oneself, "*tout autre est tout autre*" which Derrida glosses as, "every other is every other other," and "is altogether other" (77). To bring the chosen people into a Oneness is the same as the act of violence of the archive, because "the gathering into itself of the One is never without violence, nor is the self-affirmation of the Unique, the law of the archontic, the law of *consignation* which orders the archive. Consignation is never without that excessive pressure (impression, repression, suppression)" (78).

The pressure to be One is the substrate not only of the archive but of the covenant. It is passed on in every generation by the exclusion of the double, the other son, the rival brother—Isaac's brother Ishmael, Jacob's brother Esau, Joseph's eleven brothers, and Joseph's son Manassah—not to mention Abraham's brother Lot, and before them Abel's brother Cain. And Sundiata's elder brother as well, all the above examples being of younger brothers supplanting the elder. The one must keep at a distance the other; the One must ban the other, consign the Other to the location that is out of place. The work of the archive is to draw that boundary between the past retained by the archons and the forgotten memories they reduced to ash. "As soon as there is the One, there is murder, wounding, traumatism." "*L'Un se garde de l'autre*," which, again, Derrida glosses in divided terms: "The One guards against / keeps some of the other. It protects *itself* from the other, but, in the movement of this jealous violence, it comprises in itself, thus guarding it, the self-otherness or self-difference (the difference from within oneself) which makes it One" (78). "The One as the Other" (78). He is not only riffing on Rimbaud here—"*Je est un autre*"—but also playing against the Hebrew Shema ("Hear O Israel, the Lord our God, the Lord is One") and the Muslim Chahada ("There is no god but Allah").

The obedience to the One has the same form of violence as the obedience to the state in the postcolony. This is Mbembe's reading of state power as that which creates, "through administrative and bureaucratic practices, its own world of meanings," what he calls a "master code," the primary code of society that governs the "logics that underlie all other meanings within that society" (103). The state then naturalizes this code as "common sense," rendering society uniform in its consciousness. From its monopoly on brute power comes this imposition of the One, as in the single party, the father of the nation, the institutionalization of the *commandement* as hegemon "in the form of a *fetish*" (103). The fetish dissimulates its power, and especially what produces it, as well as the repression of any possibility of alternative figures of power, repression of opposition as other.

The violence that springs from this Oneness—in the archive, in the state, in the credos that follow—consists in forgetting the violence involved in the act of constituting oneself as One. Every archival move to include turns to this violence because it excludes others so as to constitute itself, and in the act turns otherness into the occasion for another act of revenge. This is how the state was built in Chad. This was the grandfather's violent commandment, which echoes Derrida's summation, as if predicting Haroun's characterization of the archonic patriarch, with these words: "*L'Un se garde de l'autre pour se faire violence* (*because* it makes itself violence and *so as* to make itself violence)" (78).

If every formulation involving the One entails the other, and is divided against itself, it is because the assumption of subjectivity entails the act of division, of splitting—of being both self and other. The violence turns on the fact that "the Other is the condition for the One" (79), the rule of the archive, the archons, and the grandfather who forgot the rule in order to complete the revenge.

Returning to *O Herói*, we find the same move suggested by Baudrillard when he postulates that the Nothingness is required for Being to exist by establishing what is in contradistinction to it, what sets it off—Being's Other. Atim is able to break with the cycles of violence that postulate the existence and exclusion of the Other so that the One might constitute itself—for "being" in Hamlet's sense of being One or Other, being or not being. Atim's refusal might have been seen as a failure to complete the injunction of the god in the desert. Or it might have been viewed as a radical opening to the future, signaled by the scene of his walking over the dune with his grandfather, now no longer bound by his call (as in the opening shots when the grandfather's calling his name reverberated throughout the quartier). Atim not only leads his grandfather, he misleads him so as to take them out of the cycles of violence begun in his time by the

Figure 10.1. Maria Bárbara and Punto del Reencontro.

Figure 10.2. Manu and trash field.

Figure 10.3. Caca and Manu at train.

Figure 10.4. Akim pointing gun at mirror.

Figures 10.5–10.6. Atim seeks revenge on bridge.

Figure 10.7. Atim seeks revenge on bridge.

Finish him off.

Figure 10.8. Grandfather in desert.

Figure 10.9. Atim points gun upward.

national leaders Habré and then Déby, both having supplanted their predecessors violently and certainly sustaining the regimes of violence for the future.[19]

This national allegory could only be supplanted by the creation of a new postcolonial archive, for which the model of trash serves in exemplary fashion. Atim, like Vitorio in *O Herói*, engages the future in the way Vitorio's prosthetic limb performs its role in the film. He enters into a cycle of exchanges that enable those separated into self and other, separated by the violence of the wars, to return home and reknit the ties of the family. Although the fathers in both films are lost, the supplements in the form of the new fathers, Vitorio and Nassara, are able to emerge because they too had lost pieces of themselves—a leg, a voice—and knew of the need to be reconstituted as whole. For each there was a specter, a prosthetic part that somehow belonged to them even as it was lost; and for each this was the necessary condition for them to create a future: "as Freud might say (this would be his thesis), there is no future without the specter of the oedipal violence" (Derrida 80). If the archive is what provides the simulation of a history on which a nation can build, and if the ashes of that archive are the result of the archival violence, its violent act of forgetting, then the burden of these two films begins the work of moving a certain Africa toward its future by deploying that image of the specter of an Oedipal violence intended to make way for an "other" archive to emerge.

11 Nollywood and Its Masks: Fela, *Osuofia in London,* and Butler's *Assujetissement*

In writing about *The Cosby Show,* Mark Reid cites critical voices that "argue that the show does not present the lived experiences of African Americans" (1993: 33–34). In contrast, we can evoke any of a number of reviews of *Precious* (2009) or *Slumdog Millionaire* (2008) for whom the "lived experiences" become overwhelming, at least before the possibility of the Cinderella ending emerges. Here is a typical example from a review of *Precious* from a newspaper called the *Herald Sun:*

> The title character of *Precious* has a way of thinking that helps her live through the unthinkable.
>
> "Every day I tell myself something's gonna happen," says Precious (impressively played by acting newcomer Gabourey Sidibe) in one of her many narrated monologues in the film. "I'm going to break through. Or someone is going to break through to me." I'm not giving away anything when I tell you that the seemingly fantastical wishes of Precious become distinctly possible by film's end.
>
> They just have to, really. For it would be impossible to make it through this punishing urban drama if there wasn't some light at the end of the long, dark tunnel of misery ahead.[1]

This raises the question of how much trash is too much: how much miserablism is too much, how much "lived experience" of raisins rotting in the sun, as Langston Hughes put it, exceeds the viewers' capacity to empathize with the victim, generating a rejection not only of the story, the character's situation, but the portrayal of the larger environment.

We can situate *The Cosby Show* in the real world of TV family sitcoms, where comforting resolutions to minicrises, to "life's" everyday situations that never ultimately unsettle, are expected before the crisis presents itself. The predictable ending is present at the outset with the predictable order whose presiding traits are confirmed at the conclusion. This brings the closure Catherine Belsey (1980) identifies with classic realism.[2]

Similarly, we situate melodramas, or especially soap operas, with their continual opening onto new crises and with equally continuous resolutions of the minicrises—not only warding off disruptions, but putting out the trash—as always restoring the clean order of life, again and again, never changing no matter how long the series lasts, no matter how many tears are shed for the poor, unfairly accused protagonists. This is the homogeneity of the "propre," in the Derridean sense of a logocentric order. It accommodates the Bakhtinian view to which Reid appeals as integrating any oppositional readings into one's own "internally persuasive discourse," which neutralizes those negative aspects of oppositionality (1993: 21). Reid appeals to this process of reterritorializing the discourse of the other so as to make sensible the black audience's acceptance of minstrelsy humor, ostensibly racist, when performed by a black performer. The humor is viewed as nonthreatening, as with the television version of Amos and Andy, despite the stereotypes of the "coon" characters: Andy, "obese, domineering, and lazy"; Kingfish, "a scheming, well-dressed con man"; and Lightnin', "a slow moving janitor" (24). All of these men conform to Bogle's typography of the coon, "no-account niggers, those unreliable ... lazy ... good for nothing more than ... butchering the English language" (Bogle 1994: 8). Similarly, the female lead, Sapphire, conforms to the minstrel stereotype as a "modernized version of a domineering mammy, who is constantly criticizing the inadequacies of her husband George" (24).

Two models of the troublesome minstrel figure present themselves for us: Fela, in performance as the wild African savage, while in political guise, the revolutionary muckracking politico; and Osuofia, the foolish, lazy, "bush" villager, mocked and dominated by his "mammy" wife, one step short of the gullible folk figure like monkey or his variants, two steps short of the trickster Leuk, or hare, whose laziness and cleverness ultimately precipitate an upheaval in an unstable order, reconstituting society as it ought to have been from the outset (Pelton 1980).

These folk characters, animal figures in human situations, must be viewed as masquerades whose connotated identities supplant the superficial denotation of their appearance. They are not what they seem, what they appear to be, but have to present their appearance as a mask in order to be comprehended as a sign for some other, unseen subject. Their meanings are unidimensional, but it requires more than one dimension to access that meaning, and it is always one degree removed from their appearance. In short, they are not simply masked but disguised. They are foolish in order to produce the meaning of the tale, which is not foolish. They are the tools of that storyteller who stands behind their figures, yet who needs them in order to speak.

In our cases of Fela and Osuofia, they are minstrel figures—not in burnt-cork blackface, but as blacks playing the role of blacks. That makes them hybrid minstrels, in Reid's terms, and the only question is whether they are performing in the service of a satirical imperative or are simply the tools of a flat "pastiche," in Jamesonian terms—lacking the parodic humor of satire, and thus its imperative of oppositionality. For the minstrel performance, race is enacted as a comic role, as in the original blackface versions played by white performers—performers of race humor, as in the *Amos 'n' Andy* radio show in the 1920s spoken by white radio actors Freeman Gosden and Charles Correll, and by black television actors Alvin Childless and Spencer Williams in the 1950s version.

In its twentieth-century iterations, as minstrelsy figures came to be played by black actors, they caricatured the images created earlier by white actors—thus blacks imitated whites imitating "blacks." Hybrid minstrels fed into blaxploitation cinema where comics played at ghetto types, not so as to mock the caricature but rather to play into the type.[3]

Lastly, satiric minstrelsy appeared in African American cinema in the 1970s, the weapon of resistance to racist representations, taking the form of parodic imitations of racist roles. A generation of Godfrey Cambridge (*Watermelon Man* 1970) and Eddie Murphy comedians quickly developed, following the emergence of blaxploitation films, veering along the precipice defined by mainstream cinema between a broadly smiling humor that laughed at the racist father in *All in the Family* without taking on directly the ugly consequences of racism. Still, an oppositional possibility was developed, and we see it manifest repeatedly in Sembène's acerbic humor as in *Xala* (1974), where the young assimilated African wedding guests speak disparagingly about blacks from whom they fled in their travels in Europe. Another example is Sembène's Dieng, in *Mandabi* (1968), a butt of the satire whose humor is placed at work in the service of oppositional cinema (Diawara 2010: 33–44).

In contrast, Fela's mask of the African man, as he calls himself in one of his greatest songs, "Gentleman," would seem to be seriously embodying the sexist figure as it simultaneously mocks the assimilated African, whom he calls the gentleman. The refrain is, "I no be gentleman at all, I be Africa man original":

I no be gentleman at all o!
I be Africa man original
. . .
Them call you, make you come chop
You chop small, you say you belly full
You say you be gentleman
You go hungry
You go suffer
You go quench
Me I no be gentleman like that
. . .
You dey go your way, the jeje way
Somebody come bring original trouble
You no talk, you no act
You say you be gentleman
You go suffer

You go tire
You go quench
Me I no be gentleman like that
. . .
Africa hot, I like am so
I know what to wear but my friends don't know
Him put him socks, him put him shoe
Him put him pant, him put him singlet
Him put him trouser, him put him shirt
Him put him tie, him put him coat
Him come cover all with him hat
Him be gentleman
Him go sweat all over
Him go faint right down
Him go smell like shit
Him go piss for body, him no go know
Me I no be gentleman like that
I be Africa man original
(http://www.songmeanings.net/songs/view/3530822107858727868/)

The cover of the *Gentleman* CD album features a baboon; Fela performs the song, in the YouTube video,[4] in a variety of outfits or semi-naked, with only the sax covering his genitals. His face in performance, in the video, in his club, in innumerable instances, as in the film, shows his face covered with paint, a sort of African-man-original's war paint—blackface war paint, as it were, enacting the powerful sound of his saxophone and voice as he intones his refusal to "wear trouser, put tie, put him singlet, and cover all with him hat," the insignia of the New African Gentleman and his old markers of alienated assimilation. One published version has the gentleman weak-kneed, "jeje":

"You dey go your way, the jeje way—the way of politeness, gentleness, unassertiveness, unmanliness."
Somebody come bring original trouble
You no talk, you no act
You say you be gentleman
You go suffer
You go tire
You go quench
Me I no be gentleman like that.

But on the YouTube version, it isn't "go quench," but "be French," that defines this lost man. His wives intone the chorus behind him, "I no be gentleman at all-o," as he growls, "I no be gentleman like that."

The saxophone wails out his black presidency message, African man, bush man—played out in the Shrine, Fela's club. Everything spiraled into the performance of the African man in Fela's life. His great compound the Kalakuta

Republic, which rose to the status of a mini-state, was attacked by the Nigerian military, who threw his eighty-two-year-old mother from a second-story window, killing her. In a subsequent attack, they burned the house, expelling all his twenty-seven wives, children, and hangers-on.

In Fela's performance of African manhood, the woman has her role as the counterpart. Fela constructs her, bizarrely, not as the liberated woman, angry, powerful, driven, like her man, the saxophone-wielding musician, but as the counter to the "lady"—to the feminist type, the equivalent of the gentleman with her class snobbery, assertiveness, and most of all, the alienated disregard for the African man's primacy:

> She go want take cigar before anybody
> She go want make you open door for am
> She go want make man wash plate for her for kitchen.

The Fela wife wore her makeup, as did the African man in performance, but hers was for dancing the "fire dance," not the gracious ballroom variety reserved for the gentleman. If the African man wore his war paint, she wore her dance paint, and her dance was to support the star in his strutting performance on stage.

> Lady
>
> If you call woman
> African woman no go 'gree
> She go say I be Lady o
> . . .
> She go say I no be woman
> She go say market woman na woman
> She go say I be Lady
>
> I want tell you about Lady: . . .
> She go say him equal to man
> She go say him get power like man
> She go say anything man do
> Him self fit do
> I never tell you finish . . .
> I never tell you . . .
> She go want take cigar before anybody
> She go want make you open door for am
> She go want make man wash plate for her for kitchen
> She want salute man she go sit down for chair . . .
> She want sit down for table before anybody . . .
> She want piece of meat before anybody . . .
> Call am for dance, she go dance Lady dance . . .
>
> African woman go dance she go dance the fire dance . . .
> She know him manna Masster

She go cook for am
She go do anything he say
But Lady no be so . . .
Lady na Masster . . .

. . .

She go say:
*(CHORUS-AFTER EACH LINE) SHE GO SAY I BE LADY O O
(http://afrofunkforum.blogspot.com/2009/03/fela-kuti-lyrics.html)

This is satiric hybrid minstrelsy as Fela's African man and African woman perform their number, mocking the Gentleman and Lady, playing their Africanness before the quartier audience in the Shrine. Fela ran for president of Nigeria, performing before the Nigerian audience, while also recording films, videos, and music recordings for the world music audience. The baboon on the cover of the *Gentleman* album is thus the satiric mask of the hybrid minstrel playing back to the racists the reflection of their bigoted imaginary, matching the Afrobeat with the image's powerful, mocking disavowal. The stronger the image, the more forceful the assertion of the manhood, the more the lady must be evoked in order that the African man's counterpart woman might be constructed. His construction requires her as his support.

Similarly, as we shall show, the figure of Osuofia, the quintessential mock villager and father, is presented in ridiculous light at the beginning of *Osuofia in London*. Unlike the African man original, he is still contained within the hybrid minstrel representation and thus continually misses his mark, falling like the country bumpkin that he is, not so as to debunk the stereotype but to represent it to the sophisticated viewer. By the end of *Osuofia in London* 2, this view is modified by our sympathy for him. Less strident that Fela, not at all overtly political, Osuofia still deploys the minstrel's mocking tones[5] so that a more "gentle" complaint against the western-biased views of Africa might be heard.

En route to both Fela's dynamic claims to manhood and Osuofia's march toward an African humanism, lie the figures of the women: Fela's twenty-seven wives, on stage, standing behind their man, his chorus in blackface, in Africana blackface, matching his own African man-blackface appearance. With *Osuofia*, the woman who appears in Osuofia's path is presented as the white gold digger, the beautiful oyimbo woman who will go so far as to put on the blackface mask of the "Africanized" woman in order to trick, or kill, Osuofia for his money.

Here then is our trash: the trashy woman who will go so far as to kill the African man for his money; or the sexy, half-nude dancers who stand behind their Fela, ready to obey their man in his fidelity to his political ideal, his careening path that ultimately takes them down along with him. These are the women who are necessary for the minstrelsy performance to work, and they are sacrificed in some sense in order that the minstrel role can be carried out. The key question for us, as we stated at the outset, is how much trash is too much? Can the performance of Fela, or Osuofia, accomplish its goals? Can Fela's oppositionality be sustained; can Osuofia's African humanism be accepted, in the end? And is the price the sacrifice of the woman, again, as some version of the trash?

Nollywood and Its Masks

What relationship might one see between the radically political Fela, a classic Fespaco film like *La Nuit de la vérité* (2004), and a Nollywood film like *Osuofia in London,* one of the most popular Nollywood films? High culture, seriousness of purpose, filmmaking techniques grounded in professional editing, camerawork, and screenwriting, all in the service of the Idea that a hermeneutic analysis engages: vision, truth, reality—all those heavy terms that have weighed down African filmmaking from its inception. The contrasting practice is termed "popular entertainment," as though this description, established when viewing films from below, constituted a definitive judgment. It is my contention that the border between such genre movies as melodramas and serious auteur films is now largely permeable, if not sensibly collapsed, and that much of the obvious distinctions between soap operas and serious dramas apply largely to the past.

In African society, Nollywood films, soap operas, along with Brazilian, Mexican, and Argentinean telenovelas, have been understood by such interpreters as Jonathan Haynes as exhibiting the anxieties over modernism. The anxiety is located on the personal level, so the cameras come in close to catch the tears, to highlight the emotional, individual moment, to record the crisis, by seeking out the most excessive displays of inner feelings. It is difficult to express the qualities of the soaps without resorting to a discourse that is already freighted with all the derogatory judgments high culture and criticism reserved for these films since their popularity took hold in the 1950s when they were dubbed "women's weepies."[6]

Nollywood is an urban film practice where urban settings are set in contrast to rural villages (Okome 1997; Haynes 2000).[7] Thus Lagos is defined as not the "bush."[8] Osuofia coming from the village is the quintessential villageois, as seen in the eyes of the urban sophisticate, and when he leaves the village it is to travel to its opposite space, London—London as a tourist postcard emblem for the modern west; London, the synecdoche for the modern city; and given Haynes's claim that Nollywood is fundamentally the product of Lagos[9] as the imaginary site for its modernity, London is the stand-in for Lagos. Modernity is figured in the city, with its luxurious living, great wealth set against poverty, and its dangers. The wealthy are seen with their high-walled compounds, guards and servants, expensive cars, flashy clothes, plush furniture, cabinets of expensive whiskey, and above all gorgeous lovers. The obsessive materialism does not accommodate itself to the notion of a truth lying hidden within a sensitive soul; rather, valuable goods are exhibited publicly and establish the primary order by which value is measured.

Nollywood films are defined by excess, where the borders that frame the images, the sentiments, the characters—the symbolic order and its limits—are violated dramatically and systematically, as in the mannerism of the neobaroque. Reality yields to magic as logos and reasonableness are banished. Haynes summarizes: "the commodity fetishism extends to walled mansions, cell phones, exercise equipment, fancy hotels and restaurants. The plots inflate common domestic problems into huge business deals and cat fights between overdressed women, and they generally show us a world closer to *Dallas* and *Dynasty* than to the reality in which virtually all Nigerians live" (2000: 3). In such settings, the supernatural makes its appearance in monstrous forms, appropriate to the visions of an extravagant Pentecostalism that has become widespread throughout West Africa. Witchcraft, sex, money, love potions, poisonings and death agonies, spirits, Mercedes: a club scene dressed in Nigerian glitter.

What does Fanta Nacro, a filmmaker given to making films like "Le truc de Konate" (1998), which is about the need for "modern" women to insist their partners use condoms, have to do with Nollywood "trash"? If we consider individual shots and scenes in their isolation from the narrative context, the differences between high and low begin to dissipate. In *La Nuit de la vérité,* the night of truth turns into a nightmare of blood filled with macabre images (see figure 7.4). However, the differences in genre and characterization between the "serious" *Nuit* and the farce *Osuofia in London* could not be greater. *Osuofia* will be our model for the analysis of its popular features and style. We will return to *Nuit* after a close analysis of *Osuofia*.

In our first glimpse of the foolish hero Osuofia, he plays the "great [white] hunter," being held up by his own four grown daughters as he attempts to train the sights of an old hunting rifle on a gazelle. He shoots, misses by a mile, and falls ignominiously as his daughters exclaim over how poor a shot he is. He chastises them, blaming them for his failure, quickly establishing for himself the role of the buffoon—or, in Bogle's terms, the coon, a bumbling, foolish loudmouth (see figure 11.1). He returns home to a wife whose size and temperament place her in Bogle's category of the Mammy—typically asexual, domineering within the homestead, mouthy, but ultimately maternal in her instinct. The daughters and mother provide the foil for the trashy vamp whom we would expect to eventually appear. In the early years of Hollywood cinema, such a figure might have been played by the "tragic mulatto" instead of a white woman, as miscegenation was a cinematic taboo. She will appear in the figure of Samantha when Osuofia eventually arrives in London.

From the opening scene, Osuofia's failures are presented by Ogoro in his relationships with his daughters and wife, that is, his failures to be an adequate father and husband. When his daughters return home from school, somewhat after the opening hunting scene, it is because they cannot pay their school fees: he blusters and tells them they are old enough to be out on their own and married and he doesn't want to wait for that until their breasts droop down to the ground. Later, when the schoolteacher appears with a solicitor from Lagos, Osuofia is again shown up by the schoolteacher's sensible, measured discourse and continues to make himself look foolish, blustering that he will take care of his daughters' fees.

Nkem Owoh's hilarious depiction of Osuofia as the stock, clownish villager provides wonderful comedy. We see him harassed on all sides for village dues, contributions to a funeral, taxes, school fees, and family needs, to which he proves incapable of paying even a single kobo. It is relevant to this character-ization that he has only daughters, now grown to high school age, with no sons to ameliorate his image of the failed, impotent pater familias.

The role of the women in this homestead of the failed father is to put up with him, to bear with his berating, exhibiting their frustration but not fear or respect. His absence of authority hasn't meant their liberation from patriarchy. Nor is it a question of that authority being based upon money, the source of agency in the age of commodity capitalism. It is as though they are living in a time where the shell of the patriarch, symbolized in the foolish figure of the failed father-husband, has become the norm, with no possibility of this being reversed.

The key moment in Osuofia's life occurs when a solicitor arrives from Lagos carrying the news of his brother's death. At first Osuofia doesn't understand the import of what is being said and bad-mouths his brother to the schoolteacher and solicitor. When the news sinks in that he will inherit his brother's consid-erable estate, he calls his daughters and wife and commands them to cry for his brother whom they hadn't seen for many years. He orchestrates their move-ments, which are turned on and off like a spigot, somehow making him, rather than them, appear all the more hypocritical. Later that evening, when the family has gathered in the living room to discuss his voyage to London to obtain the inheritance, each daughter tells him what she wants him to bring back. The smart one wants books, the pretty one a miniskirt and clothes, a Mammy Watta wig, high heel shoes; another desires cosmetics. When the daughters are gone, he tells his wife he is concerned about the daughters preserving their chastity, especially the one who wants the miniskirt. "This one wants a miniskirt," he complains: "from short skirt to pants, pants to naked." And then, "I don't want any pregnancy. I trust Oku, but all the others can open their legs."

At every point "Master Osuofia," as the schoolteacher dubs him, causes us to laugh at him. We join in the sophisticates' superior laughter at the country bumpkin, setting ourselves up for the same kind of lesson Oyono delighted in creating in Le Vieux nègre et la médaille (1956) where the reader comes to re-alize that joining in with the narrator's mocking laughter at the old man is to share in the racist perspective of the dominant colonial discourse, and that the "vieux nègre" would ultimately prove himself to be the voice of the liberal humanist's higher values, thus acting as corrective to the colonialist mockery mimed by the narrator. But before we can arrive at that point, "le vieux nègre" will have to suffer the full extent of his ignominy. For Osuofia that debasement, that completion of the image of his foolishness, can only occur in London, just as for Oyono's "vieux nègre" it could only have occurred *en ville,* in the big city. We are in the grips of modernism's Manichean aesthetic, where the signifiers of modernity are saturated with images of the west and of the urban center. For Nigeria, that is, for Nollywood, that heart of modernity is Lagos, and in *Osuofia in London* the stand-in for Lagos is London, where it is best represented by the "modern" British woman.

Osuofia must go to London to identify himself and collect the money. He is first picked up at the airport by a chauffeur in his brother's enormous stretch limousine, but he soon manages to get himself lost when he leaves the limo and runs after what he takes to be another African who is boarding a bus. He finds himself on his own, alone and defenseless before all that assaults him. Big Ben rings, and he has to cover his ears at the noise. The Tower Bridge opens to let a boat pass, and he laughs with amazement, to the amusement of passersby. The foolish villager has now become, in the sight of all who see and encounter him, the foolish Nigerian, or actually, the foolish African. An earlier generation of Parisian Africans squirmed with discomfort at the images of Africans in Ghana enacting the grisly rituals of a Hauka ceremony (Rouch, *Les Maîtres fous,* 1955). For the popular audience back home, however, the image of this foolish Nigerian villager has made *Osuofia in London* one of, if not the most popular of Nollywood films. This has been made possible only because Osuofia remains the object of knowing laughter instead of becoming an oppressed victim of racial or modernist prejudice. He is the Amos 'n' Andy, Stepin Fetchit, before the NAACP's protests were able to make such figures appear impossibly old-fashioned and denigrating.[10]

Nollywood now produces a range of sexually empowered women—witches, matrons, errant daughters, prostitutes, and above all "modern" women negotiating their lives around a range of urban and occult forces (Haynes). The figures of the "modern" woman Osuofia encounters in London provide the occasion for the enactment of African anxieties around modernity (Haynes). Osuofia arrives in a mod London where miniskirts and Big Ben define the tourist imaginary. We see the street scene through his eyes while at the same time witnessing the spectacle he makes of himself. Thus, when he hops on a tourist bus and sees an elderly couple kissing, he is shocked—to our amusement. When a female policewoman berates and chastises him, speaking in exasperated tones, we understand her "normal" reaction and can only shake our heads at the foolish responses and behavior of someone who thinks he can capture a pigeon in Regents Park and eat it.

The crowds around him scoff and call in the police, and we experience that shared discomfort of the external viewer who looks on at the scene with frustration and humor. Most importantly, though we might wish to respond sympathetically to an African outsider who disapproves of a young woman sitting on the steps of a public building in Trafalgar Square, her legs apart, happily reading a brochure, skirt hitched up, though we might compare customs "back home" where such behavior of a young woman would earn her father's slap, we would still understand that Osuofia was not home, not permitted to reproach her, to take off his jacket to cover her legs, to address her at all, much less cor-rect her behavior. But Osuofia is the foil whose foolishness makes comfortable the audience's hidden sense of the normal, and when the young woman throws off his jacket and tells him to "fuck off"—three times, because he didn't catch it the first time—we might have said, along with the frustrated policewoman, he should have known better (see figure 11.2).

We might have shared her feelings of self-righteous indignation as she slaps him to the amusement of the three young people standing by, might have said he ought to have known better, that his home ways might be good for him alone, but not for her, and in fact not good even for women in his home—not even good for him. We might have said, cultural relativism to hell—there are limits to how far we ought to go in understanding the other. We might have not only demanded that he understand different ways and conform to them in the home of others, but that he and his home must change as well. In short, the incomplete agenda of colonialism might well have reemerged in this scene where Osuofia brings out the feminist empowerment in the west, the anxiety of the African male in encountering it, and, indirectly, the entire weight of the cultural en-counter between the two worlds. This is what the director Kingsley Ogoro might have been seeking to elicit in his audience, and we can only speculate whether this address to a Nigerian modernist audience, waving its remote control at the VCD player, might have elicited the urban sophisticate's laughter at Osuofia's naiveté, his clumsy attempts to reassert some dignity to the man's position in a precarious world, especially facing the dangers of being a Nigerian in London where any overt revelation of a Nigerian social consciousness carries enormous risks.

Those dangers would not have appeared particularly manifest to the British audience for whom the young woman's thrice-repeated "fuck off" would have seemed natural; where her rights had been violated; where Osuofia's faults were due to his ignorance, if not to the flaws of his culture. Ogoro was selling his laughs to the Nigerian audience, but the British audience would have joined hands, at least partly, with the Nigerian urbanites who found Nkem Owoh's Osuofia so humorous.

We have been prepped now for fifty minutes for Osuofia's grand entry into London to lead to his contact with his brother's girlfriend Samantha and his solicitor Ben Okafor, the two central figures with their roles as grifters, modern minstrels in this mixed semi-hybrid minstrel show, semi-satiric minstrel show.[11] Reid's differentiation between the forms of hybrid minstrelsy turns on the issue of serious commitment,[12] with Reid claiming that hybrid minstrel humor is lacking in social engagement: "Hybrid minstrel humor necessarily lacks any significant dramatization of African American life. Accurate comic portrayal of such would require some emphasis upon the political purposes of African-American humor—a 'psychological leverage . . . and . . . a weapon for survival against the harsh treatment' by oppressors of African American people" (1993: 28).[13] The interesting situation here is that the setting for mocking and testing the mockery of rural African stereotyping is not in urban Nigeria for the second half of *Osuofia in London Part 1,* but in London where the issue of playing blackface minstrelsy is echoed back to the Nigerian audience through the white characters who are the spectators of Osuofia's bush antics. This deprives the African audience of the opportunity for suturing with characters whose outsider, "sophisticated" perspective they might otherwise have shared. And we would expect the black assimilated solicitor Ben Okafor to provide just such a perspective as he is suave, urbane, and ostensibly very much in control of himself and his racial identity. But this proper British solicitor is a minstrel con man who wears two masks: for himself, the black, clever, assimilated, and educated African; and for Osuofia, the kind, helpful brother. This split becomes a performed identity, not only for himself but for the black audience that is witnessing his act of putting on the mask. He is one step away from Osuofia whose broad smile has not, or not yet, been deconstructed before our eyes. That will require in part 2 the return to Africa, where the patriarch will ultimately be redeemed by his generosity and the affirmation of the foundations of African culture. However, while still in London, both Ben and Osuofia must be seen as figures defined in the split location occupied simultaneously by the contemporary colonized and colonizer. Not a third space, but a space where one can be only that which one seems.

The meeting with Ben Okafor sets Osuofia off as pigeon of the white gold-digger woman and the black con man. The latter's false mask marks Osuofia as well, since we know from the outset that Osuofia's grief for the loss of his brother was also (comically) assumed, and that his rights to his brother's estate and fiancée are also equally compromised. We never meet that brother; never know whether Samantha actually poisoned him, as she later attempts to do to Osuofia back in Nigeria as a last resort to get his money; never know whether that brother wanted Osuofia to inherit his limousine, mansion, and wealth, or fiancée. Never know if his brother was like Ben Okafor, another minstrel in the play of London's commodity consumerist culture. What we do know is that Osuofia's real challenge will lie not in obtaining that money,[14] not in breaking through the racist codes of a foreign culture he can never understand, but rather in managing his encounter with his brother's conniving girlfriend—with this British woman, and with the western liberated sexual economy that represents the ultimate challenge to his African notions of manhood.

For Osuofia, Samantha is the new kind of Mammy Watta, the one whose "wig" he feared his daughter would want to begin wearing, leading to who knows what kinds of misbehavior with the neighborhood boys. Samantha represents the ultimate challenge to patriarchy in terms of an African farce. Osuofia meets Samantha as she is sunning on the grounds of Osuofia's brother's estate. She receives him after Jeeves the butler has greeted Osuofia and brought him to her. In this scene, it is almost as though she were the owner and he the intruder and guest. But as Ben is actually colluding with her to cheat Osuofia of his brother's inheritance—which Osuofia has not yet been able to obtain legally—neither Osuofia nor Samantha actually have the right to take possession of the property. In fact, the only one we might say is legitimately occupying the house is Jeeves, whose role, like his name, appearance, accent, and comportment are completely stereotypical. Jeeves is the resident "butler" while the other two are intruders. All three remain, however, as occupants, with Osuofia telling Samantha he intends to inherit her along with the rest of the property. She confides in Ben shortly after this initial meeting that she is barely able to continue the masquerade with this impossible boor, but she manages to continue the deception.

This situation is unstable. Samantha seduces Osuofia just enough to persuade him to sign the phony documents, which he cannot in any event actually read. When she is subsequently double-crossed by Ben, she grabs back the signed documents from him, informs Osuofia of Ben's perfidy, and flees with him to Africa. The second part of *Osuofia* consists of her increasingly "going native" while retaining enough of the British "identity" to become a "bad copy." In the end, Osuofia wins her heart by forgiving her after she attempts to poison him. He displays the warm generosity of the African community and she admits to her conniving, repents, and returns to England where she belongs. Meanwhile Osuofia has given most of his money away to the members of his community who were in dire need and is now restored to the good graces of his wife, daughters, neighbors, and fellow villagers. He has also somehow become wiser, if not any more powerful than when we first saw him. It is as though Eshu the trickster had visited him with the death of his brother, and now after having traveled to England and returned, he has become not the alienated been-to but the true son of the community.

In another setting, he might have encountered Mammy Watta, as in Henri Duparc's *Caramel* (2004) or in Safo's *Jezebell* (2007) and ended up dead after coming too close to the dangerous presence of the female deity. But Samantha is more like an instrument of Eshu instead of the water goddess herself. She is the vehicle for the trickster's ruse, the persistent con artist willing to go to any lengths, including marrying and poisoning Osuofia in order to get his money. When Osuofia forgives Samantha, she repents, confesses, and recognizes her unsuitability as Osuofia's wife. She had merely assumed the mask of the African woman, had turned to the hybrid white minstrel role of the white person who has gone native—we see her change her hair to dreds, dress in a wrapper, and cook him "African" food—in order to trick Osuofia out of his money.

Just as Osuofia had made himself look comical on the eve of his departure to London as he dressed, walked, and spoke in what he took as an English manner, Samantha too looked out of place as she carried wooden faggots on her head, learned to use the outhouse, and pounded the mortar with the pestle. But at no point in this entire trajectory, until she confessed, did we have a sense that we could access her as a genuine subject. Even her confession, though honest, is instrumental in winning Osuofia's sympathy, and he lards her with money as she returns to England. In other words, she is *always* appearing to us as someone who is putting on a performance for the purpose of extracting money from Osuofia. Her beauty, seductive poses, and displays of affection are the precise counterparts to Osuofia's stereotypical actions and words in England that function to convey to the spectator the image of someone being fitted into a role—exactly like Ben Okafor fitting himself into the mirror image of the British solicitor. The fact that Ben and Samantha were con artists whereas Osuofia was the country bumpkin did not change the fact that all three were something less than full subjective agents precisely because of their subservience to stock roles. They were servants of their own performances that were continually being staged for others, performances that made one a traitor to his African client, another a seductive gold digger, and the third a foolish villager. They were trapped in the roles in which they were cast, like Fela's wives who were cast for their roles as performers on stage and stoic victims of their husband's persecutors off stage. His wives were gorgeous because they wore their makeup for the camera, spectacular as exotic dancers, singers, and martyred wives. Samantha, too, made herself spectacular and exotic, albeit in contrast to Osuofia, in contrast to Fela's wives. But they all pose the central question of attempting to gain access to agency through performance, especially when the roles are typecast.

Because it is genre cinema and conventional emotion provides the masks, we imagine that we are encountering something less endowed with actual subjectivity than our own, less capable of taking actions they obviously should, and therefore lacking an agency with which we could identify. The characters don't convey people we would recognize (or value) in the sense of normal human subjects. In short, they pose the problem of whether their subject positions are assumed knowingly and willingly, or unconsciously and by coercion. They pose the central problem of agency, of becoming a subject, of *assujetissement.*

Butler defines *assujetissement* as involving both recuperating the power and authority that is exercised over oneself, and resisting that power (subjecting oneself to power and assuming the position of becoming a subject). Although she doesn't use the terms, the former appears passive, the latter active. Subjection to power in Foucault entails subjection to a discourse that preceded the subject, that embodies the values imposed on society through the apparatuses of power. For Althusser, those apparatuses are those anonymous institutions (ideological state apparatuses) that form the subject as individuals respond to ideological interpellations. The subject accepts these external forms, discourses, apparatuses, institutions, by responding in ways that conform to the expectations placed upon her, in adopting the language, behavior, and thinking expected of her. She and others become what they misrecognize in these encounters, subjects formed in the perception of the imagos encountered in the return of their gaze. They see themselves in the image reflected in the mirrored gaze of the Other, and as they accept that image for and as themselves, they subject themselves to the power that generates that image of them. They subject themselves, but also en-subject, or make themselves into subjects (they *assujettissent* themselves).

They "subject" themselves: Samantha sees herself seen as the beautiful blond white woman; Osuofia as the African abroad; Ben as the Oreo assimilated African. Each plays these roles, but imperfectly, dishonestly, unwillingly. Osuofia feigns grief at his brother's death and then will not sign any papers until the end, signaling his imperfect integrating into the role of the dupe. Samantha cannot go native; Ben cannot rest easy as the perfect English solicitor. Only Jeeves can be a Jeeves because he has no power to resist his *assujetissement* as the perfect English butler since he has already been named as such, like Stepin Fetchit.

Samantha plays at the gold digger as well; she is subject to the role of the dishonest player, so that when she repents and assumes her guilt, she subjects herself to the liberal humanist norms of decency that Osuofia extends to her. His own subjecting of himself to those norms, like those of his fellow villagers, prevails in redefining him as well, as reintegrating him back into the community. Eshu's work is done: the guilty woman assumes her role as penitent, subordinates herself to his authority, and at the same time accedes to the larger authority of the cultural norm that says English must remain English, must subject themselves to Englishness, while the African must do the same. Each is brought under the authority that codes identities, gender roles, and community. If Samantha had previously subjected herself to Osuofia's brother, which we cannot know, it would have been to an African man who had, himself, accepted, like Ben Okafor, a subjection to Englishness, because, as she tells us, she cannot, will not, cook. She is modern, and Osuofia's brother, like his home, chauffeur, butler, and girlfriend, was undoubtedly the modern subject as well.

Thus we have the two sets of wives whose subjection defines the texts into which they are inscribed. Fela's wives, in the service of their husband's ideals, the anti-ladies whose subjectivities were ultimately placed in the service of the revolutionary order that Fela came to embody, and Osuofia's wives who ultimately enabled his restoration to the "African" order of the those who could never really become "gentlemen." Butler's point about this process of *assujetissement* is that the subject ultimately subjects itself willingly to the threat of violence and power. Samantha indeed repents after she is caught, and Fela's wives see themselves as embodying the ideals of their husband's revolutionary politics. They assume their own subordination in an order that places them under the authority that gives definition to their subjectivity (*Fela Kuti: Music Is the Weapon* [2004]; Olaniyan, *Arrest the Music* [2004]).

The question of their agency in this context might then be tied to their subordinated roles as objects in the larger processes that give them definition, what Butler calls the conditions of their subordination. "Where conditions of subordination make possible the assumption of power, the power assumed remains tied to those conditions, but in an ambivalent way; in fact, the power assumed may at once retain and resist that subordination. This conclusion is not to be thought of as (a) a resistance that is *really* a recuperation of power or (b) a recuperation that is *really* a resistance. It is both at once, and this ambivalence forms the bind of agency" (Butler 13).

At this, we leave Samantha and Fela's wives caught in this bind between recuperation and resistance. Each has assumed a subject position, but at a price that demands they turn the power of subordination back upon themselves. The one returns home a more humanist English woman; the others, expelled from their homes by the Nigerian soldiers, are returned to their audience as martyrs in the cause of revolution. In both, they are instances of a pop culture whose conditions impose these possibilities upon them as women in the service of their husband's ideals, subject to a power they assume with their own assumption of subjectivity.

Their "lived experiences" become the conditions of possibility for an agency and subjectivity that extends beyond the questions of performance or minstrelsy to the ways we now must reconfigure as the central issues of postcolonial representation—the issues that lie at the core of the entertainment apparatuses of music videos and Nollywood films where the question of subject position and agency turn out to be central.

If agency arises out of the tension between recuperation and resistance, without agency there still subsists behind the mask the disembodiment of the human figure, the devalued puppet-figures of wealth, evil, corruption, the formulas for trashy people. The masqueraded figure leaves us at a permanent distance from the acting subject underneath the mask. The mask is a projection outward; the subject lies hidden beneath—a presumed subject; an unseen, unheard subject; the simulacrum of the subject, since the mask always evacuates subjectivity from choice.

If Butler shows that the subject takes her form by submitting to power, so too does Bakhtin present the process of coming-to-consciousness in a similar light. Reid depends upon this for his concept of minstrelsy, and thus evokes Bakhtin's position in the following passage from *The Dialogic Imagination*: "Human coming-to-consciousness . . . is a constant struggle between these two types of discourse: *an attempt to assimilate more into one's own system, and the simultaneous freeing of one's own discourse from the authoritative word,* or from previous earlier persuasive words that have ceased to mean" (Bakhtin, cited by Reid 21; my emphasis). Both the acceptance of an already existent discourse and the act of reshaping it, resisting it, resemble Butler's recuperation of power and resistance to it. There is one act of assimilation—but through two seemingly different subject positions. When Bakhtin refers to "one's own system," it is as if the subject whose system is in question were single or unified. But if it were double or split, or of a materiality that couldn't be reduced to something homogeneous, but were more plastic, heterogeneous, then the absorption of another's discourse, or the subjecting of the self to that discourse could also be partial or divided: recuperation/resistance.

Butler's account of the subject's position in *assujetissement* is that it is doubled or split in its relationship to power, as the two positions occur, even if not simultaneously, in the same subject. For Butler, this is the ambivalence that forms "the bind of agency." Similarly, for Reid the response to minstrelsy and its tendentious human figures is equally a split or divided one, entailing an uneasy laugh, a recognition of, say, Eddie Murphy's exaggerated simulacrum of the cool or foolish black man as a mask being played at—a performance whose reflexivity is highlighted instead of concealed (being and playing at the mask of Stepin Fetchit). This is like melodrama where the over-the-top emotions, the excesses, along with the overly plush furniture, the excessive appeal to expensive cars, clothes, sexiness, and palatial mansions could be equated with the act of putting it on. The greater the exaggeration, the more the division between the subject position of assuming and inhabiting the external mask denoting the fabulous, the supernatural power and wealth, and the resistance to the naturalization of the mask with the image of the "simple human being" who just got lucky or made a deal with Satan (*Jezebell, Amsterdam Diary* [2005]).

The division in tendentious minstrelsy is between the blackface one puts on and the person revealed to be underneath the mask once the paint is washed off. The outer mask becomes the object, and when so obviously put on, as when Osuofia dresses to walk, behave, and speak like the proper Englishman, we laugh at him and his naiveté. When the villageois appears in London before an Englishman, it is the Englishman's bemused response that provides the audience's site for focalizing their emotional response—sharing the disparagement of the bush African, like that of the reader in Oyono's *Vieux nègre et la médaille*. The villageois becomes an object of humor, just as later, when Osuofia comes to his brother's mansion in London and first sees Samantha sunbathing in the bikini, she becomes the object of our gaze, of his gaze, if not that of the Jeeves the butler's gaze. When the characters exceed the mask and are shown assuming a role to be played for the other, as in Butler's example of drag, they display an agency that becomes apparent as they are viewed as putting on the mask. We see this especially in the scene of the barrister Ben before the mirror.

Ben's characterization fits what has been called in colonial African discourse the "bad copy." This is the assimilated African who has assumed the manners, style, and accent of the Englishman but not the moral fabric, not the colonialist's higher mission or ethical values. He is alienated from his traditional African culture, which provided him with the basis for his moral values, but having been alienated from the society, he has nothing left underneath besides self-interest and naked desire. Joyce Cary's Mr. Johnson is a prototype. He is unscrupulous; and so too is Ben unscrupulous. What might he have to do with a bad conscience, which betrays the workings of an overactive superego, an internalized agency of repression whose strength depends upon the very libido it represses, and thus turns back the libidinal energy upon itself?

For Butler, this is the manner in which melancholy, reflexively repressive, also works; Butler finds in melancholy the foundational psychic position from which an eventual subject will emerge. The bad conscience ceases to be an exceptional, failed subject position, but rather the basis for all subject formation, and indirectly all subject positions. The bad conscience "trashes" the ego, with the subject turning back on itself. The bad copy turns its unrepressed desires outward, without impediment. And yet, the central scene in *Osuofia in London* part 1 is one in which Ben, the bad copy, gazes at himself in the bathroom mirror and chastises himself for tolerating and playing up to the bushman who is Osuofia.

In this scene, Ben has just met Osuofia, who refuses to understand why he can't simply take the money his brother left him and leave. Ben insists he sign for it. Osuofia doesn't realize that what he is being asked to sign is a document that would leave Ben in a position to make off with all the funds; Ben doesn't realize Osuofia can't write. More importantly, Osuofia can't accept that Ben is a genuine Nigerian since he can't even pronounce his own name Okafor properly. Ben, who has cultivated his RP accent, laughs when cued to do so but not without becoming infuriated: he is trapped, by his attempts to deceive Osuofia, into playing the bad copy, playing against what he has managed to turn against himself, forcing him to confront the constructedness of his imago thus undoing the mirror stage's imaginary self-deceptions, its "méconnaissance."

Taking a break from his meeting with Osuofia, Ben retires to his office bathroom where he stares at himself in the mirror: Ben (white checked shirt; unhappy expression): "I hate these semi-literate [slight pause] foreign clients. They get me so mad. [pidgin accent] They get me so annoyed I give me problems of wahala. Ahh!" The camera pulls back to a medium shot that now shows Ben from his rear left side, revealing his face and body reflected in the mirror. He is leaning both hands on the sink. The slightly pinkish tones of his shirt, reflecting the walls, are accentuated by the purple tile. His more purple feelings of frustration, his unwonted blurting out of Nigerian pidgin is an expression of annoyance over the "foreign" pidgin-speaking client whom he cannot control (see figure 11.3).

Jazz music comes up. "When I get annoyed, I start to lose my British accent. Mmm?" (Now frontal close-up of his face, seen from the point of view of his reflection in the mirror. He tilts his head, unhappily ejaculating): "Ehhh! My cultivated [slight pause, slight shift in weight and position of head, reassuming role] natural [pause] English accent. I start to speak like my father [then an octave higher, again in pidgin tones]. And I don't like it. Ohh! (tsk)." (Looks down. Images flips between close-up frontal shot, and over-the-shoulder mirror shot.) "You laughing at me. You think I have a problem. You think I have a [pause] coconut problem" (see figure 11.4). (Looks down.) "Okay, calm down, calm down." (Turns on cold water tap.) "Okay. [rinses hands] Deep breath [loud jazz tones. Tight close-up, head tilted to side slightly. Stares at himself, chin up.] Stiff upper lip. God save the queen." (Camera back to over the shoulder, giving us view of what he is examining, as he tilts his head from one side to another, shaking the water off his hands.) "Ben Okafor [accent on last syllable], solicitor." (Smiles, opens his hands.) "Excellent. How can I help you?" (Smiles and nods his head; see figure 11.5.) Camera now closes in on image in mirror alone, and we see only that reflection as he walks out. Back in his role, mask in place, ready to return to Osuofia.

The mirror provides direct visual images of Ben's role-playing, his rehearsal for the performance, his split verbal and visual self, his subject position that both recuperates and resists the power that chastises and punishes, but that also empowers him. He is "bad" as the "bad copy," the baddest "bad nigger," who is strong and immoral, like Eshu, a master of speech and a victim of his own strength, since it turns against him to punish him, as his conscience, for being the "coconut." He remains faithful to his character till the end, double-crossing Samantha after she succeeds in getting Osuofia to sign the papers, and then being outfoxed by her and Osuofia as they flee back to Nigeria, outside of his power to reach them.

Butler never parses the term "bad" in her use of "bad conscience," since the meaning of the phrase is already self-evident. But in a study of trash, bad is only a stage on a journey to or from value, where loss is bad and gain is good. Punishment marks the loss of value, though the position of the one who punishes stands above the loss except when it has become internalized as part of the subject being punished. When there is a trickster mask or, say, as in the case of Eshu, a penis, it is more than what it seems: a giant bridge for people to pass over, an unsteady bridge from which those who attempt to cross will fall and be lost.[15] All these images of Eshu imply for Pelton an assurance of meaning carried by the trickster subject. But that is only if we read *assujetissement* unilaterally, as if bad means good in the end (the trickster ultimately in the service of a higher order). In the economies of trash, bad is bad, as well as good, and the service of the trickster lies in both meanings. Not in a sublimation; not in a teleological purpose.

Trashy women like Samantha, trashy bad copies like Ben, are both worthless *and* empowered figures: like the film deserving of censorship, but that turns that censorship on itself, in the mirror, making it part of the plot, like a bad conscience that makes the libido the very substance of the superego or bad conscience and its repressive force. For Butler, the bad conscience is a consequence of the incorporation of loss and is manifest in melancholy, or in mourning, since for her, the unhappiness that is due to loss takes a form so that the difference between mourning and melancholy is attenuated, as in late Freud where the role of the death drive assumes the central role (*Civilization and Its Discontents, The Ego and the Id*).

The trickster's mourning turns on the masking of the emotion so as to deceive others, as Osuofia does when he finally gathers that his dead brother has left him his inheritance. But that performance, extended to the rest of his family who are forced to perform for the lawyer, is blatantly excessive and makes apparent its own falseness, becoming the occasion for mocking Osuofia and the poor status of village patriarchy. He has suffered no real loss since he is only a comic figure of the failed patriarch, failed village authority, with nothing left to lose. The situating of loss is difficult to place, until the end of the film, when it seems that there is really something of worth at stake, the community itself for whose sake Osuofia has returned with the money and with Samantha. Only then could a Hegelian unhappy conscience emerge, or a Nietzschean and Freudian bad conscience, Butler's progenitors for the psyche that ultimately takes form as the subject—a subject that depends upon loss, mourning, melancholy, and the return of the desires against the self because of the repression incurred by loss. Loss does not speak until the melancholic turn against the self has occurred, and it is not "worked through" but permanently ensconced within the psyche.

This is the basis for the divided subject, a subject not only passive and active, but both an emerging self or subject and a self-punishing subject; a self that can accomplish this only in self-reflexivity, as in the bearer of a mask that regards himself in the mirror and chastises himself for his "coconut" problem, or, in the States, for his "Oreo" problem, his educated speech and his "wahala," his received and assumed pronunciation (RP English), his being his father's true son and his father's false son—a Nigerian and an Englishman—for whom each is devalued in terms of the other. Trash now turning against itself by assuming its self in the mask. The more the one side seeks to impose itself on the other, the more its repressive force acts to assert itself. In other words, Ben Okafor cannot suppress the son of his father without that son turning back on himself. The Nigerian father, the English queen, two divided ideals in one breast, two forced selves warring to contain the trash of the other. As Ben in London gives primacy to the Englishness, Ben the coconut gives recognition to a father who cannot be excluded, especially as Osuofia is there in front of him, telling him, like his father, how to speak and what to do. *The more the bad copy makes his effort, the more the effort shows*, the more the imago in the mirror turns into a reflected image that he cannot assume or subjugate, that he cannot *assujetir*. Méconnaissance and connaissance war with each other in the figure of the masquerade. The bad conscience works through them both, undoing the work of the bad copy, which has to rehearse how to put on the mask again, to deny itself—its progenitor, its skin color, its accent, its clothing, its origins, its office setup—in order to be itself. Fela's African gentleman meets Ben Okafor through their masks. And when we consider that Samantha will "go native" in order to trick Osuofia out of his wealth, that he is worried about his daughters wearing miniskirts, it becomes clear that all the characters, to one degree or another, wear masks that turn against themselves.

Just as Butler finds in the bad conscience the basis for *assujetissement*, upon which all subject positions are grounded, so too are all the characters to some extent "bad copies." This follows from Butler's extraordinary repudiation, or redaction, of her earlier and most famous contention, that gender is a consequence of a performance, an "imitative structure" whose inner working is captured in our apprehension of drag as the visible collateral exteriorization of gender performance—an imitation that is open about itself. The redaction comes in the form of asking what occasions the performance, and the answer lies in disavowal and repudiation that organize that performance (1997: 145). She refers to this disavowal as "dissatisfied longing" and "unacknowledged loss," an "ungrieved loss" that is "refused and incorporated in the performed identification" (145). As in melancholy, which entails an incorporation of loss and the refusal to let it go, so too gender comes to be viewed by Butler as being "in part" the "acting out" of unresolved grief (146).

The performance becomes an "allegorization" that works to stabilize gender, and that, in drag, takes the form of allegorical fantasies. This allegorical enactment and performance becomes visible in drag—gender performing itself. This is precisely equivalent to what Ben Okafor is enacting before the mirror, except that in place of gender, it is Britishness, and, in particular, the African form of Britishness called the "coconut," or, in old colonial discourse, the bad copy. Drag is the bad copy in skirts and a bra; coconut acting and speaking is Englishness in a solicitor's suit, in his good offices, where his act is in the service of the god who plays with lives and money, Eshu. Drag plays at its game of "being," but pronouncing it is not being it: he is *not* that woman he plays at being, and thus the homosexual possibility is excised from the heterosexual economy. Similarly, what is exorcised by the coconut disavowal is the Africanness of the father, or, Butler would say, "the possibility" of what is being disavowed.

It may be fair to argue that not all identities are the same, not all formed in identical ways; that not all disavowals are identical. But there is a pattern in identity formation that entails loss, disavowal and renunciation, and an acting out of the grief occasioned by the loss. There is a strong undercurrent of loss that underlies *Osuofia* from the outset: loss of patriarchy, of dignity, of agency, of a subject who can act for himself and speak to others on their terms, who can "be" on their level. The loss, for Butler, is conveyed in terms of "heterosexual melancholy," that is, a melancholy "by which a masculine gender is formed from the refusal to grieve the masculine as a possibility of love" (146). Correspondingly, "A feminine gender is formed (taken on, assumed) through the incorporative fantasy by which the feminine is excluded as a possible object of love, an exclusion never grieved, but 'preserved' through heightened feminine identification" (146).[16] The shift to loving and excluding an Africanness that is the butt of the humor, denied and repudiated as a matter of course, a matter of being the modern citizen of Lagos, the modern subject in a world of objects and wealth that confers power, is central to the "bind of agency" that also places Ben Okafor before that mirror as he finds his speech, despite himself, subject once again to the authority of the father he wishes to renounce. As the villageois is excluded as the object of modern identity formation, not grieved, and yet preserved in the figure of Osuofia, the modern, absent, lost brother become the stabilized point of an identity for the spectators to assume.

Through the mechanisms of the mask, laughing at the bumpkin position comes about with external figures, like the Londoners laughing at Osuofia or like the schoolteacher who presents the corrective voice telling Osuofia what is the proper way to greet a stranger. That distance suggests that were the masquerade figure to become the self-reflexive subject, the possibility of assuming a new subject position could become allegorically performed, unless he has been reduced to nothing but his mask. There is such a character in that position, the opposite of the divided African character like the solicitor Ben Okafor or the McDonald's Eastern European server or the Pakistani shopkeeper, and it is Jeeves.

Jeeves has one name; he is there with the mansion as an object that functions, like a thing, like the toilet, that Osuofia has to learn to use. He performs the role of butler, speaks like the butler, is incapable of laughing at Osuofia or desiring Samantha, because there is nothing there beneath the mask, there is no person underneath the minstrel blackface or, in this case, the English whiteface, since he identifies entirely with the imago. We see him as an imago, homogeneous and undivided, and therefore with no interiority, no interior subjectivity, and most importantly, no agency.

In a sense, all the English characters in the film are like that. They are entirely what we perceive them to be. The bemused English gentleman, the outraged girl on the steps who says "fuck off" to Osuofia when he is bothering her are entirely predictable because they are, like objects, homogeneous in the roles as English gentleman and angry mod English girl. The only ones in England who are less predictable, less uniform in their reactions, besides the divided Ben Okafor, are the McDonald's server, who is an East European foreigner, and the Pakistani shopkeeper. They have to deal with an unusual predicament offered by Osuofia that requires them, outsider-insiders themselves, to exercise authority over the outsider Osuofia, an authority they themselves lack as non-English immigrants.

The relationship between *assujetissement* and trash emerges on the level of the subject where recuperating and resisting authority, and ultimately incorporating the fundamental loss that sustains the exclusion on which an identity is stabilized depends upon relations of power and understandings of value on which the subject position is based. The role of submission, the force of resistance, depends on the relationship of higher and lower, superior and inferior, master and slave. From Hegel's unhappy conscience to Althusser's response to interpellation, to Nietzsche and Freud's "bad conscience," there is always a stronger, superior, ideal-ego, a figure that stands behind the screen when the voice of the Master is heard and heeded. The subject emerges from the interaction with that voice, so that "subjection to" becomes active subject formation, and "submission and mastery take place simultaneously" (Butler 1997: 116). The more the subject submits, the more it accedes to the position from which mastery can be assumed as a subject. The cyclical patterns through which trash passes from disvalued to hypervalued, from economies of loss to economies of gain, from discarded to recuperated, move together here in Butler's parsing of Althusser's *assujetissement* in which submission is recast "precisely and paradoxically as a kind of mastery" (117). Melodrama will lengthen this process so that by the end, what was lost is recast in satisfaction as recovery and gain. But trash is not separable from value in this way: the recovered object of worth carries with it the marks of its trashiness, without which there is no gain or value. Thus the objects of *récupéré* art are of worth only to the extent that we recognize that they have been reconstituted from objects deemed to be worthless, like found objects, discarded computer parts, garbage tossed onto the heap.

This is where Nollywood trashiness has its strength: it displays its masks and masking performances as though they were rehearsals for parts, rather than pure being imitated in its quiddity. Like the simultaneity of the positions of the master and slave, it sustains the imaginary positions of a moral universe and a neobaroque performance. If Brooks sees that moral universe as foundational,[17] he ignores the necessary connection to the disavowal of that moral basis that is preserved by the stabilized gender, class, and race performances that depend on the unacknowledged exclusions. The identities that are key to melodrama, to Nollywood, and to those films that borrow the clothes of these genres obey the same logic as that of gender formation, with "an exclusion never grieved, but 'preserved' through heightened feminine [or race] identification" (146).

La Nuit de la vérité and Nollywood

If *La Nuit de la vérité* shares elements of melodrama and the underlying moral order with the Nollywood film, it does not share the excessiveness in the characters that make visible the split within them, the split over recuperation and resistance to authority. *Nuit* assumes homogeneous subjects in its characters, like the figure of the Englishman and girl on the steps; it is closer to Jeeves in its portrayals, and not the East European McDonald's server or barrister Ben Okafor when he is staring into his bathroom mirror.

Rather, in *Nuit,* if a character assumes a mask, like Edna, the president's disturbed wife, it is as a public persona that breaks down in private, in the bedroom at the beginning or with her own husband and guards at the tomb of her son. When she breaks with the mask and sets up the killing of the colonel and then grills him, it is behind the lines, outside the gaze of the public, in the hidden spaces of exception—spaces out of place, outside the order, where trash is normally thrown. There, it isn't so much her self appearing after being hidden underneath a mask but rather a crazy other that surges forth, as if the subject that strove to hold itself together, to deal with mourning, had failed to contain its melancholy. The melancholic self, with its empty space within, created by the mourning and incorporation of the dead son, by the refusal to accept his death, now prevails over the fragile external self she tries to put on for others.

Unlike the divided Ben, or Osuofia in London and in Nigeria, she cannot occupy two places at the same time, and neither can Colonel Theo who killed and castrated her child. Both have incorporated the murdered boy, both cannot let him speak, both are extreme melancholic figures haunted by a trauma that continues to elicit deferred reactions and that is responsible for their ultimate demise. They thus lack the agency entailing recuperation and resistance as they fail to resist, resulting in a homogeneous subjectivity. In this, the serious auteur *Nuit,* though apparently so radically marked by the split in characters due to trauma and deferred reactions, portrays that gap between interior self and public personas as due to mental illness, not to the basic nature of their roles, their characters.

In contrast, in Nollywood, as in melodrama, the split between the mask (say, of extravagant wealth, beauty, power) and "just plain folks" underneath the minstrel's mask is normal, not the sign of a mentally disturbed person or victim of a trauma. It is "normal" in a world where excess is normalized everywhere—physically and materially—all around them in the houses, cars, furniture, makeup and especially in the emotions. In *Nuit* we have the excess, but it isn't normalized; it is present, but presented as abnormal.

The interesting point is that, abnormal as it is, it is nonetheless there, more and more in film today, even in films that purport to be serious auteur cinema. In Sissako's story of Chaka and Mele in *Bamako* (2006), a film ostensibly about the trial of the World Bank and Wolfowitz; there in a host of other Africa films, like *O Herói* (2004) where the protagonist Judite weeps before the cameras in despair of ever finding her lost son; there in Haroun's *Daratt* (2006) when the protagonist Atim points his gun at the mirror, like Al Pacino in *Taxi Driver* (1976). And it is there in Sembène's *Faat Kine* (2000) and *Moolade* (2004). In all these films, torn figures perform the same division implicit in agency between recuperation and rebellion that the characters cannot resolve.

Melodrama resolves this split. At the end of *All That Heaven Allows* (1955), as Rock Hudson lies in a coma and the deer appears at the window, Jane Wyman looks out and the underlying moral force of the universe is once again affirmed: resolution, joy, closure, wholeness seal the end of the story.

In *Nuit,* however, Edna's madness ends when she is shot by her husband; closure must cover over that violence, must forgot what had taken place in the violence of the colonel's killing and castration of the boy, in his grilling, being roasted till he turns bright red, by Edna (see figure 7.2). The national unity cannot be forged without the national archive burying and forgetting that memory, so that a single future can be forged, so that the children can learn the right lessons about being citizens of one nation (Renan, Derrida, Nora).

As the serious films now open our gaze to the horrors of the bodies floating down the river, figured in the nightmares of the colonel, and to the revenge killings of the mad witch Edna, the differences in purpose and characterization between the melodrama and the serious film become attenuated. This is because the work of forgetting and excluding on which the authorized archives of national identity have been based in the past, the work of the patriarchal archons to establish the authority to which the subjects must subject themselves, and against which they need to stage their revolts (Derrida, *Archive Fever*), has been vitiated, and the barriers to the forgotten horrors that had been held back no longer can be sustained. Djibril Diop Mambety was right when he had Gana tell Ramatoulaye that the time of the hyenas has come. Gradually Bouki and Golo and the rest of the figures of the forest have come crowding in, holding up their masks in glee and greed, dancing the dance that they must have learned from Eshu, the insatiable trickster who wore a hat with red on one side and black on the other, and who laughed when no one could say in truth what color his hat really was. Are these the figures of Nollywood's nightmares, or of the films like *Ezra* (2007), *Nuit,* or *O Herói* that bear the scars of the current traumas of today?

Loss and Trash

The loss of Osuofia's brother is what goes unacknowledged in *Osuofia in London.* By openly faking the grieving, Osuofia denies the loss—that is, the loss of the allegorical Africa that is "never grieved" but "preserved" through the figure of Osuofia, whom we can read as the figure in drag who performs the fantasy of the village African. Specifically, the loss of Osuofia's brother is the loss of the one who has gone abroad (or gone to the city and become the lost daughter, as in Aidoo's "In the Cutting of a Drink" [1970]), become rich, and forgotten about his family back home. This is a double loss—the loss of the African expat to the culture into which he has become assimilated, and that of his original African culture that has lost their son. The loss of the "real Africa" of the village to the glitzy city—the loss of a certain "Africa" that steals the Diallobe soul (*L'Aventure ambiguë* [1961]), steals the "boy" (*Une Vie de boy* [956]), steals the mind and soul of the young men and women in the African Story of the twentieth-century narrative, in which they take off for the city never to be seen or heard from again, lost to the oyimbo.

So the loss of Osuofia's brother lies at the heart of *Osuofia in London* where Osuofia's journey to London places his family and the entire village at risk in that in his quest to get the inheritance in the name of all of them, to bring back the golden egg of the future that lies in London (Lagos), he might never return. And the loss of his brother will have been the model for his own.

We know nothing about this brother, except from his choices of fiancée, lawyer, house, chauffeur, limousine, and so on. All those choices circle around a central figure who occupies the space of an aporia, as he is lost/unknown/unseen and unmourned. But his fiancée Samantha conveys the taste of the been-to who has found someone who is the opposite of Osuofia's first wife— Samantha, the sexy blond who has no children, cannot cook, and connives to steal his brother's inheritance. A rich man's white plaything. And there is Osuofia's brother's lawyer, not a staid Englishman with conservative tastes, but the mod, successful Nigerian city slicker who will stop at nothing to enrich himself. The chauffeur, the butler, the fancy estate, all bespeak not only wealth but English signifiers of wealth, untold wealth, white man's magic wealth, big city wealth, the dream of wealth beyond the wildest imagination of the poor villagers of Osuofia's home who can ask only for small things like a skirt, books, or at most help in finishing building their modest, unadorned houses—modest, old-fashioned, unadorned lives, in the imaginary of the big city. The aporia that is at the heart of London lies at an infinite distance from Osuofia's home, which signifies a tongue-in-cheek version of "Africa."

The ungrieved and unacknowledged loss is of the Africanness that lies behind the mask of that "Africa" that is still there as "home" in the countryside, awaiting the return of its lost sons and daughters, hoping not to have lost them to the cities, to Lagos. And the Mercedes, the overstuffed couches, smart phones, and above all the important business deals that signify power and wealth are placed repeatedly in relation to that poor country cousin, still waiting helplessly for the return of the long-lost child from whom they have not heard for so long that he or she must be gone for good. From the beginning, from Aidoo's *No Sweetness Here* (1972), this was the motif of modernity and its discontents:

> He danced with one of the women. She laughed when he spoke Fante. Then
> he danced with another woman. She took him to a place with bright light. It
> was there that she screamed at him. "Any kind of work is work! You villager,
> you villager, who are you!" he tells us she said. This girl, she had painted her
> face too. But in the bright light my nephew knew her. He put his hands on her
> shoulders to calm her but she threw them away. A sister treating her brother so!
> But she did not know him. When she did recognize him, she only laughed. And

Figure 11.1. Osuofia the hunter.

Figure 11.2. Osuofia: "You're telling me, fuck off?"

Figure 11.3. Ben looks at self in mirror.

Figure 11.4. "You think I have a coconut problem?"

Figure 11.5. "Excellent, 'How can I help you?'"

she did not come home with him. She is a bad woman, a woman who will take a man to a corner of a dance in the city. (44)

The ungrieved and unacknowledged loss is of the Africa that lies behind the mask of the Osuofia minstrel figures: "home" for Mansa, in Aidoo's story, who will reportedly be returning for Christmas; home awaiting still the return of its lost daughter, hoping not to have lost her to the city, to Accra, Lagos, Dakar.

Nollywood romances have given us the vision of what she has become in the city. *Desperate Women* (Obi 2006), *Blood Sister* (Chikere 2003), *Dangerous Sisters* (Obinali 2004), *Campus Queen* (Kelani 2004), *Jenifa* (Ayinde 2008), *Jezebel* (Safo 2007), *Beyonce* (Arase 2006), bearing the name of the rich and famous, providing the "stable" gender identities on the foundation of ungrieved losses, unacknowledged exclusions, giving us modernity's misrecognition of itself in the exaggerated performances, the quasi-drag, minstrel performances of urbanity.

12 Trash's Last Leaves: Nollywood, Nollywood, Nollywood

A number of Nollywood films are marked by an obsessiveness, leading to frustration in the spectator. This can take on monstrous proportions, like the "object a" that Žižek identifies with the stage of capitalism marked by extreme consumerism (Žižek 1992). The patterns of materiality in African cinema could be traced through their use of characteristic objects that are placed in relationship to subjectivity as it takes form under various stages of capitalism.

The connection between loss and trash brings us to the connection between subject, divided in *assujetissement,* and object whose value defines it as more or less trashy or as more or less precious. In my previous book on African cinema, I traced these stages of subject-object relations, following Žižek, as the subject position became increasingly fragile and divided, and as the object morphed from the original nonmaterial form of object a (*l'objet a*) to one of monstrous material proportions.[1] A summary of this shift can be seen in the following description of three moments of change Žižek traces using Hitchcock's films.

The first period of Hitchcock's films is linked to liberal capitalism, the second to imperialist state capitalism, and the third to "postindustrial" state capitalism. In the first period, obstacles to couples that stir "the desire for reunification," are "grounded in the classic ideology of the 'autonomous' subject strengthened through ordeal." The pattern is built around the role of the paternal figure. It begins with an initial stage where it enjoys its position of authority, which is ultimately asserted in the film's conclusion; thence to the resigned paternal figure of the second stage, which "evokes the decline of this 'autonomous' subject to whom is opposed the victorious, insipid 'heteronomous' hero." Finally, writes Žižek, "it is not difficult to recognize, in the typical Hitchcockian hero of the 1950s and early 1960s, the features of the 'pathological narcissist,' the form of subjectivity that characterizes the so-called 'society of consumption'" (Žižek 1992: 5).

Žižek goes on to associate these phases, each with their characteristic modalities of desire and subjectivity, with corresponding objects whose crucial role in each film is determinant of its mode. The first of the objects is described as the familiar Hitchcockian device, the "McGuffin," which is actually "'nothing at all,' an empty place, a pure pretext whose sole role is to set the story in motion" (1992: 6). In further elaboration, Žižek identifies the McGuffin with *l'objet a,* "a gap in the centre of the symbolic order—the lack, the void in the Real setting in motion the symbolic movement of interpretation" (8). The McGuffin whose absence drives the action is like El Hadj's Xala, invisible yet central to his decline—the fall of the autonomous subject, until his recovery at the end as the community comes together in an "Africanized" ritual cure. Žižek identifies the "classic ideology of the 'autonomous' subject strengthened through ordeal" (1992: 5) with this first phase of Hitchcock's films, where the possibilities of taking action within an economy of the autonomous subject corresponds with liberal capitalism.

If liberal capitalism and the autonomous subject are in play here, it would seem that their positive features that normalize western ideological values cannot be translated directly into our African model, and this would be because the benefits and powers that are inevitably bestowed on that subject are reserved for the wealthy Other—be it the European or the Europeanized African bourgeois subject. But if these idealized values had once been associated with Europe, infinitely distant, or with the Plateau in Dakar once reserved for the toubabs, now Europe has come to Lagos. Nollywood features cars that are prominently displayed in shiny, powerful images; they consistently evoke an impossible dream of wealth ensconced behind the high walls, behind the dark glass of the cars, behind the broad shoulders of the guards stationed to protect and keep riffraff at a distance (*Beyonce* [2006], *Jezebell* [2007], *Formidable Force* [2002], and so on).

Following the absent object a, the second kind of object Žižek describes has a material form, and its function is to act as the object of exchange between characters whose relationship takes on a meaningful dimension as a result of that exchange.[2] In this stage, it is less the autonomous subject functioning in a liberal capitalist economy than the "heteronomous" subject functioning within a system of imperialistic state capitalism. The objects become more concrete at this point, as we can see in the example of the corpse in Bekolo's *Les Saignantes* (2005), giving us what Žižek refers to as "a little-bit-of-Real": a disruption intrudes on the subjects' autonomous space, forcing them to come into a relationship, a symbolic relationship marked by strife and disharmony, and by the creation of an environment in which negotiation becomes necessary. Without such objects, there is no coalescing of peoples and issues around a central concern. This failure of the symbolic order to assert its presence without this artifact of the dead man attests to the diminished presence of the "big Other," the figure on which the authority of the Name of the Father relies.[3]

With the third stage, we are comfortably located in the familiar terrain of Nollywood films where the subjects are marked by a lack so profound as to disenable them, depriving them of subjectivity and agency throughout the films, until the very end when an inevitable, impossibly impermeable barrier is lifted. Objects have now taken on enormous dimensions (Žižek's example would be the monument stone carvings of the presidents in the cliffs of Mount Rushmore in *North by Northwest* [1959]). Objects of enormous proportions, diminished agency for subjects, reduction of the law of the father to a whispered suggestion at best—the symbolic order is in crisis. The features of a well-ordered society governed by respected rules, disciplined visual images corresponding to the logos of the symbolic order, all are now in disarray. With the ultimate expression of pathological narcissism and consumerism out of control, the third stage serves as a gateway to the psychic dislocations and stylistic exuberance of the neobaroque. This stage was anticipated with Mambety's *Hyènes* (1992) when the solidarity of the community fell apart in the face of the double assault of the phallic mother Ramatoulaye, with her infinite global wealth, and all the multitudes of refrigerators, air conditioners, shiny leather boots—*xaliss*, money, and more money speaking the language of the city whose vertiginous growth is signaled at the end of the film as the bulldozers drive away the last of the creatures of nature while Dakar looms menacingly on the horizon.

Nollywood now emerges, a short step from Ramatou (*Hyènes* 1992) to Beyonce (Safo 2010), one that passes through the figure of Mammy Watta (Haynes 32, Dogbe 227) and her infinite incarnations.[4] When the married Nana Ekua makes a "pact with the devil" in *Jezebell* (Safo 2007) by agreeing to Susu's promises of wealth, seduced into a lesbian relationship, abandoning her responsibilities to her husband, turning from frowsy housewife to sex bomb, she does so by becoming a devotee of "Jezebell," the classic Mammy Watta figure, rising out of the ocean, with her light skin, green eyes, long hair, and, here, evil powers to bestow wealth at the price of motherhood (see figure 12.1). *Efuru* (1966) returns under the sign of the crisis in patriarchy, now once more the *mère dévorante*. Safo's *Jezebell* skirts on the edges of self-parody in this revision of the familiar warnings against the liberated woman. The unlimited power unleashed by esoteric forces combines with the seeming helplessness of the normal social order, the autonomous subject, to resist it. Why can't Raj marry Ciera, in *Beyonce*, but is continually frustrated in his attempts to forge a relationship with the woman he loves? Why does Beyonce always succeed in defeating the couple Ray-Ciera, in killing Ciera, in forcing Raj to marry her, when in scene after scene Raj demonstrates his love for Ciera and dislike of Beyonce? In *Jenifa*, why does Jenifa not see that she is launched on the superficial path of the lifestyle of the rich and famous that will only destroy her in the end, and that winds up leaving her with AIDS and her best friend Becky dead from the ravages of unconstrained sexual acts, anal intercourse, and a fistula that leaves her smelling repulsive? In *Blood Sister* (2003), why does the evil sister Esther (played by Genevieve Nnaji) always succeed in convincing her mother that Gloria, Esther's sister, has been disobedient, when it is Esther's jealousy and wicked nature that we the spectators can all so easily perceive? Why does Gloria trust her evil sister, so that Esther moves in with Gloria's family, succeeding in poisoning her sister and taking her place with Gloria's husband Kenneth? Why does Kenneth not see the traps Esther sets for him, the evil nature of Esther, her success in alienating his children and her oppression of them? Why can't he stop Esther when his children suffer? Why does it take Gloria's ghost to return and respond to the losses incurred by Esther's evil actions? *Blood Sister*, like many others, ends with a long-delayed retribution where evil finally pays the price needed for goodness to assume its rightful place in the world.

In *Formidable Force* (2002) why can't Nike disencumber herself of Bill throughout the film when she has been given opportunity after opportunity to do so? She saves Bill, and in return he forces her to hide him in her room, pulling a gun on her and threatening her with horrific punishments if she betrays him. He is seen by the film's spectators and by Nike as a vile gangster, hunted by the police and another violent gang, and he represents the ultimate threat to her. Yet she is inexplicably drawn to him, not able to account for it even to herself. Throughout he represents a threat of death to Nike and her family; throughout she fails to turn him in to the police, to turn him out of her life. And by the end, when all the menace is lifted, he turns from a hulking brute into a handsome and honorable lover.

That quick turnabout at the end seems to occur repeatedly in the films I have seen. (Admittedly a limited sample. Yet what would not be a small sample for an industry that produces more than a thousand films a year?) *Beyonce* (2007) is a film in which a horrible, outrageous woman, with infinite wealth, faceless goons operating at her beck and call, and desires that will brook no refusal—a woman who disfigures her rival in love and breaks her lover's will until he timidly submits—is finally shot in the last scene, while the disfigured, dead rival returns alive in a taxi to watch and insure that her hit man carries out his job. The target is a woman called Beyonce, a woman without a conscience, a bad copy of the original global star of the same name. The ultimate spoiled rich girl here is the daughter of the president, and thus the social figure to whom nothing can be refused. She is Lagos turned into all the fears of the dark night side of the city, in the form of the bad woman.

She is monstrous as a subject since the absence of the bad conscience, the lack of the lack in her life, exposes her to the monstrous form of the objects that designate a desire that is unbounded, unchecked by social or superego constraints. Her huge bed is monstrous; and she fills it with the handsome boy already promised to another. Her desire for him stops at nothing, like the cars she drives and gives to him, expensive black models, sleek, shiny, large, dangerous, always available, infallible. All, like her mansion, bed, and liquor cabinet, is unbounded, as in a neogothic romance.

Žižek's cluster of the third stage object/subject/socioeconomic system, involving the figure of "pathological narcissism," is associated with late capitalism or globalization. This figure appears in quasi-parodic form when located on the terrain of the postcolony where globalization corresponds with the inevitable disappearance of the paternal superego altogether and its replacement with the completely dominating figure of the maternal superego. The kinds of objects that come to inhabit this landscape now assume gigantic and monstrous proportions.[5]

Beyonce is such an object, someone for whom an autonomous subjectivity would appear impossible to circumscribe as she is both infinitely pathological and pathetic in her narcissism. Yet her girlfriends recognize this and openly laugh as she blusters and assumes the role of powerful sexy woman, setting out to conquer whatever her heart desires and destroy whatever blocks her path. Wealth and power, demonstrably undeserved and unchecked by bad conscience, another bad copy of the Lagos's ruling autocracy held up for a judgment that comes almost as an afterthought in the final moments of a four-hour film.

In *Formidable Force*, Nike is just the opposite. Although the daughter of yet another wealthy Nigerian man, with the luxury of Lagos represented as usual in villa–car–plush furniture mise-en-scène, Nike is unprepossessing, all too easily dominated by a stranger whom she helps after seeing him lying by the side of the road where he has been shot. As soon as Bill is in the car, she becomes incapable of freeing herself from his grip. We gradually see things her way: see her fascination and attachment validated; see him emerge as the valiant journalist enmeshed in the struggle to save the country; see her transformed into his savior, with him ultimately dependent upon her to rescue him and save the country.

The object that links Nike and Bill, that represents the space in which their subjectivities become capable of acting, is a tape. And although this film is far from being either "perfect" as in the well-made commercial film, or "imperfect" as in the revolutionary mode of alternative and committed cinema, it is still "pretty good" as an exhibition of a cinema that is defined by a mode and materiality that flirts with the disruptive potentialities of trash.

In Nollywoodian terms, the film turns on a love relationship between the rich but decent Genievieve Nnaji character, Nike, and Bill, a cameraman who discovers the plot of an evil politician to set the country into turmoil in order to come to power and enrich himself. Gangsters, fear, love, danger, shifts in fortune—the usual stuff of an overstuffed Nollywood plot would seem to join this film to dozens of others. However, the camerawork immediately announces itself as distinctive, the music is at the least tolerable and at times actually works to augment the action, instead of drowning out the dialogue as is often the case in Nollywood films. Most importantly, the style uses effective film noir visuals, and the character of Bill is successfully captured by Nollywood star Hanks Anuku, who speaks with an American accent.[6]

Formidable Force brings together many of the elements I wish to analyze, enabling us to take a stab at understanding them in terms of materiality, with its objects and landscape, and subjectivity, and with its bad copies, bad consciences, and the tension between submitting to dominant forces and assuming the power to act. What brings all this together is the surprising turn late in the film in which Bill's true role is revealed. Not that of a gangster on the run, shot by his rivals, as we supposed at the outset; not a fugitive from the police because of his having killed a policeman, as we had also earlier surmised; not the evil rapist Nike fears at the beginning when he draws a gun on her, his rescuer, and forces her to take him to her bedroom. None of these things that we are led to think about him, and that his menacing gestures and appearance convey, defines who he is. He is a hero whose identity is hidden, and whose ability to take action, to move even, is continually stymied.

For Manthia Diawara, it is mobilization, mobility, that defines the aspiration of Nollywood film. In this film, with its silly Nike-brand title,[7] it is the helpless Nike herself who becomes a runner who cannot be caught and a fighter whom men cannot defeat. She ultimately decides to cast her lot in with Bill, somehow trusting him and sensing his truthfulness. He lets her in on his story, and the importance of the tape.

The revelations about the tape come in a flashback, as Bill has been recaptured by Chief Collins's men and is rendered helpless, tied to a chair. Nike surreptitiously enters his room and he whispers the secret of where the tape is hidden. Bill had been filming at Chief Collins's campaign party, held to support his candidacy for office as governor. The chief determines at the party that the police commissioner, whom he has suborned, is the only one, besides his accomplices in the government, to know about their corrupt use of $10 billion of imported weapons intended to destabilize the country. The chief shoots the commissioner in private and has his body stashed in the trunk of Bill's car, setting Bill up as the supposed killer. Bill has overheard and filmed the dialogue between the chief and the commissioner, and the tape holds the incriminatory evidence. In their dialogue, the chief asks the commissioner how he did it, and the commissioner explains that he forged signatures. The chief states they will divert the arms and spread them around the country to create havoc, after which they will foment a military coup and enrich themselves (this serving to allegorize the ills of the Abacha regime).[8] Bill returns to film the rest of the party after capturing this moment on tape. Meanwhile, the chief calls the defense minister to tell him he has shot the police commissioner and they can pin the murder on Bill, a "nobody" whom it will be easy to blame.

We see Bill videoing this party using a large handheld camera. When he finishes and tells the chief he is going, the chief asks when he will have the tape. Bill tells him it will take two days to prepare it—thus focusing our attention on the tape. The chief states he hopes the tape of the party will be good, and Bill responds,

Why not. I am an American-trained cinematographer.
CHIEF: I can hear it.
BILL: Besides, this is a digital camcorder that I've got. *[Bill leaves, placing the camcorder on the roof of his Mercedes as he removes the tape, holding the tape up between his fingers like a hidden treasure.]* (see figures 12.3 and 12.4)

The shiny camcorder in close-up, and the tighter close-up of the tape, prepare us for its role as fetish object, the object that sets all the action in motion:

it explains Bill's flight when the police flag him down and discover the corpse of the commissioner in his trunk, the shot Bill receives in the arm, and the reason why Nike finds him alongside the road. All this is unleashed as he leaves the party to the accompaniment of the refrain of the song that pervades the film:

> Nowhere to run, I got no place to hide. [As music comes up, Bill puts his hand on the camera. The lyrics continue:]
> Enemies surrounding me on every side.
> Eyes open wide, looking for me.
> Who do I trust? Who can help me?
> Somebody's trying to get me down.
> But . . .
> You're a survivor.

We don't know exactly how Bill came to dispose of the tape after his flight, and when he is recaptured toward the end, and manages to whisper to Nike where to find it and what to do with it, the words he states to her are inaudible to the film's spectators. The tape has become the magical gris-gris that will keep the vicious Chief Collins from killing him since the chief needs the tape and can't get it without Bill confessing where it is. As for Bill, whose family they have already murdered in the effort to locate him, he now fears nothing from them since, as he tells them:

> BILL: You are talking to a dead man. [Looking savagely at the chief.] Death is a meal we all shall eat one day. It comes hot or cold. However it comes, I don't care. (see figure 12.5)

Nike comes to him in the dead of night, is told about the tape, and takes off. After a few mishaps, she locates it, secretes it in her bra, and gets it to the police. The rescue and happy ending reuniting Bill and Nike follow rapidly.

The scene of her locating the tape is crucial. As is usually the case in Nollywood films, it is a prosperous-looking Lagos, unencumbered by traffic jams or dilapidated streets or buildings, that provides the setting for most of the action concerning Nike and her family, and the wealthy and powerful figures vying for power. But the tape is the hidden, occult object that will overturn the unjust order of wealthy rulers, and to find it Nike has to go to a poor section of town, where broken-down cars are scattered on a lot, and where dangerous men are ready to threaten her. She locates the very wreck Bill had described, goes down on her hands and knees, and digs in the dirt until she uncovers the package containing the tape (see figure 12.2).

The location of trash is not haphazardly chosen. The buried tape, lying under the car wreck in the slums of the city, has the material form of a magical modern instrument that can record the truth and expose the lies, disrupting the structures of evil power so as to restore a proper order, enabling Bill and Nike to be united as they were supposed to be all along. It is like a recovered talisman, one that was created by the bad copy of some Maltese falcon. Like some Sam Spade who was essential in locating the hidden Maltese falcon and punishing its ravishers, Bill, the Americanized cameraman, shoots both literally and figuratively. As in a Hollywood noir involving a mysterious stolen statue, in the Nollywood version shooting and recording the truth are always acts of creating another bad copy for the lovers of "trashy" and "meretricious" images.

The "trash" that Nike unearths in the film is like a purloined letter, a signifier with quasi-magic properties and hidden content. There are several magical properties about this object that bear on our central thesis in this chapter, starting with its function with relation to the subjects. We can say that the tape ties Bill to Nike. When he whispers into her ears that she must unearth it and get it to the police, she doesn't know what is on the tape or what it signifies. All she knows is that he told her that if she fails, he will be killed. She has gone from being his hostage, captive, and eventually, despite her reluctance to acknowledge the appeal he has for her, his lover, ultimately to be married according to the final intertitles of the film. The transformation in their relationship is due to some kind of magic that changes a dangerous criminal who has invaded her house and placed her family at risk to a courageous, indomitable, righteous man to whom she can now openly acknowledge her attraction. In other words, she passes from subjugation to acceptance, the subject through whom the Other now speaks. The tape speaks her desire, and the Bill she was drawn to becomes the Bill who saves the country. Her subject positions multiply.

In his well-known "Seminar on the Purloined Letter," Lacan writes, "The plurality of subjects, of course, can be no objection for those who are long accustomed to the perspectives summarized by our formula: *the unconscious is the discourse of the Other*" (2002: 147). Here Lacan refers to the well-known figure of the letter that, in the Poe story, is placed in plain view of the detectives searching for it the better to hide it. The letter was first intended for the queen, and its discovery by Minister D compromised her. The minister steals it by substituting another letter in its place, and then filching the original. The queen turns to the police commissioner to recover it, but with his failure to turn up the letter after assiduously searching the minister's lodging for eighteen months, Detective Dupin is put on the case. Dupin visits the minister, spots a nonchalantly placed crumpled letter on the mantle, and deduces what the ordinary police could not figure out, that it was hidden by being placed in plain view. Dupin then manages the same subterfuge as the minister, replacing the original with a crumpled copy.

For Lacan, the initial interest in the tale springs from the repetition compulsion evident in the repeated act of substituting one letter for another. The substitution of the "letter" that functions to communicate between two parties, and whose contents become less significant than the actual presence of the letter itself, evokes the role of the signifier, and more generally of the symbolic order through which the subject is constituted.

The constitution of the subject, in relation to the symbolic order, depends upon the incorporation of the discourse of the Other ("the unconscious is the discourse of the Other"), leading us to two of Butler's key notions concerning melancholy, loss, and *assujetissement*. The first is that submission to the Other is constitutive of the subject; but also, as we have stated, that resistance to that submission functions equally in the constitution of the subject. The second is that subject positions are multiple. The repetition of the scene, as in a repetition compulsion, denotes the actions indicative of a trauma or loss that returns after the event and whose repetition marks the failure to work through the loss, failure to mourn it, failure to resolve it.

Resolution might suggest the successful coming to a subject position where contradictory elements are resolved: for Lacan, "plurality of subjects" is a consequence of a plurality of subject positions taken with regard to the internalized Other, and the expression of that discourse of the Other is equally plural, equally multiple, as is the case of a signifier whose place on a chain is always defined by its distance from, difference from other signifiers. Lacan's interest in the Poe letter is that its function evokes that of the signifier, something that becomes a "thing" or object in the symbolic order only when its position is defined by its relationship to other signifiers, and more importantly, when its relationship to the original Other whose discourse it repeats is given its form through processes of transposition, displacement, substitution so that the original discourse has been altered. Loss is transferred into something that becomes manageable for the subject. Trash is recovered, reinserted into a new economy, a new discourse, while its original form is there, like the letter, visibly placed before our eyes although we cannot see it: in a position that can become "out in the open" only when its hidden sense is unveiled.

The tape that Nike digs up, salvages, and manages to keep, despite her twice being attacked and chased, is exactly like the queen's letter. We do not hear its contents, though the primal scene of violence that it records has been witnessed by us. It is put to use so as to "save the nation," as in Poe's tale where its disposition entails saving the queen. It passes between subjects so as to establish the relationship between them, just like the signifying system that both enables relationships between subjects to be formed and simultaneously disguises the primal scene of violence on which the repression of the Other and its incorporation into the unconscious is based.

What better Other, here, than the corrupt chief whose agents are deployed so as to enable him to take control over the nation by unleashing intercommunal violence and then presenting himself as the savior of the nation. But this evil Other is in competition with the good Other, Bill. Initially taken to be the dangerous enemy, Bill proves to be different, an Americanized movie star Other whose role is not only to defeat evil but to do so through the deployment of his powerful digital camera and its specially constructed recording device that deploys the very object on which the entire tale, the entire film, with all its "formidable force," depends: the video tape!

Of course that tape, which the enemy Chief Collins commands and expects to be delivered in two days, does not contain what he had expected. For Lacan, this is the core of the Poe letter, namely that its contents have one meaning for one subject and another for a different subject. "This example demonstrates indeed how an act of communication may give the impression at which theorists too often stop: of allowing in its transmissions but a single meaning, as though the highly significant commentary into which he who understands integrates it, could, because unperceived by him who does not understand, be considered null" ("Seminar on Purloined Letter"). Lacan distinguishes between the signifier—with its fluidity and multiplicity of meanings, depending on its position, on who hears and receives it, the context into which they place it—and the communication of bees that is unidimensional and single, unambiguous, direct. The tape holds a mystery; the bees' message is open, without a hidden side. The tape is both object and site of projection of different subjects; both a segment of trash to be dug up and then duplicated, before its new powers can be unleashed, and a porter of truth that will transform and salvage the lost nation, the all-but-lost Bill, the confused and desperate Nike; transforming the film that started in one place identified with commonplace dangers and attractions and ending in another with great stakes.

The place of the tape in this economy of trashy cinema is somehow different from that of the usual symbols of excessive consumerism because it rewrites the familiar monstrousness of the object universe of globalized Nollywood with the hidden message it has inscribed. Like the content of the reels of film in *Aristotle's Plot* (1996), it works its magic through the technology of the modern recording, the video camera whose eyes and ears serve to expose the plotters and to save the nation, the wrongly accused, and the rightfully joined with union of Bill and Nike. As we have already witnessed the scene it has recorded (with a camera whose presence is now inferred by the diegetic one used by Bill, and that thus becomes self-referential),[9] we know what to expect. Yet the actual working of the tape is somehow outside the world that the gangsters and evil politician have been controlling through their limitless power, their "formidable force." We cannot access the contents of the tape or its own potential formidable force. That is what sets this film apart from the others that turn so comfortably to the evangelical Christian messages we have come to expect in Nollywood film that turn to transcendental sites for their reassurance.

The tape is a signifier, in its materiality and out-of-placeness, as in the reading Lacan gives of the purloined letter. Here it is a signifier and magical talisman, both symbolic and real, both signifying and performing, and masking what is being expressed. It comes closest to our utilization of trash as both trope and material object; object a and the "little bit of real," McGuffin and monstrous thing. It brings together those separated by the impossibility of communicating, of narrating, or of being unified in an identity formulation by forcing the subjects to occupy positions that provide them with the roles needed to relate to each other. This explains Lacan's reading of the signifier as always linking one to another, despite all attempts to freeze the signifier into a fixed position. The image he uses for the signifier is realized in the tape as Nike literally unearths it from its fixity in order to open its contents to the world, passing from Bill's hand to hers to the police commissioner's:

> It is the realist's imbecility, which does not pause to observe that nothing, *however deep in the bowels of the earth a hand may seek to ensconce it, will never be hidden there, since another hand can always retrieve it, and that what is hidden is never but what is missing from its place,* as the call slip puts it when speaking of a volume lost in a library. And even if the book be on an adjacent shelf or in the next slot, it would be hidden there, however visibly it may appear. For it can literally be said that *something is missing from its place only of what can change it: the symbolic. For the real, whatever upheaval we subject it to, is always in its place; it carries it glued to its heel, ignorant of what might exile it from it.* (http://www.lacan.com/purloined.htm; my emphasis)[10]

If the real is always in its place, the signifier is always missing from the fixed place when it is read/retrieved by another. The signifier carries the mark of its absence, its difference from other terms, but also the difference in its recording of the sender's intention and the receiver's understanding. That difference results in the trashing of any originary meaning since "something is missing from its place only of what can change it: the symbolic" (C'est qu'on ne peut dire *à la lettre* que ceci manque à sa place que de ce qui peut en changer, c'est-à-dire du symbolique—which can be translated as "For one cannot literally claim that something is missing from its place except for what could change of it, that is to say, the symbolic").[11] Trash is precisely what is out of its proper place, which is lacking in its place. That is why it is appropriate that the term Lacan uses to characterize the letter, the bearer of signification, is trash—litter, refuse:

> And to return to our cops, who took the letter from the place where it was hidden, how could they have seized the letter? In what they turned between their fingers what did they hold but what did not answer to their description. *"A letter, a litter": in Joyce's circle, they played on the homophony of the two words in English. Nor does the seeming bit of refuse the police are now handling reveal its other nature for being but half torn.* (http://www.lacan.com/purloined.htm; my emphasis)[12]

The tape moves around all these registers, disrupting the movement of the narrative from its original charge as a noir crime film to a political drama, passing through the leaves of the romance novelette to its happy conclusion. In his most eloquent passage on the purloined letter and its movement through the various gazes and perspectives that endowed it with meaning, Lacan writes, "Writings scatter to the winds blank checks in an insane charge. And were they not such flying leaves, there would be no purloined letters" (http://www.lacan.com /purloined.htm). ("Les écrits emportent au vent les traites en blanc d'une cavalerie folle. Et, s'ils n'étaient feuilles volantes, il n'y aurait pas de lettres volées" [17]. My translation would be, "Writings carry to the wind blank bills/drafts from a wild and crazy cavalry charge. And if they weren't flying leaves, there would be no stolen letters.")

For all its borrowings and bad copies, its crazy violence, its violent excesses, the *traites en blanc* of *Formidable Force* are gathered into the tape whose contents sustain Bill's bluster, "You are talking to a dead man. . . . Death is a meal we all shall eat one day." Bemused and vexed, all the chief can do is to make empty threats. The purloined letter passes on from Poe's ironic prose to Benson's Nollywoodian posturing captured in the camcorder's truth.

This is the trash of Nollywood that is so much at the center of the debates over African cinema. For Diawara (2010), there is a new wave cinema that clearly participates in the same genres attributes expected of this highly commercialized cinema: crime and passion flics, like in *Viva Riva!* (2011), in which director Djo Tunda Wa Munga "transforms the American gangster movie genre into a metaphor for the plague of civil war in Central Africa" (http://www .tinymixtapes.com/film/viva-riva), or Bekolo's "gangsterish" intellectualized action film *Aristotle's Plot* (1996) and his darkly sexual political drama *Les Saignantes* (2005). Teco Benson's *Formidable Force* may be just another Nollywood video film, even if shot with more style and originality, even if more visually compelling due to its superior camera technique and effective use of film noir mise-en-scène. It may be just another one of the thousands of video films edited too quickly, with dialogue that is often stilted; just another romance with two major stars, Genievieve Nnaji and Hanks Anuku,[13] whose faces and bodies are used to fill the screen, whose close-up emotional outbursts (especially Anuku's, in this case) are the familiar stuff of melodramatic cinema. But it is also something that effectively succeeds in recuperating the trashiness of low-grade stock into recycled footage with narratives that have clearly revived the moribund cinema of Nigeria and instilled great life into something we would not necessarily identify with new wave African cinema, as Diawara describes it, but rather something he calls correctly a "popular cinema," one now grounded in a "new social imaginary" (Diawara 2010). The effervescent, almost joyful action for the sake of action translates into a "mobility" that is so visceral that it informs a plethora of difference genres and is able to move us beyond the bland uniformities of corporate consumerist filmmaking that defines so many Hollywood productions. For Diawara, what binds Nollywood films in their "deep structure" is "a physical and psychological mobility in the face of current dislocation and Afro-pessimism, from Nigeria to the rest of the continent" (179). Diawara takes that movement and extends it to those "existential paradoxes" where the forces at play assume the bold quality of "formidability," often presented in Yoruba terms as given "the life force by the ancestors or by God" (179).

The happy conclusions that resolve melodrama, that evoke the movement toward resolution of the soap operas, and that Belsey identifies with classical realism and its conservative political values (1980), appear tacked on to these films. They are divided against themselves, with the formulaic ending bringing less a comfortable resolution than an expected finale, one that is largely outweighed by what preceded it. The endings often put off the encounter with the loss we identified with subjectivity and agency, ungrieved and unacknowledged loss on which ground the figure of the woman and the African would be built. Here the loss of the elusive object of desire, returned in the mysterious form of the tape whose message will ultimately come out, be heard, and enable evil to be punished, appears to be as comforting as the reformist ending of *Jenifa* where the newly conscientized Jenifa, who has paid for her wayward lifestyle by contracting AIDS, will now become an emissary for public health reform, and her errant sisters will either repent and rediscover happiness and love, or die miserably like Becky, stinking from the fistula that she "undoubtedly deserves" because of her practicing anal intercourse. Her death is presented as comforting as the shot out of nowhere that finishes off that "rotten" president's daughter Beyonce. Or the just retribution of Gloria the good sister, killed by her "evil sister" Esther, in *Blood Sisters*, when Gloria returns as a ghost to haunt her tormentor and murderer.

As familiar and predictable as the message written at the end of *Moolaade* (2004), these endings are now being remade in such formulaic and corny terms in Nollywood as to approach self-mockery or parody, like the minstrelsy truths they embody. We are at a threshold of trashiness in cinema that approaches the "Divine" aesthetics of John Waters, barely *not* tongue-in-cheek, mostly dancing around the fun of the tongue-in-cheek, as Beyonce's extravaganzas of romantic rhetoric are openly mocked by her friends, mimicked and mimed in hilarious spoofing. And as the evil actions of all the unstoppable villains—gangsters, women who aspire to dominate, rich men who would rule others or the nation— are paraded beyond the powers of anyone else to control, we approach a line that is essential to melodrama where farce and sentiment converge. We are in a realm of freedom unknown to African film before (Barlet, Diawara), a realm that has released emotion and imitation into the shameless spaces where bad copies and bad consciences are finally allowed to play out their full emotional charge. We are where Mammy Watta and Eshu had always been waiting for us, before the detours of serious business could be finished. What Diawara calls mobility in popular Nollywood films (2010, chapter 3) we need to extend totally, not simply in the aspirations for the life of the wealthy and powerful, but for the release from the "bondage" (Kenneth Nnebue, *Living in Bondage*, 1992, launches Igbo video films [Haynes, 62])—and not simply the bondage of films to educate an audience about truth or reality, but the bondage of the representative language of the cinematic symbolic order.

It might take 1,500 films a year to fill the large spaces of such a newly crafted imaginary, and Nollywood is testing those limits with a frenzy. Ironically, this freedom is due to the compulsive reiterations of formulas that "work," formulas derived not only from *Living in Bondage* and other original Nollywood films, not only from the theatrical style and language of Yoruba traveling theatre, but from the immensely popular soap operas and melodramas appearing on television screens across the continent. These products of global consumer capitalism foster models that Nollywood copies and then submits to a market of the streets laced with piracy so beautifully delineated by Brian Larkin as generating its own imperfect cinematic aesthetic (2008).

The bad copies of the Nollywood films are copies of copies, bad copies, that is, of bad copies, themselves accorded low cultural capital in inverse relation to their high economic capital. What freedom they attain is due to the capacity of such reiterations to evoke all the powers of obsessive repetitions: theft, piracy, bad consciences, imitations of imitations: the power of cinema as Kine Pravda was never so effectively captured in this perverse formula provided by Diawara in his celebration of the popular: "By stealing from Hollywood the star system, the dress style, the music, by remaking Western genre films, and by appropriating the digital video camera as an African storytelling instrument, Nollywood is, in a sense, *a copy of a copy that has become original through the embrace of its spectators*" (185; my emphasis).[14]

Like the purloined letter, it is the tape that serves as the hidden trope, or trope of the hidden value in this cinema of digital video storytelling.

The images scattered to the wind in Nollywood films are continually relegated to the rubbish bin by celluloid film standards. Yet the works of Teco Benson, Tunde Kelani, and Kingsley Ogoro have succeeded in recapturing the African imaginary precisely through the effectiveness of those flying leaves. The audiences have responded to the broad gestures of farce so wonderfully played by Nkem Owoh as Osuafia, have created an international star like Genievieve Nnaji whose talents to move from romance to crime film to evil sister rival those of Hollywood's most versatile actresses, and others like Hanks Anuku who have created a wildly successful popular crime cinema. The inspiring new wave auteur filmmakers can carry African cinema to the major festivals while the work of Nollywood carries its own sense of African narratives to the people. As Fanta Nacro and Teco Benson have shown, both cinemas carry the insane charge of images infused with all the trashiness associated with violence, melodrama, excess, and destruction but also inform that trash with new regimes of value that open us to new cinemas whose possibilities carry us beyond the fixed boundaries of the postcolonial identity.

Trash is defined ultimately by what is valueless, within an order that places value on some particular quality, like monetary worth. But the lesson of the purloined letter is that the value of the letter placed in one position changes when

Figure 12.1. Jezebell green eyes.

Figure 12.2. Digging up the tape.

Figure 12.3. Bill and his camcorder.

Figure 12.4. The tape.

Figure 12.5. "Death is a meal we all shall eat one day."

it is reversed, cycled into another reconstituted location, one invisible to those looking in only one direction in the initial order. The glance that reverses estimates of value set the letter in motion. "And if they stop at the reverse side of the letter, on which, as is known, the recipient's address was written in that period, it is because the letter has for them no other side but its reverse" (Lacan, "Seminar on the Purloined Letter" 1972). From Bataille's transgressive positions *below* and the *old mole* to Butler's *assujetissement* and the bad conscience, it has been the goal of this study to open the glance that falls on African cinema to the possibilities of reversals in conventional estimates of value, so that what was dismissed as trash would be now welcomed in the manner of *récupéré* sculptures, not so as to revive "art" with new forms, but to redefine African cinematic practices in all their vitality. In the process, I discovered that trash could not be separated from regimes of value, from value itself, and that the combat that African cinema undertook at its inception cannot be carried forward in today's films without considering the ways we understand value in African terms. The combat has been to elaborate a perspective from "below," from the trash heap, where *déchets* are lost and then restored as *humains*—not as an oxymoron but as a transvaluation.

Notes

1. Bataille, Stam, and Locations of Trash

1. "Beyond the cemetery rose the Dungle, a piazza of flattened refuse, ringed by cardboard huts behind which rose mounds of garbage. The Dungle did double duty as a municipal garbage dump and a derelict community erected on a platform of filth, human waste and the jetsam of the more discerning scavengers. The people who skittered crablike over its stinking, gull- and rat-infested ridges were absolutely the lowest human creatures in the Caribbean caste system. These nameless scavengers were shunned by all as worse ghouls than the mythical God-cursed 'gwine-gog' hogs and hideous 'gorgon' devils who had snakes instead of eyes. Unwelcome even in the humble hierarchy of the ghetto, the inhabitants of the Dungle were not spoken of by anyone, their very existence acknowledged only by an assiduous avoidance of the precinct" (White, 2006: 113). A memorable scene in Jimmy Cliff's *The Harder They Come* (1972) occurs when the Cliff character Ivan, down on his luck and at his lowest point, joins the scavengers on the Dungle as he sings "Many Rivers to Cross."

2. Julio García Espinosa, "For an Imperfect Cinema" (1971). "Nowadays, perfect cinema—technically and artistically masterful—is almost always reactionary cinema. The major temptation facing Cuban cinema at this time—when it is achieving its objective of becoming a cinema of quality, one which is culturally meaningful within the revolutionary process—is precisely that of transforming itself into a perfect cinema."

3. Cf. Gwendolyn Brooks, who, in "The Lovers of the Poor," captures in perfectly satirical terms the condescending patronizing position of the rich white Chicago bourgeoisie as they descend on the ghetto to distribute their charity. Here is a selection from the longer poem:

> Their guild is giving money to the poor.
> The worthy poor. The very very worthy
> And beautiful poor. Perhaps just not too swarthy?
> Perhaps just not too dirty nor too dim.

The full version is available on line at http://www.poets.org/viewmedia.php/prmMID /15871.

4. On "socius," see Deleuze, ANTI OEDIPE ET MILLE PLATEAUX. Cours de Vincennes:

> I would like to pursue the problem of the economy of flows; last time, someone wanted a more precise definition of flows, more precise, that is, than something which flows upon the socius. What I call the socius is not society, but rather a particular social instance which plays the role of a full body. Every society presents itself as a socius or full body upon which all kinds of flows flow and are interrupted, and the social investment of desire is this basic operation of the break-flow to which we can easily give the name of schizz. (http://www.webdeleuze.com/php/texte.php?cle=119&groupe=Anti+Oedipe+ et+Mille+Plateaux&langue=2)

Jason Read glosses the term "socius" as follows, beginning with Althusser's "society effect" and then Deleuze and Guattari:

> 12. What Marx is outlining with this idea of an Asiatic despot, and what Deleuze and Guattari underscore, is the fact that because a mode of production is constituted as a contingent encounter of different political and social processes, an encounter which is continually threatened by its own unraveling, it must produce, artificially as it were, its own stability. This production of stability entails in part a coding (or recoding) of desire; or rather, a production of a particular subjectivity that recognizes itself and its desires in the mode of production. Marx refers to this production of subjectivity through what he calls the "inorganic body" from which subjectivity is produced; that is, the mode of production reproduces itself by providing the raw material of subjectivity in the form of "inorganic" material of beliefs, language, and desires (G 490/398). Althusser names this dimension, or problem, the "society effect" (l'effet de société).
>
> The mechanism of the production of this "society effect" is only complete when all the effects of the mechanism have been expounded, down to the point where they are produced in the form of the very effects that constitute the concrete, conscious or unconscious relation of the individuals to the society as a society, i.e., down to the effects of the fetishism of ideology (or 'forms of social consciousness'—Preface to A Contribution . . .), in which men consciously or unconsciously live their lives, their projects, their actions, their attitudes and their functions as social (Althusser and Balibar 1970: 66).
>
> In one of the un-credited citations of Reading Capital Deleuze and Guattari rename this problem the socius. Deleuze and Guattari stress what the definition offered above eclipses—that this society effect, or socius, must also and at the same time be a cause; that is, it must have its own particular effects and productivity.
>
> . . . the forms of social production, like those of desiring production, involve an unengendered nonproductive attitude, an element of anti-production coupled with the process, a full body that functions as a socius. This socius may be the body of the earth, that of the tyrant, or capital. This is the body that Marx is referring to when he says that it is not the product of labor, but rather appears as its natural or divine presuppositions. In fact, it does not restrict itself merely to opposing productive forces in and of themselves. It falls back on [il se rabat sur] all production, constituting a surface over which the forces and agents of production are distributed, thereby appropriating for itself all surplus production and arrogating to itself both the whole and the parts of the process, which now seem to emanate from it as a quasi-cause. (AO 10/16)

Every society, or social machine, has an aspect that appears as the condition, or cause, rather than the effect of the productive relations, the desires and labors of society. Paradoxically, this "quasi-cause" appears to be a cause of production, because it is itself not productive, or, more precisely, "anti-productive." It appropriates the excessive forces of production, distributing some for the reproduction of society and wasting most (in the form of tribal honors, palaces, and ultimately war). Eugene Holland underscores the centrality of "anti-production" of an expenditure that is at once useless (constituting a vast appropriation of productive forces for excess and expenditure) and useful (reproducing the relations) and thus does not fit within a neat Marxist conceptualization of "forces" and "relations" of production (Holland 1999: 62–63).

The socius is not an effect but a cause, a production of authority, prestige, and belief, what is referred to as both the recording of production and the production of recording. However, Deleuze and Guattari's reinscription of the society effect as cause is not an actual deviation from Althusser but rather a return of Althusser's concept of the "society effect" to his most important theoretical innovation, "immanent causality." While several Althusserians dismiss the idea of the "society effect" as a wrong turn for Althusser (e.g., Callari and Ruccio 1996: 2), Balibar continues to use and expand on this concept, arguing that the "society effect" and the particular mode of subjection it entails must be thought in terms of its own particular materiality and effectivity (Balibar 2002). Jason Read, "A Universal History of Contingency," in *Borderlands* 2.3 (2003), available at http://www.borderlands.net.au/vol2no3_2003/read_contingency.htm.

5. Bataille marks the processes of both appropriation and expenditure as linked to the body's activities, and to insure that the full engagement of the body with both eating and shitting is evoked, he cites his model of the great disrupter, de Sade: "Verneuil makes someone shit, he eats the turd, and then he demands that someone eat his. The one who eats his shit vomits: he devours her puke" (95). Bataille might be said to be grasping for what Kristeva will come to identify with abjection, but her purpose in evoking the abject is to set out an agenda for the consolidation of the ego, its dependency on processes of ejection that enable it to give definition to itself. Bataille's notions are far less stabilizing: he intends to disrupt a dominant social, economic, and political order whose stifling orderliness is grounded in an underlying structure of domination. His examples have the refreshing feel of naïve youth: he imagines societies in which "religious organization of a given country *is developing*" to be most amenable to "the freest opening for excremental collective impulses (orgiastic impulses) established in opposition to political, juridical, and economic institutions" (94). This make-believe society is surely what he imagines some non-western location to furnish—a people not yet corrupted into the materialistic and alienated conditions of "development." The latter condition that marks the powerful classes in their abilities to acquire and consume—to appropriate, to expropriate, to ingest, to consume—all precedes the "heterogeneous" processes that follow upon all acts of consumption. In short, the powerful eat, as in the eating of the weak; the poor are shit, are shit out, are turned into the leftovers of those who have swallowed them up. Food, land, people, these are transformed by the dominant processes of global metabolic activities; they are incorporated into a single process, ingestion, but are expelled into a heterogeneous mass that we can call the dung heap, the trash pile, the rubbish tip, into which everything deemed useless is expelled. They do not challenge the consistency of homogeneity—they are its condition for existence. The homogeneous is established, according to Bataille, "by everywhere replacing *a priori* inconceivable objects with classified series of conceptions or ideas" (96). The order that marks the symbolic structuring of knowledge, for example, results in the privileging of the scientific epistemologies over the "popular conceptions of the world," and the result, in philosophy as in other branches of disciplinary thought, is a flattening of authorized knowledges that results in "the homogeneity of the world" (96).

6. Ibid., 97. Heterology "*ceases to be the instrument of appropriation, and now serves excretion: it introduces the demand for the violent gratifications implied by social life*" (97; his emphasis). Decay becomes, for him, "an end in itself" (99), not a means to serve future insemination, growing, creation, but an end of appropriation, the process that itself eventuates in the imposition of servility: "appropriation in its most overwhelming form

historically devolves on slaves" (99); and, "as soon as one attacks the accursed exploitation of man by man, it becomes time to leave to the exploiters this abominable appropriative morality." The heart of the issue comes to this: "To the extent that man no longer thinks of crushing his comrades under the yoke of morality, he acquires the capacity to link overtly not only his intellect and his virtue but his *raison d'être* to the violence and incongruity of his excretory organs, as well as to his ability to become excited and entranced by heterogeneous elements, commonly starting in debauchery" (99).

7. "A genuine TANU [TANGANYIKA African National Union] leader will not live off the sweat of another man, nor commit any feudalistic or capitalistic action" (cited in Ferguson 75).

2. Rancière

1. As we will see, this binary itself is subject to further parsing by Rancière who defines the modernist program for art into two directions: one is represented by Barnett Newman, which he associates with the Kantian-Lyotardian sublime, and which I imagine in the form of highly abstract forms like white on white. The second appears to be the opposite, as in installation art pieces that employ the everyday object placed into unaccustomed spaces, effecting a sense of the oddity of conjoining the real and the unreal, the figurative and the abstract. Both are versions of the aesthetic regime.

2. See also Boughedir's five "tendencies," ranked in order of social values: 1. the sociopolitical tendency; 2. the moralist tendency; 3. the self-expressive tendency; 4. the narcissistic individual tendency; 5. the cultural tendency. In Ferid Boughedir, "Les Grandes tendances du cinéma en Afrique noire, " *CinémAction* 26 (1983): 48–57. Published in "L'Image apprivoisée," in *L'Afrique* 914 (July 12, 1978): 185–87; in *Le cinéma africain de A à Z* (Brussels: Organisation Catholique International du Cinéma, 1987); and in translation as "African Cinema and Ideology: Tendencies and Evolution" in June Givanni, ed., *Symbolic Narrative/African Cinema* (London: BFI, 2000).

3. In a paper titled "Women and the Dynamics of Representation," Dr. Abena Busia called for proper representation of women in Nigerian movies saying, "There is a need to redress the discrepancies about how we are seen. We should never underestimate the differences between how we are seen and how we see ourselves because when it becomes abuse, we fight." Busia's points were echoed by other women, including Mrs. Abima Fashola, First Lady of Lagos State, who spoke at the conference on Nollywood hosted by African Women in Film Forum held in Lagos on June 26, 2010, and convened by the African Women in Development Fund. (http://www.nollyzone.com/news/fashola-ireti -doyle-others-condemn-nollywood%E2%80%99s-image-of-women/; accessed July 19, 2010). Mrs. Fashola condemned the exploitation of women in Nollywood, echoing voices calling for the improvement or censorship of Nollywood's representation of women. This matches the calls of others for Nollywood to present a more positive image of Nigeria to the outside world.

4. E.g., Abderrahmane Sissako, Safi Faye, Jean-Pierre Bekolo, Idrissou Mora Kpai, or Jean-Marie Teno, who have deployed mixed genres encompassing both fictional and nonfictional dimensions, as we have seen in the narrative voices of the cineaste, narrator-character, or native guide in one way or another. *Aristotle's Plot* and *Bamako* offer two striking examples.

5. "The Novelist as Teacher" (1965) in *Morning Yet on Creation Day*, reprinted in *Hopes and Impediments*; "The Role of the Writer in a New Nation" (1964).

6. This corresponds to the pre-aesthetic period in which art was considered to work in the service of the public good, of "ethics": "The first schema of artistic possibility [Rancière] denominates is the 'ethical regime of images,' epitomised by Plato's *Republic*, and reprised in Hegel's vision of Ancient Greek culture. Here art is judged according to its utility for reflecting the collective ethos of a society or people. As Rancière puts it: 'In the ethical regime, works of art have no autonomy. They are viewed as images to be questioned for their truth and for their effect on the ethos of individuals and the community' (Rancière, 2002: 135)." Toni Ross, "*Material Thinking*: The Aesthetic Philosophy of Jacques Rancière and the Design Art of Andrea Zittel," in *Studies in Material Thinking* 1, no. 2 (April 2008), http://www.aut.ac.nz/material_thinking/materialthinking2/issues /Toni.pdf, accessed July 19, 2010.

7. In an entry to the website "Mute" (dated November 14, 2006), Melanie Gilligan challenges Rancière to explain how this redistribution of the sensible that gives political voice to those previously not heard differs from any capitalist revision of the distribution of the sensible intended to give voice to new products, i.e., to sell by changing the vision of what is exciting and new. Gilligan writes,

> You describe politics as a temporary disruption of the "distribution of the sensible," which you define as the established social order "determining what presents itself to sense experience"—in other words, what can be sensed, thought and felt. Politics happens when those who have been afforded no part in this distribution, "the part of no part," make themselves perceptible, and in so doing reconfigure the field of the sensible, an organisation which is never absolute. You identify various examples of such re-orderings, for instance in the 19th c, worker-intellectuals read and wrote "high" literature instead of militant or popular forms. This dissolved the unitary identities allotted to them in the sensible order (i.e.—the worker as he who has no time to do anything but his own work) and exercised what you have called "the power to declassify" (*On the Shores of Politics*). It is easy to see how, by extension, this relates to your conception of politics as "a theatrical and artificial sphere" ('*L'Entretien avec Jacques Ranciere*', *Dissonance no.1*) where the part of no part can use appearances and dissimulation to shift and confuse roles.
>
> However, politics as disruption of the sensible order finds a parallel in commerce—particularly in the present—where profits are increasingly made through reordering and subverting existing visual, affective and semiotic codes.

Gilligan goes on to give examples in commerce or the military in which new ways of viewing and presenting the world, from advertising to "shock and awe" are used, not to change existing ratios of power but to perpetuate them. This, she avers, is Marx's position on capitalism itself as always undergoing revolutionary change.

> We could add that this extends far beyond industrial production to the differentiation of new markets, new desires, and new subjective dispositions. Creating the differences integral to the reproduction of capital requires re-organising the field of experience. The current "established order" constantly undergoes such re-orderings, yet inequality in wealth and privilege is unaffected and continues to worsen. These redistributions effected by capital can make visible or further obscure those who are excluded from the sen-

sible order—i.e. the working-class as part of no part, immigrant laborers, the impoverished inhabitants of the third world slums, for instance. However, without a change in economic conditions, which are not reducible to economic science as a form of "political representation" (*The Philosopher and His Poor*), it is difficult to see how the excluded can actually stage a disordering of roles to significant effect without being condemned to enact the infinite repetition of these performances. What distinguishes the politics you describe from the re-orderings prevalent in commerce today? Would you say that economic conditions could only change through such reorganisations of the sensible order and if so, how can the part of no part create consequential disturbances when the current distribution (in so far as it is determined by capital) relies on such re-orderings? (Gilligan)

In turning to economism and marketing strategies, Gilligan reproduces the regime of sensibility that originally enabled the structuring of politics as the expression of class interest.

8. "Pape Samb left rural Senegal as a ten-year-old orphan, traveling to the capital city of Dakar. He has spent the last forty years there, in a fishing village squeezed between factory yards in the portside industrial park of Belaire. Samb has remained single, and his tiny one-room shack has just enough space for his hammock. The wealth of his life lies in his devotion to Sheikh Amadu Bamba (1853–1927), the Sufi saint central to the Mouride Way. Samb paints wall murals as a devotional task. He has no formal training; his inspiration comes from dreams, his hand guided by the saint. Samb's graffitist tag is 'Papisto Boy,' and his greatest achievement is a mural covering three long exterior walls of one of Belaire's factories" (137).

"Two-meter-tall portraits of Bamba and other Mouride luminaries appear beside revolutionaries like Martin Luther King, Kwame Nkrumah, and Nelson Mandela. Politicians range from Jimmy Carter to Che Guevara, and medical pioneers, philosophers, and the pope all find places. Heroes of popular culture are prominent, and Bob Marley and Jimi Hendrix are given pride of place as hallowed "messengers." Portraits appear in mystical configurations from Papisto's dreams and visions. For example, the Senegalese singing star Coumba Gawlo is embraced by the curving staircase of the infamous 'Slave House' of Gorée Island, as she looks to its haunting 'door of no return'" (Roberts and Roberts 127).

9. In 1992, at the first edition of Dak'Art, Moustapha Dime (Senegal 1952–1998) won the Grand Prize for his sculpture *La Dame de la culotte*. This object, made from a large tree trunk into which the artist carved only breasts and inserted a large spike topped with a bit of scavenged plastic netting for a neck, head, and hair, achieved recognition for one of Senegal's now most famous avant-garde styles: recuperation. Recuperation, while readily translatable into English, does not signify an international movement or style, although artists using its methods exist around the globe. As a technique, it involves the collection of items easily found within the artist's environment, and then the conversion of those objects, often through as little artistic intervention as possible, into works of art. Recuperation, additionally, possesses some unique attributes: it is defiantly a sculptural phenomenon—even two-dimensional artists find themselves working in a more three-dimensional mode if they are using recuperation techniques—and it is defined by its connection to urbanity and to the local environment of the cities in which its artists live. Only large urban

cities are capable of producing the critical mass of cast-off items necessary to sustain the intensive sorting and salvaging operations that provide raw materials to recuperation artists.

The Dak'Art editions have provided a unique forum for viewing the multiple recuperation strategies used by artists around the world. In Dak'Art 2006, wire and bottle-top "fabrics" by Ghanaian El Anatsui shared space with a door barricaded from entry by barbed wire fencing strung with discarded gloves and hats by Cote d'Ivoire's Jems Koko Bi. In 2004, Cameroonian Joseph Francis Sumegne's Les Neuf Notables took over one corner of the National Gallery with its over-life-size village elders made from rebar, tires, beads, bones, and automobile parts. The same year two broken windshields formed a transparent barrier through which a plastic and resin male figure charged in *Crash* by Sumegne's compatriot Issac Essoua. In the 2008 edition, following in Dime's footsteps, Senegalese Ndary Lo was a co-winner of the Grand Prix Leopold Sedar Senghor for his *Muraille Verte*, a room-sized installation of welded rebar tree people rooted in sand, seed pods, and dried leaves laid on top of mirror plates. Lo confesses that with the success he has garnered over the last decade with his recuperation sculptures, he no longer salvages the rebar from the industrial zone of Mbao, just on the outskirts of Dakar where he lives. "I can't find enough of it by myself," he laments, "so now he buys the rebar from the factories. But, he winks, the sand he "recuperated" himself from the tiny reforested area just in front of the industrial city, known as the Mbao Forest.

Susan Kart, "The Phenomenon of Recuperation at the Dar'Art Biennale," *African Arts* (September 22, 2009), http://www.thefreelibrary.com/The+phenomenon+of+recuperation +at+the+Dak%27Art . . . -a0206055413 (accessed July 19, 2010).

10. On "police," Ranciere writes,

> I do not . . . identify the police with what is termed the "state apparatus." The notion of a state apparatus is in fact bound up with the presupposition of an opposition between State and society in which the state is portrayed as a machine, a "cold monster" imposing its rigid order on the life of society. This representation already presupposes a certain "political philosophy," that is, a certain confusion of politics and the police. The distribution of places and roles that defines a police regime stems as much from the assumed spontaneity of social relations as from the rigidity of state functions. The police is essentially, the law, generally implicit, that defines a party's share or lack of it . . . The police is thus first an order of bodies that defines the allocation of ways of doing, ways of being, and ways of saying, and sees those bodies are assigned by the name to a particular place and task; it is an order of the visible and the sayable that sees that a particular activity is visible and another is not, that this speech is understood as discourse and another as noise. It is police law, for example, that traditionally turns the workplace into a private space not regulated by the ways of seeing and saying proper to what is called the public domain, where the worker's having a part is strictly defined by the remuneration of his work. Policing is not so much the "disciplining" of bodies as a rule governing their appearing, a configuration of occupations and the properties of the spaces where these occupations are distributed. (1999: 29)

In another definition, Rancière defines police as an "organizational system of coordinates that establishes a distribution of the sensible." It is responsible for, or accounts for, the division of the community into its various social strata—groups, social positions, and functions. What is central for our concerns is that this division is what accounts for those who participate in the social system and those who are excluded: those who thus become visible to the community as members of society, and those who do not; those who are heard, and those not; those who can speak, and those not (2009b: 3).

11. A simple example might be a way of seeing a given object, say an independent avant-garde film, as belonging to "the world of cinema," rather than being a vaguely artistic expression of something not really film; or vice versa, seeing in crassly commercial film something that participates in a world of visual arts accessible to the analyses of film studies. In terms of the political landscape, it would consist in a character like Bigger Thomas or Sembène's Black Docker, or his beggars and handicapped figures, being viewed as members of the community, not outsiders; or of the Invisible Man being recognized as a human being, etc.

12. Cf. Elizabeth Harney, "Art at the Crossroads: Senegalese Art in the 1960s." She describes the revolt against the stifling atmosphere of Senghor's official state doctrines of Negritude with the formation of the Village des Arts, and especially the new movement Laboratoire Art-Agit, "a multimedia performance group comprised of artists, cultural workers and intellectuals whose main agenda was to liberate artists from dependence on the state. Artists such as Issa Samb, Babacar Traoré, and Youssouf John, staged impromptu demonstrations and performances outside of official gallery and theater openings, bringing art back to people in the streets and calling into question the authenticity of invented traditions of the Negritude movement" (75). They deployed improvisation and audience participation against a notion of officially sanctioned art. In Nkiru Nzegwu, ed., *Issues in Contemporary African Art* (Binghamton, NY: International Society for the Study of Africa, 1998).

13. When I first viewed *Touki Bouki* (1973) in Yaounde, the audience emerged from the showing scratching its head, asking what "that" was all about. My sense of a surrealist venture saved the film for me; we were at the time of Dikongue Pipa's *Le Prix de la liberté* (1978) and Daniel Kamwa's *Pousse-Pousse* (1976), not of Godardian experimentalism. Diop stood alone those years.

14. Bureau of Public Secrets, http://www.bopsecrets.org/SI/2.derive.htm: "One of the basic situationist practices is the *dérive*,(1) a technique of rapid passage through varied ambiences. Dérives involve playful-constructive behavior and awareness of psychogeographical effects, and are thus quite different from the classic notions of journey or stroll.

"In a dérive one or more persons during a certain period drop their relations, their work and leisure activities, and all their other usual motives for movement and action, and let themselves be drawn by the attractions of the terrain and the encounters they find there. Chance is a less important factor in this activity than one might think: from a dérive point of view cities have psychogeographical contours, with constant currents, fixed points and vortexes that strongly discourage entry into or exit from certain zones" (Guy Debord).

15. This is the commonest argument against "anticolonialism" as grounded in the same presuppositions or values as colonialism, even in the attempt to reverse them. Spivak's critique of postcolonialism often follows along these lines.

16. Along similar lines, Roberts and Roberts record innumerable examples of the way that the image of Amadou Bamba is viewed as an encounter in which the subject of the paintings, the saint or his adherents, are actively engaged: "Mourids state that images

of Amadou Bamba and his family are active sources of potency and power. The images offer protection, prosperity, benevolence, healing, and reversal of misfortune. . . . The Saint's image possesses powers [i.e., his *baraka*]" (24).

"Whenever you see Amadou Bamba's image . . . you feel hope being released inside you. You feel happiness being released inside you just by looking at the image" (45).

"The image of the Holy Man prevents me from going in a bad direction because the image is a protection. In addition, the image attracts all kinds of good things to the store . . . The image attracts good things and repels evil. . . . The image gives me confidence. One can just look at the picture and see an image, but I look to see the inside of the Holy Man. . . . I know that I have the power of the Holy Man inside me" ("A Dakar Cobbler," cited in Roberts and Roberts 48).

17. To illustrate this point, Rancière writes that metapolitics in the past could be seen in Marxism's reading of productive forces and relations of production as explanatory mechanisms of social forms, but the revolution that Marxism advocated could only come about, he claimed, "after a revolution within the very idea of revolution of the forms of sensible experience as opposed to a revolution of state forms" (33–34). This statement demonstrates most clearly the gap between the older national liberationist thinking, best exemplified by Fanon, and Rancière's call for a new form of sensible experience, a new understanding of revolution.

18. This is the burden of Diawara's *We Won't Budge* (2003) and *In Search of Africa* (1998) in which he obstinately defends the African market, and by implication and statement, consumerism, the sources that produce wealth, trade, and ultimately more successful market economies in Africa. He sees no benefit in the misery of poverty, the glories of which Césaire sings, that Sissako celebrates, in a blackness that stands free from western domination and values, apart from the material bases for the good or even the okay life. Before that freedom and celebration can take place, there must be food and wine on the table to provide for the celebration. The African market is one place to celebrate it; its close proximity to neoliberal trade values is not particularly vilified.

3. The Out-of-Place Scene of Trash

1. "Although within the body blood flows in equal quantities from high to low and from low to high, there is a bias in favor of that which elevates itself, and human life is erroneously seen as an elevation. The division of the universe into subterranean hell and perfectly pure heaven is an indelible conception, mud and darkness being the *principles* of evil as light and celestial space are the *principles* of good: with their feet in mud but their heads more or less in light, men obstinately imagine a tide that will permanently elevate them, never to return, into pure space. Human life entails, in fact, the rage of seeing oneself as a back and forth movement *from refuse to the ideal, and from the ideal to refuse* [my emphasis]—a rage that is easily directed against an organ as *base* as the foot" (Bataille 1989: 20–21).

2. Rancière 2004: 298. As the "subject" of human rights became associated with victims of human rights abuses, they were increasingly seen as those who were helpless to do anything about the violations, and they received their rights only as a kind of humanitarian gesture. "Human" rights became "humanitarian" rights since in reality it seemed that the only ones who actually enjoyed those rights were citizens of nations inasmuch as the rights were attached to a "national community as such" (298).

3. In his extraordinary text, Dominique LaPorte presents the history of how shit came to pass from a fertilizing and beautifying substance to that which is seen to be opposing purity and health. He carries the burden of shit, as does this text, in its manifestations as a trope as well as a material object. Thus, in a marvelous section, he quotes a French edict of 1539 that suggests that cleansing the city functions in the same way that one cleanses language: "If language is beautiful, it must be because a master bathes it—a master who cleans shit holes, sweeps offal, and expurgates city and speech to confer upon them order and beauty" (7). Secondly, he evokes the "hierarchy of waste" that develops when the city is placed under the ordinances that require order and practices to insure health, a pattern that inscribes trash with the same features as those of the population in its divisions of higher and lower (28).

4. Cf. Stam's take on hybridity in "Beyond Third Cinema" (2003).

5. "*Parergon:* neither work (*ergon*) nor outside the work (*hors d'oeuvre*), neither inside nor outside, neither above nor below, it disconcerts any opposition but does not remain indeterminate and it *gives rise* to the work" (Derrida 1987, 9). See also his point that when we look at a painting, the frame is seen as part of the wall when looking at the painting itself, and is seen as part of the painting when looking at the wall (67). In yet another iteration of trash, it fits Derrida's definition of the parergon.

6. Many rivers to cross
   But I can't seem to find my way over
   Wandering I am lost
   As I travel along the white cliffs of Dover

   Many rivers to cross
   And it's only my will that keeps me alive
   I've been licked, washed up for years
   And I merely survive because of my pride

   And this loneliness won't leave me alone
   It's such a drag to be on your own
   My woman left me and she didn't say why
   Well, I guess I'll have to cry

   Many rivers to cross
   But just where to begin I'm playing for time
   There have been times I find myself
   Thinking of committing some dreadful crime

   Yes, I've got many rivers to cross
   But I can't seem to find my way over
   Wandering, I am lost
   As I travel along the white cliffs of Dover

   Yes, I've got many rivers to cross
   And I merely survive because of my will . . .

7. Increasingly we are seeing scenes from other films around the world with similar settings in garbage dumps, like *District 9* (2009), *Waste Land* (2010), *Slumdog Millionaire* (2008), along with the older Cissé film *Nyamanton* (1987).

8. Rancière, 2009c: 22–31. In brief, Rancière defines these three images thusly: the naked image is "the image that does not constitute art, because what it shows us ex-

cludes the prestige of dissemblance and the rhetoric of exegeses" (22). The ostensive image "asserts its power as that of sheer presence, without signification. But it claims it in the name of art. It posits this presence as the peculiarity of art faced with the media circulation of imagery, but also with the powers of meaning that alter this presence: the discourses that present and comment on it, the institutions that display it, the forms of knowledge that historicize it" (23). The metamorphic image "involves an idea of the relations between art and image that much more broadly inspires a number of contemporary exhibitions. According to this logic, it is impossible to delimit a specific sphere of presence isolating artistic operations and products from forms of circulation of social and commercial imagery and from operations interpreting this image" (24). Examples of the naked image include well-known photographs of the Holocaust; of the ostensive, classical painting; and of the metamorphic, installation or conceptual art (*Future of the Image* [2009c] 2009).

9. Sembène's familiar neologism, "mégotage" is derived from *mégot*, French for a cigarette butt. Piecing together the footage, shot on the cheap, defines the economical style developed in early African cinema.

10. An interesting example of this is the Jewish genizah, a storehouse for writings with sacred text of some form or other inscribed on it, to be disposed of by being "buried" rather than destroyed—thus a sort of cemetery for writings. The Cairo genizah lasted for millennia, and became not only an invaluable source of historical materials, but also inspired the novelist Amitav Ghosh in his novel *In an Antique Land* (1994).

11. Moser cites Tournier and Douglas in defining this undifferentiated mass as the zero degree of rubbish: in "what Tournier calls 'the soft white mass of refuse' . . . the particular object was engulfed, intact, save for a few chips. Undifferentiated, they are doomed in whole to the process of 'pulverization, dissolution and rotting' that, according to Douglas, effects the transition of the impure object (for it is still perceived as an object) to the status of rubbish" (95). In passing to that state of nothingness, the object must lose any remnants of its identity, its memory being lost: "Debilitation of this memory goes hand in hand with removal of the waste-object and the material transformations that it endures" (97).

12. In a key scene early in the film, Ivan comes to Hilton's residence to beg for an audition. He sees a quartet sing for Hilton who waits impatiently in his Mercedes convertible for them to finish before he says, "I can't use that," and drives off.

13. Larry Summers, president, World Bank, December 12, 1991 (http://www .whirledbank.org/ourwords/summers.html, accessed February 11, 2011). In addition to the passage quoted in this chapter, Summers wrote,

> 'Dirty' Industries: Just between you and me, shouldn't the World Bank be encouraging MORE migration of the dirty industries to the LDCs [Less Developed Countries]? I can think of three reasons:
> 1) The measurements of the costs of health impairing pollution depends on the foregone earnings from increased morbidity and mortality. From this point of view a given amount of health impairing pollution should be done in the country with the lowest cost, which will be the country with the lowest wages. I think the economic logic behind dumping a load of toxic waste in the lowest wage country is impeccable and we should face up to that.
> 2) The costs of pollution are likely to be non-linear as the initial increments of pollution probably have very low cost. I've always thought that under-

populated countries in Africa are vastly UNDER-polluted, their air quality is probably vastly inefficiently low compared to Los Angeles or Mexico City. Only the lamentable facts that so much pollution is generated by non-tradable industries (transport, electrical generation) and that the unit transport costs of solid waste are so high prevent world welfare enhancing trade in air pollution and waste.

3) The demand for a clean environment for aesthetic and health reasons is likely to have very high income elasticity. . . . Clearly trade in goods that embody aesthetic pollution concerns could be welfare enhancing. While production is mobile the consumption of pretty air is a non-tradable.

14. The sovereign stands outside the state as that which founds its order by force, and inside its juridical order, empowered to suspend the validity of the law (1998: 15). That is, logically it precedes the social contract, yet at the same time it functions within the social contract state as its ultimate foundation of power over the citizenry.

15. In the biblical account, the Jews of Exodus were wanderers in the desert, the place of exception where their confrontation with what Agamben calls the "Force of Law" meant that their existence could assume only the quality of "bare life" because their lives were defined entirely by confronting the presence of "Ha-Shem," a lord whose name (Ha-Shem means the Name) and whose rules conveyed only the necessity to acknowledge him. Later, as the Jews were placed into concentration camps, during World War II, they faced the same exigency: the acknowledgment of the force that enclosed them in the space that was created to be apart from that of normal life, the camp. There they had numbers burned into their arms and learned that bare life meant life without meaning or purpose, life of subordination to the sovereign power of their masters.

16. Cf. Amnesty International on Bemba's atrocities visited on the Pygmies during the Congo wars (http://www.amnesty.org.au/svaw/comments/20168/). *Slate* reported on it as well (http://www.slate.com/id/2097314/entry/2097322).

17. Tutsi forces under Paul Kagame designated themselves *inyenzi* (cockroaches) indicating that they swarmed forward with an unstoppable force.

4. Globalization's Dumping Ground

1. Although the high numbers of deaths and ugly punishments such as cutting off the hands of Africans who failed to meet their quotas were shocking enough, they were not unique. The story of the region as well as of Leopold's Congo is narrated in popular terms in Adam Hochschild's *King Leopold's Ghost*.

2. Cf. report of 2002 titled: "Making a Killing: The Diamond Trade in Government-Controlled DRC"

> Amnesty International: 'What do you do when someone is shot dead in your diamond concessions?'
> Diamond company official: '*Nothing*.' (1)
> 1. Introduction
> Every day blood is being spilled in the diamond fields of the Democratic Republic of Congo (DRC), and nobody in the international community is even talking about it. In the capital Kinshasa, the government is able to announce, unchallenged, its commitment to an international system aimed at breaking the links between the diamond trade and human rights violations,

(2) while in Mbuji-Mayi, the hub of the country's diamond industry, serious abuses directly connected to the diamond trade are occurring on a daily basis, largely unchecked.

Dozens of people are being shot dead every year in the diamond fields of Mbuji-Mayi. Still more are being shot and wounded, often seriously. Dozens, including many children, are being held without charge in appalling conditions by security forces who have no formal authority to detain them.

Most of the victims are suspected to be responsible for illegal mining in the diamond concessions. The shootings occur mainly within the concessions, where most of the victims have no legal right to be. But none of this diminishes their entitlement to their basic rights, which include the right to life, the right not to be subjected to cruel, inhuman and degrading treatment or punishment and the right to a fair trial.

In some cases, the victims may themselves be armed, or be with an armed escort, and therefore pose a genuine threat to the safety of those guarding the concessions. But in the majority of cases these suspected illegal miners are not armed and the use of firearms against them cannot be justified. Shooting them dead, in such circumstances, amounts to extrajudicially executing them.
(http://www.amnestyusa.org/document.php?id= 46C1966AA44FF65A80256C4F0025CEA4&lang=e)

3. In a recent report on the website Petroleum News, we have this appreciation of Trafigura:

Trafigura is a Dutch company accused a few years ago of dumping some 500 tons of toxic material off the shores of Ivory Coast, with reported loss of ten lives and thousands of intoxicated victims. In January of this year Trafigura was one of the strongest three candidates for "Most Irresponsible Corporation" out of a group of 400 companies identified by a civic organization called "Public Eye on Davos" that shadows the World Economic Forum at Davos. The company has also been named in connection with the Iraqi Oil for Food scandal that rocked the United Nations. Up to 2004 Wilmer Ruperti, a prominent contractor for Petroleos de Venezuela, who has been investigated in Venezuela and the U.S. for his business deals, represented the company in Venezuela. We do not know if Mr. Ruperti is associated with Trafigura for the purposes of this Ecuadorian venture. Trafigura was created by two associates of the notorious international, financial buccaneer Marc Rich. The associates, Claude Dauphin and Eric de Turkheim, are the owners of Trafigura. It is important to mention that two of the four accepted bids for the Ecuadorian contract were presented by companies (Trafigura and Glencore) that still are associated or have been associated in the past with Marc Rich.

According to the reports from Ecuador Trafigura bid $79 per ton of gas. This was the low bid, as Glencore bid $85,76 per ton, Anglo Energy bid $89,9 per ton and FLOPEC $91,10 per ton. The first thing that seems noteworthy is that Trafigura has been charging the Ecuadorian government $116 per ton for this service, $27 more than the amount of their current bid. This strongly suggests that either Trafigura has been overcharging Ecuador or that they are underbidding now, in an effort to win the contract. In countries with a high level of corruption it is frequent to see winning bids that are far too low but, once the contract is awarded, costs are allowed to escalate by the company receiving the services. (http://www.petroleumworld.com/Ed07080301.htm)

5. Agency and the Mosquito

1. In the connection between feces and money in "From the History of an Infantile Neurosis" (1955), Freud emphasizes that an interest in money is libidinal rather than rational in character, and that it thus relates back to excremental pleasure. The various terms in the sequence *filth = money = gift = child = penis* are thus treated as synonyms.

2. "I shall speak about women's writing: and *what it will do*. Woman must write her self: must write about women and bring women to writing, from which they have been driven away as violently as from their bodies—for the same reasons, by the same law, with the same fatal goal. Woman must put herself into the text—as into the world and into history—by her own movement" (Cixous 245). "Write! and your self-seeking text will know itself better than flesh and blood, rising, insurrectionary dough kneading itself, with sonorous, perfumed ingredients, a lively combination of flying colors, leaves, and rivers plunging into the sea we feed" (Cixous 260).

3. Spectators occupy a split site of viewing, a site that is not clearly or comfortably identified through the certitudes of the film, but that is constituted "asymmetrically"—that is, in a location that is unseated, jostled off-center, *by the gaze of the film back onto us*. This is how Žižek describes this effect: "I can never see the picture at the point from which it is gazing at me, i.e.: the eye and the gaze are constitutively asymmetrical" (1998: 125).

4. The scene brings to mind Soyinka's *Death and the King's Horseman*: when Elesin enters into the market, he is surrounded by his women, the market women who rule this unruly space where even the authority of the ruler cannot keep the Iyaloje's tongue from chastising Elesin for failing in his duty to commit ritual suicide and for chasing skirts.

6. Trashy Women

1. The proper term would be "Roma" in English, "Rom" in French.

2. Cf. Elizabeth Harney's account of the factory setup by Senghor in *In Senghor's Shadow: Art, Politics, and the Avant-Garde in Senegal, 1960–1995*. At Senghor's orders, it was established in Thies in 1965 under Papa Ibra Tall and produced impressive tapestries that evoked Negritude themes. The tapestries are occasionally exhibited still, though the factory was closed when I visited it in 2006.

3. Most notably the *Village des Arts*, which was founded in 1977 after some artists broke with the state École. Diouf closed the Village in 1983 after a series of unpleasant maneuverings with the artists. The more radical *Laboratoire Agit Art,* led by Issa Samb, Babacar Traore, and Youssouf John, brought demonstrations and street art to the scene. Multimedia creations reflected a sensibility that moved toward late modernism, again eschewing state patronage.

4. Her dancing entailed, and encouraged, the *ventilateur,* an erotic dance involving bending over and rotating her buttocks. The women perform it erotically in prison; Karmen's version is more muted, but still evocative. The dance has since been declared illegal in public performances in Senegal.

5. In a letter of December 22, 1897, Sigmund Freud wrote to Wilhelm Fleiss, "Birth, miscarriage, and menstruation are all connected with the lavatory via the word Abort (Abortus)" (240). In German, this word does effectively carry these different meanings.

Freud was to further develop these reflections in his "Three Essays on the Theory of Sexuality" (1905d), where he describes the phases of libidinal development from birth onward. The retention of fecal matter initially corresponds with an intention to use it for masturbatory purposes. The whole meaning of the anal zone is thus reflected in the fact that "few neurotics are to be found without their special scatological practices, ceremonies, and so on, which they carefully keep secret" (187).

However, another link, that between fecal matter and money, emerged in listening to the discourse of obsessive patients; this link is expressed in one of the traits of the anal character, avarice. Freud writes in "Dreams in Folklore" (1958 [1911]): "How old this connection between excrement and Gold is can be seen from an observation by Jeremias: gold, according to ancient oriental mythology, is the excrement of hell" (187).

Based on these associations, Freud establishes a symbolic equation that he phrases as follows: "In the products of the unconscious—spontaneous ideas, phantasies, and symptoms—the concepts *faeces* (money, gift), *baby* and *penis* are ill-distinguished from one another and are easily interchangeable" (128). When the child perceives that woman does not have a penis, the latter is conceived as being detachable and is thus analogous to excrement when it is separated from the body. In the same text, Freud underscores the importance of this equivalence in terms of the object: "Defaecation affords the first occasion on which the child must decide between a narcissistic and an object-loving attitude. He either parts obediently with his faeces, 'sacrifices' them to his love, or else retains them for purposes of auto-erotic satisfaction and later as a means of asserting his own will" (130). The love object that must be renounced (the mother of childhood), the lost object, will be identified by the Unconscious with feces, the body's most intimate product, which must necessarily be relinquished; this marks the onset of the dynamics of loss, mourning, and melancholia.

Returning to the connection between feces and money in "From the History of an Infantile Neurosis" (1918b [1914]), Freud emphasizes that an interest in money is libidinal rather than rational in character, and that it thus relates back to excremental pleasure. The various terms in the sequence *filth* = *money* = *gift* = *child* = *penis* are thus treated as synonyms and represented by shared symbols.

In his "New Introductory Lectures on Psychoanalysis" (1933a), Freud completed his views: According to infantile theories of sexuality, the child is born from the intestine as a piece of feces; defecation is the model for the act of being born. "A great part of anal erotism is thus carried over into a cathexis of the penis" (101), he writes (Dominique J. Arnoux, http://www.enotes.com/psychoanalysis-encyclopedia/feces).

6. Ma Penda calls his "Monsieur le coq" when Karmen visits her in bed, and both of them laugh over this. This corresponds to Karmen's feelings for him: affectionate, but light.

7. Boni. "La Mère, le marché"—market of food, of clothes, of those comings and goings that draw people together for needs that begin with the sediment of life, but go on to its adornment: the essentials of city life in Djomo-La-Lutte: "Au marché de Djomo-La-Lutte, la surprise n'a pas cours et le reproche ne se vend guère. Des denrées alimentaires de première nécessité. Des feuilles, des écorces d'arbres, des pagnes par rangées, par brassées, des chaussures de forêt ou de savane. De quoi nourrir, habiller, chausser, parer, soigner l'âme et le corps de la tête jusqu'aux pieds . . ." (At the market of Djomo-the-Struggle, surprises don't usually happen and reproaches are hardly to be found. Foodstuffs of the most basic kind. Leaves, bark of trees, cloth by the yard in neat rows, armfuls, shoes for the forest or the savannah. What you need to eat, dress yourself, to wear on your feet, to adorn yourself, to care for the soul and the body from head to toe; 13).

With its own food, its local spices and herbs, its own pagnes, its bazins, its sandals, its stalls and stalls, at times extending in all directions like a world unto itself, the market gives to the city or the town an atmosphere, if not an identity, a space that cannot be assimilated to the European urbanscape. It forms "un autre univers" [another universe], one in which the beauty of the women is noticed, formed, and sold. In the midst of the mud, a diamond: "Toi aussi dans le marché?" [You too here in the market?] Niyous asks his friend, Bakari-Service. "'Je ne sors pas de là, jo!' répond l'ami avec assurrance. Et comme pour lui en mettre plein la vue: '. . . c'est que, j'ai un de ces diamants ici . . . dans le marché-aux-tresses. Viens, viens voir'" (17) ["I don't leave it, jo!" the friend answers with assurrance. And as if to put on a show for him, ". . . it's that, I've got one of these diamonds here . . . in the market for braiding women's hair. Come, come and see."]. Niyous and Bakari-Service then make their way to that "other" universe of the women where the new space is being forced, one that is neither this nor that, but the meeting place, the rendezvous of all the women's cultures: "Bakari-Service et Niyous se dirigent vers *un autre univers* où l'on rencontre les mêmes transactions, la même soif de consommation. Mais où les traditions et les cultures se côtoient ou se mélangent. Ils aperçoivent les hangars du marché-aux-tresses qui ne sont pas encore les salons de coiffeur super équipés de Bellevue. Qui ne sont plus la natte ancestrale de grand-mère" [Bakari-Service and Niyous make their way toward *another universe* where one finds the same transactions, the same thirst for consumption. But where traditions and cultures find themselves side by side or mixed together. They perceive the sheds of the market for braiding women's hair which weren't yet the super-equipped hairdressing salons of Bellevue. And which are not grandmother's ancestral braiding either.] (Boni 17; my emphasis).

8. "The danger which is risked by boundary transgression is power. Those vulnerable margins and those attacking forces which threaten to destroy good order represent the powers inhering in the cosmos" (Douglas 2002: 199).

9. In fact, the singing of a Mourid dirge in this scene occasioned the reprobation of Mourid authorities who ordered their talibes to threaten to burn down the theater where *Karmen Geï* was scheduled to be shown. The showing was withdrawn, and the film was never shown in Senegal (personal communication from Ramaka).

7. Trashy Women, Fallen Men

1. See also *Dissensus*: "For Rancière, genuine political and artistic activities always involve forms of innovation that tear bodies from their assigned places and free speech and expression from all reduction to functionality. They are forms of creation that are irreducible to the spatio-temporal horizons of a given factual community. In other words, the disruption that they effect is not simply a reordering of the relations of power between existing groups: dissensus is not an institutional overturning. It is an activity that cuts across forms of cultural and identity belonging and hierarchies between discourses and genres, working to introduce new subjects and heterogeneous objects into the field of perception" (2010a: 1–2).

2. Cf. Peter Brooks's famous definition of the "moral occult": "is not a metaphysical system, it is rather the repository of the fragmentary and desacralized remnants of sacred myth. It bears comparison to unconscious mind, for it is a sphere of being where our most basic desires and inner dictions lie, a realm which in quotidian existence may

appear closed off from us, but which we must accede to since it is the realm of meaning and value. The melodramatic mode in large measure exists to locate and to articulate the moral occult" (1995: 5).

3. Rancière, 2009c: 22; "naked images," whose indubitable, innate claims cannot be subject to conflicting interpretation, or even to interpretation itself. His examples are drawn from famous concentration camp photos. We might take the now familiar image of the hooded prisoner being tortured at Abu Ghraib, or earlier photographic shots of Ethiopian children starving during the drought. Yet Rancière also claims that the image is "never a simple reality" but rather is constituted as an operation that establishes a relationship between what is said and what is seen (6). What is to be said in front of the image of the tortured man at Abu Ghraib is also being said for us. The word hasn't disappeared, but in a sense has submerged the image by its force. Rancière would assert that the mimetic function has been transformed into something more direct, what he calls "the imprint of the thing, the naked identity of its alterity in place of its imitation," or, more importantly, "the wordless, senseless materiality of the visible instead of the figures of discourse" (2009c: 9).

4. Here is Gabriel Rockhill's gloss of these two regimes, in Rancière's *The Politics of Aesthetics*: "The aesthetic regime abolishes the hierarchical **distribution of the sensible** characteristic of the **representative regime of art**, including the privilege of speech over visibility as well as the hierarchy of the arts, their subject matter, and their genres. By promoting the **equality** of represented subjects, the indifference of style with respect to content, and the immanence of meaning in things themselves, the aesthetic regime destroys the system of genres and isolates 'art' in the singular, which it identifies with the paradoxical unity of opposites: *logos* and pathos" (2009b: 81). In contrast to the aesthetic regime, the representative regime is not simply a regime of resemblance or mimesis, but rather is one that adheres to the following axioms: "the hierarchy of genres and subject matter, the principle of appropriateness that adapts forms of expression and action to the subjects represented and to the proper genre, the ideal of speech as act that privileges language over the visible imagery that supplements it" (91). The representative regime is appropriate to a society dominated by notions of high culture whose principle of hierarchy reflects the social order; the aesthetic regime democratizes, in the sense of rendering equal, that order. An example of the latter for Rancière would be Flaubert, who was indifferent to aesthetic hierarchy as to social privilege. I see the representative regime as corresponding to the dominant form of "serious" African cinema in its first decades under the impress of Senegalese, Malian, and Burkinabe filmmakers. The aesthetic regime more closely corresponds to the melodramatic and Nollywood forms.

5. For Rancière, notions of policing, politics, dissent, and consent to an established order are all organized around a concept relatively close to hegemony: that is, in Gramscian terms, manufactured consent to a perspective on the universe where the shared perceptions provide common understandings that reinscribe dominant social values. Dissensus, then, shakes up that order, what Rancière calls the sensible order, "by confronting the established framework of perception, thought and action with the 'inadmissable'" (2009b: 85). The function of the police is to provide and maintain the borders that determine the categories of the sensible order as fixed and determined, those presuppositions to which "consensus" is normally given. The challenge to this "natural" order is the proper sphere of politics, that is, "acts of **subjectivization** that separate society from

itself by challenging the 'natural order of bodies' in the name of **equality** and polemically reconfiguring the **distribution of the sensible**. Politics is an anarchical process of **emancipation** that opposes the logic of **disagreement** to the logic of the **police**" (90).

8. Opening the Distribution of the Sensible

1. Cf. Gwendolyn Brooks, "The Lovers of the Poor," skewers the position of the bourgeois givers of charity:

> Their guild is giving money to the poor.
> The worthy poor. The very very worthy
> And beautiful poor. Perhaps just not too swarthy?
> perhaps just not too dirty nor too dim
> Nor—passionate.

The full version is available online at http://www.poets.org/viewmedia.php/prmMID /15871.

2. When interviewed, she is introduced by her husband's name; when she presents herself, she uses her own name.

3. Sembène's famous term, meaning a film constructed of bits and pieces of shots, as a cigarette is pieced together by the remainders of tobacco in discarded butts (*mégots*).

9. Abderrahmane Sissako's *Bamako* (2006) and the Image

1. El Anatsui's use of found objects, recycling trash, fits directly into one of the themes of this study. His own comment highlights this turn to an art whose vitality is not subject to the former constraints of representational art: "Art grows out of each particular situation, and I believe that artists are better off working with whatever their environment throws up" (http://africa.si.edu/exhibits/gawu/index.html; accessed July 6, 2011).

2. Rancière: "This subordination of the 'image' to the 'text' in thinking about poems also founded the correspondence to the arts, under its legislation. If we take it as given that this hierarchical order has been abolished, that the power of words and the power of the visible has been freed from this common measurement system for two centuries, the question arises: how should we conceive the effect of this uncoupling?" (2009b: 39).

3. 2009c: 23. Whereas Duchamps might have presented his famous "Fountain" (urinal) in 1917 so as to evoke this sense of presence per se, it would have been more difficult, if not impossible, to attempt to accomplish this with Holocaust images in 1945, or in present-day Israel, as the "obtuseness" of the image cannot occlude all discourses under all circumstances.

4. As has been the case with other African contemporary filmmakers of note like Bekolo, Haroun, Mambéty, and Nacro (especially in their short films), and Teno's recent work, *Lieux sacrés* (2009). Diawara points out many more "new wave" filmmakers similarly moving into new arenas (Diawara 2010).

5. During the campaigns of 2005–2006, Wade's name was sprayed, attesting to his accomplishments, on walls surrounding new buildings of hotels along the corniche whose beaches Wade had sold out to Kuwaiti and other investors, a devastating betrayal of the patrimony of the beaches Senghor had promised to the people of Senegal for their posterity.

6. At this point I am going to turn increasingly to the term "sentence" instead of relying solely of Rancière's term "text" to convey that use of the word that implies a meaning, or imposes a meaning, on a film or novel. Sentence-image, for him, is the site of a contemporary struggle under what he terms the aesthetic regime. But our concern is less with this westernized regime than that bound up in the problematic of representation, what he calls the representative regime. Indeed, the courtroom trial scenes are clearly part of the latter regime, while the scenes outside the courtroom fall increasingly into the former.

7. I am grateful to Sarah Hamlin for her observation about Sissako's use of this technique, whereby the camera remains still, like an old-fashioned still camera, while various figures cross the screen horizontally. He uses this technique notably in *La Vie sur terre* (1999). The effect is to give a static quality to the scene while marking the activity of those passing in and out of the screen. The contrasting techniques of cinema, tracking or panning, carry the eye of the viewer with the figure in motion, as if the viewer were witnessing directly the figure instead of remaining motionless in a fixed location.

8. "The first archivist, the first to discovered the archive, the archeologist and perhaps the archon of the archive. The first archivist institutes the archive as it should be, that is to say, not only in exhibiting the document but in establishing it" (1996: 55).

10. The Counter-Archive for a New Postcolonial Order

1. In a memorable scene in Mohsen Makhmalbaf's *Kandahar* (2001), we witness one-legged men racing to acquire prosthetic limbs that were parachuted into a medical clinic in Afghanistan.

2. Sarah Coffey, at the University of Chicago website on Theories of Media, presents the Derridean notion of the prosthesis thus: "Jacques Derrida also examines writing as a prosthetic device, which he terms 'the supplement.' Yet Derrida approaches the prosthetic supplement, not as Heideggerian amputation, but as a neutral term that "*signifies* nothing, simply replaces a lack" ("Derrida" 921).

> For Derrida, the supplement represents not only the act of writing, but also the precarious relationship between terms like "speech" and "writing," which he argues should not be stacked in a hierarchy, but rather viewed as supplementing one another. Derrida explains his position on the relationship between writing and the body when he asserts "that in what one calls the real life of these existences 'of flesh and bone' . . . there has never been anything but writing; there have never been anything but supplements, substitutive significations which could only come forth in a chain of differential references" (919). Writing determines how we perceive existence, identified by lack as much as by supplementation.
>
> Derrida's student, Bernard Stiegler, built on his teacher's arguments about the supplement, stressing the prosthesis of writing and memory: "What is exceeded is the essential fallibility of a person's memory that, as living, is mortal; the supplement of writing allows that person to confide the trace of his or her intuitions, which become as a result transmissible, to future generations" (Stiegler 245). Within the concept of the supplement, Stiegler compounds living and dead, interior and exterior. His argument returns to the double nature of prosthesis as extension and amputation when he writes, "the supplement, marking the default of origin, does nothing but try and fill this default in;

and yet, in doing so, it can only affirm it as necessary . . ." (260). Like Derrida, Stiegler does not use the supplement as a device for separating the artificial and the real, but rather as a concept that is inseparable from existence, and in which many seeming oppositions collapse together. Stiegler 2001: 238–70.

Accessed April 26, 2011. http://csmt.uchicago.edu/glossary2004/prosthetics.htm (Jacques Derrida from *Of Grammatology.* 1967. *Art in Theory: 1900–1990,* ed. Charles Harrison and Paul Wood [Oxford: Blackwell, 1996], 918–23).

3. For cinema verité, the truth lies in not concealing the act of filming and consequently in the unrehearsed nature of the reality to be revealed. It conceives of its honesty as lying in the refusal to direct the actors before the camera, but to engage them as participants in the act of creating the film. Neorealism is completely given to staging, using the full apparatus of the cinema, but in the service of representing the fundamental truth of the situation—such situations being typically those involving social struggle, class conflict, economic and political issues.

4. A doubling of the audience, of the witnessing, whose effect is reproduced in *Bamako* with the audience that witnesses the testimonies at the trial.

5. Cf. Peter Brooks on melodrama and its moral basis in what he calls the "moral occult" (*The Melodramatic Imagination* [1995]).

6. In further elaboration, Žižek identifies the McGuffin with *l'objet a,* "a gap in the centre of the symbolic order—the lack, the void in the Real setting in motion the symbolic movement of interpretation" (8). Žižek identifies the "classic ideology of the 'autonomous' subject strengthened through ordeal" (1992: 5) with this first phase, wherein the possibilities of taking action within an economy of the autonomous subject corresponds with liberal capitalism, and the absent object that accounts for the economy of desire would be *l'objet a.* Relations of power inevitably drive the autonomous subject into situations and ordeals that appear insurmountable.

7. The objects/subjects/socioeconomic system clusters here are marked by the figure of "pathological narcissism" associated with late capitalism or globalization—a figure who appears in mocked dress when located on the terrain of the postcolony where globalization corresponds with the inevitable disappearance of the paternal superego. In *Looking Awry* (1991), Žižek describes the disorder in the family generated under these circumstances: "The father is absent, the paternal function (the function of the pacifying law, the Name-of-the-Father) is suspended and that vacuum is filled by the 'irrational' maternal superego, arbitrary, wicked, blocking 'normal' sexual relationship (only possible under the sign of the paternal metaphor)" (1999: 99). For the figure of the monstrous in African cinema, we would not turn to the failed despots, the Popauls of the second group of objects, but to those multitudinous shocking figures of disruption and fearfulness that embody the spiritual realm of evil forces, the favored haunt of contemporary video filmmakers in Nigeria. Demonic figures, insurmountable forces motivated by desires associated with greed and lustfulness—all are markings of the absence of the paternal superego.

8. According to Lacan, speech develops by the substitution of the signifier for the prohibited object of desire; the chain of terms that constitute the acts of signification is built on this initial act of repression and internalization.

9. This resembles that phase of post–World War II neorealism dubbed "Rose," as in De Sica's *Miracle in Milan* (1950).

10. With an array of blogs like http://www.nairaland.com/nigeria/topic-37322.0.html #msg839008, we now have threads like "Genevieve Nnaji Is Still The Hottest Sex Symbol In Nollywood"—her list of films now exceeds sixty.

11. This will be the theme of chapter 11 in which Butler bases subjectivity on subjugation.

12. Sigmund Freud's "Mourning and Melancholia," 14: 239–60; Freud (1923); Melanie Klein; Cathy Caruth; Dominick LaCapra.

13. Sundiata's actions, if not precisely revenge, still fit under the model of deferred actions, and here deferred obedience.

14. In *Archive Fever,* Derrida presents Yerushalmi as in conversation with the ghost of Freud, thus evoking the father figure whose commandment has passed. He further presents Freud as having displaced Moses, just as Moses himself had been displaced by the sons who had risen up and killed him (in *Moses and Monotheism*).

15. Derrida 1998: 61. We almost expect de Niro's words in *Taxi Driver* (1976) to come out of Atim's mouth when he points the gun in the mirror: "You talkin' to me?" This is a cinematic ghost.

16. It is both the basis for an archive and the contents of an archive, and the contents dictate the form of the substrate.

17. Derrida associates this violence of repetition with the obsessiveness of the death instinct, taking this point from Freud's work on the death instinct. In Derridean terms, each act of repetition, of re-marking a text, alters and denies the original as a new context provides new meanings with each iteration.

18. A covenant repeated on Yom Kippur with the injunction to remember to forget Amalek, Amalek being remembered as the evil enemy who attacked the Israelites from the rear in the wilderness.

19. Ironically, with my rereading of these words in July 2011, Senegal's Wade has agreed to ship Habré back to Chad for trial under Déby! He reneged a week later when the "international" community objected.

11. Nollywood and Its Masks

1. http://www.heraldsun.com.au/news/special-reports/leigh-paatsch-film-review -precious/story-e6frf8r6-1225826799700 (accessed February 4, 2010). Similarly, for *Slumdog,* the accumulation of material detritus that Danny Boyle presents as the "lived experiences" in the slums of Delhi overwhelm this blogger: Well yes these things do happen in India. However the problem is when you show every hellish thing possible all happening to the same person. Then it stretches reason and believability and just looks like you are packing in every negative thing that Westerners perceive about India for the sake of "crowd pleasing." Because audiences and jury members "feel good" when their preconceived notions are confirmed. On the flip side, nothing disquiets a viewer as much as when his/her prejudices are challenged. So Boyle does the safe thing.

Let's say I made a movie about the United States where an African American boy born in the hood, has his mother sell him to a pedophile pop icon, after which he gets molested by a priest from his church, following which he gets tied up to the back of a truck and dragged on the road by KKK clansmen. Then he is arrested and sodomized by a policeman with a rod, after which he is attacked by a gang of illegal immigrants, and then uses these life experiences to win "Beauty and the Geek."

Even though each of these incidents have actually happened in the United States of America, I would be accused of spinning a fantastic yarn that has no grounding in reality, that has no connection to the "American experience" and my motivations would be questioned, no matter how cinematically spectacular I made my movie. At the very least, I wouldn't be on 94% on Tomatometer and a strong Oscar favorite. (http://greatbong.net/2008/12/29/slumdog-millionaire-the-review/)

2. "The movement of classic realist narrative toward closure ensures the reinstatement of order, sometimes a new order, sometimes the old, but always intelligible because familiar. . . . The epilogue common in nineteenth-century novels describes the new order, now understood to be static" (Belsey 1980: 75). Thus the epilogue in *Jane Eyre* reestablishes harmony "through the redistribution of the signifiers into a new system of differences which closes off the threat to subjectivity, and it remains only to make this harmonious and coherent world intelligible to the reader, closing off in the process the sense of danger to the reader's subjectivity" (75–76).

3. An early African example appears in the series of films called *Matamata and Pilipili* (1996), played by Congolese actors before the camera of a Belgium priest, Van Hoerst, whose goals were to produce comic situations that served pedagogical and religious moralist purposes. For instance, one episode shows Matamata, a large, gangling, foolishly smiling figure, deciding to return to school after he sees other men his age reading newspapers, which he cannot read. To return to school, he has to cut off his moustache and shorten his pants to conform to the rules governing children's school uniforms. He begins to learn proper reading and writing, and repeats his lesson, as he walks home, "Je suis, je suis, je suis." The foolish figure of what Bogle would call the coon lacks only the high-pitched falsetto as a Stepin Fetchit in order to capture the full stereotype—but as the films were silent, he was saved by the subtitles.

4. http://www.youtube.com/watch?v=wfyEIq9QJhU.

5. As was the case in Oyono's *Le Vieux nègre et la médaille* (1956). Oyono's villageois manages to turn the tables on those who thought they had permission to laugh at him, and who thus find themselves caught in the trap set for them when they joined in the laughter in the novel's opening farcical scenes.

6. For Adorno, popular culture on film and radio had little to do with art. They were a business whose ideology was "to legitimize the trash they intentionally produce" (Horkheimer and Adorno 2002: 95). This business was based on what Adorno referred to as "Fordist capitalism," with mass production techniques used in the cultural sphere.

7. Both Okome and Haynes stress that Nollywood is essentially an urban film phenomenon. I see its urbanism defined in relation to a village identity that sets off that of the city. On its urban nature, Okome stated in 1997, "These video dramas now form one of the most significant ways in which the city discusses itself, its superficial modernity and its strange attachment to traditional life. In many ways, these dramas construct the city in its own image . . . they provide a new and refreshing way to look at this city. This is a medium of the city, created and nurtured in the city for its own benefit" (75).

8. Haynes qualifies this dichotomy by indicating that "magical" forces associated with "traditional" Africa are located in the city as well as the country. However, this notion of magic and traditionalism is framed by contemporary understandings—invented, in the same way that Ranger means invented when he proposed colonial discourse as the location for the construction of notions of modern and traditional.

Haynes indicates that both Yoruba and Igbo films are set predominantly in the city, and uses a discourse based on "modern" and "traditional" for his analysis. Thus, "Personality and identity are presented as complex and layered [in *Living in Bondage*] and it is the more modern and individualized part that falls prey to the devouring city. One might be tempted to say that it is a traditional moral scheme and narrative imagination that figures the dramas of city life as one of ritual murder—except that the urban vampire story is one propagated in the cities, by city dwellers, to make sense of their own condition." He concludes, "We are then not really dealing with a polarized opposition where modernity and the urban scene are on one side, and tradition, magic, and the rural village are on the other" (80–81).

I would argue that the imaginary that gives us urban and village nonetheless constructs them as different, and that when the naïve and gullible or foolish figure is required, as in the early scenes of *Jenifa*, it is the "villager" who serves that role. The same is true of *Osuofia*.

9. "Many of the films have traditional village settings . . . but most are set in Nigeria's cities, above all in Lagos" (2). "If one had to choose a single image to express the culture of the videos, it would undoubtedly be a Mercedes Benz" (2). None of this means that "modern" Lagos is not also the site for magical forces, or "traditional" magic. It means the imaginary of the city is set off by the imaginary of the village. In addition, "Production and marketing for all of southern Nigeria is centralized in Lagos" (Haynes 70).

10. In the 1946 film *Song of the South*, Hollywood produced the ultimate Uncle Tom character in the "loveable" Uncle Remus. Now Disney refuses to permit distribution of that film in video form (Cripps). Eleven years after *Song of the South*, Harry Belafonte played the love interest against Joan Fontaine in *Island in the Sun* (1957), but the Production Code Administration censorship demanded cuts that eliminated all but the most anodyne scenes between the mixed lovers. Even in the hot Carmen atmosphere of the 1954 *Carmen Jones*, sexual passion turns quickly to the "buck's" violent jealousy and murder of Carmen, while the love scenes are played out tamely. Poitier and Belafonte set the limits of what the black male star could achieve in the 1950s and early 1960s, and the most to be expected was humanist idealism of major roles in *Guess Who's Coming to Dinner* (1967) or *The Defiant Ones* (1958). The change to sexually empowered males would have to wait until 1971 for blaxploitation features like *Shaft* and *Sweet Sweetback's Baadasssss Song*.

11. Cf. Mark Reid's denominations of contemporary African American films in *Redefining Black Film* (1993). Hybrid minstrel shows entail black actors playing blackface roles, like the humorous minstrelsy figures, while satiric hybrid minstrel shows entail black actors mocking the stereotypes of such shows as they play at them. Examples of the latter would be Eddie Murphy, whereas the prime example of the former would be *Cotton Comes to Harlem* (1970). Hybrid minstrel shows are oppositional in that black actors and directors now are taking central roles, but playing the scenes for laughter avoids any reference to realistic issues facing the black community. The overtly political satire of Godfrey Cambridge and Dick Gregory evokes the stronger discourse of oppositionality marked by the radicalization of the black protest movement during the 1970s and marks the third form of minstrelsy, satiric (28).

12. This distinguishes it from Jameson's requirement that the postmodernist text be marked by a pastiche that eschews parody. For Jameson, pastiche is flat, lacking a hu-

morous target because of postmodernist distancing from the ethical or moral imperatives of committed literature—maintaining a distance from the humanist tradition (1991: chapter 1).

13. Reid 1993: 28. Nollywood generally eschews the serious dramatization of social issues, unlike most of what had been the practice of African cinema. The occasional ventures to do so, after much carping at the triviality of Nollywood's entertainment values, have quickly disappeared, or morphed into evangelical imaginary representations of sorcery and divinity. Cf. Birgit Meyer's work on evangelical influences in Ghanaian film and Socrate Safo's one film dealing with AIDS, quickly followed by more conventional social comedies and action films like *Amsterdam Diary* (2005). See Birgit Meyer and Annelies Moors, *Religion, Media, and the Public Sphere* (2006).

14. Just as Dieng's real challenge in *Mandabi* (1968) entailed more than cashing in his money order.

15. We are singing for the sake of Eshu
     He used his penis to make a bridge
     Penis broke in two
     Travellers fell into the river.
     (Pelton 45)

16. Correspondingly: "A feminine gender is formed (taken on, assumed) through the incorporative fantasy by which the feminine is excluded as a possible object of love, an exclusion never grieved, but 'preserved' through heightened feminine identification" (1997: 146).

17. What Brooks defines as melodrama's "moral occult" is the following: it "is not a metaphysical system, it is rather the repository of the fragmentary and desacralized remnants of sacred myth. It bears comparison to unconscious mind, for it is a sphere of being where our most basic desires and inner dictions lie, a realm which in quotidian existence may appear closed off from us, but which we must accede to since it is the realm of meaning and value. The melodramatic mode in large measure exists to locate and to articulate the moral occult" (18).

12. Trash's Last Leaves

1. See Harrow, *Postcolonial African Cinema*, chapter 5, "Toward a Žižekian Reading of African Cinema."

2. A key example might be the reels of film in *Aristotle's Plot*. In this stage, it is less the autonomous subject functioning in a liberal capitalist economy than the "heteronomous" subject functioning within a system of imperialistic state capitalism.

3. Lacan identifies this diminished presence with the algorithm S(A), i.e., "Sujet de l'Autre barré" (subject of the barred Other; 1968), which Žižek glosses as "the insignia, the index of the father's impotence: a fragment of reality which functions as the signifier of the fact that the 'big Other' is barred, that the father is not able to live up to his Name, to his symbolic Mandate" (1992: 8).

4. One of the most beautiful of which is the late Henri Duparc's *Caramel* (2004), another "popular" film, though equally auteurist under the able direction of Duparc, about which I wrote the following description for the Duparc website after his demise:

Caramel. Elle est de teint clair, comme la beauté qui surgit des eaux. Nous ne savons pas d'où elle est venue, mais un jour elle était là, attendant de voir "Mangala, Fille des Indes," le film que son père aimait. Ce film merveilleux intègre divers moments de tous les films antérieurs de Duparc, y compris des posters et des clips, car le héros, Freddie, est le propriétaire—gérant d'une salle de cinéma. Une salle sur le point de fermer définitivement. C'est là qu'il rencontre Caramel, nom qui lui vient du goût de caramel que son visage évoquait pour son père. Ils tombent amoureux l'un de l'autre; la soeur de Freddie fait tout son possible pour subvertir leur amour, mais elle n'est plus que l'obstacle qui le rend encore plus savoureux. Elle est grosse, comique, pas séduisante. Caramel est svelte et belle, avec un doux et beau sourire et l'allure avec, . . . irrésistible.

Ah, c'est comme cela que les choses se passent avec Mammy Watta. Et quand survient l'inévitable, et qu'elle ferme les yeux de Freddie avec ses mains, elle, la Mammy Watta depuis longtemps partie vers le seul pays où l'amour vrai existe, nous voyons le mythe du rêve urbain prendre forme vivante sous nos yeux. Chez Duparc, la romance a toujours été présente, mais la formule tout à fait juste l'éludait jusqu'à ce qu'il trouve sa Mammy Watta. Elle apporte aux sentiments une notion africaine de transgression et de transcendance, deux des caractéristiques essentielles qui permettent à l'imaginaire débridé, au fantastique d'atteindre son point culminant. L'imaginaire de la fantaisie et le désir: ils résument tout ce que les "pères" du cinéma africain voulaient éliminer.

(http://www.henriduparc.com/?f=hommage&int=4)

5. The spiritual realm of evil forces, the favored haunt of contemporary video film-makers in Nigeria and Ghana, is inhabited with demonic figures, insurmountable forces motivated by desires associated with greed and lustfulness—all the markings of the absence of the paternal superego—are here translated into an African imaginary of what Denise Paulme (1986) called "la mère dévorante," and that we can take as a response to the conditions associated with the pandemics now facing much of Africa: AIDS, "la crise," "la conjunction," and the nightmare scenarios of brutal war, violence, and violation.

6. An interview with Anuku (variously named Hank or Hanks) reads like Nollywood fan mag dialogue: "In Moviedom I Am a Chameleon—Hank Anuku, June 19, 2007":

Hank Anuku, Nollywood actor, is not only associated with the role of the bad guy in the movie industry, he is an actor that abandons his jeeps to ride on heavy racing motor bikes on the streets of Lagos. Hank was living in the United States of America before returning to Nigeria. Although his accent is American, he is deeply rooted in the African culture and cherishes his people. He bares his mind on several issues including his relationships with women. Excerpts:

WHEN did you begin your acting career and how did you enter the entertainment industry?

I always told people that I started from heaven because that was where my father and Creator is. This dates back to many years ago. I don't know the exact date.

Did you begin your acting here in Nigeria or overseas?

I have done some stuff overseas before I came here. When I came home on vacation years ago, I met Regina Askia and she asked me to do some work with her. Earlier, I did an Igbo freak called The Skeleton with Mr. Fidelis Duka. (http://nigeriamovies.net/news/news118.php; accessed June 19, 2011)

7. Nike Men's Air Force Formidable II: "This Finish Line Exclusive is a lightweight, comfortable and durable basketball shoe made for the indoor courts but is tough enough for the outdoor courts. The large-volume, visible Air-Sole unit in the heel provides maximum protection" (http://reviews.finishline.com/9345/Nike_Men_char39_s_Air_Force _Formidable_II/nike-mens-air-force-formidable-ii-reviews/reviews.htm?sort=rating& dir=asc).

8. Chief Collins: "We will divert the arms in every state in this country and that will make the government most unpopular. As soon as we are able to cause confusion and chaos throughout the country, we will strike, and the people will shout, Hallelujah, the Messiah has come to save us. Don't you know we make much more money during military regimes?"

9. Another structural element that evokes Lacan's description of the glances in "The Purloined Letter" where the exchanges of glances, between the queen, the minister, the police commissioner, and Dupin are made possible by the signifier—the letter—whose meaning for each is different, and whose positions are all constructed by that signifier.

10. Ce serait trop leur demander sans doute, non en raison de leur manque de vues, mais bien plutôt du nôtre. Car leur imbécillité n'est pas d'espèce individuelle, ni corporative, elle est de source subjective. C'est l'imbécillité réaliste qui ne s'arrête(29) pas à se dire que rien, si loin qu'une main vienne à l'enfoncer dans les entrailles du monde, n'y sera jamais caché, puisqu'une autre main peut l'y rejoindre, et que ce qui est caché n'est jamais que *ce qui manque à sa place*, comme s'exprime la fiche de recherche d'un volume quand il est égaré dans la bibliothèque. Et celui-ci serait-il en effet sur le rayon ou sur la case d'à côté qu'il y serait caché, si visible qu'il y paraisse. C'est qu'on ne peut dire *à la lettre* que ceci manque à sa place que de ce qui peut en changer, c'est-à-dire du symbolique. Car pour le réel, quelque bouleversement qu'on puisse y apporter, il y est toujours et en tout cas, il l'emporte collée à sa semelle, sans rien connaître qui puisse l'en exiler.

11. I am grateful to Safoi Babana-Hampton for this translation, which she glosses thus: "It seems to me that the English translation on that web site conveys the exact opposite meaning of the French original (at least the first portion of it). I believe it should read: 'For one cannot literally claim that something is missing from its place except for what could change of it, that is to say, the symbolic.'

"If I'm right, Lacan is claiming that the space left by a hidden/missing object never coincides fully with just the physical object itself, but something more, which he designates as 'the symbolic' (perhaps in reference to the signifying value the object carries in a larger signifying network or chain of signifiers, in the same way a book that is lost in the library points not only to the book itself, but to its position/relation to other books in the library catalog. For even though the book is missing, its presence is implied by its position in the larger catalog system). That's my humble attempt to decipher the inscrutable Lacan" (personal communication, June 30, 2011).

12. He concludes this paragraph with, "A different seal on a stamp of another color, the mark of a different handwriting in the superscription are here the most inviolable modes of concealment. And if they stop at the reverse side of the letter, on which, as is

known, the recipient's address was written in that period, it is because the letter has for them no other side but its reverse."

"Et comment en effet, pour revenir à nos policiers, auraient-ils pu saisir la lettre, ceux qui l'ont prise à la place où elle était cachée? Dans ce qu'ils tournaient entre leurs doigts, que tenaient-ils d'autre que ce qui ne répondait pas au signalement qu'ils en avaient? A letter, a litter, une lettre, une ordure. On a équivoqué dans le cénacle de Joyce sur l'homophonie de ces deux mots en anglais. La sorte de déchet que les policiers à ce moment manipulent, ne leur livre pas plus son autre nature de n'être qu'à demi déchiré. Un sceau différent sur un cachet d'une autre couleur, un autre cachet du graphisme de la suscription sont là les plus infrangibles des cachettes. Et s'ils s'arrêtent au revers de la lettre où, comme on sait, c'est là qu'à l'époque l'adresse du destinataire s'inscrivait, c'est que la lettre n'a pas pour eux d'autre face que ce revers." Pp. 16–17 Le Séminaire sur "La lettre volée" prononcé le 26 avril 1955 au cours du séminaire Le moi dans la théorie de Freud et dans la technique de la psychanalyse fut d'abord publié sous une version réécrite datée de mi-mai, mi-août 1956, dans La psychanalyse n° 2, 1957, pp. 15–44 précédé d'une "Introduction," pp. 1–14. C'est cette version qui est ci-dessous proposée. (1) LE SÉMINAIRE SUR "LA LETTRE VOLÉE" (http://www.bibliotheques-psy.com/spip.php?article1007).

13. Or Genevieve Nnaji and Hank Anuku . . . both have their names spelled differently on different credits and their websites.

14. That the spectators of Nollywood film, or should we say, its consumers, appreciate its qualities while it is considered as nothing but low trash by the aficionados of celluloid cinema might be likened to the varying appreciation of the same message in "The Purloined Letter," as Lacan states, "This example demonstrates indeed how an act of communication may give the impression at which theorists too often stop: of allowing in its transmission but a single meaning, as though the highly significant commentary into which he who understands integrates it, could, because unperceived by him who does not understand, be considered null."

Bibliography

Abani, Christopher. *Graceland*. New York: Farrar, Straus, and Giroux, 2004.
——. *Song for Night: A Novella*. New York: Akashic Books, 2007.
Achebe, Chinua. *Morning Yet on Creation Day*. London: Heinemann Educational Books, 1975.
——. "The Novelist as Teacher." In *African Writers on African Writing*, ed. G. D. Killam. London: Heinemann, 1973.
Adiche, Chimamanda. *Purple Hibiscus*. Chapel Hill, NC: Algonquin Books of Chapel Hill, 2003.
Agamben, Giorgio. *Homo Sacer: Sovereign Power and the Bare Life*. Stanford, CA: Stanford University Press, 1998.
——. *Means without End: Notes on Politics*. Trans. Vincenzo Binetti and Cesaire Casarino. Minneapolis: University of Minnesota Press, 2001.
Aidoo, Ama Ata. *No Sweetness Here*. 1970; Garden City, NY: Anchor, 1972.
D'Almeida, Irène A. *Francophone African Women Writers: Destroying the Emptiness of Silence*. Gainesville: University Press of Florida, 1994.
Alloula, Malek. *The Colonial Harem*. Trans. Myrna and Wlad Godzich. Minneapolis: University of Minnesota Press, 1986.
Amnesty International. "Angola: Lives in Ruins: Forced Evictions Continue." January 2007. Accessed July 2010. http://www.amnestyusa.org/angola/reports/page.do?id=YCR0854005000E.
——. "Making a Killing: The Diamond Trade in Government-Controlled DRC." Accessed July 10, 2010. http://www.amnestyusa.org/document.php?id=46C1966AA44FF65A80256C4F0025CEA4&lang=e.
Anderson, Warwick. *Colonial Pathologies: American Tropical Medicine, Race, and Hygiene in the Philippines*. Durham: Duke University Press, 2006.
Antelme, Robert, Annie Mahler, and Jeffrey Haight. *The Human Race*. Evanston, IL: Malboro Press, 1992.
Anuku, Hanks. Interview. Accessed June 19, 2011. http://nigeriamovies.net/news/news118.php.
Appiah, Kwame Anthony. "Is the 'Post-' in 'Postcolonial' the 'Post-' in 'Postmodern'?" In *In My Father's House*. New York: Oxford University Press, 1993.
Armah, Ayi Kwei. *The Beautyful Ones Are Not Yet Born*. Oxford: Heinemann, 1968.
Arnoux, Dominique J. "Feces." *International Dictionary on Psychoanalysis*. Accessed August 16, 2010. http://www.enotes.com/psychoanalysis-encyclopedia/feces.
Assman, Aleida. "Beyond the Archive." In *Waste-Site Stories: The Recycling of Memory*, ed. Brian Neville and Johanne Villeneuve. Albany: State University of New York Press, 2002.
Ba, Mariama. *Une Si longue lettre*. Dakar: Les Nouvelles éditions africaines, 1980.
Ba, Thierno. *Lat Dior ou le chemin de l'honneur: drame historique en huit tableaux*. Dakar: Les Nouvelles éditions africaines, 1987.

Barlet, Olivier. *African Cinemas: Decolonizing the Gaze*. London: Zed Books, 2005.

Bataille, Georges. *Visions of Excess: Selected Writings, 1927–1939*. (1970). Trans. Allan Stoekl. Minneapolis: University of Minnesota Press, 1989.

Baudrillard, Jean. *Impossible Exchange*. Trans. Chris Turner. London: Verso, 2001.

———. *Simulations*. Trans. Paul Foss, Paul Patton, Philip Beitchman. NewYork: Semiotexte, 1983.

BBC News. "Trafigura." Accessed July 30, 2010. http://news.bbc.co.uk/2/hi/programmes /newsnight/8417913.stm.

Belsey, Catherine. *Critical Practice*. London: Routledge, 1980.

Benjamin, Walter, Michael W. Jennings, Brigid Doherty, and Thomas Y. Levin. *The Work of Art in the Age of Its Technological Reproducibility, and Other Writings on Media*. Cambridge, MA: Belknap Press of Harvard University Press, 2008.

Bhabha, Homi K. *Location of Culture*. London: Routledge, 2004.

Bogle, Donald. *Toms, Coons, Mulattoes, Mammies, and Bucks: An Interpretive History of Blacks in American Films*. New York: Continuum, 1973/1994.

Boni, Tanella. *Une Vie de Crabe*. Dakar: Les Nouvelles Editions Africaines du Sénégal, 1990.

Bornowsky, Eli. "Notes on the Politics of Aesthetics." Fillip4 Fall 2006. Accessed August 2010. http://fillip.ca/content/notes-on-the-politics-of-aesthetics.

Boughedir, Ferid. "African Cinema and Ideology: Tendencies and Evolution." In *Symbolic Narrative/African Cinema: Audiences, Theory and the Moving Image*, ed. June Givanni. London: British Film Institute, 2008.

———. "Les Grandes tendances du cinéma en Afrique noire." *CinémAction* 26, 1983: 48–57.

Boulter, Jonathan. *Melancholy and the Archive: Trauma, History, and Memory in the Contemporary Novel*. London: Continuum International Publishing Group, 2011.

Brand, Dione. *In the Full and Change of the Moon*. Canada: Alfred Knopf, 1999.

Breton, Andre. *Manifestoes of Surrealism*. Trans. Richard Seaver and Helen R. Lane. Ann Arbor: University of Michigan Press, 1972.

Brooks, Gwendolyn. "The Lovers of the Poor." Accessed January 20, 2011. http://www .poets.org/viewmedia.php/prmMID/15871.

Brooks, Peter. *The Melodramatic Imagination: Balzac, Henry James, Melodrama, and the Mode of Excess*. New Haven: Yale University Press, 1995.

Busia, Abena. "Women and the Dynamics of Representation." In *African Women in Film Forum*. Lagos, Nigeria: June 2010. July 2010.

Butler, Judith. *Gender Trouble*. New York: Routledge, 1990.

———. *The Psychic Life of Power*. Stanford: Stanford University Press, 1997.

California Newsreel. *Karmen Gei*, September 8, 2009 http://newsreel.org/nav/title.asp ?tc=CN0134.

———. *Si-Gueriki*. September 8, 2009. http://www.newsreel.org/nav/title.asp?tc=CN0154.

Caruth, Cathy. *Unclaimed Experience: Trauma, Narrative, and History*. Baltimore: Johns Hopkins University Press, 1996.

Cazenave, Odile M. *Femmes Rebelles: Naissance d'un nouveau roman Africain au féminin*. Paris: L'Harmattan, 1996.

Césaire, Aimé. "Barbare." In *Négritude: Black Poetry from Africa and the Caribbean*, ed. Norman R. Shapiro. London: October House, 1970.

———. *Cahier d'un Retour au Pays Natal*. 1939; Paris: Présence africaine, 1983.

———. *Discours sur le colonialisme.* Paris: Présence africaine, 1955.

Chakrabarty, Dipesh. "Of Garbage, Modernity, and the Citizen's Gaze." In *Habitations of Modernity: Essays in the Wake of Subaltern Studies.* Chicago: University of Chicago Press, 2002.

Chakravarty, Sumita S. "The Erotics of History: Gender and Transgression in the New Asian Cinemas." In *Rethinking Third Cinema,* ed. Anthony Guneratne and Wimal Dissanayake. London: Routledge, 2003.

Cham, Mbye. *Black Frames: Critical Perspectives on Black Independent Cinema.* Boston: MIT Press, 1988.

Chamoiseau, Patrick. *Solibo Magnificent.* Trans. Rose-Myriam Réjouis and Val Vinokurov. New York: Pantheon Books, 1997.

Cixous, Hélène. "The Laugh of the Medusa." In *New French Feminisms,* ed. Elaine Marks and Isabelle de Courtivron. New York: Schocken Books, 1980.

Cixous, Hélène, and Catherine Clément. *The Newly Born Woman.* Minneapolis: University of Minnesota Press, 1986.

Coffey, Sarah. *The Chicago School of Media Theory.* Accessed October 14, 2009. http://lucian.uchicago.edu/blogs/mediatheory/keywords/prosthesis/.

Comaroff, Jean, and John Comaroff, eds. *Law and Disorder in the Postcolony.* Chicago: University of Chicago Press, 2006.

Coronel, Gustavo. "Corruption in PetroEcuador and PDVSA: The Marc Rich Connection." August 15, 2010. http://www.petroleumworld.com/Ed07080301.htm.

Culler, Jonathan. "Rubbish Theory." *Framing the Sign.* Norman: University of Oklahoma Press, 1988: 168–84.

Davies, Nick. "Melilla: Europe's Dirty Secret." *The Guardian.* April 17, 2010. http://www.guardian.co.uk/world/2010/apr/17/melilla-migrants-eu-spain-morocco. Accessed April 25, 2010.

Debord, Guy. *Society of the Spectacle.* London: Rebel Press, 1967.

Deleuze, Gilles. January 25, 2010. http://www.webdeleuze.com/php/texte.php?cle=119&groupe=Anti+Oedipe+et+Mille+Plateaux&langue=2.

Derrida, Jacques. *Archive Fever: A Freudian Impression.* Trans. Eric Prenowitz. Chicago: University of Chicago Press, 1996.

———. *The Truth in Painting.* Trans. G. Bennington and I. McLeod. Chicago: University of Chicago Press, 1987.

Diawara, Manthia. *African Films: New Forms of Aesthetics and Politics.* Munich: Prestel, 2010.

———. *In Search of Africa.* Cambridge: Harvard University Press, 1998.

———. *We Won't Budge: A Malaria Memoir.* New York: Basic Civitas Books, 2003.

Dogbe, Esi. "Elusive Modernity: Portraits of the City in Popular Ghanaian Video." In *Leisure in Urban Africa,* ed. Paul Tiyambe Zeleza and Cassandra Rachel Veney. Trenton, NJ: Africa World Press, 2003.

Douglas, Mary. *Purity and Danger.* (1966). New York: Routedge, 2002.

Espinosa, Julio Garcia. "For an Imperfect Cinema." Trans. Julianne Burton. *Jump Cut* 20 (1979): 24–26, http://www.ejumpcut.org/archive/onlinessays/JC20folder/ImperfectCinema.html. November 14, 2010.

Falola, Toyin, and Matthew M. Heaton. *A History of Nigeria.* New York: Cambridge University Press, 2008.

Fanon, Frantz. *The Wretched of the Earth.* 1961. Trans. Constance Farrington. New York: Grove Press, 1968.

Ferguson, James. *Global Shadows: Africa in the Neoliberal World Order.* Durham, NC: Duke University Press, 2006.

Foster, Gwendolyn Audrey. *Captive Bodies: Postcolonial Subjectivity in Cinema.* Albany: State University of New York Press, 1999.

———. *Women Filmmakers of the African and Asian Diaspora: Decolonizing the Gaze, Locating Subjectivity.* Carbondale: Southern Illinois University Press, 1997.

Freud, Sigmund. *The Ego and the Super-Ego, The Ego and the Id.* 1923; trans. Joan Rivière, ed. James Strachy. New York: Norton, 1960.

———. "From the History of an Infantile Neurosis." *The Standard Edition of the Complete Psychological Works of Sigmund Freud.* London: Hogarth Press, 1955. 17: 7–122.

———. *General Psychological Theory,* ed. Philip Rieff. New York: MacMillan, 1976.

———. "Mourning and Melancholia." In *The Standard Edition of the Complete Psychological Works of Sigmund Freud.* London: Hogarth Press, 1955. 14: 239–60.

Gabriel, Teshome. *Third Cinema in the Third World: The Aesthetics of Liberation.* Ann Arbor, MI: UMI Research Press, 1982.

Gadjigo, Samba. *Ousmane Sembène: The Making of a Militant Artist.* Bloomington: Indiana University Press, 2010.

Garritano, Carmela. "Restaging the Past: The Rewriting of the Tale of the Beautiful Daughter by Abrahams, Tutuola, Ogali, and Aidoo." In *African Images: Recent Studies and Text in Cinema. The Annual Selected Papers of the African Literature Association,* ed. Maureen N. Eke, Kenneth W. Harrow, and Emmanuel Yewah. Trenton, NJ: Africa World Press, 2000.

GHanaweb, Nov 25, 2008. Accessed Nov 26, 2008. USAAFRICADIALOGUE@googlegroups.com.

Givanni, June, ed. *Symbolic Narrative/African Cinema: Audiences, Theory and the Moving Image.* London: British Film Institute, 2000.

Greatbong. "*Slumdog Millionaire*—The Review." December 29, 2008. http://greatbong.net/2008/12/29/slumdog-millionaire-the-review/

Guneratne, Anthony, and Wimal Dissanayake, eds. *Rethinking Third Cinema.* London: Routledge, 2003.

Harney, Elizabeth. *In Senghor's Shadow: Art, Politics, and the Avant-Garde in Senegal, 1960–1995.* Durham: Duke University Press, 2004.

Harrow, Kenneth. "On Duparc's *Caramel.*" http://www.henriduparc.com/?f=hommage&int=4.

———. *Postcolonial African Cinema.* Bloomington: Indiana University Press, 2007.

Haynes, Jonathan, ed. *Nigerian Video Films.* Athens: Ohio University Center for International Studies, 2000.

Head, Bessy. *Collector of Treasures and Other Bostwana Village Tales.* London: Heinemann Educational, 1977.

Hochschild, Adam. *King Leopold's Ghost.* Boston: Houghton, Mifflin, 1998.

Holland, Eugene W. *Deleuze and Guattari's Anti-Oedipus: Introduction to Schizoanalysis.* London and New York: Routledge, 1999.

Horkheimer, M., T. W. Adorno, and G. Schmid Noerr. *Dialectic of Enlightenment: Philosophical Fragments.* Stanford, CA: Stanford University Press, 2002.

Ian, Marcia. *Remembering the Phallic Mother.* Ithaca: Cornell University Press, 1993.

Jacob, Catherine. "Sky Probe: Scandal of Waste Sent to Africa." Sky News. August 15, 2010. http://news.sky.com/home/uk-news/article/15224628.

JALA, Journal of the African Literature Association. February 2010. http://www.africanlit.org/publications.htm.

Jameson, Fredric. Postmodernism, Or, the Cultural Logic of Late Capitalism. Durham: Duke University Press, 1991.

Kane, Cheikh Ahmidou. Ambiguous Adventure. Trans. Katherine Woods. London: Heinemann, 1972.

Kart, Susan. "The Phenomenon of Recuperation at the Dar'Art Biennale." African Arts. Sept 22, 2009.

Kawash, Samira. Dislocating the Color Line: Identity, Hybridity, and Singularity in African-American Narrative. Stanford, CA: Stanford University Press, 2001.

Klein, Melanie. "Mourning and It Relation to Manic-Depressive States." International Journal of Psycho-Analysis 21 (1940): 125–53.

Kristeva, Julia. Powers of Horror: An Essay on Abjection. Trans. Leon S. Roudiez. New York: Columbia University Press, 1982.

Kuti, Fela. "Gentleman." February 2011. http://www.songmeanings.net/songs/view/3530822107858727868/.

———. "Lady." February 2011. http://afrofunkforum.blogspot.com/2009/03/fela-kuti-lyrics.html

———. Music Is the Weapon. Los Angeles: Geffen Records, 2004.

Lacan, Jacques. "Seminar on the Purloined Letter." Le séminaire sur "La Lettre volée." Trans. Jeffrey Mehlman. "French Freud" in Yale French Studies 48 (1972). January 2011. http://www.lacan.com/purloined.htm. French version: http://www.bibliotheques-psy.com/spip.php?article1007.

Lacan, Jacques, and Bruce Fink. Ecrits: A Selection. New York: W. W. Norton, 2002.

LaCapra, Dominick. Writing History, Writing Trauma. Baltimore: Johns Hopkins University Press, 2000.

LaPorte, Dominique. History of Shit. Trans. Nadia Benabid and Rodolphe El-Khoury. Boston: MIT Press, 2002.

Larkin, Brian. Signal and Noise. Durham: Duke University Press, 2008.

Laye, Camara. L'Enfant noir. Paris: Plon, 1953.

Lyotard, Jean François. Enthusiasm: The Kantian Critique of History. Trans. Georges Van Den Abbeele. Stanford, CA: Stanford University Press, 2009.

Mbembe, Achille. "Necropolitics." Public Culture 15, no. 1 (2003): 11–40.

———. "On Politics as a Form of Expenditure." In Law and Disorder in the Postcolony, ed. Jean Comaroff and John Comaroff. Chicago: University of Chicago Press, 2006.

———. On the Postcolony. Berkeley: University of California Press, 2001.

Meyer, Birgit, and Annelies Moors. Religion, Media, and the Public Sphere. Bloomington: Indiana University Press, 2006.

Michaelsen, Scott, and David E. Johnson. Anthropology's Wake: Attending to the End of Culture. New York: Fordham University Press, 2008.

Miller, R. D. A Study of Schiller's "Letters on the Aesthetic Education of Man." Harrogate, North Yorkshire: Duchy Press, 1986.

Minh-Ha, Trinh T. Cinema Interval. New York: Routledge, 1999.

Mitchell, Timothy. Rule of Experts: Egypt, Techo-Politics, Modernity. Berkeley: University of California Press, 2002.

Morgan, David. *Visual Piety: A History and Theory of Popular Religious Images.* Berkeley: University of California Press, 1998.

Morrison, Toni. *The Bluest Eye.* New York: New American Library, Plume, 1970.

——. *Tar Baby.* New York: Signet-New American Library, 1981.

Morton, Stephen, *Gayatri Spivak: Ethics, Subalternety, and the Critique of Post Colonial Reason.* Cambridge: Polity, 2007.

Moser, Walter. "The Acculturation of Waste." In *Waste-Site Stories: The Recycling of Memory*, ed. Brian Neville and Johanne Villeneuve. Albany: State University of New York Press, 2002.

Mudimbe, V. Y. *The Idea of Africa.* Bloomington: Indiana University Press; London: J. Currey, 1994.

——. *The Invention of Africa: Gnosis, Philosophy, and the Order of Knowledge.* Bloomington: Indiana University Press, 1988.

Mulvey, Laura. "Visual Pleasure and Narrative Cinema." *Screen* 16, no. 3 (Autumn 1975): 6–18.

——. "*Xala*, Ousmane Sembene 1976: The Carapace That Failed," *Third Text* 16–17 (Autumn/Winter 1991): 19–37; reprinted in *Colonial Discourse and Post-Colonial Theory*, ed. Patrick Williams and Laura Chrisman. New York: Columbia University Press, 1994: 517–34.

Neville, Brian, and Johanne Villeneuve, eds. *Waste-site Stories: The Recycling of Memory.* Albany: State University of New York, 2002.

Nzegwu, Nkiru, ed. *Issues in Contemporary African Art.* Binghamton, NY: International Society for the Study of Africa, 1998.

Okome, Onookome. "Loud in Lagos: Home Video." *Glendora Review* 2, no. 1 (1997): 75–83.

Okri, Ben. *The Famished Road.* London: Cape, 1991.

——. *Stars of the New Curfew.* London: Secker and Warburg, 1988.

Olaniyan, Tejumola. *Arrest the Music! Fela and His Rebel Art and Politics.* Bloomington: Indiana University Press, 2004.

Oyono, Ferdinand. *Le Vieux nègre et la médaille.* (1956) Paris: Union Générale d'éditions, 1979.

Paatsch, Leigh. Review of *Precious. Herald Sun.* February 4, 2010. http://www.heraldsun.com.au/news/special-reports/leigh-paatsch-film-review-precious/story-e6frf8r6-1225826799700.

Pelton, Robert. *The Trickster in West Africa.* Berkeley: University of California Press, 1980.

Rancière, Jacques. *Aesthetics and Its Discontents.* Trans. Steven Corcoran. Cambridge, Malden, MA: Polity Press, 2009a.

——. *Dis-agreement: Politics and Philosophy.* Trans. Julie Rose. Minneapolis: University of Minnesota Press, 1999.

——. *Dissensus.* Trans. Steven Corcoran. New York: Continuum, 2010a.

——. "L'Entretien avec Jacques Rancière." *Dissonance* 1, April 2010b.

——. *La Fable Cinématographique.* Broché, 2001.

——. *The Future of the Image.* (2007). Trans. Gregory Elliot. New York: Verso, 2009c.

——. *The Politics of Aesthetics.* (2000). Trans. Gabriel Rockhill. New York: Continuum, 2009b.

————. "Who Is the Subject of the Rights of Man?" *South Atlantic Quarterly* 103, no. 23 (2004): 297–310.

Read, Jason. "A Universal History of Contingency." *Borderlands* 2, no. 3 (2003). March 2010. http://www.borderlands.net.au/vol2no3_2003/read_contingency.htm.

Reid, Mark. *Redefining Black Film.* Berkeley: University of California Press, 1993.

Robert, Pelton. *The Trickster in West Africa:* Berkeley: University of California Press, 1980.

Roberts, Allen, and Mary Nooter Roberts. *A Saint in the City: Sufi Arts of Urban Senegal.* Los Angeles: UCLA Fowler Museum of Cultural History, 2003.

Senghor, Léopold Sédar. "New York, New York." In *The Negritude Poets,* ed. Ellen Conroy Kennedy. New York: Thunder's Mouth Press, 1989.

Shakespeare, William. *Hamlet.* Cambridge, U.K.: Cambridge University Press, 2003.

————. *Macbeth.* Basingstoke: Palgrave Macmillan, 2006.

————. *The Tragedy of Anthony and Cleopatra.* Oxford: Clarendon Press; New York: Oxford University Press, 1994.

Shohat, Ella, and Robert Stam, eds. *Multiculturalism, Postcoloniality, and Transnational Media.* New Brunswick: Rutgers University Press, 2003.

————. *Unthinking Eurocentrism: Multiculturalism and Media.* New York: Routledge, 1994.

Sky News, Guardian.co.uk. Feb. 18, 2009. February 25, 2009. http://news.sky.com/skynews /Home/UK-News/Sky-Probe-Reveals-Recycling-Scandal-As-Broken-TVs-Are -Shipped-Over-to-West-Africa.

Soyinka, Wole. *Death and the King's Horseman.* New York: Hill and Wang, 1975.

————. *The Road.* London: Oxford University Press, 1965.

Stam, Robert. "Beyond Third Cinema: The Aesthetics of Hybridity." In *Rethinking Third Cinema,* ed. Anthony Guneratne and Wimal Dissanayake. London: Routledge, 2003.

Stiegler, Bernard. "Derrida and Technology: Fidelity at the Limits of Deconstruction and the Prosthesis of Faith." In *Jacques Derrida and the Humanities: A Critical Reader,* ed. Tom Cohen. Cambridge: Cambridge University Press, 2001. 238–70.

Summers, Larry. February 11, 2011. www.whirledbank.org/ourwords/summers.html.

Taylor, Clyde. *The Mask of Art: Breaking the Aesthetic Contract-Film and Literature.* Bloomington: Indiana University Press, 1998.

Thompson, Michael. *Rubbish Theory.* New York: Oxford University Press, 1979.

Walcott, Derek. *Dream on Monkey Mountain.* In *Dream on Monkey Mountain and Other Plays.* New York: Farrar, Strauss, and Giroux, 1970.

————. *What the Twilight Says: Essays.* New York: Farrar, Strauss, and Giroux, 1998.

Weissman, Fabrice, ed. *In the Shadow of "Just Wars."* Ithaca, NY: Cornell University Press, 2004.

White, Luise. "Cars Out of Place." In *Tensions of Empire,* ed. Frederick Cooper and Ann Laura Stoler. Berkeley: University of California Press, 1997.

White, Timothy. *Catch a Fire: The Life of Bob Marley* (1983). New York: Macmillan, 2006.

Williams, Raymond. *Marxism and Literature.* Oxford: Oxford University Press, 1977.

Yosef, Raz. "Traces of War: Memory, Trauma, and the Archive in Josef Cedar's *Beaufort.*" *Cinema Journal* 50, no. 2 (Winter 2011): 61–83.

Young, Robert. *Colonial Desire: Hybridity in Culture, Theory and Race.* London: Routledge, 1995.

Žižek, Slavoj, ed. *Everything You Always Wanted to Know about Lacan (But Were Afraid to Ask Hitchcock).* London: Verso, 1992.
———. *Looking Awry.* (1991). Cambridge, MA: MIT Press, 1998.
———. *The Žižek Reader,* ed. Elizabeth Wright and Edmond Wright. Maiden, MA: Blackwell, 1999.

Filmography

Absa, Moussa Sene. *Tableau ferraille*. 1998. ADR Productions, Canal Horizons, Kus Productions, La Sept Cinéma, MSA Productions. Senegal. 92 min.

Aduaka, Newton. I. *Ezra*. 2007. Amour Fou Filmproduktion. Nigeria. 110 min.

Arase, Frank Rajah. *Beyonce*. 2006. Venus Films. Ghana. 120 min.

Ayinde, Muyideen Sasili. *Jénífà*. 2008. Olasco Films. Nigeria. 226 min.

Ba Kohbio, Bassek. *Sango Malo*. 1990. Les Films Terre Africaine. Cameroon. 95 min.

Bekolo, Jean-Pierre. *Aristotle's Plot*. 1996. JBA Production, BFI. France, Zimbabwe. 70 min.

———. *Quartier Mozart*. 1992. Kola Case, Cameroon Radio Television. Cameroon. 80 min.

———. *Les Saignantes*. 2005. Quartier Mozart Films, é4 Television. France, Cameroon. 92 min.

Benson, Teco. *Formidable Force*. 2002. Reemy Jes Nigeria Ltd. Nigeria. Part 1: 55 min; part 2: 53 min.

Blomkamp, Neill. *District 9*. 2009. Peter Jackson. Julian Clarke Wingnut Films, QED Internation, Key Creatives, Wintergreens Productions. South Africa. 112 min.

Bourlard, Tristan. *Matamata and Pilipili*. 1996. Bilan du Film Ethnographique Musee de l'Homme, Paris and Belgium. 55 min.

Boyle, Danny. *Slumdog Millionaire*. 2008. Celador Films, Film Four, Pathé Pictures International. India. 108 min.

Brooks, Mel. *The Producers, aka "Springtime for Hitler."* 1968. Brooksfilms Production. 135 min.

Buñuel, Luis. *Los Olvidados*. 1950. Ultramar Films. Mexico. 81 min.

Camus, Marcel. *Black Orpheus*. (1958). Ed. Antonio Carlos Jobim. New York, Verve: Universal Music Distribution, 2008. 100 min.

Caton-Jones, Michael. *Shooting Dogs aka "Beyond the Gates."* 2005. CrossDay Production Ltd., ARTE, BBC Films. Rwanda. 115 min.

Chaplin, Charles. *The Great Dictator*. 1940. Charles Chaplin Productions. United States. 126 min.

Chikere, Tchidi. *Blood Sister*. 2003. Great Movies Industries, Great Future Production. Nigeria. 120 min.

Cissé, Souleymane. *Baara*. 1978. Mali. 90 min.

———. *Finye*. 1982. Mali. 100 min.

———. *Yeelen*. 1987. Atriascop Paris, Burkina Faso Ministry of Life and Culture, Centre National de la Cinématographie (CNC). Mali. 105 min.

Dangarembga, Tsitsi. *Everyone's Child*. 1996. Media for Development Trust. Zimbabwe. 90 min.

Daniels, Lee. *Precious*. 2009. Lionsgate Entertainment, Lee Daniels Entertainment. United States. 109 min.

Deal, Carl, and Tia Lessin. *Trouble the Water*. 2008. Elsewhere Films, Louverture Films. United States. 90 min.

Diawara, Manthia. *Rouch in Reverse.* 1995. San Francisco: California Newsreel. 52 min.

Dikongué-Pipa, Jean-Pierre. *Le Prix de la liberté.* 1978. Cameroun Spectacles. Cameroon. 90 min.

Djadjam, Mostéfa. *Frontières.* 2002. Vertigo Productions. Algeria. 102 min.

Dornford-Mays, Mark. *U-Carmen e-Khayelitsha.* 2005. Spier Films. South Africa. 120 min.

Duparc, Henri. *Caramel.* 2005. Focale 13. Côte d'Ivoire. 88 min.

Eduardo Coutinho. *O Fio da Memoria* (The Thread of Memory). 1991. Cinefilmes. Brazil. 115 min.

Gamboa, Zézé. *O Herói.* 2004. David and Golias, Les Films d'Après midi, Gamboa and Gamboa. Angola. 97 min.

George, Terry. *Hotel Rwanda.* 2004. United Artists, Lions Gate Entertainment. United States. 122 min.

Gerima, Haile. *Teza.* 2008. Nigod-Gwad Productions. Ethiopia. 140 min.

Gomes, Flora. *The Blue Eyes of Yonta.* 1991. Arco Iris, Eurocreation Productions, Instituto Portuges de Cinema, Radio Television Portuguesa, Vermedia. Guinea Bissau. 90 min.

Haroun, Mahamat-Saleh. *Daratt.* 2006. Chinguitty Films, Entre Chiens et Loup, Goi-Goi Productions. Chad. 96 min.

Henzell, Perry. *The Harder They Come.* 1972. International Films, Xexon Pictures. Jamaica. 120 min.

Hondo, Med. *Soleil O.* 1967. Grey Films, Shango Films. Mauritania. 98 min.

Imasuen, Oduwa Lancelot. *Without Shame 1 and 2.* 2005. Elonel International Ltd. Nigeria. 98 min.

Kaboré, Gaston. *Wênd Kûuni.* 1982. Direction du Cinema de Haute Volta. Burkina Faso. 75 min.

——. *Zan Boko.* 1998. Atria Films. Burkina Faso. 95 min.

Kamwa, Daniel *Pousse-Pousse.* 1976. DK7 Communications. Cameroon. 100 min.

Kelani, Tunde. *Campus Queen.* 2004. Mainframe Films and Television Productions. Nigeria. 100 min.

Kpaï, Idrissou Mora. *Si-Gueriki.* 2003. Centre National de la Cinematography. Benin. 63 min.

Levi, Dani. *Führer, Mein—The Truly Truest Truth about Adolf Hitler.* 2007. Arte, Bayrischer Rundfunk (BR). Germany. 115 min.

Loreau, Dominique. *Divine Carcasse.* 1998. Underworld Films, Carré-Noir RTBF, Centre du Cinéma et de l'Audiovisuel de la Communauté Française de Belgique, Office de Radio et Télévision Bénin, Sindibad Films. Belgium, Benin. 78 min.

Makhmalbaf, Mohsen. *Kandahar.* 2001. Bac Films, Makhmalbaf Productions. Iran. 85 min.

Mambéty, Djibril Diop. *Le Franc.* 1994. Waka Films. Senegal. 44 min.

——. *Hyenas.* 1992. ADR Productions, Thelma Film AG. Senegal. 110 min.

——. *Parlons Grand-Mère.* 1989. Mali. 34 min.

——. *La Petite Vendeuse de Soleil.* 1999. Maag Daan. Waka Films. Senegal. 45 min.

——. *Touki Bouki.* 1973. Cinegrit, Studio Kankourama. Senegal. 85 min.

Minh-ha, Trinh T. *Reassemblage: From the Firelight to the Screen.* 1983. United States. 43 min.

Munga, Djo Tunda Wa. *Viva Riva!* 2011. uFilms, Formosa Productions. Democratic Republic of the Congo. 98 min.

Nacro, Fanta. *Un Certain matin*. 1991. Burkina Faso. 13 min.
———. *La nuit de la verité*. 2004. Acrobates Film, Les Films du Defi. Burkina Faso. 100 min.
———. *Puk Nini*. 1995. Atriasco Paris, Les Films du Defi. Burkina Faso. 32 min.
———. *Le Truc de Konate*. 1998. Les Films du Defi. Burkina Faso. 33 min.
Ngangura, Mweze. *Pièces d'identité*. 1998. Congo, Belgium. 93 min.
Ngangura, Mweze, and Benoît Lamy. *La Vie est belle*. 1987. Congo, Belgium. 85 min.
Obi, Ernest. *Desperate Women* 1 and 2. 2006. Elonel International, Ltd. Nigeria. 98 min.
Obinali, Obi Callys. *Dangerous Sisters*. 2004. Hallmark Films. Nigeria. 173 min.
Ogoro, Kingsley. *Osuofia in London*. 2004. Kingsley Ogoro Production. Nigeria. Part 1: 83 min.; part 2: 85 min.
Ouédraogo, Idrissa. *Le Cri du coeur*. 1994. Les Films de l'Avenir, les Films de la Plaine. Burkina Faso. 86 min.
———. *Yaaba*. 1989. Arcadia Films, Les Films de l'Avenir, Thelma Film AG. Burkina Faso. 90 min.
Pontecorvo, Gillo, and Franco Solinas. *The Battle of Algiers*. 1993. Santa Monica, California: Rhino; New York: Axon Video. 121 min.
Preminger, Otto. *Carmen Jones*. 1954. Carlyle Productions. United States. 105 min.
Raimi, Sam. *Evil Dead*. 1981. Renaissance Pictures. United States. 85 min.
Ramaka, Joseph Gaï. *Karmen Gei*. 2001. Canal+ Horizons, Crédit d'Impôt Cinéma et Télévision, Euripide Productions, Film Tonic, Les Ateliers de l'Arche, Sofica Sofinergie 5, Téléfilm Canada, UGC International, Zagarianka Productions, arte France Cinéma. Senegal. 82 min.
Raymont, Peter. *Shake Hands with the Devil: The Journey of Roméo Dallaire*. 2004. White Pine Pictures. Canada. 90 min.
Safo, Socrates. *Amsterdam Diary*. 2005. Movie Africa Production. Ghana. 148 min.
———. *Jezebell*. 2007. Movie Africa Production. Ghana. 120 min.
Sauper, Hubert. *Darwin's Nightmare*. 2004. Mille et une Production, Coop 99. Austria. 107 min.
Sembène, Ousmane. *Borom Sarret*. 1963. Senegal. 20 min.
———. *Camp de Thiaroye*. 1987. S.N.P.C., ENAPROC, Films Domireew, Films Kajoor. Senegal. 153 min.
———. *Ceddo*. 1976. Films Doomireew. Senegal. 120 min.
———. *Emitai*. 1971. Films Doomireew. Senegal. 121 min.
———. *Faat Kine*. 2000. Films Doomireew. Senegal. 120 min.
———. *Guelwaar*. 1992. Channel 4, Doomireew, France 3 Cinéma, Galatée Films, New Yorker Films, Westdeutscher Rundfunk (WDR). Senegal. 115 min.
———. *Mandabi*. 1968. Comptoir Français du Film Production, Films Doomireew. France, Senegal. 105 min.
———. *Moolade*. 2004. Ciné-Sud Promotion, Centre Cinematographique Morocain, Cinétéléfilms, Direction de la Cinematographie Nationale, Films Doomireew, Les Films Terre Africaine. Senegal. 124 min.
———. *La Noire de . . .* 1966. Films Domireew. France, Senegal. 65 min.
———. *Tauw*. 1970. Senegal. 24 min.
———. *Xala*. 1974. Société Nationale de Cinématographie/Filmi Doomireew. Senegal. 123 min.

Sganzerla, Rogério. *Red Light Bandit.* 1968. Urano Filmes. Brazil. 92 min.

Sissako, Abderrahmane. *Bamako.* 2006. Archipel 33, Chinguitty Films, Mali Images. Mali. 115 min.

——. *Heremakono.* 2002. Duo Films, Arte France Cinéma. Mauretania. 92 min.

——. *La Vie sur terre.* 1999. Centre National de la Cinematographie (CNC), Haut et court, La Sept Arte. Mauritania, Mali, France. 62 min.

Sissoko, Cheick Oumar. *Finzan.* 1992. Kora Films. Mali. 107 min.

——. *Nyamaton.* 1987. Mali. 90 min.

Teno, Jean-Marie. *Afrique, je te plumerai.* 1993. Les Films du Raphia. Cameroon. 88 min.

——. *Chef.* 1999. Les Films du Raffia. Cameroon. 61 min.

——. *Clando.* 1996. Arte, Les films du Raphia. Cameroon. 98 min.

——. *Lieux sacrés.* 2009. Les films du Raphia. Cameroon. 70 min.

——. *Le Malentendu colonial.* 2004. Les films du Raphia. Cameroon. 78 min.

Waters, John. *Female Trouble.* 1974. Dreamland. United States. 89 min.

Whitecross, Mat, and Michael Winterbottom. *Guantanamo.* 2006. Films4, Revolution Films. United Kingdom. 95 min.

Zwick, Edward. *Blood Diamond.* 2006. Warner Bros Pictures. United States. 143 min.

Index

Page numbers in italics indicate illustrations.

Brand, Dionne: *In the Full and Change of the Moon*, 9
Breton, André, 8
Brooks, Gwendolyn, 283n3, 300n1
Brooks, Peter, 259; moral occult, 298n2, 302n5, 306n17
Buñuel, Luis, 67
Busia, Abena, 286n3
Butler, Judith: *assujetissement*, 250–51, 253, 255–57, 259, 274, 282; bad conscience, 254–57, 259, 270; mourning and melancholy, 139–43, 148, 153, 154, 254, 256–58, 260–61, 274, 297n5

Césaire, Aimé: *Cahier d'un retour au pays natal*, 20, 26–27, 36, 52, 171, 196, 199; negation, 19
Chakrabarty, Dipesh, 9, 11, 102, 103–104, 105, 113; social science, 102
Chakravarty, Sumita, 103–104, 110–11, 126, 152; *The Red Lantern*, 111
Chamoiseau, Patrice: *Solibo*, 21
Chikere, Tchidi: *Blood Sister*, 268–69, 278
cinéma vérité, 206, 302n3
Cixous, Hélène, and Cathérine Clément: *The Newly Born Woman*, 128, 296n2
Cliff, Jimmy: *The Harder They Come*, xii, 63–67, 70–71, 79, *80–81*, 92, 283n1, 292n6
Coffey, Sarah: prosthesis and supplement, 204, 301n2
Commodity, 23, 29, 51–54; commodity capitalism, 8, 26–27, 245, 248; commodity consumerism, 51; commodity festishism, 113, 205, 218, 220, 244
consensus. *See* Rancière, Jacques
Consumption. *See* Bataille, Georges, appropriation
Cosby Show, The, 237
Culler, Jonathan, 60; Stevengraphs, 68–69
Cultural bias, 102

Dangarembga, Tsitsi, 58
Daniels, Lee: *Precious*, 237
Daratt. *See* Haroun, Mahamat-Saleh
Deal, Carl, and Tia Lessin: *Trouble the Water*, 170–76
Debord, 45–46, 290n14
Déchets humains, 1, 41, 50, 57, 70, 74–75, *81*, *82*, 137, 177
Deferring, 224, 227–28
Dérive, 290n14

Derrida, Jacques: *Archive Fever*, 196, 225, 227–30, 261, 301n2, 303n14, 303n17; messianicity, 199–200; parergon, 57, 292n5
Diawara, Manthia, ix, xi, 3, 33, 239, 271, 277–79, 291n18, 300n4; African cinema categories, 33; consumerism, 291n18; mobility, 271, 277–79
Dime, Moustapha, 114
Dirt, 60–61, 62–63. *See also* Douglas, Mary
Dissensus. *See* Rancière, Jacques
Distribution of the sensible. *See* Rancière, Jacques
Documentary Filmmaking: Grierson, 173; Vertov and Kino-Pravda, 173–74
Douglas, Mary, 1; dirt ("matter out of place"), 60–63, 68, 111, 215, 293n11, 298n8
Duparc, Henry: *Caramel*, 126, 307n4

Eshu, 255
Espinosa, Julio Garcia, 283n2
Exchange value, 51, 140; *The Harder They Come* and, 66, 67; *Karmen Gei* and, 112, 113, 117, 125; *O Herói* and, 204
Expenditure (excretion). *See* Bataille, Georges
Ezra, 29

Faat Kine. *See* Sembène, Ousmane
Faye, Safi, 127
Fela, 39, 238; "Gentleman," 239–40, 242; "Lady," 241–42; wives, 251–52
Ferguson, James: Summers, 21–24, 92; commodity fetishism, 23, 25, 26, 27–28
Foucault, Michel: heterotopia, 12
Freud, Sigmund, 141; *The Ego and the Id*, 140, 256; feces and money, 112, 296n1, 296n5; *Moses and Monotheism*, 223, 303n14

Gabriel, Teshome, 16, 30, 33, 158
Gamboa, Zézé: *O Herói*, 203–20; and realism, 9–12. *See also* Archive, the; Melodrama; Prosthesis; Supplement
Garritano, Carmela, 103–104; tale of the handsome gentleman, 103
Genizah, 293n10
Gerima, Haile: *Teza*, x
Gilligan, Melanie: on Rancière, 287n7
Gomes, Flora, 44
Gueye, Mor, 46

Hamlet, 141, 157, 223–26
Hamlin, Sarah, 301n7

and garbage, 10–13, 17; material and, 15; recuperation, 13; and Shohat, 3; trash and low culture, 3, 7, 8

Standpoint epistemology, 170–72

Stoeltje, Beverly, and Edna Bay: *Si-Gueriki* notes, 159–61

Summers, Lawrence, 198–99; dumping of toxic waste in Africa and, 293n13. *See also* Ferguson, James

Supplement, 204–209; logic of, 221, 301n2

Teno, Jean Marie: *Afrique, je te plumerai,* 49; *Clando,* 49; *Lieux sacrés,* 49; *Le Malentendu colonial,* 145

Theorization of trash. *See* Douglas, Mary; Thompson, Michael

Thompson, Michael, 68–70

Trafigura, 84–92, 295n3

Trash, 1–6, 7–29, 57–83; cinema as, 24, 30, 53, 275; definitions, 1; detritus, 11–12, 37, 40, 51, 79, 84, 86, 114, 216, 303n1; dungle as, 65, *81;* trash aesthetics (John Waters), xii, 53, 60, 67, 115; "trashy people," 12, 36, 41, 65, 73, 252; "trashy women," 48, 59, 97, 99, 105–25, 126–69, 242, 244, 255; trope of, 60, 273. *See also Déchets humains;* Dirt; Douglas, Mary

Trauma, 142, 154, 214, 223

"Le Truc de Konaté," 2, 127

Use value, 50, 66, 68, 112; in *The Harder They Come,* 66; in *Karmen Gei, 125;* in *O Herói,* 204, 211

Vie sur terre, La. See Sissako, Abderrahmane

Walcott, Derek: *Dream on Monkey Mountain,* 21; "What the Twilight Says," 20

Waste, 5, 10, 22, 58, 60, 71, 76, 78, 91, 105, 190, 292n3, 293n11; dungle and, 283n1; propriety and, 106; toxic, 8, 23, 84–92; Waters, John: *Female Trouble,* 60, 67. *See also* Trash, trash aesthetics

Weissman, Fabrice, 21, 138

Winterbottom, Michael: *Guantanamo,* 154

Wolfowitz, Paul, 198

World Bank, 198

Young, Robert, 10

Žižek, Slavoj, 100, 296n3; McGuffin (as objet a), 209, 266–67, 275; phallic mother, 163; three object/subject/socioeconomic systems, 209–11, 214, 217, 266–69, 302n7

KENNETH W. HARROW is Distinguished Professor of English at Michigan State University with specializations in African literature and cinema. He has taught at l'Université de Yaoundé and l'Université Cheikh Anta Diop in Dakar. He is the author of *Thresholds of Change in African Literature; Less Than One and Double: A Feminist Reading of African Women's Writing;* and *Postcolonial African Cinema: From Political Engagement to Postmodernism* (IUP, 2007). He has edited numerous collections on such topics as Islam and African literature, African cinema, and women in African cinema.